Neorealism, States, and the Modern Mass Army

This study constructs a neorealist theory of crossnational military emulation. The theory of emulation invites us to rethink neorealism as a theory of organizational effects, and not just state behavior and systemic outcomes. States have always imitated the best practices of one another: the latest in military weaponry, industrial processes, regulatory policy, even entire organs of state such as central banks. This deliberate imitation is an enduring feature of the international system. In the late nineteenth century, a diverse array of countries, including the United States, Japan, Brazil, Argentina, and Chile, imitated the military system of Germany. Because countries so different from one another imitate identical military practices and come to have similar military organizations, the explanation for these outcomes cannot be found in the peculiarities of their national culture, history, or traditions. What, then, explains this puzzle? The causes of military emulation, this book argues, are to be found not in the cultural, political, historical, or institutional attributes of states, but outside of them in their external security environment. This work is a qualitative comparative study, and it offers three rich – and uncommon – historical cases: Argentina, Brazil, and Chile.

João Resende-Santos is Associate Professor of Government in the Department of International Studies at Bentley College. He received his Ph.D. from Harvard University and previously taught at the University of Pennsylvania, Harvard University, and the University of Pittsburgh. He has published articles in *Security Studies, Latin American Politics and Society,* and *Latin American Research Review.*

South America, 2006

Neorealism, States, and the Modern Mass Army

JOÃO RESENDE-SANTOS

Bentley College

CAMBRIDGE
UNIVERSITY PRESS

CAMBRIDGE UNIVERSITY PRESS
Cambridge, New York, Melbourne, Madrid, Cape Town, Singapore, São Paulo, Delhi

Cambridge University Press
32 Avenue of the Americas, New York, NY 10013-2473, USA

www.cambridge.org
Information on this title: www.cambridge.org/9780521869485

First published 2007

Printed in the United States of America

A catalog record for this publication is available from the British Library.

Library of Congress Cataloging in Publication Data

Resende-Santos, João, 1966–
Neorealism, states, and the modern mass army / João Resende-Santos.
    p.   cm.
Includes bibliographical references and index.
ISBN-13: 978-0-521-86948-5 (hardback)
ISBN-13: 978-0-521-68965-6 (pbk.)
1. Military art and science – South America – History – 19th century.   2. Military art and
science – South America – History – 20th century.   3. Military art and science – Germany –
History.   4. Military art and science – France – History.   5. South America – History,
Military – 19th century.   6. South America – History, Military – 20th century.   I. Title.
UA612.R47   2007
355′.03308–dc22   2006033390

ISBN   978-0-521-86948-5 hardback
ISBN   978-0-521-68965-6 paperback

I dedicate this book to my Mom and Dad, Dinora and Vasco

Contents

List of Tables and Figures

Acknowledgments

The process of writing a book is lonely and arduous, but the final product is rarely the lone effort of the author. This project has been long in the making and the final product has benefited from the generous contributions and encouragement of a great many people. While the flaws and shortcomings of the book are mine alone, I wish to thank all the people, friends, and reviewers who have read and listened to numerous permutations and early drafts of my theory of emulation over the years. They have helped me sharpen the argument and encouraged me to open new spaces. My ability to express my gratitude is small compared to their contributions. I begin by thanking, collectively, the faculty and graduate students at my various home departments at the University of Pennsylvania, Dartmouth College, the University of Pittsburgh, Harvard University, and Bentley College.

I wish also to thank a number of individuals. Ben Frankel has not only been my biggest cheerleader and supporter, his jokes kept me going when the going got tough. Jorge Domínguez always has been a mentor, a wonderful teacher, and a friend. Jennifer Sterling-Folker and Jeffrey Taliaferro are great friends and comrades-in-arms in opening up new spaces in neorealist theory. I am grateful to Joe Grieco, whose early interest and encouragement helped in ways that went beyond the project itself. His interest in my emulation argument while I was still a graduate student was pivotal in the evolution of this book. Dan Deudney and Rudy Sil were patient, generous, original, and brilliant; their expansive ideas and unconventional insights inspired me and gave me models to emulate. Avery Goldstein, Michael Mastanduno, Robert Pape, Michael Desch, William Bernhard, James Henz, Christopher Gelpi, Randy Schweller, Peter Feaver, Ed Rhodes, Ashley Tellis, Mlada Bukovanky, David Rousseau, and Susan Martin have been generous with their time and insightful comments, as well as with career advice. Stephen Biddle always has been encouraging and supportive. With the support of the Mellon postgraduate fellowship, the political science faculty and graduate students of the University of Pittsburgh offered a stimulating environment for me to sharpen my argument. I am grateful to Barry Ames, mentor and friend over the years. While at Pittsburgh, my theory on crossnational emulation benefited greatly from the many conversations with Juliana Martínez-Franzoni, whose quick and brilliant mind had been working on emulation in public policy areas. My colleagues at Bentley College have been loyal, patient, and encouraging. Anne Rawls shared her wisdom and experience and offered advice throughout the revision process. I am grateful to Catherine Musinsky, who offered her time and talent helping me proofread and prepare the illustrations. Finally, I wish to acknowledge the wonderful staff at the Biblioteca do Exército and Arquivo Histórico do Exército, Rio de Janeiro, Brazil, and the Archivo Histórico del Estado Maior General del Ejército, Buenos Aires, Argentina.

Military Emulation in the International System

From the time humans began to organize into political collectives, states have imitated the best practices of one another: the latest in military weaponry, industrial processes, regulatory policy, even entire organs of state, such as central banks. This deliberate imitation – and the resulting crossnational convergence that results from it – has been a recurring feature of the international system. Today this crossnational borrowing can range from simple copying of new stand-alone technologies to more complex forms such as nuclear proliferation and emulation of industrial policy. In the 1980s much public discourse in the United States focused on the need to adopt Japanese corporate governance, production-line practices, and even Japan's education policy. Meanwhile, on the other side of the Pacific, the Japanese were busy xeroxing U.S. securities regulations. A century earlier, the United States, Japan, Brazil, Argentina, Chile, France, and a number of other countries emulated, to varying degrees, Prussia's famed Imperial Army. These countries avidly copied Prussia's general staff, field regulations, armaments, conscription system, even its uniforms and marshal music. In some cases this foreign military influence proved superficial and fleeting, in others more lasting. The occasional tourist today in downtown Santiago, Chile may witness a military parade and identify vestiges of this past in the Chilean army's goose-stepping and spiked helmets. Meiji Japan's voracious copying of Western practices is the most familiar and notable historical case of large-scale, sustained crossnational borrowing.

Less well known is the extensive copying of the Prussian / German military system by the major South American republics during the last quarter of the nineteenth-century. Starting with Chile in 1885, the South Americans began importing the Prussian mass army. This period marks the founding of their modern military establishments. They recreated their armies on the basis of foreign models, embodying a radical departure from established practices and traditions. The South Americans, along with Meiji Japan, France, the Ottomans, and others, invested considerable treasure and political capital remaking their military systems – a process in itself fraught with political peril and organizational upheaval. They did so by introducing practices that were alien to their own societies and traditions.

Equally puzzling is that, despite becoming avid importers of Germany's Imperial army, before 1870 they copied the French army extensively. Before and after 1870 they used the British Royal navy as the sole model for their navies. Remarkable, too, is that the South Americans appeared to be unfazed by the wider social and political ramifications of importing the mass army. The mass army not only represented a different stage of warfare, but it also entailed changes beyond the military itself. Its adoption was socially and politically disruptive. Its underlying principle of the nation-in-arms meant, in practice, universal conscription, which everywhere put strains on state-society relations. It altered the domestic political power balance between the executive and other branches, between the central government and the provinces, between the state and society.

These late nineteenth-century emulators of Prussia/Germany were geographically dispersed, culturally and politically disparate, in different stages of social and economic development, shared little in common with each other and even less with Prussia, yet each attempted to refashion its military along the lines of Prussia's (see Table 1.1). A constitutional democracy imported military practices from the paragon of militarism and monarchism. Poor, weak, and peripheral countries copied the ways of the rich and powerful. Latin South America, whose ruling aristocracy was educated in and consumed everything French, had much closer cultural and historical affinity to Latin Europe than Prussia, with whom even commercial and diplomatic ties were thin at the time.

States rich and poor, new and established, culturally homogenous and fragmented, Western and non–Western, republican and dictatorial, deliberately engaged in large-scale efforts to reconstitute their military establishments on the basis of the same foreign model. Since countries so different from each other imitated identical military practices, and came to share similarities in their military organization, the explanation for these outcomes cannot be found in the peculiarities of their national culture, history, or traditions. What, then, explains this puzzle? The causes of military emulation are to be found not in the cultural, political, historical, or institutional attributes of states, but outside of them in their external security environment.

This study explains crossnational military emulation – the deliberate systematic imitation of the military technology, organization, and doctrine of one country by another. It develops an area of neorealism (structural realism) that has been overlooked by critics and defenders alike. I construct a neorealist theory of emulation to explain four key aspects of military emulation:

- why states emulate the military practices of other states
- when they emulate (the timing of emulation)

TABLE 1.1. *Selected Major Episodes of Military Emulation in South America, 1870–1930*

Country	Emulation Start Date	System Emulated
Chile	1885	Germany
Ecuador	1895	France
Ecuador	1903	Chile
Peru	1896	France
Argentina	1899	Germany
Venezuela	1904	Chile
Colombia	1907	Chile
Bolivia	1910	Germany
Paraguay	1913	Germany
Paraguay	1926	France
Brazil	1906	Germany
Brazil	1919	France
Non–South American Cases		
Japan	1866	France
Japan	1878	Germany
France	1870	Germany

Note: As a proxy for the start of emulation, I use the date when military training missions are contracted. In most cases this is misleading, since emulation typically starts much earlier, and not all cases of emulation involve training missions.

- what model, or country, they choose to emulate (as well as why and when they may "switch" to other models)
- the speed and scale of their emulation efforts

The work is a qualitative comparative study, and it offers three rich, and uncommon, historical cases: Argentina, Brazil, and Chile. I examine each case across a sixty-year time span, 1870–1930, which allows me to analyze them longitudinally before and after the start of military emulation. The research is based exclusively on primary documents drawn from military and diplomatic archives in the countries under study. I want to stress right away that this work is neither structured nor intended as comparative theory testing, whereby I might address competing explanations systematically. My sole purpose here is to unearth a neglected dimension of neorealism, refine it, test it, and build a new and better neorealist theory of emulation. I will address issues raised by alternative explanations as they pertain to particular points under discussion.

The Argument

This book is about the relationship between the state, military organization, and the state system. While the empirical story I tell deals with military modernization in Argentina, Brazil, and Chile over a century ago, the theory I develop is about the timeless relationship between external security, the organization of violence, and the international system. It is about the political foundations of violence in the system and the political criterion states use to organize the instruments of violence. I explain why the three South American governments decided to import military practices alien to their own societies. My theory is about why governments make the security decisions they do and how the structure of the international system constrains and molds their choices. The book is about the behavioral and organizational outcomes in a realm in which states lack a higher authority to protect them, provide for their welfare and safety, or adjudicate their relations. In the absence of such authority, this relationship and these outcomes have characterized the life of states with monotonous persistence and frequency despite the great many changes in political forms and internal conditions they have experienced. The South Americans were neither the first nor the last to engage in cross national borrowing.

Emulating the best military practices of others is an enduring behavioral pattern in the international system, irrespective of the many changes in forms, shapes, and sizes of states or the endless variety in their internal makeup. Given the centrality of power and conflict in the state system, it is not surprising that the emulation of violence technology would be so pervasive. Cross-national emulation is thus a product of the underlying nature of the international system, not the peculiar characteristics or aims of individual states. Emulation is one of the two main predictions in neorealism, as elucidated more fully in the next chapter.[1] Neorealist theory is based on two key predictions about the behavior of states: they will balance against external threats and they will emulate the best practices

---

[1] My interpretation of neorealism is based exclusively on the works of Kenneth N. Waltz, principally *Theory of International Politics* (Reading, MA: Addison-Wesley, 1979). Other works by Waltz cited include: Kenneth N. Waltz, "The Emerging Structure of International Politics," *International Security* 18, no. 2 (Fall 1994): 44–79; "Realist Thought and Neorealist Theory," *Journal of International Affairs* 44, no. 1 (Summer 1990): 21–38; "Reflections on *Theory of International Politics*: A Response to My Critics," in *Neorealism and Its Critics*, ed. Robert O. Keohane (New York: Columbia University Press, 1986): 322–47; "The Origins of War in Neorealist Theory," in *The Origin and Prevention of Major Wars*, ed. Robert I. Rotberg and Theodore K. Rabb (Cambridge: Cambridge University Press, 1989): 39–52; *Man, the State, and War* (New York: Columbia University Press, 1959). Neorealism is also often referred to as structural realism by Waltz and others. See Robert O. Keohane, "Theory of World Politics: Structural Realism and Beyond," in Keohane, ed., *Neorealism and Its Critics*, 158–203; Barry Buzan, Charles Jones, and Richard Little, *The Logic of Anarchy: Neorealism to Structural Realism* (New York: Columbia University Press, 1993); Fareed Zakaria, "Realism and Domestic Politics: A Review Essay," in *The Perils of Anarchy: Contemporary Realism and International Security*, ed. Michael E. Brown, Sean Lynn-Jones, and Steven E. Miller (Cambridge, MA: MIT Press, 1995): 462–483; Colin Elman, "Horses for Courses: Why Not Neorealist Theories of Foreign Policy?" *Security Studies* 6, no. 1 (Autumn 1996): 7–51.

of one another.[2] The explanation for balancing and emulation can be found in the theory's three foundational assumptions about the international system. First, the international system is an anarchic realm. As I elaborate in Chapter 2, from the assumption of anarchy we are able to derive logically other ubiquitous features of the system. Among the most important characteristics are its conflictual or competitive nature, self-help imperative, and the insecurity and uncertainty that pervade the life of states. From the assumption of anarchy, we also derive the long-standing realist verities about the international system – the centrality of power and military force in the relations of states. The second assumption is that the primary actors in the system are states. The third assumption is that security is their highest end. Even among realists, there are disagreements over these assumptions and their implications, and none more so than the third. To these I will return later.

My argument is: First, military emulation is a security-enhancing strategy in response to external threats. In the face of major threats, military emulation is the quickest and most dependable way to increase power and bolster security. Timing, pace, and scale will correspond with the timing and magnitude of external threats. At a more general level, it is the result of states' preoccupation with relative *competitive effectiveness*, or its overall capacity to meet the changing requirements of viability and success in the system. Relative competitive effectiveness is a comprehensive notion, the core of which is the state's military capabilities and its fiscal-administrative-coercive apparatus. States put a premium on their relative competitive effectiveness. While they continually worry about how well they are organized and equipped, when faced with episodes of major threats they will engage in sustained restructuring and re-tooling in order to keep up with and adjust to the changed minimum requirements of competition.

Second, emulation is a form of balancing behavior. States adopt various measures and strategies to respond to threats and keep up with the power of others. Neorealism maintains that states balance against threats in one of two generic strategies or in their combination: A state may adopt a strategy of alliance-making or coalition with others (external balancing), or it may choose to mobilize its domestic resources (internal balancing). A state may align with others and pool collective resources to deal with a common threat, or it may choose to muster its own domestic resources. Military emulation is a form of internal balancing. Realist scholars, like their critics, have focused exclusively on the former type of balancing and neglected the latter – even though the two predictions are inextricably linked. Overlooked too is that predictions about emulation, and all forms of large-scale internal balancing, entail organizational consequences. This is not a study of whether or not

---

[2] Waltz, *Theory of International Politics*, 118, 124, 127–28.

states balance, a debate settled by the works of Walt and others.[3] Rather, it examines what they often do internally when they engage in a particular kind of internal balancing; why there is variation in the pace and scope of their efforts, while occasionally highlighting some of the organizational ramifications of this form of internal mobilization.

Third, I build on the neorealist assumption that states exist in an international system which is dynamic and competitive. Thus it is a system that presses states continually to attend to how well they are internally organized and equipped for that competition. Whether firms in the market or states in the system, units in competitive realms are continually pressed to ensure they are internally well organized and equipped to thrive and to survive. States are especially preoccupied with the relative size and effectiveness of their military power.[4] They worry about the consequences to their security and autonomy of falling behind. States continually attend to the relative strength of their military power, although qualitative improvements such as large-scale emulation occur in spurts and tend to be discontinuous. The distinction here is fine but important. Pressure of competition spurs states to worry about relative competitiveness, but it is episodes of sustained direct threat that press them to make improvements in their tools and methods of competition. Put differently, crossnational emulation in the system will be sporadic, clustered, uneven, and discontinuous.

Military emulation is driven by a competitive security logic. It is a response to external threats, and will correspond to the timing and scale of external threats. When faced with a major threat, emulating the military organization and technology proven most effective is the surest and quickest strategy for a state to bolster its military power and enhance its security. Since timing, pace, and scale are functions of threats, emulation, especially large scale, is discontinuous rather than continual. Emulation is only one of several possible strategies states adopt to enhance their security. I specify the conditions under which states will choose emulation over other internal balancing strategies, such as innovation and arms buildup. I will show that whether and how much states emulate will be influenced by the availability of external balancing options, whether in the form of alliances or indirect free riding on the power of others. Finally, all states – big and small, great powers and secondary states, even innovation-capable states – emulate.

Fourth, states emulate on the basis of proven effectiveness, which is a political criterion. This proposition is one of the amendments I introduce into Kenneth Waltz's original formulation. As discussed in the next chapter,

---

[3] Stephen Walt, *The Origins of Alliances* (Ithaca: Cornell University Press, 1987); Barry Posen, *The Sources of Military Doctrines: France, Britain, and Germany Between the Wars* (Ithaca: Cornell University Press, 1984).

[4] Barry Posen, "Nationalism, the Mass Army, and Military Power," International Security 18, no. 2 (Fall 1993): 80–124, 82.

Waltz claims that states emulate the most powerful in their numbers, and that emulation occurs among adversaries. I rectify these two related flaws by showing that states, including adversaries, emulate prevailing international best practices. Given their preoccupation with competitive effectiveness, states prefer to emulate only practices and technologies demonstrated to be the most effective among synchronic alternatives. In the area of military emulation, states use battlefield performance, especially victory in war, as the truest observable measure of effectiveness. States thus emulate the military system that emerges victorious in great power wars. It may often be the case that the military system drawing the most emulation appeal is that of the most powerful state in the system. Likewise, in the absence of a test of effectiveness, emulators may reasonably use aggregate power as an approximation. However, it is useful to keep the distinction between proven effectiveness and capabilities, since the two will not always coincide. (Indeed, some versions of realist theory, such as power transition, and much of the work in industrial economics, posit that innovation and best practice will be introduced by challengers.) Proven success in war provides states with a closer approximation of the true utility of certain military practices. It reduces the uncertainties that surround such practices.

Similarly, states display a selective approach to emulation. They emulate specific categories of military capabilities. The United States, Japan, and the South Americans copied elements of the kaiser's army, but it was to the British Royal Navy they looked as naval model. There may have been reasonable squabbles over whether Britain was the most powerful overall among the great powers – the primus inter pares – during the last quarter of the century, but they all emulated Germany's victorious mass army. In each category of military capabilities, or military mission requirements, states emulate only what has been tested and proven successful among existing alternatives.

States are continually preparing for the next war by copying the best practices of the previous war. This appears irrational, since these practices often turn out to be inappropriate or obsolete for the next war. That states repeatedly do so reinforces the point about proven effectiveness. A further conundrum for states is that, in the end, borrowed best practices may or may not prove effective in terms of purchasing greater security or enhancing military power because of faulty copying, failure to copy ancillary practices, inability to integrate properly and utilize borrowed methods, or simply the lack of the necessary human skill and know how. Yet in the context of structural uncertainty and insecurity, and as security competition stiffens, emulating the proven and tested best practices of others remains a sensible strategy that offers states speed and greater certainty in building up their power.

Fifth, as mentioned already, the timing, pace, and scale of military emulation will vary with shifts in the intensity of external security competition in the state's immediate strategic environment. The ability to account for when, how quickly, and how much emulation takes places is crucial, because it sets apart the neorealist theory of emulation from competing theories, especially ones that give causal primacy to cultural factors. Simply put, the higher and more intense the threat level, the deeper and more sustained the adverse shift in the external security environment, the more rapid and large scale the emulation. Rather than place all explanatory weight on shifts in the global distribution of power, as Waltz does, I emphasize the importance of the state's local strategic environment.

I borrow the structural elements of Walt's balance of threat theory and offense-defense theory, both of which emphasize the importance of changes in the state's immediate security environment. Like Walt, I argue that it is more reasonable to examine state behavior in terms of the source, direction, and nature of security threats in its immediate strategic setting, rather than just the narrower variable of global distribution of capabilities.[5] The nature, source, and intensity of the security dilemma that inheres in the system are not the same for all states, even if the underlying logic of behavior is the same. Nor is it one global or uniform security dilemma stemming from the global distribution of capabilities. Local or geographically clustered subsystems of power balancing, and local patterns of amity and enmity shape the immediate security environment of states, especially secondary states. Unless they have global capabilities, states give more significance to threats and adverse shifts that are local and immediate. The qualitative measure of threat levels stresses the importance of military (technology, doctrine, deployment) and geographic factors (advantages and liabilities, terrain, proximity). In addition, I argue that a state's level of threat will be affected by the availability of external balancing options. The availability of allies and free-riding opportunities lowers threat level, and dampens the scale and pace of emulation; while the absence of such options heightens the threat and spurs greater emulation, all else being equal.

In summation, the book is about what causes states to emulate the military technologies and organizational structures of others. The topic of military emulation is understudied in international relations theory. The few works on the topic are either descriptive or emphasize cultural explanations. Few,

---

5 Walt, *Origins of Alliances*. A good deal of debate is involved here, especially Walt's use of perceptual factors, which I exclude. See Michael E. Brown and Sean Lynn-Jones, "Preface," in *The Perils of Anarchy: Contemporary Realism and International Security*, ed. Michael E. Brown, Sean Lynn-Jones, and Stephen E. Miller (Cambridge, MA: MIT Press, 1995): ix–xxi; Benjamin Frankel, "The Reading List," *Security Studies* 5, no. 1 (Autumn 1995): 183–94; Robert Powell, "Anarchy in International Relations Theory: The Neorealist-Neoliberal Debate," *International Organization* 48, no. 2 (Spring 1994): 313–44; Sean Lynn-Jones, "Offense-Defense Theory and Its Critics," *Security Studies* 4, no. 4 (Summer 1995): 660–91; Charles Glaser and Chaim Kaufmann, "What is the Offense-Defense Balance, and Can We Measure It?" *International Security* 22, no. 4 (Spring 1998): 44–82.

if any, base their analysis on systematic, archival empirical supports.[6] Unlike other works, I develop a fresh and powerful theory of emulation to explain why states emulate, when they do so, why they discriminate among whom they choose to emulate, and why there is variance in the speed and magnitude of their emulation efforts. In building a theory of emulation, I work within structural realism. I connect some previously unconnected ideas and open up new spaces. I correct and refine flaws and clarify some major concepts.

To do this requires that I limit the scope of the book. My work focuses exclusively on why states emulate and not on the results or efficacy of their emulation. The success or failure of emulation does not concern me; only the underlying causes and substance of the process itself. It is natural to ask whether emulation actually results in improved military effectiveness given all the energy and resources states devote to it. Since effectiveness is a product of a number of variables, and ultimately can only be known in combat, I focus instead on the state's attempt and efforts to improve its power. This distinction is worth highlighting because cultural explanations often conflate the results and effectiveness of emulation with the effort itself. I do not focus on the wider scale military, political, cultural, social, or any other hypothesized consequences and secondary effects of military emulation. Military emulation has state-making effects. These organizational effects are not the primary focus of the book, though I make preliminary observations on some of these effects.

WHAT IS MILITARY EMULATION?

Military emulation is the deliberate imitation by one state of any aspect of another state's military system that bears upon its own military system. This emulation brings the emulator's military (or specific components of it) into reasonably close correspondence with the model being emulated. Emulation, as a generic form of state behavior, is the voluntary, purposeful, and systematic imitation by one state of the techniques and practices of another. Crossnational emulation occurs in a wide variety of areas and by an equal variety of state and nonstate entities. Although I focus on state-directed emulation in the military area, states have also emulated one another's economic,

---

[6] See the edited volume by Emily O. Goldman and Leslie C. Eliason, *The Diffusion of Military Technology and Ideas* (Stanford: Stanford University Press, 2003). See also Emily O. Goldman, "Cultural Foundations of Military Diffusion," *Review of International Studies* 32, no. 1 (January 2006): 69–91; *The Culture of National Security: Norms and Identity in World Politics*, ed. Peter J. Katzenstein (New York: Columbia University Press, 1996); David B. Ralston, *Importing the European Army: The Introduction of European Military Techniques into the Extra-European World, 1600–1914* (Chicago: University of Chicago Press, 1990); Frederick M. Nunn, *Yesterday's Soldiers: European Military Professionalism in South America, 1890–1940* (Lincoln: University of Nebraska Press, 1983).

regulatory, administrative, and even constitutional practices.[7] While private, nonstate entities, such as business firms, may also engage in emulation domestically or internationally, the kind of emulation examined here is characterized by a centrally coordinated, national-level planning.

As noted above, emulated practices and techniques may range widely from industrial, to military, to public administration, to policy and regulatory measures. Emulation in all forms, by firms or states, whether in economic or military areas, is driven by the same pressures of competition and based on the same political criterion. The theory I develop applies to emulation in all areas, including both state-directed and nonstate emulation provided they share one quality in common – they are realms organized on the basis of anarchy and self-help. In essence, emulation is a process by which states observe, learn, and copy the ways and practices of one another – though the process itself implies nothing about its causes. Conceptually, emulation is akin to, but different from, diffusion. The latter term is a purely descriptive notion that says nothing about the causes, nature, intent, direction, or content of the process. Emulation leads to the diffusion of best practices, though it is not the only path of diffusion and isomorphism in the system.

Three aspects of this definition must be emphasized at the outset. First, military emulation is a conscious, voluntary, and deliberate act. It involves a deliberate decision to copy, in part or in whole, the military system of another country. To be sure, there are any number of other ways in which certain state practices spread and converge. Historically, external coercion and imposition have been salient in the life of states. Similarly, there are likely to be ambiguous cases bordering between voluntary emulation and coercion. For instance, many states today adopt standardized economic and regulatory policies, even restructure their administrative apparatus, as a result of so-called structural adjustment programs dictated by the International Monetary Fund (IMF). The European Union acts as a force of convergence and standardization among its members. One commonality in all three types of crossnational diffusion and convergence is the central role of power differentials.

Second, emulation results in similarity, but we cannot realistically expect an identical, carbon copy to result. As Waltz noted, similar is not the same as identical. Emulation is not perfect replication, for there are practical and human limits to exact copying.[8] There has always been a good deal of debate in the literature, across various disciplines, as to whether foreign borrowing results in replicas, or whether states simply graft borrowed practices onto

---

[7] A classic work is D. Eleanor Westney, *Innovation and Imitation: The Transfer of Western Organizational Patterns to Meiji Japan* (Cambridge: Harvard University Press, 1987). See also *National Diversity and Global Capitalism*, ed. Suzanne Berger and Ronald Dore (Ithaca: Cornell University Press, 1996).

[8] Robert Boyer, "The Convergence Hypothesis Revisited: Globalization But Still the Century of Nations?" in Berger and Dore, eds., *National Diversity*, 29–59.

old ones, resulting in hybrids. We expect that emulators use foreign models as more than general exemplars, templates, or intellectual guides.[9] The cases examined here show that states attempt to retain the fidelity of borrowed practices. The degree of similarity between any two systems, or the fidelity of the emulation, is an empirical question.

Last is a point related to similarity. A distinction needs to be maintained between emulation as a process, as a deliberate strategy involving explicit intent and discernible measures, from the efficacy of the outcome. That is, emulation can be said to take place irrespective of whether or not the emulator is able to employ effectively the borrowed technology or organizational practice. The dexterity or efficacy with which emulators employ borrowed practices is conceptually apart from the process of borrowing, and requires different explanatory variables. The question of why some emulators are more prodigious is historically and theoretically interesting, but lies outside this study.

This study focuses exclusively on emulation processes in the military sphere. I focus on emulation decisions and efforts in the areas of military organization (conscription, general staff and command structures, and officer formation) and weapons technology. I deliberately omit from focus those matters pertaining to doctrine – the set of precepts and prescriptions that tell the military how to structure, deploy, and apply these main components. Although it is outside the purview of this study, and less visible, it should be noted that large-scale military emulation engenders doctrinal changes.

The military, unlike most other state organs, uniquely lends itself to studying the entire emulation process. Its relative insulation, centralized and hierarchical internal organization, its more or less clearly defined functions and internal procedures, clearer organizational boundaries, its location on the border between domestic and international – all these qualities allow us to trace closely the entire emulation process. For analytical convenience, I limit my definition and research focus to strictly military components of the process, even while recognizing that the overall processes of military emulation may involve or bleed across any number of other organs of state and ancillary practices.

Military emulation ranges from simple garden-variety borrowing of discrete practices to large-scale, sustained efforts of the kind engaged in by the South Americans. In this study I concentrate on the upper ranges of military emulation, but the theoretical framework I construct accounts for variance across the entire range of military emulation. As I explain later, my research design allows me to investigate each case across a long historical time frame, allowing me to observe episodes of emulation and nonemulation. Small-scale, one-time emulation, whether in military or nonmilitary areas,

---

[9] Colin J. Bennett, "How States Utilize Foreign Evidence," *Journal of Public Policy* 11, pt. 1 (January–March 1991): 31–54.

is the most common form of crossnational borrowing. The most frequent and widespread, but also superficial, kind of military emulation in the system is the imitation of specific weapons technologies, equipment, uniforms, or discrete battlefield tactics. The South Americans of the early nineteenth century often emulated only superficial elements of the leading powers. In the postwar period the military emulation of most visibility and concern has been that of nuclear weapons and nuclear technology. What about the upper ranges of military emulation?

For our purposes here, the term military emulation denotes a *large-scale* and *sustained* process encompassing the entire military system, rather than simple garden variety borrowing or one-time discrete copying. My interest is in explaining larger-scale historical events. I isolate this upper range of internal balancing, which entails qualitatively as well as quantitatively deep and sustained mobilization of the human, material, organizational, and technological resources of the state.

Military emulation of this scale is measured in terms of years and decades, not months. It depicts the restructuring, or modernization, of the country's entire armed forces based explicitly on an existing foreign model.[10] The large-scale military emulation of post–1870 France, Turkey, Meiji Japan, Chile, and the other major South American powers involved the restructuring and modernization of not only the military's armaments and equipment but also its internal organization and doctrine. Although it is a lengthy, sustained process, military emulation has discernible starting and ending points. As a process it displays a certain degree of coherence and continuity with respect to its contents, sequencing, and goals. Military emulation is a different kind (qualitatively and quantitatively) of military reform. The distinction is important, since reforms, or modernization, can occur in the absence of emulation, although I will use all three terms interchangeably.

I expect large-scale military emulation of the kind examined here to occur at major strategic junctures: during episodes of significant external shock, or deep and sustained adverse shifts in the state's strategic environment. In other words, neorealist theory is explicit about the conditions under which we observe balancing behavior, whether it involves small- or large-scale efforts. I use the term "strategic juncture" as a proxy description of significant adverse shifts in the state's level of vulnerability. Such critical junctures may be of natural, economic, or military kind, triggering substantial disruption or collapse of existing institutions, practices, and technologies, or exposing their

---

[10] Modernization is used here to refer to the process whereby existing institutions, technologies, or practices are brought into close correspondence with those widely considered to be more effective among all existing alternatives at any one time. The term does not connote any unilinear teleology, normative judgment, or optimization. I will often use the terms military modernization, emulation, and reforms interchangeably in my discussion of the South American cases of large-scale emulation.

weakness or obsolescence. The notion of strategic junctures as a trigger or catalyst for major restructuring of state institutions is familiar.[11] At these junctures the state is prompted to undergo thorough restructuring and improvement of existing domestic arrangements and practices. The appearance of major security threats, such as the threat of invasion and war, or the military buildup of a rival, combined with geographic and other strategic liabilities, constitute such junctures.

In the military sphere, large-scale emulation often, but not exclusively, accompanies major wars.[12] Beyond the immediate impact on the military establishment itself (especially for the vanquished), such wars often trigger significant changes in the local or international balance of capabilities, as well as alterations in the relative standings of states. In the wake of Napoleonic France's victories, the major continental powers of Prussia, Austria, and Russia modernized their military systems (and imitated the French).[13] Nowhere was this modernization and emulation more pronounced than in defeated Prussia. Little more than half a century later it was France that feverishly modernized and emulated its archrival after the defeat in 1870.[14] As we shall see, South America during the 1870–1930 period experienced three critical junctures that upset the regional system of power balancing.

RETHINKING NEOREALIST THEORY

Neorealism has a latent theory of emulation. Neorealist theory predicts that states will emulate the successful practices of one another. Specifically, Waltz argues that states emulate successful military weapons and strategies.[15] Waltz's predictions on military emulation, taken together with the core predictions of neorealism, form a coherent and testable set of propositions to form a stand-alone theory of cross-national emulation. However,

---

[11] Peter J. Katzenstein, *Small States in World Markets: Industrial Policy in Europe* (Ithaca: Cornell University Press, 1985); Stephen D. Krasner, "Approaches to the State: Alternative Conceptions and Historical Dynamics," *Comparative Politics* 16, no. 2 (January 1984): 223–46; Peter Gourevitch, *Politics in Hard Times: Comparative Responses to International Economic Crises* (Ithaca: Cornell University Press, 1986). See also essays in *The State and American Foreign Economic Policy*, ed. G. John Ikenberry, David A. Lake, and Michael Mastanduno (Ithaca: Cornell University Press, 1988).

[12] Posen, "Nationalism," 87.

[13] Gunther E. Rothenberg, *The Art of Warfare in the Age of Napoleon* (Bloomington: Indiana University Press, 1978); Robert M. Epstein, *Napoleon's Last Victory and the Emergence of Modern Warfare* (Lawrence: University Press of Kansas, 1994).

[14] Allan Mitchell, " 'A Situation of Inferiority': French Military Reorganization After the Defeat of 1870," *American Historical Review* 86, no. 1 (February 1981): 49–62, and *Victors and Vanquished: The German Influence on Army and Church in France After 1870* (Chapel Hill: University of North Carolina Press, 1984).

[15] Waltz, *Theory of International Politics*, 127, and "The Emerging Structure."

Waltz's original formulation, while showing the way, has a number of flaws, which I will elaborate on and correct in the next chapter. Presently, there is no theory of emulation in neorealism aside from a loose collection of propositions that are undeveloped, inconsistent, and incomplete. To construct such a theory, several amendments of neorealism are necessary, albeit consistent with neorealism's explanatory logic.

My main objective is to develop a neorealist theory of emulation. My intention is to open up new spaces, both in IR theory in general and neorealism in particular. My work unearths an undeveloped dimension of neorealism – its second image reversed logic. It refines and extends a powerful theoretical tradition to new questions, to a new empirical puzzle, to new (non-European) historical cases, and in new directions hitherto overlooked. Given the central theoretical standing of emulation (and balancing) in the theory, correcting and elaborating its treatment of emulation involves reexamining neorealism's entire explanatory infrastructure and inner logic. While explaining an historical puzzle, the work shows the theory has much greater explanatory reach, and greater empirical and historical application, than both critics and defenders recognize.

Efforts to refine and extend neorealism face many obstacles, not the least of which is Waltz's own opposition. If his reply to Elman and others is any indication, Waltz seems content with a theory that loosely explains only a "few big and important" outcomes.[16] He continues to view efforts to enhance the theory's determinacy and causal specification as reductionist, as efforts to place more weight on the theory than it can bear. This study shows we can enhance the determinacy of the theory without altering its spare conception of structure or compromising its elegance and economy. Another objection might be that, given this study's comparative case design and its aim to explain emulation behavior of individual states, the theory of emulation that I construct strays too far from systemic patterns and outcomes and too close to explaining foreign policy. The objection is unwarranted. After all, patterns and outcomes in the system are generated by unit behavior. Indeed, my aim is to show precisely how structure limits and shapes the decisions and choices of states. Neorealism and its theory of emulation, which I develop, make testable claims about state behavior, while remaining faithful to structural level causal properties. Waltz associates theories of foreign policy with unit-level causes. The neorealist theory of emulation that I construct is a theory of structural causes and the logic of behavior in anarchy.

The theory of emulation, once developed, invites us to reconsider the entire architecture of neorealist theory. It offers us an elegant and robust

---

[16] Kenneth N. Waltz, "International Politics Is Not Foreign Policy," *Security Studies* 6, no. 1 (Autumn 1996): 54–57. See also, Waltz, "Reflections," in Keohane, ed., *Neorealism and Its Critics*.

explanation of why states emulate and why there is variance in their emulation efforts, but it also gives us an insight into the nature of the state's development over time. Large-scale military emulation, like other forms of sustained internal mobilization, invariably entail changes that extend beyond organs and matters of state that are strictly military in character. I argue that neorealism is a theory of organizational effects. It treats the state as the highest political organization whose primary function is protection against the insecurity of the external realm.[17] The exigencies of the external realm, and its continually changing requirements for survival and viability, condition the organizational development and not just external behavior of states. Competition has organizational consequences. The proof is not so much Waltz's trademark argument-by-analogy to microeconomics, but is instead to be found in the first four chapters of Theory of International Politics. Each one of neorealism's two main predictions about the behavior of states entails organizational consequences. These twin organizational effects are derivatives of internal balancing: anarchic structure not only presses states continually to retool and reorganize but it induces them to follow similar transformations and trajectories.

The theory's inner logic is about the organizational effects of competition in anarchically organized realms. States simply cannot engage in large-scale internal mobilization, especially in core areas relating to the organization and management of military power, without the process leaving major scars, imprints, or spin-offs. Both processes, propelled by the pressures of external competition, involve or trigger changes in the state's internal arrangements from the size, differentiation, and functions of its organizational apparatus to social-economic and political conditions. We need not place too ambitious a claim on neorealism or the theory of emulation in this regard. At a minimum, we need to make explicit this dimension of the theory. The entire architecture of neorealism points to an outside-in causal framework, one which gives us important clues into the state's organizational development. Waltz's famous second image formulation posited that state attributes and internal arrangements determine their external behavior in the international system.[18] The second image reversed, as famously elaborated by Gourevitch, posited that the international system has causal weight in shaping and conditioning the internal organization and not just the behavior of states.[19] Internal balancing is the avenue through which the system works its organizational effects on states.

---

[17] This conception of the state appears in fragmented form in Waltz, *Theory of International Politics*, 118, 130–31, 177–78, 181, 183. This conception is similar to that in the Historical Sociology Works of Tilly, Skocpol and others.

[18] Waltz, *Man, the State, and War.*

[19] Peter Gourevitch, "The Second Image Reversed: The International Sources of Domestic Politics," *International Organization* 32, no. 4 (Fall 1978): 881–911.

This aspect of neorealism is both underdeveloped by neorealists and over-looked by critics. Neorealists have yet to explicate a coherent set of propositions about organizational effects of anarchic realms. I suspect that this underdevelopment of the theory is the result of the exclusive attention paid to external forms of balancing, even though intuitively we expect that contending units in self-help realms will turn mainly to internally directed efforts to bolster their relative competitive effectiveness.

This study lies at the heart of neorealism's core logic and does what Waltz failed to do. It elaborates neorealism's theoretical infrastructure, brings greater determinacy and specification to its causal framework, and does so while remaining faithful to its structural logic and without undermining its economy and elegance. More critically, my book shows that Waltzian neorealism – so widely criticized as ahistorical and unable to account for one of its main units of analysis, does have something useful to say about states and their historical development. I am suggesting, therefore, that much more is implicated, theoretically and historically, in the process of military emulation. Crossnational military emulation is not just the leading pathway through which military organizations change, develop, and follow common trajectories. It is also an avenue through which we can examine the historical development of states and their shared organizational-technological transformations.

THE STUDY IN WIDE ANGLE

This is a work of theory and history; one that marries Waltz to Tilly. A study of crossnational emulation reveals a number of theoretical and historical issues hitherto unnoticed in neorealism and largely unconnected in IR debates. Neorealism has been widely and correctly criticized for not having any account of the state.[20] I will address this more fully later. Suffice it is to say that neorealism's silence regarding the nature and historical development of the state is not the result of any theoretical inadequacy but of underdevelopment and neglect. Recasting neorealism as a theory of organizational effects allows us to extend the theory to account for aspects of the state's macrohistorical development.[21]

The realist tradition across the millennia has emphasized the centrality of power and violence in the life of states. Clearly, if power competition

---

[20] Michael Mastanduno, David A. Lake, and G. John Ikenberry, "Toward a Realist Theory of State Action," *International Studies Quarterly* 33, no. 4 (December 1989): 457–474; Stephen Hobden, *International Relations and Historical Sociology: Breaking Down Boundaries* (London: Routledge, 1998); Fred Halliday, *Rethinking International Relations* (Vancouver: University of British Columbia Press, 1994).

[21] Charles Tilly, *Coercion, Capital, and European States, A.D. 900–1990* (Cambridge: Basil Blackwell, 1990); Theda Skocpol, *States and Social Revolutions: A Comparative Analysis of France, Russia, and China* (Cambridge: Cambridge University Press, 1979).

and organized violence are central to the international system as well as to the state formation process, then realism can speak to this larger historical process. The theory of emulation is self-consciously embedded in the long-standing realist verity regarding the centrality of power and violence in the life of states. These insights run parallel in a number of other fields of theorizing, especially historical sociology. Tilly and others have shown the organizational effects of war making on the state's development over time. While Hobbes provides the intellectual lineage of the idea that the anarchy of the external realm drives the organization of hierarchy internally, Hintze and the German Historical School provide the first coherent scholarly elaboration of the political-organizational effects of the international system.

The realist tradition has always had a latent second image reversed perspective dating to Thucydides and later Hobbes. It is a tradition attentive to how the requirements of power and security in the interstate system, shapes, and constrains the organization of the state. The Hobbesian state was an organizational solution to a double security dilemma, an internal and external security dilemma. The neorealist contribution to Hobbes's original insight of the state as an organizational solution to insecurity of the external realm is that, as the minimum requirements of external security and competitive effectiveness change, so too must the form and organizational attributes of the solution. Since large-scale military emulation involves restructuring the central fiscal-administrative-coercive apparatus of the state edifice – and to the extent military organization and warfare are at the heart of state formation – it is likewise a pathway for the historical development of the state. Moreover, the theory of emulation posits that this change in the form and particulars of the organizational solution will tend to follow predictable paths and similar transformations across states.

The theory of emulation posits a causal relationship between the anarchy of the external realm and the development and articulation of hierarchy in the domestic realm. I argue that this theory of emulation leads to a broader neorealist theory of the state, though this is a subject matter for another book. I do not claim that neorealism has a full-blown theory of the state. Neorealists must proceed carefully here so as not to overreach, given the demands of a fully developed theory of the state. Nevertheless, neorealism and its theory of emulation can speak to an important dimension of the state's organizational development. I also argue that the main conceptual pillars of this theory of the state are contained inside neorealism as originally formulated by Waltz. No amendment or ad hoc reductionist amplification of the theory is required.

Developing a theory of crossnational emulation is the first big foundation piece for understanding a major aspect of the state's historical development. Military emulation – as all forms of large-scale internal balancing – has much broader theoretical and historical implications. But in IR debates today, and in the interpretation and application of neorealism, there is a marked tendency to view world politics in static terms. The realist tradition is particularly guilty. Internal balancing, warfare, efforts to increase competitive effectiveness and the like, are viewed in static, narrow terms – snapshots in the life of states, divorced from the ramifications that follow from these major episodes. Efforts to enhance competitive effectiveness are neither neutral nor superficial in their impact.

Military emulation is the primary avenue through which military organizations develop, change, and follow common organizational-technological transformations. The theory of emulation captures a big part of the relationship binding the state, the organization of violence, and the state system, but it cannot presuppose to capture all complexities and intricacies. The theory offers an elegant and persuasive explanation of large-scale military emulation and its impact on matters directly pertaining to the design and organization of the military. It cannot tell us, for it cannot capture, all the details and variance in the state's organizational development. Just as emulation ranges from simple to large scale, however, so too the second image reversed effects of international competition will vary from simple to complex outcomes and organizational consequences – some either too subtle, too intricate, or delayed to be visible to an elegant systemic theory. Yet the theory can illuminate some aspects of this larger process.

In the South American cases, large scale military emulation gave rise to a number of spill-over effects and ramifications that extended beyond parts of the state that were strictly military in character. Leaving aside the many ancillary changes or the altered relationship between state and society, for example, large-scale military modernization resulted in great physical expansion of the military establishment. Not only was modernization itself expensive, maintaining the larger organ of state, in turn, demanded greater extraction and improvement in the state's extractive capacity. As Brewer, Tilly, and many others have articulated in crisper and more elegant language, two further ramifications stemmed from this: expansion of the state's role and greater organizational (bureaucratic) elaboration. If war and war making capacity are at the center of state formation, as Tilly and others have shown, then no other intellectual tradition in international relations is better equipped to address a big part of the state's historical development than realism. Indeed, much of the so-called war-centric accounts of state formation in sister disciplines, such as history and sociology, though far richer and multicausal, are realist insofar as they give central importance to warfare, military capacity, and external political competition in the state's organizational development.

These organizational effects of anarchic competition are nowhere more visible than in the central fiscal-administrative-coercive apparatus of states. While state development cannot simply be reduced to its central edifice, the formation, growth, and transformation of its central apparatus occupies an extensive terrain in the sum of its development. At major historical junctures, the mobilization and mustering of human and material resources will usually entail reform and restructuring in the rest of the state apparatus, the economy, and society – a point anticipated by Porter, Tilly, Barnett, Posen, Mann, Howard, and others.[22] Large-scale military emulation of the kind engaged in by the South Americans was accompanied by ancillary changes in areas not strictly military in character. Its repercussions were visible in societal, political, and even constitutional areas. It required, or triggered, major changes in the rest of the state apparatus as well as the state's overall relationship to the economy and society. For example, it is not possible to understand fully the emergence of public primary education, the rise of the state's economic role, or the beginnings of national arms manufacturing industry in countries like Brazil, Chile, and Argentina without reference to this period of internal mobilization and emulation.

The state's macrohistorical development is driven by both universalizing and homogenizing forces as well as forces of particularism.[23] The neorealist theory of the state does not deny the role of internal forces in the organization and development of the state. The sum total of the state's development, and its internal conditions and arrangements, involve much more than interstate war, war preparation, and organizing military power in pursuit of security. Indeed, in Latin America as elsewhere, far more bloodshed has been spilled within than between states. The theory does suggest that this historical process has an external dimension that bears upon many areas of the state's evolution. In particular, the theory posits that the choices states make in the design and organization of its central edifice are guided by the requirements of international competition.

Waltz's structural realism is also the subject of criticism for its alleged inability to account for change in the system. I will address this matter in the

---

[22] I borrow from the following works: Bruce Porter, *War and the Rise of the State: The Military Foundations of Modern Politics* (New York: Free Press, 1994); Tilly, *Coercion, Capital, and European States*, and "War Making and State Making as Organized Crime," in Peter Evans, Dietrich Rueschemeyer, and Theda Skocpol, eds., *Bringing the State Back In* (Cambridge: Cambridge University Press, 1985): 169–91; Michael N. Barnett, *Confronting the Costs of War: Military Power, State, and Society in Egypt and Israel* (Princeton: Princeton University Press, 1992); Michael Mann, *The Sources of Social Power*, 2 vols. (Cambridge and New York: Cambridge University Press, 1993); Michael Howard, *War in European History* (London: Oxford University Press, 1976); Geoffrey Best, *War and Society in Revolutionary Europe, 1770–1870* (Leicester: Leicester University Press, 1982); Thomas Ertman, *Birth of the Leviathan: Building States and Regimes in Medieval and Early Modern Europe* (Cambridge: Cambridge University Press, 1997); John Brewer, *The Sinews of Power: War, Money and the English State, 1688–1783* (Cambridge, MA: Harvard University Press, 1988); Karen A. Rassler and William R. Thompson, *War and State Making: The Shaping of the Global Powers* (Boston: Unwin Hyman, 1989); Anthony Giddens, *The Nation-State and Violence: A Contemporary Critique of Historical Materialism*, vol. 2 (Berkeley: University of California Press, 1987); Brian Downing, *The Military Revolution and Political Change: Origins of Democracy and Autocracy in Early Modern Europe* (Princeton: Princeton University Press, 1991).

[23] I thank Rudy Sil, University of Pennsylvania, for this expression.

concluding chapter. In view of emulation – its obvious implications for the organization of the state as well as crossnational convergence – this accusation against neorealism is at odds with the actual theoretical narrative. However, we should note that it is not entirely clear what critics mean by "change." At which of the three tiers of structure should we expect change? Depending on the nature, form, or level of change anticipated, neorealism views some forms of change as possible and other forms impossible in anarchic realms. A closer reading of neorealism uncovers a theory that anticipates both stasis and change in the system; a system of dismaying persistence as well as dynamism.[24]

CROSSNATIONAL EMULATION AND CONVERGENCE

Since the first state-units began interacting to form an anarchic interstate system, emulation has been part of the life of states. Whenever one unit developed a practice, institution, or technology that enhanced its competitive position, such practices or methods were emulated by others in the system. In the wake of the Peloponnesian wars, the Spartan development of hoplite warfare was quickly copied throughout the region. That it took over three centuries for the combination of Spanish conquistadores and the new states of South America to defeat the native Araucanian Nations was in part due to the latter's successful and adept adoption of European weapons and tactics. The Maratha states of present-day India made conquest a costly affair for the British when in the late 1700s they began to adopt Western military weapons, and even hired some European military advisers.[25] The grand studies of McNeill and Parker examine how organizational and technological innovations in one part of early modern Europe and after were quickly imitated and adopted throughout the region and beyond.

As Table 1.1 shows, the South American republics were neither the first nor the only ones to emulate the French and German armies at the close of the nineteenth century. A good number of them, for instance, selectively emulated the Prussian general staff alone.[26] Mitchell and Posen provide insightful accounts of mutual emulation behavior between France and Germany throughout the nineteenth century.[27] By the turn of the century emulation had spread through much of the region, including Ecuador, Colombia,

---

[24] Jennifer Sterling-Folker, "Realism and the Constructivist Challenge: Rejecting, Reconstructing, or Rereading," *International Studies Review* 4, no. 1 (Spring 2002): 73–97.

[25] Geoffrey Parker, *The Military Revolution: Military Innovation and the Rise of the West* (Cambridge: Cambridge University Press, 1988), 136.

[26] On this point see Trevor N. Dupy, *A Genius for War: The German Army and General Staff, 1807–1945* (Englewood Cliffs: Prentice-Hall, 1977).

[27] Mitchell, "A Situation of Inferiority;" and *Victors and Vanquished*; Barry Posen, "Nationalism"; David B. Ralston, *The Army of the Republic: The Place of the Military in the Political Evolution of France, 1871–1914* (Cambridge: MIT Press, 1967).

Venezuela, Guatemala, El Salvador, Bolivia, and Peru. On the periphery of Europe at this time, several states engaged in large-scale, sustained military emulation.[28] Diverse states such as Russia, the Ottoman Empire, China, Egypt, the United States, and Japan launched modernizing emulation programs with varying degrees of scale and success. In many cases, these states contracted official military missions from the European great powers after whom they sought to model their new military system. In the period of the war of the Crimea to the First World War, the French and German armies were the most emulated in the world.

That the international system conditions the state's core organizational makeup, among other internal aspects of its development, is not a novel idea.[29] Nor is the idea that crossnational convergence and borrowing take place in the system, as Veblen, in his brilliance and originality, first explored in one of the earliest scholarly treatments of the subject.[30] Veblen was especially fascinated by why some societies were more prodigious in adopting and utilizing borrowed foreign practices. For Gerschenkron, geopolitical competition was pivotal in the industrial and political development of states, leaving different institutional imprint depending on the onset of competition and level of technology.[31] The works of Gourevitch, Rogowski, and others carry on the long-standing inquiry into how the international economic system conditions the organization of the state as well as its internal political arrangements. The English school has always inquired into the global spread of state practices. Classical liberalism from Ricardo to modernization theory viewed crossnational emulation and convergence as both desirable and inevitable. Much of the international development literature recognize the importance of crossnational borrowing in late development, and the advantages "late modernizers" derive from product-cycle diffusion and emulation of early industrializers.[32] Theories of imperialism, especially

---

[28] Ralston, *Importing the European Army.*

[29] Ronald Rogowski, *Commerce and Coalitions: How Trade Affects Domestic Political Alignments* (Princeton: Princeton University Press, 1989); Gourevitch, "The Second Image Reversed"; E. L. Jones, *The European Miracle: Environment, Economies, and Geopolitics in the History of Europe and Asia,* 2nd ed. (Cambridge: Cambridge University Press, 1987); *The Expansion of International Society,* ed. Hedley Bull and Adam Watson (Oxford: Clarendon Press, 1984). See also Peter A. Gourevitch, *Politics in Hard Times: Comparative Responses to International Economic Crises* (Ithaca: Cornell University Press, 1986).

[30] Thorstein Veblen, *Imperial Germany and the Industrial Revolution* (Ann Arbor: University of Michigan Press, 1966 [1915]); Westney, *Innovation and Imitation.* See also Ellen Kay Trimberger, *Revolutions from Above: Military Bureaucrats and Development in Japan, Turkey, Egypt, and Peru* (New Brunswick: Transaction Books, 1978); Rudra Sil, *Managing "Modernity": Work, Community, and Authority in Late-Industrializing Japan and Russia* (Ann Arbor: University of Michigan Press, 2002).

[31] Alexander Gerschenkron, *Economic Backwardness in Historical Perspectives: A Book of Essays* (Cambridge: Belknap Press of Harvard University Press, 1962).

[32] Berger and Dore, eds., *National Diversity.*

dependency theory and world systems theory, saw generative and homogenizing forces at work in the global capitalist system and in the relations between core and peripheral societies.[33] Theories of hegemonic war, long cycles, and power transition make implicit assumptions about the role of emulation in epochal change in the system.[34]

ALTERNATIVE EXPLANATIONS

To claim that countries copy the best practices of one another may seem, prima facie, intuitive and uninteresting. That the technology and organizational practices of the leading military system of an era reappear crossnationally is common in history. Why they do so, however, is a matter of intense theoretical debate in IR theory. My aim is to construct a neorealist theory of emulation. I do not wish to rehash the often stilted and formulaic debates between neorealism and competing theories; suffice it to note that neorealism is at a distinct disadvantage because of its underdevelopment. Alternative explanations merit far more careful elucidation, serious scrutiny, and empirical testing than possible here. It is with reluctance that I mention them here.

Crossnational military emulation lends itself to competing explanations at all three main levels of analysis – organizational, domestic political, and international. It is an inviting subject matter for explanations in both rationalist as well as reflectivist, or ideational, traditions. Moreover, the character of the historical cases themselves – secondary states, Latin America – is tempting to those who view behavior of such states as distinct or unique. Such explanations are easily dismissed, for all states engage in emulation.

A related explanation commonly used to interpret the national security behavior of secondary states is regime insecurity.[35] It posits that the foreign

---

[33] Fernando Henrique Cardoso and Enzo Faletto, *Dependency and Development in Latin America* (Berkeley: University of California Press, 1979); Emmanuel Wallerstein, *The Modern World System: Capitalist Agriculture and the Origins of the European World-Economy in the Sixteenth Century* (New York: Academic Press, 1976).

[34] Robert Gilpin, *War and Change in World Politics* (Cambridge: Cambridge University Press, 1981); Paul M. Kennedy, *The Rise and Fall of the Great Powers: Economic Change and Military Conflict from 1500 to 2000* (New York: Random House, 1987); George Modelski, *The Long Cycle* (Seattle: University of Washington Press, 1987).

[35] Stephen R. David, *Choosing Sides: Alignment and Realignment in the Third World* (Baltimore: Johns Hopkins University Press, 1991); Robert Rothstein, "The 'Security Dilemma' and the 'Poverty Trap' in the Third World," *Jerusalem Journal of International Relations* 8, no. 4 (December 1986): 1–38; *The Insecurity Dilemma: The National Security of Third World States*, ed. Brian Job (Boulder: Lynne Reinner, 1990). See also Robert L. Rothstein, "Epitaph for a Monument to a Failed Protest? A North–South Retrospective," *International Security* 42, no. 2 (Spring 1988): 725–52; Mohammed Ayoob, *The Third World Security Predicament: State Making, Regional Conflict, and the International System* (Boulder: Lynne Reinner, 1995).

and security policies of secondary states are driven by internal threats; by the necessities of regime survival facing weak and vulnerable rulers. This explanation appears to fit nicely in the context of Latin America, given its turbulent political history and interminable bouts of civil wars, military coup d'état, and repression. The military traditionally has been viewed as an instrument of repression, the praetorian guard of wretched leaders. This explanation, however, cannot account for the wide variety of states that engage in emulation, let alone its timing, pace, and scale. More critically, there is no logical reason why insecure leaders would opt for large-scale military emulation; the creation of a large, professional, and institutionally autonomous military undercuts their rule. Weak leaders will prefer servile, subjectively controlled militaries. As for the three historical cases studied here, regime insecurity was never a factor during the period examined.

Unit-level explanations, such as domestic political battles and organizational behavior, are popular explanations for crossnational emulation. I argue that system-level structural material factors alone suffice to account for the overall variance in military emulation across states. The theory of emulation developed in this study does not claim to account for all the variance in military emulation. This is not a weakness. No structural theory can make such a claim. By definition, all theories leave out some unexplained variance. Indeed, some measure of unexplained, or residual, variance is likely to accompany all episodes of military emulation, especially its timing, pace, and scale. The theory of emulation need not be preoccupied with eliminating all residual variance as long as predicted outcomes fall within expected ranges. Nor is there any need to attempt some integrative explanatory scheme that tries, uneasily, to marry neorealist structural framework with reductionist variables. I am skeptical of such schemes for various reasons, not the least of which is their loss of economy and reductionism. The fact that states of varying domestic and military organizational conditions engage in the same external behavior indicates that the explanation for their common behavior must necessarily lie elsewhere. More important, I suspect that unit-level factors, such as the level of domestic political opposition for example, are themselves partly a function of the intensity of external pressures. Unit-level factors, such as regime insecurity and domestic politics, cannot provide satisfactory explanations for why states emulate and whom they emulate. Domestic-level factors may be interesting in highlighting individual details but are unnecessary in explaining the sources and overall pattern of variance in military emulation.

The subject matter (military organizational change) and the historical cases (Latin America) force us to consider seriously the weight of these factors. Military organizational and domestic political explanations are too numerous and too divergent to allow a just and thorough explication here. Military organizational and domestic political factors will affect variance in timing, pace, and scale of emulation at the margins. They fill in the range predicted by the theory of emulation. The point here is not that the neorealist theory of emulation is flawed or ought to engage in reductionist incorporation of such factors, but to underscore the reality of the process of military emulation.

For students of Latin American politics, the beginning and end of any analysis of politics and society in the region is the military and its political role. Matters involving changes in military organization, missions, or internal procedures turn our attention to military organizational explanations. Military emulation is ultimately about organizational change – the destruction or reform of antiquated but deeply entrenched institutions and their replacement by new ones. Nothing in the military organization literature leads us to conclude this is a smooth and automatic process, let alone one driven by forces outside the organization.[36] I expect, for example, that intramilitary opposition will play a role in determining the exact timing, pace, and scale of military emulation. It would be unrealistic to expect otherwise. Large-scale military emulation everywhere will have its defenders and its opponents, winners and losers, inside the organization. It is first and foremost a challenge to entrenched interests vested in the existing status quo inside and outside the military. Large-scale military emulation involves the redistribution of power and resources, unavoidably leaving behind winners and losers. It has enormous consequences domestically in terms of the distribution of power: between government and society, central and regional power centers, executive and other branches, between reformers and standpatters within the military. These correspond to the main sources, or loci, of opposition: civil society, regional governments, provincial power brokers, congress, and antireform factions within the military.

Most works that have examined crossnational emulation have adopted some form of cultural, or ideational, analysis to explain emulation behavior and choices. In general, cultural explanations have been popular and long-standing in the literature on crossnational emulation. Explanations that posit social, cultural foundations of state behavior constitute a wide-ranging and heterogeneous research program, with as many formulations, methodologies, and theoretical labels as there are works. The best and most familiar

---

[36] I rely mainly on these works: Stephen Van Evera, *The Causes of War: Power and the Roots of Conflict* (Ithaca: Cornell University Press, 1999); Scott D. Sagan, "The Perils of Proliferation: Organization Theory, Deterrence Theory, and the Spread of Nuclear Weapons," *International Security* 18, no. 4 (Spring 1994): 66–107; Kimberly Marten Zisk, *Engaging the Enemy: Organization Theory and Soviet Military Innovation, 1955–1991* (Princeton: Princeton University Press, 1993); Jack Snyder, *The Ideology of the Offensive: Military Decision Making and the Disasters of 1914* (Ithaca: Cornell University Press, 1984); Stephen P. Rosen, *Winning the Next War: Innovation and the Modern Military* (Ithaca: Cornell University Press, 1991); Stephen Van Evera, "The Cult of the Offensive and the Origins of the First World War," *International Security* 9, no. 1 (Summer 1984): 58–107; Posen, *The Sources of Military Doctrine*.

works embrace approaches such as sociological institutionalism, constructivism, military organizational culture, and strategic culture. To avoid confusion, I will use the generic label social theory, though I will often refer to the umbrella term cultural analysis.[37] Whether we attach the adjective social or cultural, it is a research program that sees ideas and shared norms, within and among states, as the foundation of behavior, interests, preferences, and what is loosely referred to as "identity." While I base my comments on individual works, it is important to note that there is no one social theory. Moreover, social theory emphasizes the causal primacy of social-cultural-ideational forces in world politics, but cultural arguments about crossnational emulation are not confined to social theory. The most sustained theorizing on crossnational emulation has come from organizational sociology, which heavily influences versions of social theory such as sociological institutionalism.[38]

---

[37] The principal works cited here are: Alexander Wendt, *Social Theory of International Politics* (Cambridge: Cambridge University Press, 1999); Jeffrey Checkel, "The Constructivist Turn in International Relations Theory," *World Politics* 50, no. 2 (February 1998): 324–48; Katzenstein, ed., *The Culture of National Security*; Elizabeth Kier, *Imagining War: French and British Military Doctrine Between the Wars* (Princeton: Princeton University Press, 1997); Thomas U. Berger, *Cultures of Anti-Militarism: National Security in Germany and Japan* (Baltimore: Johns Hopkins University Press, 1998); *Tamed Power: Germany in Europe*, ed. Peter J. Katzenstein (Ithaca: Cornell University Press, 1997); Alastair Iain Johnston, *Cultural Realism: Strategic Culture and Grand Strategy in Chinese History* (Princeton: Princeton University Press, 1995); John G. Ruggie, "Continuity and Transformation in the World Polity," *World Politics* 35, no. 2 (January 1983): 261–85; Richard K. Ashley, "Untying the Sovereign State: A Double Reading of the Anarchy Problematique," *Millennium* 17, no. 2 (Summer 1988): 227–62; Mlada Bukovansky, "The Altered State and the State of Nature: The French Revolution in International Politics," *Review of International Studies* 25 (1999): 197–216; Robert Cox, "Social Forces, States, and World Orders: Beyond International Relations Theory," in Keohane, ed., *Neorealism and Its Critics*, 204–54; Martin Hollis and Steve Smith, *Explaining and Understanding in International Relations* (Oxford: Clarendon Press, 1990); Yosef Lapid, "The Third Debate: On the Prospects of International Theory in a Post-Positivist Era," *International Studies Quarterly* 33 (1989): 235–54; Yosef Lapid and Friedrich V. Kratochwil, eds., *The Return of Culture and Identity in IR Theory* (Boulder: Lynne Rienner, 1996); Ted Hopf, "The Promise of Constructivism in International Relations Theory," *International Security* 23, no. 1 (Summer 1998): 171–200; Alexander Wendt, "Anarchy Is What States Make of It: The Social Construction of Power Politics," *International Organization* 46, no. 2 (Spring 1992): 391–425; Martha Finnemore, *National Interest in International Society* (Princeton: Princeton University Press, 1997), and "International Organizations as Teachers of Norms: The United Nations Educational, Scientific, and Cultural Organization," *International Organization* 47, no. 4 (Fall 1993): 565–97. See also Dana P. Eyre and Mark C. Suchman, "Status, Norms, and the Proliferation of Chemical Weapons: An Institutional Theory Approach," in Katzenstein, ed., *The Culture of National Security*, 79–113.

[38] The seminal work remains *The New Institutionalism in Organizational Analysis*, ed. Walter W. Powell and Paul J. DiMaggio (Chicago: University of Chicago Press, 1991). The pioneering work in this area is John W. Meyer and the so-called Stanford School of Sociology. See John W. Meyer, "The World Polity and the Authority of the Modern Nation-State," in *Studies of the Modern World-System*, ed. Albert J. Bergesen (New York: Academic Press,

There are different grades of social-cultural arguments in IR today, but they unite around the common proposition that the foundations of state behavior are ideational, not material cultural, not political. Despite the variety of cultural theories populating the IR literature, they also have in common a rejection of realist theories and all other materialist accounts of state behavior. Moreover, they are motivated by the desire to explain change in the international system which, they argue, neorealism cannot. The current wave of cultural theorizing explains military-strategic behavior as a cultural phenomenon. The general thrust of these cultural arguments is that national security affairs – namely, the state's perception of its external environment, its security needs, its responses, strategy, and measures – are constructed and filtered through culturally accepted norms and values or shared ideas. Social theory makes a more profound claim about states and world politics. Namely, that ideas and norms have constitutive, not just regulative, properties.

The growth of cultural, or ideational, analysis in security studies has been impressive, yielding a number of fresh and pioneering works. The works of Goldman and others examine the cultural foundations of crossnational emulation and military technological diffusion.[39] A number of works, for example, have argued that the military policy and strategies of states are products of their national political-military culture.[40] Other works trace state security behavior to military organizational culture.[41] More sophisticated and pioneering cultural analysis in IR can be found in the works on strategic culture, which explain national security behavior and military policy as results of each state's political-military culture.[42] Less sophisticated versions of cultural theory make claims about cultural matching, or compatibility, whereby states emulate others based on cultural affinity. Thus, Prussia's emulation by the South Americans and Japanese would have been based on cultural compatibility. Another version of cultural matching posits that emulation will occur only insofar as global norms (embodied in specific practices and

---

1980), 41–70; *Organizational Environments: Ritual and Rationality*, ed. John W. Meyer and W. Richard Scott (Newbury Park: Sage, 1992); *The Institutional Construction of Organizations: International and Longitudinal Studies*, ed. W. Richard Scott and Soren Christensen (Thousand Oaks: Sage, 1995). The most lucid version of sociological institutionalism in IR are the works of Finnemore, *National Interest*, and "International Organizations." See also Theo Farrell, "World Culture and Military Power," *Security Studies* 14, no. 3 (Spring 2005): 448–88.

39 Goldman, "Cultural Foundations."

40 Berger, *Cultures of Anti-Militarism*; Katzenstein, ed., *Cultural Norms and National Security*.

41 Jeffrey W. Legro, *Cooperation Under Fire: Anglo–German Restraint During World War II* (Ithaca: Cornell University Press, 1995), and "Military Culture and Inadvertent Escalation in World War II," *International Security* 18, no. 4 (Spring 1998): 108–42.

42 Johnston, *Cultural Realism*; Kier, *Imagining War*, and "Culture and Military Doctrine: France Between the Wars," *International Security* 19, no. 4 (Spring 1995): 65–93.

organizations) are compatible with national culture.[43] A permutation of this argument gives causal primacy to the extent of cultural tolerance present in a society or among its elite. Emulation will occur under conditions of cultural tolerance, and will be obstructed or delayed in situations where elites defend traditional orthodoxy or the national culture is resistant to change. Since Latin America's culture is often portrayed as conservative, intolerant, hierarchical, and tradition-bound because of its Catholic heritage, presumably this version of cultural analysis will not find much empirical support. Other familiar, if also less sophisticated, forms of social theory are prestige arguments, which claim that policies and choices of states are driven by prestige goals. For reasons that are likely more ethnocentric than theoretical, prestige arguments are usually associated with the behavior of developing countries and small states.

As exemplified by these works, there is no one cultural, or social, theory in IR. The concept of culture is variously defined – and a notoriously difficult concept in social science. Cultural analysis in IR locates causal variables at three main levels of analysis or some intricate interplay of multiple levels: organizational, domestic, and international. Some scholars define culture as historically grounded and society bound, while others adopt global formulations. Traditionally, the concept has denoted national difference and uniqueness. Thus, each state has its own unique cultural makeup that shapes its own distinct brand of external behavior. States having different cultures will behave differently. Works in this line of cultural arguments focus on the peculiarities of national-level culture, whereby contingent, historically grounded and unique cultural values and norms of individual states determine their external behavior. States are viewed as culturally-bound actors. This is the most common form of cultural analysis in IR, and has anthropology as its intellectual font. Accordingly, cultural analyses, such as the ones mentioned above, make opposite claims regarding state behavior and emulation specifically. Works that locate cultural causes inside the state, at the organizational or national cultural level, posit cultural uniqueness that blocks or distorts external behavior, like emulation, that neorealism sees as common and reoccurring across all states. Presumably, national cultural distinctiveness supersedes international norms and global cultural models. While the unlikely assortment of states that emulated Prussia did not seem to mind, unit-level cultural explanations expect states to preserve jealously their own unique practices and reject those of others. Unit-level cultural explanations are simply unsustainable, given the variety of states (and their military organizations) that behaved similarly.

Versions of social theory, or cultural analysis generally, that pose a more compelling challenge to neorealism are those that give causal primacy to

---

[43] Jeffrey T. Checkel, "Norms, Institutions, and Cultural Identity in Contemporary Europe," *International Studies Quarterly* 43 (1999): 83–114, and "The Constructivist Turn."

structural, or third-image, forces. Amidst the latest flowering of cultural analysis in IR, third image social theory, which gives causal primacy to global cultural norms and standardized (global) models of statehood, has a carefully refined and articulated theory of crossnational emulation. In contrast, the realist tradition has been conspicuously silent. Indeed, many of its accounts are deceptively similar to neorealism's. Paradoxically, both neorealism and systemic social theory predict emulation and convergence in the system. Both offer structural accounts. Both see the political and organizational development of the state as occurring within a larger, external context rather than as purely the products of self-contained processes and histories. For one, system structure consists of ideational or social forces, while in the other, structure is material in composition. The theoretical chasm between the two traditions is great. Each, in addition, is based on metatheoretical, epistemological presuppositions that are irreconcilable and, ultimately, unverifiable in the case of social theory.

Although most third-image social theories embrace an elaborate, if ambiguous, interplay between structural, process, and unit-level variables, they share a common emphasis on the global social-cultural structure, or social environment, of states. Social theory sees social-cultural, not material, forces at work in the international realm that shapes and molds the behavior and internal makeup of states. Variants in social theory make an even bigger theoretical turn. Moving beyond the moderate social theorizing of Wendt, who allows for the presence of some material factors with independent causal weight, a number of social theorists reject an independently constituted material base. Rather, they argue, material forces are socially constructed. More accurately, their meaning and role are intersubjectively derived. Material power and interests of states are socially constructed.

Third-image social theory appears to be well suited to explain crossnational emulation and its resulting interstate isomorphism. Global social structure constitutes, or socializes, states. We should add, however, that many social theorists, and social theory in general, commit to the principle of reciprocal constitution or codetermination between actors and structure. Following Wendt, we can bracket the unit-level, or bottom-up social construction in order to elucidate the top-down process. Third-image social theory, in other words, has its own version of the second image reversed, whereby global social-cultural forces construct and transform the identity, preferences, and attributes of states. Put differently, the international system is a realm of social construction, or socialization. Emulation is a process of social-historical construction. This is a tailor-made explanation for emulation. One implication is that we ought to see continual emulation by states.

In third-image accounts, such as sociological institutionalism, the nature and organizing principles of state-actors in the system are constructed and reconstructed through global social interaction and collective practices which define the appropriate nature, purpose, attributes, preferences, and behavior of statehood. The world polity defines for all states appropriate organizational and technological practices.[44] States, in other words, are organizational embodiments of world-cultural norms and models, from which they learn and emulate the meaning, attributes, and practices of statehood. International social-cultural structure is constitutive and generative. For Finnemore, states are socialized by international organizations, rather than disembodied collectives in the world polity.[45] The state's social construction is both an ideological (normative) and organizational process.

The modern sovereign territorial state itself is a collective norm; a socially selected and mutually empowered (or legitimated) form organizing political space that precludes other possible forms.[46] Its symbols and practices of statehood – its organs, policies, behavior, self-image, etc. – are products of historical social construction. Emulation becomes a social process whereby states internalize socialized beliefs about what kinds of interests to have, what aims are appropriate, what practices are acceptable, and so on. State behavior and choices are guided by a "logic of appropriateness," emulating standardized global models and practices deemed most appropriate or legitimate. Collectively held standards of appropriateness, for instance, determine which military technologies, practices, or methods of organization and warfare are acceptable and, alternatively, which practices or technologies are taboo.[47] (Of course, this does not explain why so many states, so often, risk pariah status and military attack in order to acquire taboo weapons technologies.) Thus, appropriate and acceptable security policies and military practices are embedded in, and legitimized by, a world political-military culture that defines appropriate national security policies, military practices and organization.[48]

Third-image critical theory claims to provide a superior explanation of state behavior even in traditional realist preserve – military and security affairs.[49] For neorealism, emulation is driven by a competitive logic, by a

---

[44] Meyer, "The World Polity," 113.

[45] Finnemore, *National Interests*.

[46] Hendrik Spruyt, *The Sovereign State and Its Competitors* (Princeton: Princeton University Press, 1994); Robert Jackson, *Quasi-States: Sovereignty, International Relations, and the Third World* (Cambridge: Cambridge University Press, 1990); David Strang, "Anomaly and Commonplace in European Political Expansion: Realist and Institutionalist Accounts," *International Organization* 45, no. 2 (Spring 1991): 143–62; *State Sovereignty as Social Construct*, ed. Thomas J. Biersteker and Cynthia Weber (Cambridge: Cambridge University Press, 1996); David Strang, "Contested Sovereignty: The Social Construction of Colonial Imperialism," in Biersteker and Weber, eds., *State Sovereignty*, 22–49;

[47] Nina Tannenwald, "The Nuclear Taboo: The United States and the Normative Basis of Nuclear Non-Use," *International Organization* 53, no. 3 (Summer 1999): 433–69.

[48] Berger, *The Culture of Anti-Militarism*, chap. 1, passim; Finnemore, *National Interests*, 19. See also Meyer, "The World Polity."

[49] See essays in Katzenstein, ed., *The Culture of National Security*.

logic of consequence. Social theory argues that emulation takes place according to a logic of appropriateness, whereby states pursue social fitness, not security per se.[50] States desire legitimation and acceptance in the larger community. Some social theorists make an important turn at this juncture of their argument. Legitimation, or social fitness, in turn, guarantees physical security. In social theory, states survive and prosper in relation to the degree to which they share and embody global legitimizing norms and practices. Thus, emulating the most appropriate and legitimate practices in the system is the best strategy to enhance social fitness, and thus to bolster security. Security becomes a social end, pursued by social means. Maximizing social fitness maximizes survival and prosperity in the system, an argument first made by Meyer and advanced most recently by Spruyt.[51] Specific types of states survive, and certain organizational and technological practices arise and spread, as a result of legitimation agreements and mutual empowerment that define interstate relations. Collective norms, and a process of mutual empowerment and legitimation, determine who the acceptable and legitimate state-actors are in the system.

That states pursue security through social fitness is potentially a powerful argument. The problem this argument poses for a neorealist refutation is not simply that it makes the same claim and prediction – security-seeking behavior. It is also that the argument does not provide us with a handle for its falsification, especially in versions of social theory that posit a process of socialization in which states are unwitting or unconscious participants. In moderate versions of social theory, which embrace positivist methods, we can test these claims against empirical evidence and verify the extent to which states and their leaders speak and act according to these and other expected observable implications. For example, one observable implication of this argument is that we should see constant, immediate, and uniform emulation of social best practices in the system, irrespective of external threats, since no state will want to risk delegitimation.

How are best practices determined? For social theory, best practice, or success, in the system is normatively, or intersubjectively, determined, rather than based on competitive utility or some other objective measure. Yet this claim is, at best, a mere assertion. It leaves unanswered the question why any one practice comes to be deemed most appropriate. It cannot tell us, *ex ante*,

[50] On distinctions between a logic of consequence and logic of appropriateness, see James G. March, *A Primer on Decision Making: How Decisions Happen* (New York: Free Press, 1994); Finnemore, *National Interests*.

[51] John W. Meyer and Brian Rowan, "Institutionalized Organizations: Formal Structures as Myth and Ceremony," in Meyer and Scott, *Institutionalized Organizations*, 21–44; Spruyt, *The Sovereign State*; Robert H. Jackson and Carl G. Rotberg, "Why Africa's Weak States Persist? The Empirical and Juridical in Statehood," *World Politics* 35, no. 1 (October 1982): 1–24; Jackson, *Quasi-States*.

which practice will come to have this shared meaning. Shared norms and understandings, not technicism, may determine best practice, but how do states come to hone in on a specific practice or embodiment. Some social theories go a step further to assert that competitive utility is intersubjectively determined, a shared norm and understanding, rather than a technical outcome. The very standards by which the technical performance, or functional value, of certain practices or organizational formats are measured and evaluated are themselves collectively shared assessments and meanings. Whereas neorealism sees victory in war as the ultimate sanction of best practice, presumably for social theory victory is intersubjectively determined. This particular claim is intriguing, but there is no falsifiable, nontautological way out. Social theory thus places ultimate causation, even for seemingly rational or instrumental action, in shared meaning and interpretation that cannot be accessed or verified.

A possible way out, or restatement of this claim, can be found in the new institutionalism literature, as exemplified in the seminal work of Powell and DiMaggio.[52] Even if we accept that best practice, or proven effectiveness, is objectively determined, the new institutionalism literature argues that it subsequently comes to have social value. The new institutionalism literature posits that behavior such as emulation may begin as rational action, as behavior motivated by instrumental goals and a consequential logic, but over time becomes infused with social value and legitimation. As practices and models become standardized and institutionalized, a collective rationality comes to characterize the emulation behavior and choices of states. State emulation decisions and choices – of technically defined best practices for rational problem-solving – become rule-following. In time, emulating best practice becomes a process of ceremony and ritual.[53] The distinction between goal-oriented action and value-oriented action collapses. As norms and practices become institutionalized, social-normative bases of action eventually displace consequential logic.[54] One implication here is that we should see crossnational emulation as more uniform, widespread, and continuous in the system. Another is that, similar to neorealism's prediction, best practices will wax and wane according to their technical performance. The notion that socially appropriate practices have prior material or technical determinants, and subsequently are endowed with shared cultural value, is attractive. At a minimum, it neutralizes the neorealist proposition. The problem with the notion is twofold. First, since it mimics the same predictions as neorealism, it has no theoretical value added. Second, it falsely attributes causal properties

[52] Powell and DiMaggio, eds., *The New Institutionalism.*
[53] Meyer and Rowan, "Institutionalized Organizations."
[54] Powell and DiMaggio, eds., *The New Institutionalism*; Meyer and Scott, eds., *Organizational Environments.*

to an effect. That is, if the prior determinants of socially accepted best practices are material forces, then those social practices are byproducts, without cultural foundations.

The explanatory limitations of social theory, and cultural analyses in IR generally, have been discussed elsewhere.[55] Systematic evaluation and testing of these theories is not possible here. Suffice to say that the variety of social-cultural theories, and variety of their methodologies, make evaluation difficult. Many social-cultural explanations, for example, make epistemological, or philosophical, claims that are ultimately unverifiable. Conceptual imprecision is also a major obstacle, though neorealism too does not escape guilt. Social theory has many moving parts, with few if any constants, which makes falsification difficult and leads to infinite regress.

Social theory accounts are flawed in a number of ways, though the diversity and divergence of these accounts complicate a general evaluation. Less sophisticated versions are easily discounted. Other, more sophisticated versions of social analysis, such as strategic culture and organizational culture, cannot be supported by the cases and archival evidence examined here. A strategic culture explanation, like organizational culture explanations, is unsustainable given the wide variety of states that emulate the same model. Cultural arguments that give primacy to national, historically bounded culture fail to account for crossnational emulation. Their claims are simply unsupported by the military emulation of the United States, Japan, Argentina, Chile, and Brazil. Human history has shown that technology spreads across different people and cultures. For it to spread there is no need for people to share the same language, custom, or sophisticated forms of social communications. Arguments about prestige, cultural affinity, or legitimacy-based cultural analysis also do not find supporting evidence in the cases studied here. While we cannot expect leaders to give theoretical reasoning for their policy decisions, there is simply nothing in the archival records to suggest South American or U.S. leaders, for example, thought of emulation in terms of legitimacy and prestige. On occasion they referred to the military practices of the "advanced" nations and "civilized" countries, but such remarks do not add up to prestige- or social fitness-seeking behavior.

In top-down approaches of third-image social theory, states emulate on the basis of socially acceptable, or appropriate, practices and symbols of statehood. This view cannot account for innovation, since it appears to rule out incentives for states to innovate. Leaving aside cumbersome and circular arguments about recursivity, this approach points to stasis, not change and

---

[55] Michael C. Desch, "Culture Clash: Assessing the Importance of Ideas in Security Studies," *International Security* 23, no. 1 (Summer 1998): 141–70; Dale C. Copeland, "The Constructivist Challenge to Structural Realism: A Review Essay," *International Security* 25, no. 2 (Fall 2000): 187–212; see also Legro, "Which Norms Matter?"

dynamism, in the system. Once extant discursive social practices become internalized, states risk ostracism and imperil their physical security by departing from accepted social fitness norms. Bottom-up and inside-out approaches to social theory face the opposite problem, so that it is unclear how any one practice can emerge as the most appropriate in the thicket of diverse practices generated by unit-level processes. At a minimum, social theory posits socialization and internalization of behavioral and constitutive norms. Presumably these are enduring. Social theories that collapse the distinction between material and ideational bases of action, for example, obstruct meaningful adjudication of the dispute over *why* states emulate, since their claims cannot be falsified. Of course, in mainstream cultural accounts we should observe military emulation in the absence of external threats. Is this observation supported by the empirical evidence in the three South American cases and across the sixty years, time span examined here?

The weaknesses of third-image cultural explanations are visible when we consider some of the observable implications of social theory for crossnational emulation. Social theory cannot account for variance in the timing, pace, and scope of emulation, and fails to explain why specific states are imitated. The first implication of third-image social theory is that emulation will be continual. We should expect emulation to be uniform, or simultaneous, across states, and we should expect emulation to follow quickly the advent of new practices. Yet the emulation of Prussia was uneven, discontinuous, and clustered. Not every state in the system emulated Prussia; the ones that did, did so for reasons pointed to by neorealism's theory of emulation. The pattern of emulation in South America during 1870–1930 was discontinuous and wave-like, not uniform and fluid, across and within the three countries. In general, large-scale emulation has always displayed a sort of punctuated equilibrium. It occurs in spurts, and these spurts correspond with changes in the strategic environment.

Second, and related, social theory cannot account for variance in emulation, specifically its timing and scope as well as variance across states. Why do some states emulate and others do not? Why do states emulate at different times, even though they emulate similar practices? The logic of social theory accounts is one that implies no variance. If emulation is driven by a logic of appropriateness, then we should expect all states to emulate rapidly and fully. Why does Chile imitate nearly every aspect of the German system, while the United States flirts with only a few? If emulation is driven by social fitness, which itself is crucial to national survival, why might some states not emulate and why do some emulators do so only partially?

Third, social theory cannot explain why states emulate specific practices of individual states; that is, it cannot explain why specific best practices are emulated. Many cultural arguments, especially sociological institutionalism, speak in terms of global or Western practices and models, but this does not tell us why the practices of particular Western countries and not others are copied. To accept the social theory explanation is to accept that the South Americans did not see any meaningful distinction among the many European mass armies. They did.

IMPORTING THE MASS ARMY IN SOUTH AMERICA

This work incorporates comparative historical case studies from Latin America to test the validity of hypotheses I generate about crossnational military emulation. These cases are theoretically valuable, and offer extensive archival materials to conduct systematic tests of theoretical predictions. Given its scale and depth, late nineteenth century military emulation in South America was of singular historical significance. For this reason alone it merits study. The impact on military organization was impressive. Military emulation in the region during the late 1880s involved, in essence, an effort to adopt the European mass army.[56] By the turn of the century the three major regional powers, Argentina, Brazil, and Chile, along with neighboring states, had adopted in full or in part the modern mass army based on German and later French models. Military emulation was so extensive and transforming that British and U.S. diplomats began to call Chile the "Prussia of South America." In Chile and Argentina, military emulation was sustained for three continuous decades, and involved the total remaking of their army establishments. Their armies fashioned themselves as tropical replicas of Germany's Imperial army. German doctrinal and intellectual imprint was lasting. Both countries continued to adhere to the German model during the interwar years. Both remained neutral during World War I and World War II (if not outright sympathetic to the Axis cause), despite heavy U.S. pressures to join the Allied cause. The social imprint of military emulation was significant as well. For some scholars, so was the political impact of emulation. For the military in all three countries intervened in politics during the succeeding decades. Modernization and professionalization proved a feeble antidote to political activism, Huntington not withstanding.

Why Latin America? Why study the behavior of secondary states through the lens of neorealism when Waltz himself maintains the theory is applicable only to great powers? The choice of empirical cases is deliberate. First, by examining empirical cases that are neither European nor great powers, I am able to construct a more demanding test for the theory I develop. I share Walt's point that incorporating non-European, nongreat power cases

---

[56] Posen, "Nationalism"; Peter Paret, "Revolution in Warfare: An Earlier Generation of Interpreters," in *National Security and International Stability*, ed. Bernard Brodie, Michael D. Intriligator, and Roman Kolkowicz (Cambridge: OG&H, 1983): 157–70; Howard, *War in European History*; Gunther E. Rothenberg, *The Art of Warfare in the Age of Napoleon* (London: B.T. Batsford, 1977).

is good for international relations theory.[57] Waltz maintains that neorealism applies only to great-power behavior, an unwarranted claim. Moreover, as noted earlier, there is a presumption in the IR literature that interstate relations of peripheral regions are either derivatives of great-power politics or are driven by idiosyncratic, region-specific factors. Yet we should not take as a given Waltz's premise that the theory is applicable only to great powers, nor accept the specious reasoning behind claims that secondary states behave differently. Structural realism is a theory of situational constraints and opportunities that all states confront; a theory of structural forces shaping and molding the behavior of actors and their internal organization. It is not a theory based on the nature or characteristics of the actors or their individual capability, as Waltz repeatedly acknowledges. It is a theory of behavior and outcomes in anarchic realms, irrespective of the nature and size of the actors. Indeed, we might just as easily say that the theory is ill-suited to study great-power behavior; that great-power behavior is not representative of the structural constraints the theory speaks of.[58] Based on the logic of structural constraints, we can reasonably argue that the extra margin of safety of great powers tempts them, at times, to act as they please. They can bear the costs of structural discipline or bypass them altogether. Perhaps the behavior of secondary states more accurately reflects the theory's structural logic.

I choose these cases in order to bring new, non-European, empirical cases into the IR field. Specifically, I wish to widen the empirical content of neorealism, and to show that it has much wider applicability than great-power politics. Indeed, Latin American cases are ideal candidates to enrich the empirical menu of IR theory. Outside of China, Japan, Turkey, Egypt, and India, no other peripheral countries have had a longer experience with foreign military influence. Aside from the region's lengthy and vibrant diplomatic history, the diplomatic-military record is well developed and its archival material extensive.

A third reason mirrors the second, namely to bring IR theory to the field of Latin American studies. As a student of both, I was always struck by the degree to which IR was so Euro-centric in its empirical focus and theory development, and by the near absence of major IR theory in the study of regional diplomatic history and interstate relations.[59] For their part, scholars working on the region have been theoretically innovative in their own right, as in the case of dependency theory and, generally, putting into crisper theoretical focus the ways in which the global structure of economic and political power affects the internal makeup and external behavior of countries in the

---

[57] Walt, *Origins of Alliances*, 13.

[58] I owe this insight to Avery Goldstein, University of Pennsylvania.

[59] There are notable exceptions. Among the best are the works of David R. Mares, *Violent Peace: Militarized Interstate Bargaining in Latin America* (New York: Columbia University Press, 2001).

periphery.[60] The reluctance to import major IR theory into studying the region retards knowledge advancement on both ends as well as perpetuates the notion that the region is somehow sui generis.[61] The pioneering work of Robert Burr pointed the way, but few scholars took up the challenge.[62] Among IR scholars there is a general impression – one not grounded in familiarity with the region's diplomatic history – that Latin America is devoid of war and security competition. I address this issue more closely in Chapter 3. More still, the notion that non-Western states somehow behave differently, or that their behavior can more easily be attributed to mimicry, has been prevalent. Indeed, given the sad history of U.S.–Latin American relations, I suspect that Latin America is often viewed as acted upon, not acting of its own volition.

Yet nineteenth-century South America was a time of war making and state making. The late nineteenth century, in particular, was a time of rapidly changing power balances. Acute, fast-moving power differentials triggered arms racing and near-war crises that rippled across the different subsystems in the region. To be sure, we do not find in Latin America's modern past the kinds of dynastic, prolonged, and global system-transforming wars of Europe.[63] For Latin Americans, especially citizens of the three countries studied here, the warfare and bitter rivalry of their past are living memories. The three big powers – Argentina, Brazil, and Chile – were locked in militarized competition since their independence, a rivalry that by the 1970s included nuclear proliferation between Brazil and Argentina.[64]

---

[60] On dependency theory see: Cardoso and Faletto, *Dependency and Development*. For an overview see João Resende-Santos, "Fernando Henrique Cardoso: Social and Institutional Rebuilding in Brazil," in *Technopols: Freeing Politics and Markets in Latin America in the 1990s*, ed. Jorge I. Domínguez (University Park: Pennsylvania State University Press, 1996): 145–94.

[61] On this point see Carlos Escúde, *Realismo periférico: fundamentos para la nueva política exterior argentina* (Buenos Aires: Planeta, 1992).

[62] Robert N. Burr, *By Reason or Force: Chile and the Balance of Power in South America, 1830–1905* (Berkeley: University of California Press, 1965).

[63] This literature is sparse. The most extensive study in English is Miguel Angel Centeno, *Blood and Debt: War and the Nation-State in Latin America* (University Park: Pennsylvania State University Press, 2002). See also Fernando López-Alves, *State Formation and Democracy in Latin America, 1810–1900* (Durham: Duke University Press, 2000). Good studies exist on individual states. See for example Oscar Oszlak, *La formación del estado argentino* (Buenos Aires: Editorial Belgrano, 1985). On more recent conflicts see the collection of essays in *Controlling Latin American Conflicts: Ten Approaches*, ed. Michael A. Morris and Victor Millán (Boulder: Westview Press, 1983). See also Keith Jaggers, "War and the Three Faces of Power: War Making and State Making in Europe and the Americas," *Comparative Political Studies* 25, no. 1 (April 1992): 26–62. The impression of Latin America as conflict-free is oddly juxtaposed to the alarm raised by policymakers and scholars alike during the 1970s and early 1980s about the seemingly uncontrollable conflicts in the region.

[64] João Resende-Santos, "The Origins of Security Cooperation in South America," *Latin American Politics and Society*, 44, no. 4 (Winter 2003): 89–126

To be sure, foreign military influence was not new to Latin America. The colonial armies and the armed forces of the independence wars were not only modeled on those of Europe but, in many instances, they were captained by European officers. The military modernization of the late nineteenth century was of a scale, intensity, and duration not previously known in the region. It marks the founding of the modern military establishments of these countries. Intensifying military competition and war, in turn, prompted a chain reaction of large-scale military emulation among the principal rivals. Large-scale military emulation in the region began with Chile in 1885, when it hired a large German military training mission to direct its modernization. Chile, though victorious in the Second War of the Pacific (1879–83), found itself in a worsened strategic environment. Small size and encirclement by historical enemies created perennial defensive disadvantages. Victory and territorial conquests in the Second War of the Pacific brought greater defensive and military mission demands as well as threats from old (Argentina) and new (United States) sources. Even before the war concluded an anti-Chilean coalition emerged, led by the United States and Argentina, intent on rolling back its gains. The war, moreover, revealed serious organizational and technological flaws in the military. Finally, Chile did not have viable external-balancing options. It comes as no surprise, then, that Chile would be the first among the regional powers to launch large-scale military emulation. Interestingly, Chile subsequently reexported the German model to other parts of the region, sending its own military training missions to Ecuador, Colombia, Venezuela, Honduras, and El Salvador.

Chile's archrival, Argentina, was second among the big continental powers to undertake large-scale military modernization, officially launching extensive military emulation in 1899. Chile's rapid and massive buildup upset the strategic balance for its historical rival, Argentina. Their antagonism dated back to colonial times, and was fueled by border disputes. Chile amassed an offensive military machine that struck fear on the other side of the Andes. Argentina's military emulation was reactive. It was building up its forces since the early 1890s, but the real threat of immediate war with Chile around the turn of the century finally led to large-scale military emulation. Brazil's military emulation was also reactive, a response to the enhanced military vigor of its Argentine nemesis. Unlike the others, Brazil moved haltingly and with great difficulty. Its stifling defensive advantages – its continental size, the vast Amazon jungle, its tacit alliance with Chile – dampened the pressures for military modernization even in the light of Argentina's buildup. By the eve of World War I these advantages were quickly eroded by the emergence of Argentina as the continent's premier military power.

Consistent with the predictions of the theory of emulation, the South Americans adopted military practices that had been demonstrated as most effective at the time, switching from one model to the next in accordance with its fortunes in great power war. During the 1870–1914 period, all three continental powers, despite bitter rivalry among them, emulated the same military system, the Prussian/German army. Their emulation is thus a telling illustration that the premium states put on proven effectiveness. The specific military system generating the most appeal and emulation in South America during that period waxed and waned with its fortunes in great-power wars: the French army prior to the Franco-Prussian war (1870), the Prussian/German army after 1870, the French again after 1918, and the United States after World War II. For naval modernization, from the early postindependence years to the 1920s, the South Americans remained faithful to the British Royal navy, despite their zealous adherence to the armies of France and Germany.[65]

In their admiration and emulation of the European armies, particularly Germany's (see Table 1.1), the three South American powers were not alone in the late 1880s. Military emulation in South America itself spread wave-like to the neighboring smaller countries. Peru and Bolivia, conquered and dismembered by rival Chile in 1883, moved quickly to modernize their militaries in their quest for revenge. Both hired French training missions, in apparent contradiction to the theory. Peru's 1896 French mission, first headed by Captain Paul Clément, remained in Peru until 1942, and was later joined by naval and air missions in 1905 and 1919. Peru first attempted unsuccessfully to contract a German mission. Germany's unwillingness to upset Chile forced Peru to turn to the next best thing. Bolivia's persistence eventually paid off, contracting a small private mission of Germans and French officers. A full German mission arrived in 1910, and would remain into the 1920s despite the war in Europe and restrictions of the Versailles settlement.[66] The head of the German mission in Bolivia, Major Hans Kundt, became a highly controversial figure. From 1920 to 1925 he served as Bolivia's chief of the general staff and minister of war. Kundt became enmeshed in internal political upheavals and partisan politics and was forced to leave in 1929. He returned to Bolivia a few years later and commanded Bolivian forces in the disastrous Chaco war of 1932.

The regional countries were part of a much broader wave of military emulation during the late nineteenth and early twentieth centuries. Several other countries, facing their own security challenges, emulated the German and French systems. Whereas the South American cases have been hidden from scholarly view, Japan, in contrast, has always been the paradigmatic case of crossnational emulation. No other country in modern history has engaged

---

[65] On the British influence see: Robert L. Scheinna, *Latin America: A Naval History, 1810–1987* (Annapolis: Naval Institute Press, 1987); Adrian J. English, *Armed Forces of Latin America: Their Histories, Development, Present Strength and Military Potential* (London: Jane's, 1985); Varun Sahni, "Not Quite British: A Study of External Influences on the Argentine Navy," *Journal of Latin American Studies* 25, no. 3 (October 1993): 489–514.

[66] León E. Bieber, "La política militar alemana en Bolivia, 1900–1935," *Latin American Research Review* 29, no. 1 (1994): 84–106.

in emulation at the same scale, intensity, and frequency. Meiji Restoration Japan undertook the most extensive program of crossnational emulation in recorded history, one that encompassed nearly every area of national life.[67] Japan was the clearest example of a state enhancing its competitive effectiveness with a sustained strategy of emulation. Western imperial encroachment had forced it to shed its self-imposed isolation, and it responded with far-reaching modernization of every area of national life. Japan's extensive military emulation began in 1866–67 with the arrival of a French mission.[68] It turned to the British Royal Navy as the model for its naval forces. France's defeat in 1870 led Japan to turn to the Prussian/German model. In 1878 the Japanese hired a large German military mission, headed by the legendary Major Jacob Clemens Meckel.[69]

Also joining the South Americans at the time was the United States, which flirted with Imperial Germany's military system during the pivotal Root Reform period.[70] Though a detailed study of U.S. military emulation is lacking, the United States is an interesting case theoretically because it was both an innovator and a great power. Military emulation in the United States was limited, selective, and syncretistic. Like Meiji Japan, U.S. military modernization was part of the larger backdrop of industrial and social modernization; it accompanied its rise as an imperial power with a blue water navy.[71] The Root reforms, while incomplete and slow to take effect, were an

---

[67] Trimberger, *Revolutions from Above*; Kennedy, *Rise and Fall of the Great Powers*, 206–09.

[68] Ralston, *Importing the European Army*. See also, Roger F. Hackett, "The Military in Japan," Robert E. Ward and Dankwart A. Rustow, eds., *Political Modernization in Japan and Turkey* (Princeton: Princeton University Press, 1964); Meron Medzini, *French Policy in Japan During the Closing Years of the Tokugawa Regime* (Cambridge: Harvard University Press, 1971); Hyman Kublin, "The 'Modern' Army of Early Meiji Japan," *Far Eastern Quarterly* 9, no. 1 (November 1949): 20–41; *Western Influences in Modern Japan: A Series of Papers on Cultural Relations*, ed. Inazo Nitobe et al. (Chicago: University of Chicago Press, 1931).

[69] Major General T. Kono, "The Japanese Army," in Nitobe, *Western Influences in Modern Japan*.

[70] This is a vast literature. I rely on the following works: Samuel P. Huntington, *The Soldier and the State: The Theory and Politics of Civil-Military Relations* (New York: Random House, 1957); Graham A. Cosmas, *An Army for Empire: The United States Army in the Spanish-American War* (Columbia: University of Missouri Press, 1971); Russell F. Weigley, *History of the United States Army* (Bloomington: Indiana University Press, 1984); William A. Ganoe, *The History of the United States Army*, rev. ed. (Ashton: Eric Lundberg, 1964); Walter Millis, *Arms and Men: A Study in American Military History* (New York: Putnam 1956); John Dickinson, *The Building of an Army* (New York: Century Co., 1922). See also Leonard Wood, *Our Military Policy: Its Facts and Fallacies* (Chicago: Reilly and Britton Co., 1916); Herman Hagedorn, *Leonard Wood: A Biography*, vol. 2 (New York: Harper and Bros., 1931). Elihu Root, *The Military and Colonial Policy of the United States: Addresses and Reports* (New York: AMS Press, 1970; originally published 1916). Roots reform measures were outlined in the War Department's *Annual Report of the Secretary of War 1899* (Washington DC: Government Printing Office, 1899): 45–46.

[71] Fareed Zakaria, *From Wealth to Power: The Unusual Origins of America's World Role* (Princeton: Princeton University Press, 1998).

important turning point.[72] Key areas of reforms, such as military education, were patterned on the German model. The single most creative force and intellectual influence in the army reform movement of this period was General Emory Upton.[73] His posthumously influential studies, especially *Armies of Asia and Europe* and *Military Policy of the United States*, became the wellspring of the Root reforms.[74] Upton argued that we may not be able to "Germanize" the U.S. military system but "we can apply the principles of common sense."[75] The United States, as an innovator, moved slowly and awkwardly in its military emulation. Since the principal source of threat was maritime, it first concentrated on building a powerful blue water fleet. More important, like Brazil, it did not face an immediate military threat. As a consequence, the process and politics of military reforms in the United States closely resembled those in Brazil.

There were numerous reasons for the South Americans and their contemporaries not to engage in large-scale military emulation, from its financial and political costs, to the inherent difficulties of organizational change, to importing practices from countries with whom they shared little cultural or historical affinity. The prospective gains from emulation were many, but so were the risks. The internal obstacles were numerous, as we might expect in matters pertaining to the distribution of political power and resources, let alone the adoption of foreign, or alien, ideals. First, military modernization is universally a politically charged and difficult process. Although the South American militaries underwent complete overhaul, and did so by incorporating alien methods and practices, change was neither smooth nor automatic. Major institutional change never is. Internal resistance was stiff. Second,

---

[72] Cosmas, *An Army for Empire*; Russell F. Weigley, *The American Way of War: A History of United States Military Strategy and Policy* (New York: MacMillan, 1973). A view from the reformers is Lieutenant Arthur L. Wagner, "The Military Necessities of the United States," *JMSI* 5, no. 19 (September 1884): 237–71.

[73] Root, *The Military and Colonial Policy of the United States*, 125. On Upton, see Peter S. Michie, *Life and Letters of Emory Upton* (New York: D. Appleton and Co., 1885); Stephen E. Ambrose, *Upton and the Army* (Baton Rouge: Louisiana State University Press, 1964).

[74] Emory Upton, *The Armies of Asia and Europe: Embracing Official Reports on the Armies of Japan, China, India, Persia, Italy, Russia, Austria, Germany, France, and England* (New York: Greenwood Press, 1968; originally published 1878), and *The Military Policy of the United States*, 4th ed. (Washington, DC: Government Printing Office, 1917). On the influence of the German model in the United States see: the War Department's *Annual Reports* from 1870 to 1900. Numerous articles appear in the flagship military journal of the day, *Journal of Military Service Institution of the United States* (*JMSI*). See also: Lt. Arthur L. Wagner, "Combined Maneuvers of the Regular Army and Organized Militia," *JMSI* 36, no. 133 (January/February 1905): 62–87; Phillip H. Sheridan, *Personal Memoirs* (New York: Da Capo Press, 1992); Lieutenant Arthur L. Wagner, *The Campaign of Königgrätz: A Study of the Austro-Prussian Conflict in the Light of the American Civil War* (Fort Leavenworth: Infantry and Cavalry School, 1889).

[75] Quote cited in Ambrose, *Upton and the Army*, 97.

military emulation in all three cases did not involve a mere question of military reforms but the organization and power of the state. These are cases where we should expect domestic politics to predominate. The mass army entailed distributional consequences – in terms of power, material interests, status, and extraction – not just inside the army but throughout the political system and society. It involved nothing less than the enlargement and strengthening of the state (and its central rulers du jour) as well as its prerogatives in the economy and society. The effects of military emulation are not neutral with respect to state-society relations, the role and size of the state, the relative bargaining position of domestic groups, and the allocation of power among them.[76] As Brewer notes, no other issue in human history has involved more bloodshed than the contest over how the state is to be organized and what powers it should have.[77] Large-scale military emulation is costly and socially disruptive. There is nothing politically facile about such processes. Yet its recurrence, in small and large scale, marks the life of states.

RESEARCH DESIGN AND METHODOLOGY

I draw on detailed comparative historical cases to test systematically the predictions I generate from each of the four key hypotheses on military emulation.[78] I explore the degree to which emulation decisions and choices in each of the three historical cases examined are consistent with the theory's predictions on the causes and variance of military emulation. Because my aim is to develop a neorealist theory of emulation, I do not intend or structure this study as a competitive theory testing endeavor. Thus, I do not incorporate into the work alternative explanations or systematically test competing explanations. I fully embrace Lakatos's principle of sophisticated methodological falsificationism, and its underlying idea that a theory can only be weakened or invalidated by a more powerful theory and not simply by empirical observations.[79] Yet putting this principle into practice would entail a much broader undertaking and a lengthier work than is possible here.

---

[76] Tilly, *Coercion, Capital, and European States*; Skocpol, *States and Social Revolutions*; Downing, *The Military Revolution*; Barnett, *Confronting the Costs of War*.

[77] Brewer, *Sinews of Power*.

[78] On theory testing, theory building, and rules of causal inference I rely primarily on: Imre Lakatos and Alan Musgrave, eds., *Criticism and the Growth of Knowledge*, vol. 4 (Cambridge: Cambridge University Press, 1970); Waltz, *Theory of International Politics*, chap. 1; Gary King, Robert O. Keohane, and Sidney Verba, *Designing Social Inquiry: Scientific Inference in Qualitative Research* (Princeton: Princeton University Press, 1994).

[79] Imre Lakatos, "Falsification and the Methodology of Scientific Research," in Lakatos and Musarave, eds., *Criticism and the Growth of Scientific of Knowledge*, 91–196. See also, King, Keohane, and Verba, *Designing Social Inquiry*; Harry Eckstein, "Case Study and Theory in Political Science," in *Handbook of Political Science*, vol. 7, *Strategies of Inquiry*, ed. Fred Greenstein and Nelson Polsby (Reading, PA: Addison-Wesley, 1975).

A good theory of military emulation must be able to account for four key aspects of military emulation: (1) why states emulate, (2) why they emulate specific military systems among all synchronic alternatives, (3) when they emulate, (4) variance in the speed and scale of the emulation process. In other words, it is not sufficient simply to explain why a state adopts military emulation as a security strategy. A good theory must also explain the variance in the timing and scale of emulation for any one state as well as across states. In addition, it needs to account for why states choose specific military systems to emulate and, if applicable, why they may switch models over time.

This is a small N study that employs qualitative research methods. It combines theory and history in a comparative case study design.[80] I ask the same set of questions in each of the three main historical cases. I systematically test the theory's predictions about all four aspects of military emulation in each case. I first outline the main predictions and hypotheses of the neorealist theory of emulation. In this and the next chapter, I clearly specify the conditions under which we expect military emulation to occur, why it occurs, how quickly and extensively, and which of the existing models states will emulate. Second, I examine each historical case to assess the degree to which behavior and outcomes correspond with the theory's predictions; to evaluate the degree to which the actions, choices, and declarations of leaders are consistent with theoretical expectations. Because I examine the historical cases longitudinally, I am able to check the full range of the independent variable against the full range of the dependent variable. That is, I effectively increase my N, or number of observations along the dependent variable.

I rely on detailed historical evidence of a specific and superior sort: archival records. I draw on documentary evidence in military and diplomatic archives in each of the three South American cases.[81] I also rely on archival materials from U.S. and British official documents. I examine systematically the same types of records in each country and across the same period of time. For example, one of the more widely used records is the annual reports of the war departments in each country. I analyzed these reports for the period

---

[80] On comparative method see: Arendt Lijphart, "The Comparable-Cases Strategy in Comparative Research," *Comparative Political Studies* 8, no. 2 (July 1975): 158–77; Walt, *The Origins of Alliances*, 11–12; Alexander George, "Case Studies and Theory Development: The Method of Structured, Focused Comparison," in *Diplomacy: New Approaches in History, Theory, and Policy*, ed. Paul Gordon (New York: Free Press, 1979): 43–68; Theda Skocpol and Margaret Somers, "The Uses of Comparative History in Macrosocial Inquiry," *Comparative Studies in Society and History* 22, no. 2 (April 1980): 174–97.

[81] The main archives consulted were: in Brazil (Arquivo Histórico do Exército [AHEX], Biblioteca do Exército, Biblioteca Nacional, Arquivo Histórico do Itamaratí); in Argentina (Servicio Histórico del Ejército, Archivo Histórico del Estado Maior General del Ejército, Biblioteca Nacional, Archivo General de la Nación; Archivo Histórico del Ministério de Relaciónes Exteriores y Culto); in Chile (Biblioteca Nacional, Biblioteca del Congresso Nacional).

1870–1930. The reports were surprisingly detailed and frank, far from the kind of bureaucratic apologia one might expect. Other archival materials include annual reports and studies by the general staff; annual reports and policy documents from the foreign ministry; diplomatic cables; diplomatic correspondence from foreign (mainly U.S. and British) legations in the region; military journals; memoirs of individual leaders and military officers; and personal historical archives of key individuals.

The study explains military emulation, but this dependent variable can be recast in a number of ways. Military emulation is a form of balancing behavior, and it is only one of a number of possible balancing strategies, as discussed in Chapter 2. The work lays out the conditions under which we expect states to emulate as opposed to other internal balancing strategies. But a measure of ambiguity is likely to intrude in our causal inference. The absence of emulation under conditions of adverse external security does not mean neorealism is proved wrong, unless we can also show absence of other forms of balancing. First, a state may engage in other forms of internal mobilization, and not emulation, or a combination of strategies. Such cases do not necessarily contravene neorealist predictions, since the state is still balancing. Nevertheless, we do expect to see some attempts, if not concrete measures, to emulate given the structural conditions we expect emulation.

The theory establishes a single causal framework, whereby the sources and variance in military emulation correspond to a single causal factor: adverse shifts in the state's strategic environment. Given certain other conditions, we expect states to engage in military emulation when facing security threats. The theory is weakened or discredited if emulation occurs in the absence of such adverse shifts, or if balancing of any kind fails to take place. The seriousness of contravening cases is a matter of debate among scholars. Isolated facts, observations, or individual anomalies are frequently pointed to as proof of neorealism's impotence. Yet, anomalies appear for any theory. What is important is only the frequency of anomalies.[82] All theories simplify and abstract from reality, thus theories that are useful will, by definition, confront anomalous observations and have unexplained residual variance. Isolated anomalies do not weaken a theory if the bulk of cases continue to fall within expected ranges.[83]

Neorealism has been the target of numerous methodological criticisms, a number of which I will correct. Of the various methodological criticisms launched against Waltz the most serious focus on falsifiability and the probabilism of its causal inference. Neorealism is hampered by poor specification

---

[82] Lakatos, "Falsification."

[83] Ronald Rogowski, "The Role of Theory and Anomaly in Social-Scientific Inference," *American Political Science Review*, 89, no. 2 (June 1995): 467–70, 470.

and indeterminacy.[84] Waltz notes that, because the theory makes only indeterminate, general predictions regarding balancing and emulation – it cannot predict precise balances or when and what will be emulated – theory testing and falsification become difficult.[85] Second, establishing causal inference with a high degree of confidence is difficult, since causal properties are also located at the level of units. Waltz can often be read as formulating a probabilistic theory.[86] Recognition of the causal interplay between structure and unit accounts for much of the loose language and imprecision in *Theory of International Politics*. In the end, Waltz comes down on the side of structure as predominant, though he fails to specify the conditions under which unit-level factors may either block or successfully resist structural pressures and imperatives.[87] There is no easy resolution for these methodological issues in social science or for the self-generated ones in neorealism. Waltz's position seems reasonable for a structural theory that wants to avoid determinism, while remaining elegant and nonreductionist. Yet he was premature in closing off the theory to increased predictive accuracy. This study enhances the theory's predictive accuracy, both by more clearly specifying the conditions under which our theoretical expectations hold as well as by explicating more clearly what these expectations and propositions are.

A final word on comparative case study designs. There are numerous advantages to such designs. The most significant advantage is that in-depth, archival-based analysis of individual cases provides a more robust foundation for comparative theory testing and application. Our conclusions from such analyses are likely to be sounder and more accurate, even if our ability to generalize may be restricted. Multivariate quantitative studies, while increasing our confidence in the generalizability of our findings, rest on cursory and often inaccurate sketches of empirical cases, resulting in generalizable but flawed conclusions. The advantages of qualitative studies notwithstanding, there are legitimate methodological questions regarding small-N studies and surrounding the use, interpretation, and completeness of archival records. As noted above, small-N studies have limitations in terms of their external validity, or generalizability, of their findings. I soften this handicap by examining the cases longitudinally as well as providing illustrative examples from other cases in the region and elsewhere. The second methodological criticism has to do with universal sins that tend to plague qualitative studies – selection

---

[84] Elman, "Horses for Courses"; Thomas Christensen and Jack Snyder, "Chain Gangs and Passed Bucks: Predicting Alliance Patterns in Multipolarity," *International Organization* 44, no. 2 (Spring 1990): 137–60.

[85] Waltz, *Theory of International Politics*, 124; Keohane, "Theory of International Politics," 172–75.

[86] Elman, "Horses for Courses."

[87] Waltz, "Reflections," attempts some of this.

bias.[88] Selection bias comes in a variety of forms. I highlight two common ones that my study may be said to exhibit: selection of cases on the basis of the outcome and specific coding of the dependent variable. That is, I examine only cases of military emulation, and do not incorporate cases of no emulation. This is accurate only partially. I ease the problem in two ways. I develop an explanatory-predictive model which clearly specifies the conditions under which emulation does or does not take place. Additionally, I examine each of the three main cases longitudinally, allowing me to look at each case before and after the historical process of emulation. In similar vein, I concentrate on the upper ranges of military emulation, on large-scale, sustained processes as opposed to episodic, garden variety emulation. I do so mainly because these instances are far more interesting. By focusing only on the upper ranges of military emulation, the study is susceptible to the methodological problem of truncation. I predict emulation to vary along a range, however, and I can test this prediction by looking at the cases longitudinally. I am able to trace each case across time along the full variance of emulation, and to determine at each phase whether or not the hypotheses and antecedent conditions were present.

The third and fourth criticisms pertain to common weaknesses in qualitative studies: the challenge of operationalizing key concepts and content analysis. Conceptual clarity and operationalizable variables are challenging for both qualitative and quantitative studies. I develop concepts with clear, consistent definitions and boundaries. I define military emulation and its key components, which allows for systematic, consistent observation across cases. Of all the key concepts used here the most challenging to operationalize is the level of threat, discussed in the next chapter. International relations theory still lacks a good theory of threats. I rely on the well-established work of Walt. As for issues relating to content analysis and interpretation of archival data, social science as a whole has been unable to eliminate all the pitfalls. More serious problems in working with archives have to do with language translations and the unity and comprehensiveness of the archival records. I make my own translations. The latter issue is far more serious. The region's repeated bouts with economic turmoil and fiscal crisis have meant that the upkeep and organization of archives have suffered. Where there are gaps in the documentary records, and there were some, I make a notation.

---

[88] King, Keohane, and Verba, *Designing Social Inquiry*, chap. 4; David Collier and James Mahoney, "Insights and Pitfalls: Selection Bias in Qualitative Research," *World Politics* 49, no. 1 (October 1996): 56–91; Barbara Geddes, "How the Cases You Choose Affect the Answers You Get: Selection Bias in Comparative Politics," in *Political Analysis*, ed. James A. Stimson (Ann Arbor: University of Michigan Press, 1990); David A. Laitin et al., "Review Symposium: The Qualitative-Quantitative Disputation," *American Political Science Review* 89, no. 2 (June 1995): 454–81.

The balance of the book is organized as follows. Chapter 2 delineates the neorealist theory of emulation. Chapter 3 is a transition chapter, an orphanage of disparate but important content. The chapter begins with a summary of the main organizational features of the Prussian/German and French armies. The second half of the chapter offers a summary of the regional South American balance of power system during 1870–1930. The section also offers a survey of the preemulation regional armies. Chapters 4 (Chile), 5 (Argentina), and 6 (Brazil) are the empirical cases, presented in chronological order of their emulation.

2

Theory of Military Emulation

"We need to adopt to our conditions," said the Brazilian war minister in 1899, "the principles and the perfections sanctioned by experience of the more advanced nations."[1] On the other side of the continent Chilean military and political leaders argued for the "necessity of reconstituting rapidly an army whose efficiency would be the guarantee of [our] security," by adopting the "methods of warfare tested previously in the Franco-Prussian War."[2] Throughout the region at the time similar pleas and recommendations were being voiced. Several thousand miles to the north, General Emory Upton, the tireless reformer, summed up his study of the German military system by stating that "I have given in brief their organization, and then have enlarged on those features which, in my judgment, we ought to imitate."[3]

Different as these countries were, in both their internal and external conditions, there were some remarkable similarities in the observations of their leaders – as if they were reading from the same script. While the South American countries emulated, in varying degrees, Germany's Imperial Army, they maintained their close attachment to Britain's redoubtable Royal Navy as the model for their naval forces. Here was another similarity. Why? These countries were discriminating in whom to emulate in different areas of military capabilities. Once again their decision appeared to be based on the same uncompromising criteria. Chile's attachment to the German army

---

[1] Brazil, Ministério de Guerra (Ministry of War), *Relatório apresentado ao Presidente da República pelo Gen. João N. de Medeiros Mallet, 1899* (Rio de Janeiro: Imprensa Nacional, 1899), 9.

[2] General Carlos Saez Morales, *Recuerdos de un soldado*, 3 vols., *El Ejército y la política*, vol. 1 (Santiago: Biblioteca Ercilla, 1934), 22; General Francisco Javier Díaz, *La guerra civil de 1891: relación militar*, 2 vols., *La campaña del norte*, vol. 1 (Santiago: Imprenta La Sud América, 1942).

[3] Emory Upton, *The Armies of Asia and Europe: Embracing Official Reports on the Armies of Japan, China, India, Persia, Italy, Russia, Austria, Germany, France, and England* (New York: Greenwood Press, 1968; originally published 1878): viii.

model resembled religious fanaticism; but Jorge Montt, its legendary naval commander and president, put it succinctly in rebuffing pressures from Germany – then the exclusive source of armaments for its land forces – to purchase German rather than British warships: "You may be right, and we may be behind the times, but we think that British-built ships are the best in the world. When you beat them then we shall be quite ready to buy our ships in Germany."[4]

The South Americans, like Meiji Japan, the United States, France, and so many other countries at the time, emulated Germany's Imperial Army. The timing, speed, and extent of their emulation varied, but they all did so for security reasons. Yet large-scale military emulation of this kind was an enormous gamble, a huge and complex undertaking. There was nothing easy about it. It carried its own risks, and there were no guarantees that imported techniques will work. It was financially onerous, requiring sustained diversion of resources from other areas and the usual guns-and-butter political battles it engenders. Large-scale military emulation entailed the elimination of old institutions and procedures, along with their vested interests, familiar arrangements, and procedures for recruitment and advancement. Socially disruptive and politically risky, leaders had plenty of reasons not to do it. Yet countries continually vest enormous resources and political capital to do so. Why do so when so much stands in the way?

This chapter constructs a theory of military emulation. The theory of emulation I develop is firmly and exclusively rooted in neorealism, as originally articulated by Waltz in *Theory of International Politics* and elsewhere. It builds on neorealism's two main predictions about the behavior of states: balancing and emulation. To build this theory of emulation requires a rethinking of Waltz and recovering neglected aspects of neorealism. We can build a theory of emulation faithful to the theoretical and explanatory architecture of neorealism while strengthening areas that have remained obscured since Waltz's seminal work was first published.

This work is faithful to Waltzian neorealism. The point merits reiterating for several reasons, but two in particular stand out. The first is the imprecision surrounding the label "realism" in the wider literature as well as the recent proliferation of realist theories in the literature. Wendt makes a distinction between Waltzian realism and what he calls post-Waltzian realism.[5] The house of realism as a paradigm is suddenly crowded with the resuscitation of classical realism, its numerous permutations, and other realisms-with-adjectives. The trend is positive for the field and the tradition. Pluralism, even within traditions, is essential. For this reason alone we need to be

---

[4] President Jorge Montt, communiqué to German minister, 1896. Quote cited in Emílio Meneses Ciuffardi, "Coping With Decline: Chilean Foreign Policy during the Twentieth Century, 1902–1972," unpublished Ph.D. thesis., Oxford University/Balliol College (1988): 80.

[5] Alexander Wendt, *Social Theory of International Politics* (Cambridge: Cambridge University Press, 1999).

careful and more precise with our theoretical labels, and avoid conflating Waltzian neorealism with other variants in the realist tradition. Legro and Moravcsik erred in their conclusions and some of the analysis, but their basic point stands regarding the reductionist trend of recent works in the realist tradition.[6] The field has witnessed the emergence of a cottage industry of works purporting to amend and improve neorealism, or structural realism. Yet these often result in reductionist classical realism with neorealist add-ons. Given my explanatory aims, Waltzian neorealism remains as powerful as it is economical. The changes I introduce – if, in fact, they even qualify as changes – are in the direction of uncovering hidden elements and extending its core logic. The additions I make, such as incorporating a security dilemma approach rather than polarity, are meant to enhance the empirical accuracy of the theory, and not to alter its core assumptions.

Second, some readers will regard my work as too critical of Waltz, perhaps even a departure. It is neither. Rather, it improves and extends Waltzian neorealism. I point out the areas that are underdeveloped, that are prematurely closed off by Waltz, or that detract and confuse (such as socialization). Waltzian neorealism is elegant and powerful, but its theory of crossnational emulation has gaps. These shortcomings are far from fatal and easily correctable. The remedy requires neither ad hoc expansion of its core assumptions nor resurrection of classical realism.

In this chapter, I elaborate the main conceptual pillars of the theory of emulation, drawing on (and rethinking) the main assumptions and propositions in Waltzian neorealism. The basics of neorealist theory are widely familiar. I build on only those concepts and assumptions directly relevant, and address criticisms of these when pertinent. The chapter will first examine Waltz's treatment of emulation and its shortcomings. I will propose a reconceptualization of neorealism as a theory of organizational effects before delving into the details of its theory of emulation. To do so requires a brief excursus on neorealism's core assumptions and conception of the system. My goal is to nest emulation behavior as part of a much larger phenomenon whereby the anarchy of the external realm presses states to put a premium on how well they are internally organized and equipped, especially in terms of the methods and technology of security competition. I will then proceed to a substantive treatment of emulation, with separate sections devoted to: emulation as a form of balancing behavior, emulation and innovation, the advantages of copying, crossnational convergence, the role of war as a selector of best practices and, finally, the conspicuous notion of socialization in the theory. The final section of the chapter will examine the determinants of threat of levels.

---

[6] Jeffrey W. Legro and Andrew Moravcsik, "Is Anybody Still a Realist?" *International Security* 24, no. 2 (Fall 1999): 5–55.

EMULATION IN NEOREALIST THEORY

Neorealism has a theory of emulation. Emulation is one of the two principal predictions of neorealism and is based on the same core assumptions of the theory. Waltz predicts two dominant, recurring patterns of state behavior: balancing and emulation. Yet this powerful prediction about emulation was never developed, and its implications thus remained hidden from view.[7]

Waltz predicts states will emulate, but he does not expand on the concept or elaborate a coherent set of propositions.[8] He maintains that states will display characteristic behaviors typical of competitors. Namely, they will emulate the successful practices of one another and, over time, come to share certain attributes. Specifically, he argues that states will emulate the military weapons and strategies contrived in the country of greatest capability and ingenuity.[9] His treatment of emulation points the way, but it remains truncated. His formulation of neorealist theory as a whole is hamstrung by poor specification and other weaknesses.[10] His predictions regarding emulation suffer from many of the same weaknesses. The theoretical cost has been that Waltz, like other neorealists, either overlooks or ignores a fertile area in theory and, as such, misses the organizational implications of these predictions.

Waltz freely claims the theory cannot predict which balancing strategies states will adopt, nor can it predict when, what, and how extensively states will emulate.[11] Part of Waltz's problem is his overreliance on the global distribution of capabilities as a predictor as opposed to a security dilemma approach which focuses on immediate threats. Furthermore, he does not attempt to account for why, or under what conditions, states will opt to emulate rather than to innovate. Competition should just as likely lead to innovation than emulation.[12] A bigger theoretical question is engaged here: namely, the spectrum of balancing strategies, and the theory's need to specify *ex ante* the conditions under which states will choose among different

---

[7] Barry Posen, "Nationalism, the Mass Army, and Military Power," *International Security* 18, no. 2 (Fall 1993): 80–124, was the first attempt by a realist to apply the concept.

[8] Kenneth N. Waltz, *Theory of International Politics* (Reading, MA: Addison-Wesley, 1979), 77, 118, 122, 124–25, 127, 128.

[9] Waltz, *Theory of International Politics*, 126, 127.

[10] Colin Elman, "Horses for Courses: Why Not Neorealist Theories of Foreign Policy?" *Security Studies* 6, no. 1 (Autumn 1996): 7–53; Thomas Christensen and Jack Snyder, "Chain Gangs and Passed Bucks: Predicting Alliance Patterns in Multipolarity," *International Organization* 44, no. 2 (Spring 1990): 137–60. For more critical perspectives see, Paul Schroeder, "Historical Reality vs. Neorealist Theory," *International Security* 19, no. 1 (Summer 1994): 108–48; Richard Ned Lebow, "The Long Peace, the End of the Cold War, and the Failure of Realism," in *International Relations Theory and the End of the Cold War*, ed. Richard Ned Lebow and Thomas Risse-Kappen (New York: Columbia University Press, 1995): 23–56.

[11] Waltz, *Theory of International Politics*, 64, 124, 179.

[12] Barry Buzan, Charles Jones, and Richard Little, *The Logic of Anarchy: Neorealism to Structural Realism* (New York: Columbia University Press, 1993): 40.

balancing strategies. In partial defense of Waltz, he appears to classify states in two categories, innovation-capable great powers and secondary states. Yet all states, big and small, including innovation-capable great powers emulate. In general, Waltz fails to elaborate the conceptual distinction between innovation and emulation, and ignores the sources and role of innovation in competitive realms. It may be fair to caution that the latter places too much burden on neorealism. At a minimum we need in neorealism a sharper sense of the full range of balancing strategies and the conditions under which states may opt for one or another or a combination.

Waltz maintains that neorealist theory applies only to great powers, and not to secondary states. This claim is unnecessarily restrictive. It is also simply at odds with the logic of a theory about outcomes and behavior in anarchic realms that should hold true irrespective of the attributes of the units. In consequence, he places all explanatory power in shifts in the global distribution of capabilities, as opposed to changes in the local strategic environment of states. Doing so gives him great coverage and economy in explaining broad patterns of state behavior but, as Walt and others have pointed out, an emphasis on shifts in the global distribution of capabilities does not give us good leverage on the behavior of nongreat powers.

Another important matter is that Waltz incorrectly maintains that states emulate on the basis of capabilities – imitating only the most powerful in their numbers. I will argue that states put a premium on proven, demonstrated, effectiveness, and will thus emulate on a criterion of proven best practices rather than aggregate capabilities. In addition, Waltz argues that emulation occurs among adversaries.[13] That is, two contending states imitate each other's best practices, rather than the best practices of third states. The findings in this study show otherwise. Consistent with the premium they place on competitive effectiveness, states emulate prevailing international best practices, whether or not these practices belong to an adversary. Indeed, we find in the cases studied here a counterintuitive outcome – that of adversaries emulating the same foreign military system. The century-long mutual emulation between France and Prussia/Germany between 1806 and 1914 shows that emulation can occur between adversaries. It is more accurate to view this emulation as occurring on the basis of proven effectiveness, since it was the military system of Napoleonic France and post-1866 Imperial Germany that set the international standard.

Last, and complicating matters further, Waltz inadvertently suggests that emulation is a product of social forces, namely "socialization." Yet how do we talk about emulation in a theory regarded as highly asocial? If emulation is a social phenomenon, and connotes processes and behavior in social realms that are hierarchically ordered, how can we talk about emulation in a realm

---

[13] Waltz, *Theory of International Politics*, 77, 124, 127. See also Waltz, "Emerging Structure." Posen, "Nationalism," restates Waltz's claim.

whose ordering principle is anarchic? In later sections I discuss Waltz's notion of socialization, showing that it is merely a descriptive notion conveying structure's disciplining effects.

A THEORY OF ORGANIZATIONAL EFFECTS

The theory of emulation is built on the main assumptions and hypotheses of neorealist theory. Waltzian structural realism is erected on three core assumptions: the international system is anarchic, states are the principal actors in the system, and security is their highest and overriding goal. These assumptions, and their observable implications, taken together generate an international system consisting of states primed for competition. Their competition, in turn, generates dual organizational effects. These assumptions and hypotheses must be developed more fully to make visible the theory of emulation as well as derive other observable implications. It is important to note that these assumptions are targets of criticism as well as disagreement as to precisely what they are. For example, Waltz's position on anarchy and its implications have come under attack from within and outside the realist school.[14] There are conflicting interpretations over what the main assumptions are (or should be), and not simply about their veracity or usefulness.[15] For instance, power and rationality are frequently cited in

[14] Waltz's anarchy assumption has been under assault from all sides, from other realists, liberalism, and social theory. See Wendt, *Social Theory*, and "Anarchy Is What States Make of It," *International Security* 46, no. 2 (Spring 1992): 391–425; Randall Schweller, "Neorealism's Status Quo Bias: What Security Dilemma?" *Security Studies* 5, no. 3 (Spring 1996): 90–121; Helen Milner, "The Assumption of Anarchy in International Relations Theory: A Critique," *Review of International Studies* 17 (1991): 67–85. For general discussions see: Robert Powell, "Anarchy in International Relations Theory: The Neorealist-Neoliberal Debate," *International Organization* 48, no. 2 (Spring 1994): 313–44; *The Perils of Anarchy: Contemporary Realism and International Security*; Michael E. Brown, Sean M. Lynn-Jones, and Steven E. Miller, eds., (Cambridge: MIT Press, 1995); Joseph Grieco, Duncan Snidal, and Robert Powell, symposium on "The Relative Gains Problem for International Cooperation," *American Political Science Review* 87, no. 3 (September 1993): 729–43; Buzan, Jones, and Little, *The Logic of Anarchy*; Daniel Deudney, "Dividing Realism: Structural Realism versus Security Materialism on Nuclear Security and Proliferation," *Security Studies* 1 (1993): 7–37, and "The Philadelphian System: Sovereignty, Arms Control, and the Balance of Power in the American States-Union, Circa 1787–1861," *International Organization* 49 (1995): 191–228. Classic liberal perspectives on anarchy are: Hedley Bull, *The Anarchical Society: A Study of Order in World Politics* (London: Macmillan, 1977); Robert O. Keohane and Joseph S. Nye, *Power and Interdependence* (Boston: Little, Brown, and Co., 1977). A conception of anarchy outside the discipline is Jack Hirshleifer, "Anarchy and Its Breakdown," *The Journal of Political Economy* 130, no. 1 (February 1995): 26–52.

[15] Robert O. Keohane, "Theory of World Politics: Structural Realism and Beyond," in *Neorealism and Its Critics*, ed. Robert O. Keohane (New York: Columbia University Press, 1986): 158–203, 166–67, identifies states, power, and rationality as the three main assumptions.

the literature as two core assumptions. There is an important question as to whether many of Waltz's famous postulates – such as self-help, the centrality of power – should be treated as auxiliary assumptions or as logical derivatives of the core.[16] Important examples are Waltz's follow-on assumptions about states, such as they can be treated as unitary actors.[17] Whereas the unitary actor postulate can be reasonably treated as supplementary, all the other claims are more properly treated as logical implications of the three core assumptions. I will focus primarily on the first and second core assumptions. While I will have plenty to say, directly and indirectly, about the state, there is no need to rehash worn debates about the assumption that states are the primary actors in world politics.

Anarchy is the linchpin assumption in neorealism, as it is for all its realist antecedents. In Waltz's three-tier definition, the system's structure comprises three elements: its ordering principle (anarchy), the nature of the state-units or specification of their functions (functionally alike), and the system-wide relative placement of states (distribution of capabilities). The implications of an anarchic ordering principle extend beyond the mere absence of a central sovereign. Unlike the domestic realm of states, organized on the principle of hierarchy, the ordering principle of the external realm of states is anarchic. Inherent to anarchic realms are certain characteristics or patterns of behavior and outcomes that can be overcome only if the system's ordering principle changes. These characteristics are mutually reinforcing, and thus magnify the behavioral effect of each one on the interacting states. From the anarchy assumption we are able to derive a number of observable implications and structural features of the system: self-help, uncertainty, insecurity, competition, and the centrality of power.

The first crucial feature is that anarchic realms are necessarily self-help realms. Self-help realms are, by implication, competitive. We need not rehearse here debates about neorealism's depiction of the system as a self-help realm.[18] In the absence of a central authority or agency that can provide and guarantee their security and welfare, states are forced to rely on their own self-help efforts. This does not mean states will never cooperate, exchange, or even free ride. It does mean that they limit the scope of their dependence on others, avoid specialization, and rely as much as possible on their own

Keohane does not view anarchy as an assumption but a "background" characterization of the system. See also Randall L. Schweller and David Priess, "A Tale of Two Realisms: Expanding the Institutions Debate," *Mershon International Studies Review* 41 (1997): 1–32.

[16] Schweller and Priess, "A Tale of Two Realisms," make a similar point.

[17] Waltz, *Theory of International Politics*, 118.

[18] Wendt, "Anarchy," never disagreed with Waltz's that the system *is* a competitive, self-help realm that starts with egoistic, competitive inclinations; they disagreed only about its endurance and transformative logic.

efforts.[19] It means, above all else, that only they can take care of themselves. It means that in its interactions with others, including disputes and other conflict interactions, the state must ultimately rely only on its own abilities and capabilities. The result is a system in which states end up duplicating each other's functions and activities, including mustering the means to assure their safety and autonomy. The problem – and the tragedy of international politics – is that self-help efforts to garner the means of security result in pernicious, but unintended, effects.

The second characteristic is that insecurity and uncertainty are inherent in anarchic realms. In order to flesh out these two implications of anarchy, we must return to neorealism's second core assumption of security-seeking states. States value security above all other goals, where security is broadly defined to include physical survival, territorial integrity, and political autonomy.[20] That is, security encompasses both physical and political dimensions, military and nonmilitary components.[21] Waltz's assumption that states pursue security above all other goals remains controversial among realists and their critics. His incautious phrasing – that states, at a minimum, seek survival and, at a maximum, universal hegemony – did not help. Moreover, his theoretical stance that state behavior and aims are determined by both structural and unit-level causes, while sensible, leaves the theory vulnerable. The assumption has split realists into offensive and defensive realists.[22] Thus, many realists and critics alike have taken aim at Waltz's security assumption, arguing that a security-seeking assumption alone is not sufficient to generate the competitive and war-prone system neorealists describe. If states only seek self-preservation, critics argue, security will be plenty. All states will feel secure. As such, neorealism cannot account for hegemony-seeking, arms racing, and war. Neorealists, these critics argue, have to smuggle in implicit assumptions about other state preferences, or distribution of interests, including imparting on some states aggressive or revisionist aims. For offensive realists, states are always primed for offense.[23] Security is always scarce, and can only be assured through maximizing more power than others.[24] Adherents of classical realism, such as Schweller, argue that

[19] Waltz, *Theory of International Politics*, 105, 143–145; Joseph M. Grieco, *Cooperation Among Nations: Europe, America, and Non-Tariff Barriers to Trade* (Ithaca: Cornell University Press, 1990), 11.

[20] Waltz, *Theory of International Politics*, 96, 104–6, 153, chap. 6, passim.

[21] Grieco, *Cooperation among Nations*; Albert O. Hirschman, *National Power and the Structure of Foreign Trade* (Berkeley: University of California Press, 1945); David A. Baldwin, *Economic Statecraft* (Princeton: Princeton University Press, 1985).

[22] Jeffrey W. Taliaferro, "Security Seeking Under Anarchy: Defensive Realism Revisited," *International Security* 25, no. 3 (Winter 2000–1): 126–61.

[23] John J. Mearsheimer, *The Tragedy of Great Power Politics* (New York: W. W. Norton, 2001).

[24] See, for example, John J. Mearsheimer, "The False Promise of International Institutions," *International Security* 19, no. 3 (Winter: 1994/1995): 5–49; Charles L. Glaser, "Realists as Optimists: Cooperation as Self-Help," *Security Studies* 5, no. 3 (Spring 1996): 122–66

the fundamental problem in the system is not really anarchy or insecurity, but the pathological aims of certain states. States have nonsecurity motives such as opportunism, influence maximization, greed and spoils, power, and revisionism. These aggressive aims drive insecurity and competition in the system.[25] Waltz can be interpreted as having an ambiguous position, though much of his language points to a defensive-positionalist argument.[26]

Waltz does not, and need not, fall back on any hidden assumptions about aggressive states. Nor is there a need for neorealism to relegate so-called aggressive behavior to unit-level causes, as defenvise realists like Van Evera and Snyder maintain. Critics underestimate the powerful effects of the pervasive, irreducible uncertainty inherent in the system. Similarly, they underestimate the effects of a state's self-help efforts on other states. States are organized solutions to the insecurity inherent in a realm lacking a central security provider or adjudicator, but one also populated by entities that imperil their self-preservation – other states. Self-preservation is not in constant danger but survival is not a static condition or idle wish, but continual striving. Not every encounter is life-or-death. It is the possibility that any one encounter might be; that any one in their numbers might pose a threat. Put differently, insecurity is structural as much because the external realm is self-help as it is the product of uncertainty pervading the system. Security competition obtains even if no state has political ambitions beyond security.

A security-seeking assumption provides a solid foundation, and is consistent with Waltz's intent. We need not append assumptions about pathological intentions; states do that themselves when dealing with each other. Did it matter whether Chile's 1883 territorial expansion was a case of aggrandizement or an attempt to lessen its age-old encirclement problem by creating more of a buffer? Anarchy's effects are not limited to states fending for themselves and adopting self-help measures to assure their safety as best they know how or as far as their capability permits. It generates a particular kind of veil of ignorance, or veil of uncertainty, for all states when they make estimates about the nature and aims of the self-help efforts of others. Security-seeking efforts, however, are not neutral, nor are they seen as such by other states.

On neorealism's maximization assumption, see Keohane, "Theory of World Politics," 174; Fareed Zakaria, "Realism and Domestic Politics: A Review Essay," *International Security* 17, no. 1 (Summer 1992): 177–98.

[25] Randall L. Schweller, *Deadly Imbalances: Tripolarity and Hitler's Strategy of World Conquest* (New York: Columbia University Press, 1998); Mearsheimer, *The Tragedy of Great Power Politics*; Fareed Zakaria, *From Wealth to Power: The Unusual Origins of America's World Role* (Princeton: Princeton University Press, 1998), and "The Rise of a Great Power: National Strength, State Structure, and American Foreign Policy, 1865–1908," unpublished Ph.D. thesis, Harvard University (1993); Randal Schweller, "Bandwagoning for Profit: Bringing the Revisionist State Back In," *International Security*, 19, no. 1 (Summer 1994): 72–107.

[26] Waltz, *Theory of International Politics*, 126. Walt's defensive realism is far more evident in his *Man, The State, and War*.

Self-help efforts entail continual striving and retooling, toward which others cannot be indifferent. The reason why the security-seeking assumption is sufficient theoretically rests on an important but overlooked characteristic of anarchic realms – uncertainty. Uncertainty is structural in self-help realms. It is structural in that it obtains irrespective of the aims, intentions, characteristics, perceptions, or the wisdom of states. Although Waltz does not systematically develop the point, the theory relies extensively on uncertainty.[27] Uncertainty magnifies structural insecurity; it is the flip side of insecurity.

Thus, the combination of the nature of the system (anarchy) and the goals of states (security) produce two crucial implications for the behavior of states, especially emulation: uncertainty and insecurity. Both characteristics are structural in that no amount of self-help efforts – nothing short of overthrowing the ordering principle of the system – can overcome them. Indeed, self-help efforts only intensify them. The international system is a realm of tragedy. As formally stated by Herz decades ago, a security dilemma is inherent in the system, wherein anarchy encourages rational behavior that leaves everyone worse off.[28] The absence of a suprastate authority that can protect states and promote their welfare, together with the fact that states pose the greatest threat to each other, produces a situation where security is always scarce, at least in the sense that it is never assured. In anarchic realms, competition for security is both unwitting and unavoidable, even if all states aim only for safety and independence.

Self-help efforts of states to provide for their own defense give rise to a competitive and insecure realm.[29] That their own self-help effort is the only true guarantor of their security is at once a source of relief and insecurity. Thus states often find themselves sliding into a counterproductive, tit-for-tat spiral of insecurity and suspicion. Undoubtedly, some self-help security efforts in the system are unnecessary, unfounded, and foolish wastes

---

[27] Robert Jervis, "Cooperation Under the Security Dilemma," *World Politics* 30, no. 2 (January 1978): 167–214; Grieco, *Cooperation Among Nations*, 45. See Jon Elster, "Some Unresolved Problems in the Theory of Rational Behavior," *Acta Sociologica* 36 (1993): 179–90, 182.

[28] John H. Herz, "Idealist Internationalism and the Security Dilemma," *World Politics* 2, no. 2 (January 1950): 157–80, and *Political Realism and Political Idealism: A Study in Theories and Realities* (Chicago: University of Chicago Press, 1951). On the security dilemma see: Waltz, *Theory of International Politics*, 64; Jervis, "Cooperation Under the Security Dilemma," and *Perceptions and Misperceptions in International Politics* (Princeton: Princeton University Press): 62–93; Barry Buzan, *People, States, and Fear: An Agenda for International Security Studies in the Post Cold War Era* (Hemel Hempstead: Harvester-Wheatsheaf, 1991); Stephen van Evera, *Causes of War: Power and the Roots of Conflict* (Ithaca: Cornell University Press, 1999); Charles L. Glaser, "The Security Dilemma Revisited," *World Politics* 50, no. 1 (October 1997): 171–201.

[29] Kenneth N. Waltz, "The Origins of War in Neorealist Theory," in *The Origin and Prevention of Major Wars*, ed. Robert I. Rotberg and Theodore K. Rabb (Cambridge: Cambridge University Press, 1989), 39–52 and *Theory of International Politics*, 118–19, 127.

of resources, to the extent that the aims of others are truly benign and self-regarding. In anarchy, this is perfectly rational even if unfounded given structural uncertainty. The dynamic is a competitive one. It varies in intensity, but states cannot escape it. What matters for the theory are not the aims and intentions of states but the effects of their self-help efforts.[30] No amount of signaling benign intentions or treaty pledges can eliminate the insecurity. In the absence of a central agent of appeal and protection, uncertainty about the present or future intentions of others cannot be eliminated. States can make informed, reasonable estimates, but ultimately they cannot know or predict with certainty the sources, timing, nature, or actual probability of threats to their security.[31]

This structural uncertainty generates even more profound effects on the behavior of states and emulation in particular. For the theory of emulation, uncertainty has two related implications. First, uncertainty means that states cannot accurately gauge their position relative to the capabilities of others, although the severity of this problem will vary with shifts in polarity.[32] Nor can they predict the minimum requirements of viable competition, especially armed competition. Perfect information about the minimum requirements of security and viability, present and future, is always beyond their reach. There are limits to their calculation, knowledge, and evaluative or predictive capacity. States cannot know beforehand the changing requirements for survival and success in the system, a limitation that has nothing to do with the cognitive or perceptual abilities of their leaders. That states do not, and cannot, go through some hypothetically optimum decision-making process says very little about how rational they are. We can ask, are states engaged in irrational behavior when they rely on emulating proven success as a shortcut to security – as opposed to relying on an exhaustive process of discovery of all knowledge and weighing of all alternatives?

Second, and directly relevant to why states emulate and the criterion they use, states cannot know or predict the best means to security. The best (optimum) means to security are beyond the reach of states, and they are averse to basing their security on untested, unverified practices. The only true measure of security-enhancing practices, under uncertainty, is the proven best practices of others, not some hypothetical optimum. States cannot accurately know or predict the minimum requirements of safety and survival or how they may change in the future. Unable to know either with any measure of confidence, states turn to emulation. They emulate on the basis of proven

---

[30] Stephen M. Walt, *The Origins of Alliances* (Ithaca: Cornell University Press, 1987); Schweller, "Realism's Status Quo Bias."

[31] For an opposing view see, Robert O. Keohane, "Institutionalist Theory and the Realist Challenge after the Cold War," in *Neorealism and Neoliberalism: The Contemporary Debate*, ed. David A. Baldwin (New York: Columbia University Press, 1993): 269–300, 282–3.

[32] A similar observation is made by Geoffrey Blainey, *The Causes of War* (New York: Free Press, 1973).

success. Deprived of prescience and omniscience, what else do states have to go on if not proven and tested best practices? As I discuss later, what prevails as best practice may be the result of technical superiority, luck, or accident. Victorious military systems attract widespread emulation. Clausewitz and others, however, remind us that victory in war is as much the result of fog and good fortune as technical excellence. It may be the case that, for unrelated reasons, the best system, technically measured, is not the one that emerges victorious. But in a world of uncertainty, victory and battle performance serve as powerful guides in the decision making of states.

Emulation does not rely on assumptions about perfect perceptual abilities, since it is structure that selects and promotes successful practices and behavior. In the area of military security, structure provides clear and unambiguous signals as to which practices and institutions are successful. In the presence of structural uncertainty, states turn to emulation as a heuristic, as a shortcut. At any one point in time, the only reasonably accurate estimate that states have of the minimum requirements of security or the best security practices is what they observe in the actions and performance of others or what it directly tests in practice. Structural uncertainty means that a state's security-enhancing decisions are judgments about future outcomes that are unknowable.[33] Uncertainty surrounds new and untested organizations or technologies; short of action in war, true utility or effectiveness cannot be known.[34] New technologies or organizations will lack the authoritative quality derived from success in battle.[35] Emulating proven best practice, viewed in this light, becomes a rational act on the part of states.

For these reasons, neorealism cannot be viewed as relying on an assumption of states as rational, defined to denote foreknowledge or optimality.[36] Neorealism's assumption on this matter is modest – states are sensitive to costs, and their decision making is consequential.[37] Rationality, as used by Waltz, refers to cost sensitivity in the state's decision making; it says nothing about the optimality or intelligence of state actions or the effectiveness of the results. If anarchic systems are characterized by structural uncertainty, then necessarily any claim about actors having perfect rationality must be viewed with doubt. Not even a loose reading of Waltz can lead to a contrary conclusion. In anarchy, there can be no such thing as perfectly rational actors, decisions or collective outcomes, if the measure of rationality is optimization. Omniscience is neither an attribute of states nor a quality of their interaction.

[33] Richard N. Langlois and Paul L. Robertson, *Firms, Markets, and Economic Change: A Dynamic Theory of Business Institutions* (London: Routledge, 1995): 18.

[34] Colin Gray, "New Weapons and the Resort to Force," *International Journal* 30, no. 2 (Spring 1975): 238–58.

[35] Gray, "New Weapons."

[36] Keohane, "Theory of World Politics," 167, 194.

[37] Waltz, *Theory of International Politics*, 76–77.

Waltz's position has been controversial and unsatisfactory to many. He makes four points regarding rationality: two directed at states and two are statements about the system. First, states are rational only in the limited sense that they are sensitive to costs, and will strive to minimize these costs. Second, states may in fact behave as they wish, and at times irresponsibly. They may act out of whim, hubris, or intelligence. At times they make decisions on the basis of flawed or corrupt information. Stupidity is never in short supply among leaders and people alike, for rationality does not protect against stupidity. Irresponsible or stupid behavior and choices, however, will prove costly in the system. Waltz's third point is: structure punishes and disciplines, a point I return to later. As long as others are making reasonably good choices, resulting in net improvement in their competitive advantage, those making poor choices can expect to pay a price.[38] Fourth and related, Waltz is here suggesting that rationality – that is, the measure or standard of rationality – is a system attribute in that the standard is set by those states making relatively better choices and strategies. Similarly, as the security dilemma reminds us, the rational self-help efforts of one state will result in undesirable – irrational – collective outcomes.

From a structural standpoint, all that matters is the relative effectiveness of a state's response, not the intricate ways in which its decision-making process led to the choice or whether the outcome was optimal.[39] The effectiveness of the response can be the product of superior calculation ability, pure luck, or stupidity. It does not matter as long as it turns out to be better than or equal to those of others in the system.[40] Moreover, the effects of its actions and choices on others will be the same regardless of whether they were based on wisdom, luck, or stupidity. For these reasons too, critiques based on perceptual-cognitive pathologies and calculative limitations become either moot or ineffectual. Indeed, neorealism predicts that, given structural uncertainty, misperceptions, miscalculations, unintended or undesired outcomes, good and bad consequences, all will characterize the behavior of states. More profoundly, structural uncertainty means that it is impossible to distinguish actions that result from misperceptions and miscalculations from those guided by accurate information or fortuitous predictions. States may succeed or fail, they may make choices that enhance or diminish security, and they may do so on the basis of *virtú* or *fortuna*. Those who do make reasonably good choices that enhance their competitive position – whether

---

[38] Kenneth N. Waltz, "Reflections on *Theory of International Politics*: A Response to My Critics," in Keohane, ed., *Neorealism and Its Critics*, 322–47, *331* and *339*.

[39] Armen A. Alchian, "Uncertainty, Evolution, and Economic Theory," *The Journal of Political Economy* 58, no. 3 (June 1950): 211–21, makes a similar point regarding the behavior of firms.

[40] Alchian, "Uncertainty." See: Terry M. Moe, "The New Economics of Organization," *American Journal of Political Science* 28, no. 4 (November 1984): 739–77. See also Waltz, "Reflections," 331.

they do so on the basis of intelligence or dumb luck – come to set the standards by which others must adjust as long as they wish to remain viable.

Emulation is a rational strategy in a context of insecurity and uncertainty. As I noted in the previous chapter, there is also an element of oddity, perhaps irrationality, in it – states preparing for the next war by imitating methods of the last. In a similar vein, the adopted methods may or may not result in improved fighting capacity. Emulation is a rational response both in the sense that it follows a consequential logic and because it is the most reasonable strategy under conditions of security competition and structural uncertainty. The rationality of state action is a procedural one, not substantive.[41] States make decisions and choices by evaluating, as best they can under structural uncertainty, the expected consequences of alternative courses of actions. Rationality refers only to the consistency between means and ends in their decision making, and not to outcomes or results. States are rational strategically, or instrumentally; they attempt to minimize the costs and risks in their self-help efforts to preserve and enhance their security. Put differently, to say that states act rationally only means that their emulation decisions and choices are subject to some instrumental calculation of net benefits of alternative strategies and models. The actual results may not be in accord with their expectations, but this does not make their decision making irrational. Whether we wish to ascribe adjectives such as "bounded" to their decision making is, in the final analysis, not that important because differences in rationality are not what differentiate states in anarchic realms.[42]

There is one last point with regard to emulation and the depiction of states as rational agents that calculate net benefits among competing alternatives. While the theory of emulation gives causal primacy to outside-in, second image reversed forces, it does not treat the state as a helpless, mindless object buffeted by invisible external forces. The dual organizational effects of external competition is not a mechanical, detached process. I argue that the connection between external forces and their articulation in the internal realm is actually a conscious one – a rational one. States monitor, evaluate, and make deliberate and discriminating choices among synchronic alternatives as they retool and reorganize internally in order to compete externally.

Competitive Realms: Behavioral and Organizational Implications

Emulation is driven by security competition. As Waltz argues, all anarchically organized realms will display emulation behavior. The competitive, anarchic

---

[41] James G. March, *A Primer on Decision Making: How Decisions Happen* (New York: Free Press, 1994).

[42] For this definition of bounded rationality see, Langlois and Robertson, *Firms, Markets, and Economic Change*, 29; March, *A Primer on Decision Making*, chap. 1, passim.

structure of the system, says Waltz, generates the principal behavioral regularities in the system – balancing and emulation – and it does so indirectly through competition and socialization.[43] I will discuss socialization separately later. Emulation is one of the main strategies for contending units. Realms organized on the principle of anarchy, as opposed to hierarchy, are unavoidably competitive in that the autonomous, self-regarding units are directly and indirectly affected by, and can neither escape nor ignore, the actions and choices of others. Strategic interdependence obtains whether or not they wish it so. Security-enhancing self-help efforts take the form of a competitive process even if the aims and intentions of states are not competitive. Others are compelled to do the same. Emulation is a quick and efficient competitive strategy.

Competitive realms are by implication dynamic. This point is vital to understanding the sources of innovation in the system. The competition inherent in the system is not static or single-play. It is ceaseless, even while its intensity varies. The international system is a realm of birth and death, rise and decline, innovation and imitation. It is a realm of struggle and motion. It is a realm of risk and uncertainty that spurs states to search and adopt (through innovation or emulation) newer, more effective instruments and strategies of competition. The system is always in a state of transition and flux, even while the principles of its arrangement remain fixed. Differentials in the natural growth of states and their capabilities are sources of this dynamism.[44] Since insecurity is structurally fixed, the security dilemma implies that the security-enhancing efforts of states never come to full rest. They may stabilize or vary in intensity over time and across states, but never cease. As Jervis's classic essay reminds us, competition in the system is neither constant nor uniform. It is variegated, broken, uneven, segmented, because states do not have the exact same vulnerabilities to the changing strategic environment. It will oscillate across states between long lulls and intense bursts.

Neorealism relies extensively on the assumption of the system as a competitive realm. Waltz's treatment of competition, however, presents us with a few conceptual difficulties. To anticipate the discussion in later sections, there are two such difficulties and flaws in Waltz's treatment. The first is his notion of socialization, discussed below, which has befuddled both followers and critics. The second is his narrow and inconsistent treatment of competition and its effects. Consistent with his microeconomics approach, Waltz attaches a good deal of importance to competitive pressures in propelling states to

---

[43] Waltz, *Theory of International Politics*, 74.

[44] Paul M. Kennedy, *The Rise and Fall of the Great Powers: Economic Change and Military Conflict from 1500 to 2000* (New York: Vintage Books, 1987); William H. McNeill, *The Pursuit of Power: Technology, Armed Force, and Society Since A.D. 1000* (Oxford: Basil Blackwell, 1983).

emulate the successful practices of others. Yet he mistakenly suggests that emulation is the only behavioral response possible. States should just as likely respond to competitive pressures by innovating.[45] Here Waltz leaves several important questions unanswered. Competition can just as likely lead to innovation or implosion; it can just as well trigger internal collapse as national renewal.[46]

Competitive Effectiveness

Competitive realms press contending units to attend to their relative capacity to compete successfully. I refer to this as competitive effectiveness. Units in anarchic realms, be they firms or states, put a premium on their relative competitive effectiveness. Their prosperity and survival as independent entities depend on it. Self-help competitive realms do not just press the contending units to find external support or undertake quantitative internal improvements. This is another way to contemplate the meaning, or implications, of balancing. The pressures of competition, though variable and episodic in intensity, spur them continually to make qualitative improvements in how well they are organized and equipped relative to one another. At certain junctures, such improvements take the form of deep, sustained restructuring and modernization. In a realm in which the use of armed force is continually possible, a state's preoccupation with relative competitive effectiveness will more directly and narrowly focus on the relative size and effectiveness of its military power. All militaries have their ideals, myths, and traditions, but none wish to fall behind.

Two implications follow from the premium states place on competitive effectiveness. First, in a realm that is dynamically competitive and in which insecurity and uncertainty are fixed, the units will be motivated by much more than the minimal goal of survival. They will seek to maximize their security-enhancing efforts. Second, emulation choices are made on the basis of proven effectiveness, as opposed to any other criteria that may emphasize cultural-ideological affinity or domestic political preferences.

Waltz is on target when he writes that competition spurs states to keep up because they fear the consequences of falling behind. But what does this mean in practice? For states, viability and prosperity in the system ultimately rests on their overall capacity to compete – in whatever form that competition takes. Security competition is not just for momentary relief and security, but

---

[45] Mathew Evangelista, *Innovation and the Arms Race: How the United States and the Soviet Union Develop New Military Technologies* (Ithaca: Cornell University Press, 1988), was one of the first to make this observation.

[46] Buzan, Jones, and Little, *The Logic of Anarchy*, 40; Daniel Deudney and G. John Ikenberry, "The International Sources of Soviet Change," *International Security* 16, no. 3 (Winter 1991–2): 74–118.

for the capacity to remain secure, defend autonomy, and sustain long-term security. A state's balancing efforts are geared to improve its short- and long-term competitive effectiveness. Because states worry about their autonomy and not just physical survival, and because physical security and prosperity depend on the underlying bases of national power, it is more meaningful to characterize them as seeking competitive effectiveness.[47] They fear the consequences of erosion in their relative competitive effectiveness not so much out of survival concerns but for their autonomy and overall capacity to compete in the future.

Competitive effectiveness, or national strength, is a comprehensive notion.[48] It comprises both military and nonmilitary components, some quantifiable and tangible, while others less so. It has external components – such as the added resources and power of an ally – but it is fundamentally an internal measure. It may be defined as the state's aggregate material and organizational resources, of which its productive base, organizational capacity, and raw military assets are key components.[49] (I accept that competitive effectiveness may also comprise intangible factors such as skill and leadership). This idea is consistent with long-standing realist definitions of national power. Competitive effectiveness is ultimately a measure of the quality and capacity of the state's central edifice, and all the human, organizational, technological, and material components on which it rests. A state's capacity to compete externally (whether in war, commerce, or simply to maintain its independence) is a function of the strength of its organizational core and resource base.[50] External strength, Clausewitz argued, depends on the strength of internal institutions and their efficiency in mustering the material and human energies of the nation.[51] (From this perspective it becomes evident why large-scale military emulation is likely to trigger changes in, or spill over into, economic, administrative, or societal spheres.)

---

[47] Waltz, *Theory of International Politics*; Grieco, *Cooperation among Nations*.

[48] Leopold von Ranke, *The Secret of World History: Selected Writings on the Art and Science of History*, trans., Roger Winer (New York: Fordham University Press, 1981); Kennedy, *The Rise and Fall of the Great Powers*.

[49] Waltz, *Theory of International Politics*, 118, 130–31, 177–78, 181, 183. See also, McNeill, *The Pursuit of Power*; Kennedy, *The Rise and Fall of the Great Powers*. Waltz, *Theory of International Politics*, 131, and 97–98, also includes some non-material components (e.g., competence, stability) in his definition of national capabilities.

[50] Charles Tilly, *Coercion, Capital, and European States, A.D. 990–1992* (Oxford: Basil Blackwell, 1990). Herz refers to the state as a "protection unit." See, John Herz, *International Politics in the Atomic Age* (New York: Columbia University Press, 1950), and "The Rise and Demise of the Territorial State," *World Politics* 9, no. 4 (July 1957): 473–93. See also interesting paper by Cameron G. Thies, "State Building, Interstate and Intrastate Rivalry: A Study of Post-Colonial Developing Country Extractive Efforts, 1975–2000," *International Studies Quarterly* 48 (2004): 53–72.

[51] Peter Paret, *Clausewitz and the State* (New York: Oxford University Press, 1976).

As noted previously, the core of a state's competitive effectiveness is the fiscal-military hub of the state apparatus.[52] Military capabilities are the most critical, at least the most immediate and tangible, components of national competitive effectiveness. Though military strength is not the only component of competitive effectiveness, in a realm where competition can be conducted by force, relative military strength becomes an important one. To the extent that the speed and scale of organized violence increases progressively, as Deudney argues, the importance of these interrelated components also increases. The tight link among these components suggests that balancing will often entail enhancing military and nonmilitary bases of power. Thus, military effectiveness, like overall national strength, is composed of a complex array of human and material factors, not just the hardware (armaments, force structure) and software (organization, doctrine) of the military. It is also a function of moral, nonmaterial aspects.[53] Military effectiveness consists of both imitable organizational, technological, and doctrinal factors but also inimitable factors such as discipline, leadership, cohesion, training, and intelligence. Biddle, Creveld, and others emphasize the role of skill and moral qualities in determining victory, combat power, and overall military performance.[54] I accept the principle of their argument, though such factors do not easily fit a material structural framework. That aside, the question becomes; If military best practice consists of inimitable, nontransferable elements, why do states emulate at all, and how can emulation be an effective security-enhancing strategy?

Last, competitive effectiveness is structurally determined. It is not a quality of the individual units, but a product of their competition. Whether or not

---

[52] The term "fiscal-military state" is borrowed from John Brewer, *The Sinews of Power: War, Money, and the English State, 1688–1783* (London: Unwin Hyman, 1989). See also Margaret Levi, *Of Rule and Revenue* (Berkeley: University of California Press, 1988); Charles Tilly, "War Making and State Making as Organized Crime," in *Bringing the State Back In*, ed. Peter Evans, Dietrich Rueschemeyer, and Theda Skocpol (Cambridge: Cambridge University Press, 1985). See also Michael Mann, *States, War, and Capitalism: Studies in Political Sociology* (Oxford: Basil Blackwell, 1988): 13–14; Joseph R. Strayer, *On the Medieval Origins of the Modern State* (Princeton: Princeton University Press, 1970): 26–32; Herz, "The Rise and Demise."

[53] Martin van Creveld, *Fighting Power: German and U.S. Army Performance, 1939–1945* (Westport: Greenwood Press, 1982). See also Herbert Rosinski, *The German Army* (New York: Praeger, 1966); Stephen Biddle, *Military Power: Explaining Victory and Defeat in Modern Battle* (Princeton: Princeton University Press, 2004). On military effectiveness, see *Military Effectiveness*, 3 vols., ed. Allan R. Millet and Williamson Murray (Boston: Allen and Unwin, 1988). For an argument about the social bases of military effectiveness see: Stephen Peter Rosen, "Military Effectiveness: Why Societies Matter," *International Security* 19, no. 4 (Spring 1995): 5–31, and *Societies and Military Power: India and Its Armies* (Ithaca: Cornell University Press, 1996).

[54] Biddle, *Military Power*; van Creveld, *Fighting Power*; Allan R. Millet, Williamson Murray, and Kenneth H. Watman, "The Effectiveness of Military Organizations," ed. Millet and Murray, 1–30.

firms are profitable has more to do with the structure of their competition than with the internal attributes of individual firms – even while to be profitable they must be able to meet the minimum requirement of effective internal organization. Anarchic structure alone determines the minimum requirements of viability in the system.

Focusing on the centrality of relative competitive effectiveness allows us to view emulation in a broader context. It also permits us to rethink the state as the unit of competition. Neorealism is more properly understood as a theory of organizations and organizational effects in competitive realms. It treats states as political units in a realm where pressures and incentives push them to behave in certain ways and not others, and shape their internal organization. States in much of the realist tradition are depicted as billiard balls, but we should not miss the fact that the realm of their interaction conditions their organizational form and attributes as well as their behavioral regularity. Building on Waltz's original formulation but departing from many of his conclusions, I argue that the international system, because it is an anarchic realm, has dual organizational effects on the contending states.[55] These organizational effects are byproducts of the system's primary behavioral exigency, balancing.

The theory of emulation does not just tell us something about emulation, a particular kind of internal balancing behavior. It pushes us to reconceptualize neorealism's two principal units of analysis, the system and the state-units. What the theory's defenders and critics ignore are the full implications of the conception of the system as anarchically organized, namely the organizational imprint inherent in such realms. Neorealism's inner logic is about behavioral regularity as well organizational effects of self-help competition. Anarchic realms are dynamic, not static. As both the intensity and quality of competition changes, so do the minimum requirements for competitive effectiveness. This is a fancy way to restate neorealism's key proposition: that states will balance. But what else does balance mean and entail beyond alliance making? In the short run, some states may have the good fortune of generous friends and fortuitous external circumstances (*fortuna*), but in the long run their viability can only be assured by their own efforts and the strength of their internal organization (*virtù*). The organizational consequences for states of these principles are manifest. Hidden in neorealism is a conception of the state consistent with long-standing realist verities dating back to Thucydides, Hobbes, and Machiavelli, namely, a conception of the state as, above all else, an organizational solution to the insecurity of the external realm.[56]

---

55 Borrowing from Tilly, *Coercion, Capital, and European States*, I adopt an organizational definition of the state.

56 The idea of the state as an organizational solution to insecurity is most clearly articulated in Otto Hintze, *The Historical Essays of Otto Hintze* (New York: Oxford University Press,

Scholars have generally focused on two of the theory's claims that received the most attention in Waltz: that states will balance against power, and that shifts in the third tier will affect the efficiency of their balancing as well as the probability of war among them. Yet defenders and critics alike have focused on system outcomes and behavioral regularities, rather than on the organizational effects on states responding to the system's competitive pressures.[57]

EMULATION AS BALANCING

The theory of emulation builds on neorealism's two key hypotheses about the behavior of states.[58] The first is that states, when confronted with challenges to their safety, will mobilize their domestic resources as well as seek external help from friends. This broad range of security-enhancing efforts, some internally directed while others externally oriented, is referred to as balancing behavior. Balancing may be broadly defined. Conceptually, it is not restricted to alignment behavior (external alliance making), though this is the usage that seems to predominate in the literature.[59] Rather, it broadly designates the concerns and subsequent efforts to keep up with and counter the capabilities-enhancing efforts and gains of others. Either way, states are doing the same thing – relying on a combination of (internal and external) efforts to respond to threats, to offset the actual or perceived relative increases in the capabilities of others.

The forms and methods of external balancing are well developed in the literature and are more readily identifiable. External balancing in the form of alliances has dominated theorizing. Here too we should widen the analysis. External balancing is not limited to military alliances; what matters is the effect of this option on the security calculations of opposing states. External balancing will range from formal and informal alliances to free riding, generically referred to as buck-passing. The point is a vital one, for the availability of external balancing options will weigh on the decisions states make about emulation as well as other forms of internal balancing. To simplify, external balancing options may or may not come in the form of formal alliances. As the historical cases studied here illustrate, the ability or opportunity to free ride on the balancing efforts of others can matter just as much as the

1975); Richard Bean, "War and the Birth of the Nation State," *Journal of Economic History* 33 (1973): 203–21; Herz, "The Rise and Demise."

[57] I thank Jeffrey Taliaferro, Tufts University, for this observation.

[58] Waltz, *Theory of International Politics*, 124.

[59] Walt, *The Origins of Alliances*; Glenn H. Snyder, "Alliances, Balances, and Stability," *International Organization* 45, no. 1 (Winter 1991): 121–42; Posen, *The Sources of Military Doctrine*; Edward Vose Gulick, *Europe's Classical Balance of Power* (New York: W.W. Norton, 1955). Waltz's version of realism is often referred to as balance of power theory. See Michael Mastanduno, "Preserving the Unipolar Moment: Realist Theories and U.S. Grand Strategy After the Cold War," *International Security* 21, no. 4 (Spring 1997): 49–88.

availability of formal alliances. Free riding is a shaky and unsustainable balancing option, but it can provide short-term relief. The reliability of all forms of external balancing, including formal alliances, is uncertain. Nevertheless, what matters most is not formality of the external balancing option, but the effects of this option on the calculations of adversaries.

Waltz devotes nearly all his attention to external balancing and the formation of power balances in the system, leaving internal balancing underdeveloped and empty of content. Waltz rightly points out that internal balancing is the more efficient – and, we should add, the most assured – form of balancing. However, he does not follow through on the matter. Under conditions of structural uncertainty, internal balancing is necessarily the most efficient and secure form of balancing, but also the most widely displayed. Waltz's uneven treatment left the impression that internal balancing is displayed only in bipolar systems. Simple intuition tells us that internal balancing is not just the more reliable and precise but also the more prevalent; the one with the most extensive and visible organizational footprint. States rise and fall in rank, they grow and contract, live or disappear, based on their ability to muster their human, material, technological, and organizational resources. In conditions of self-help and uncertainty, the primary and dominant form of balancing behavior must necessarily be internal, irrespective of polarity. States often will rely on external balancing, and some are so weak and poor as to have no other recourse. Still others, though resource rich, have the luxury of an external security provider, as in the classic cases of postwar Germany and Japan. Yet even in such extreme cases, some level of internal mustering will take place.

Military emulation is a form of internal balancing. As elaborated in the next section, it is only one of several internal mobilization strategies, which involve quantitative and qualitative mustering of the state's human, material, organizational, and technological resources. It is a distinct, stand-alone strategy, but it is usually not exclusive. At the upper range of internal balancing, states are likely to be engaged simultaneously in multiple forms of internal balancing. Not all forms of internal balancing involve deliberate imitation of the best practices of others; raising troop levels, increasing military expenditures, or redeploying armed forces may be done with an eye on what others are doing but involve no emulation. On the other hand, emulation may be only a small part of a much larger internal-balancing strategy, as is often the case with innovation-capable states.

When faced with sustained major threats, states rely primarily on internal means. Thus, all else being equal, a response that relies solely on external means is ruled out by the theory. As system polarity changes, questions pertaining to the propensity and efficiency of one form or another can only be questions about external, not internal, balancing.[60] Indeed, external

---

[60] Waltz, *Theory of International Politics*, 163–72.

balancing can only supplement, not supplant, internal forms regardless of polarity. To claim otherwise is to abandon the self-help assumption. As long as the system remains an anarchic, self-help realm, internal balancing will be the dominant form. There is a dynamic interplay between the two forms of balancing. Internal balancing may be the dominant form, but its scale and intensity will vary with the availability and reliability of external balancing options. This point is crucial because external balancing constitutes one of the biggest factors conditioning the timing, pace, and scope of emulation.

Internal balancing has state-building consequences. If it is large scale and sustained, it will leave behind organizational consequences. All forms of large-scale internal balancing will leave an organizational residue or imprint, all the more so when it is large in scale and sustained over time. This organizational imprint will be both distinct and targeted when internal balancing takes the form of emulation. The organizational footprint of major, sustained internal balancing is most clearly visible on the state's fiscal-administrative-coercive apparatus (though even run-of-the-mill quantitative mustering of resources will likely leave some residue). At certain historical junctures, internal balancing will involve the creation, redesign, development, and restructuring of the state's organizational edifice. As we might expect, the locus of externally induced organizational effects will be the fiscal-administrative-military hub of the state apparatus. Though our focus is on the central edifice, as Porter, Brewer, and others have argued, changes in the state's organizational hub nearly always implicate or reverberate in other areas of the state machinery and beyond.[61] In general, the character, scope, and durability of organizational effects and side-effects will depend upon the intensity and durability of the international competition. The more sustained, intense, and total the competition, the greater the organizational effects.

Emulation as Internal Balancing

The second prediction is that states will emulate the ways and practices of each other.[62] The questions are: What is the connection between balancing and emulation, and what are their wider consequences on the state's organizational makeup? The anarchic structure of the international system generates twin organizational effects on states. Anarchic structure presses states to make continual improvements in the organizational-technological backbone of national power, and it propels them toward common improvements. It does so via internal balancing. In other words, internal balancing is the

---

[61] Bruce Porter, *War and the Rise of the State: The Military Foundations of Modern Politics* (New York: Free Press, 1994); Brewer, *Sinews of Power*. See also Karen A. Rassler and William R. Thompson, *War and State Making: The Shaping of the Global Powers* (Boston: Unwin Hyman, 1989).

[62] Waltz, *Theory of International Politics*, 127.

TABLE 2.1. *Simplified Balancing Strategies*

External	Free Riding	Formal Alliance	
	Buck-Passing		
Internal	Countermeasuring	Innovation	Emulation
	Balancing Strategies		

vehicle through which external competitive pressures translate into organizational effects. When internal balancing entails or is accompanied by emulation, these organizational effects reappear internationally as common transformations. Internal balancing is a range, and at its lower end the organizational effects will either be absent or negligible. Balancing at all levels will entail the mustering or improvement of military power and all that underlies it, since such capabilities remain the most direct means to security. At certain junctures much more will be required than just an adequate supply of men, money, and arms. A state's overall ability to muster, deploy, and utilize its men and arms effectively rests upon a less visible, less dramatic foundation. Confronted with serious and sustained threats, the state will be forced to restructure and retool the organizational-technological bases of its national power.

Internal balancing, which itself consists of a number of discrete measures and policies, is only one of several major categories of balancing strategies. Although these measures and strategies often bleed into one another, for analytical convenience we can distinguish among five major security-enhancing strategies: emulation, innovation, countermeasuring, and the two main forms of external balancing, free riding and formal alliance (see Table 2.1). Two quick points are worth mentioning about these broad categories of strategies. First, states generally will rely on more than one, thus we expect to find some overlap or bleeding across strategies. Second, this simple taxonomy is silent on their efficiency, scale, and permutations. The latter two strategies involve externally oriented mustering. I discuss innovation separately below. The first three strategies are forms of internal balancing, and we may think of them as progressing from quantitative efforts (countermeasuring) to qualitative ones (innovation, emulation). I expect states to move along the quantitative-qualitative continuum as the scale and duration of threats increase, but the trajectory is not linear.

On a separate point, there is some debate about bandwagoning as a distinct form of external balancing. Bandwagoning entails the joining or appeasement of the source of the threat as opposed to taking measures to counter it.[63] Although neorealism expects states to balance against and not

[63] Stephen M. Walt, "Alliance Formation and the Balance of World Power," *International Security* 9, no. 4 (Spring 1985): 3–43, and "Alliance, Threats, and US Grand Strategy: A Reply to Kaufman and Labs," *Security Studies* 1, no. 3 (Spring 1992): 448–82; Snyder,

bandwagon with threats, bandwagoning is possible. Waltz discusses the unusual and highly restrictive circumstances under which it arises. Beyond the restricted conditions Waltz specifies, bandwagoning is anomalous in neorealism. For our purposes here, we can simply discount it.

Countermeasuring is an elastic category of internal mobilization. Countermeasuring strategies involve quantitative increases in arms, men, and finances to offset increases in an adversary's power. They may also include repositioning, redeploying, and retooling of forces, organizational rearrangement, and reconfiguring existing methods in order to thwart an adversary's measures. Countermeasuring may entail significant changes and large-scale efforts that may often accompany or bleed into emulation and innovation. Its salient characteristic is that it does not consist of devising or introducing new ways and practices. Rather, it involves quantitative increases and reconfiguration of existing human, organizational, and technological resources. At major strategic junctures countermeasuring is insufficient. Nonetheless, it is the one strategy that affords states the highest level of certainty and control. From the standpoint of neorealist theory, we expect countermeasuring to be the most common balancing strategy, and the one most likely to accompany emulation at all levels.

In practice, states rely on a combination of security-enhancing strategies when responding to threats. They will first turn to strategies that are more readily available and easily executed, followed by or in parallel with efforts whose implementation and results are longer term. As such, we expect to find, in the first instance of military emulation cases, some degree of countermeasuring. The greater the threat, the more likely we are to see multiple forms of internal balancing (leaving aside external balancing options). Thus, we expect to see all episodes of emulation preceded by countermeasuring as well as continued reliance, or blending, of such efforts in the overall emulation process. Indeed, a closer inspection of the South American cases shows some types of countermeasuring, such as armaments buildup, simply transform into the emulation process, as countries acquire weapons technology of the model being emulated.

For analytical convenience, we assume that states are choosing between only emulation and innovation. The more theoretically interesting question is not why secondary emulate, but why primary states choose emulation

"Alliances, Balances, and Stability." See also Douglas J. Macdonald, "*Origins of Alliances*: Book Review," *Journal of Politics* 51, no. 3 (August 1989): 795–97; Michael N. Barnett and Jack S. Levy, "The Domestic Sources of Alliances and Alignments: The Case of Egypt, 1962–73," *International Organization* 45, no. 3 (Summer 1993): 369–96; Michael N. Barnett, "High Politics Is Low Politics: The Domestic and Systemic Sources of Israeli Security Policy, 1967–1977," *World Politics* 42, no. 4 (July 1990): 529–62; Schweller, "Bandwagoning"; Eric J. Labs, "Do Weak States Bandwagon?" *Security Studies* 1, no. 3 (Spring 1992): 383–416; Robert G. Kaufman, "To Balance or to Bandwagon? Alignment Decisions in 1930s Europe," *Security Studies* 1, no. 3 (Spring 1992): 417–47.

rather than innovation. Why did France, which had conquered nearly all of Europe and revolutionized warfare, emulate Germany? The biggest theoretical challenge for neorealism and its theory of emulation is predicting which balancing strategy, or combination, states will choose. I believe the matter of which balancing strategy states will choose is ultimately indeterminate, since so much of it is dictated by a range of contingencies facing individual states. The indeterminacy stems from two sources. One, states typically rely on multiple strategies, particularly as threat levels increase. Two, whether or not states choose emulation is often the result of a delicate constellation of factors, none of which can be anticipated. Nevertheless, we can better specify the conditions under which states are more likely to choose one or another. The crux of this question turns on emulation and innovation as balancing strategies.

EMULATION AND INNOVATION

The theory of emulation understands innovation and emulation to be the only dominant strategies at critical junctures. Although Waltz is vague on the point, I argue that all states emulate, including innovation-capable states (the great powers). Innovation-capable states, like the United States in the late nineteenth century, will engage in both innovation and emulation. Under what conditions might states innovate rather than emulate, and vice versa? The theory of emulation benefits from but does not require an accompanying theory of innovation. It can simply take innovation as given without losing its explanatory power and usefulness. A theory of emulation does require clarifying the conceptual distinctions between emulation and innovation and specifying the conditions under which states will adopt one or the other.

Emulation and innovation are distinct processes. In commonly accepted definitions, innovation involves the invention of new, previously unknown practices, or the recombination of existing ones in new ways. Innovation is discovery of new knowledge, normally resulting in technical-scientific advance and improved performance. Emulation, on the other hand, essentially involves copying proven innovations. It may be possible to consider emulation as a kind of innovation – from the standpoint of the emulator who, in effect, is adopting something new. For those states who emulate, emulation is a kind of innovation insofar as it is qualitative departure from their existing practices.[64] Moreover, the process of emulation may shade into, or inspire, innovation as emulators recombine or reconfigure borrowed practices. However, it is useful to maintain the conceptual distinction.

[64] Alchian, "Uncertainty," 218.

Neorealist theory does not account for the sources of innovation in the international system. Nor does it explain differences of innovativeness across states.[65] It cannot explain which particular state, for example, status quo, challenger, or secondary, will innovate. It may not need to. The theory assumes that innovation is a matter of capabilities. It is far more interested in the effects of innovation and the structural dynamics that give rise to it, rather than place and time of innovation. This may not be sufficient theoretically. Such indeterminacy papers over big questions regarding the nature of behavior in the system, especially as they pertain to the debate between defensive and offensive realists.

The deep source, or cause, of innovation is easily explained by neorealism. Put broadly, the competitive nature of the state system engenders both innovation and borrowing.[66] Innovation is endogenous to competitive realms. It arises from the same deep structural forces that give rise to balancing and emulation behavior. Like all forms of self-help efforts, it is aimed at bolstering competitive effectiveness. All competitive realms have built-in incentives for innovating, since the prospective payoffs of successful innovation are great. Emulation may bring security payoffs, but the payoffs from successful innovation are likely to be greater.

Given the competitive advantages that result from successful innovation, states that possess the necessary material-technical-scientific capacity will innovate, all else being equal. The rate of innovation will increase with the intensity of competition. The international system, like the market, generates ceaseless technical and organizational innovation.[67] The system is in constant motion because of it. Neorealism expects the system to display continuous innovation as a result of the striving and jockeying among contending states – constant striving and jockeying to avoid falling behind as a result of what others have done as well as in anticipation of what they might do. In other words, when we look at how states think about and practice innovation, their actions display both an action-reaction dynamic as well as a prisoners' dilemma dynamic. Competitive systems have built-in incentives

---

[65] Evangelista, *Innovation and the Arms Race*, chap. 1, passim.

[66] A similar point is made by E. L. Jones, *The European Miracle: Environments, Economies, and Geopolitics in the History of Europe and Asia*, 2nd ed. (Cambridge: Cambridge University Press, 1987): 45.

[67] On innovation in the market I rely on the following works: James M. Utterback, *Mastering the Dynamics of Innovation: How Companies Can Seize Opportunities in the Face of Technological Change* (Boston: Harvard Business School Press, 1994); F. M. Scherer, *Industrial Market Structure and Economic Performance*, 2nd ed. (Boston: Houghton Mifflin, 1980); Giovanni Dosi, "Sources, Procedures, and Microeconomics Effects of Innovation," *Journal of Economic Literature* 26, no. 3 (1988): 1120–71; Maria Brouwer, *Schumpeterian Puzzles: Technological Competition and Economic Evolution* (Ann Arbor: University of Michigan Press, 1991); Geoffrey M. Hodgson, *Economics and Evolution: Bringing Life Back Into Economics* (Cambridge: Cambridge University Press, 1993).

for contenders to engage in innovation. If successful, innovation brings with it enormous (albeit short-lived) first-mover advantages.

At a descriptive level, we can classify states into innovation-capable states and emulators. That secondary states will always emulate is incontrovertible, for they typically lack the resource-technological bases. Waltz associates innovativeness with capabilities, arguing that contending states will emulate the military strategies and weapons of the state of greatest ingenuity and capability.[68] It is not surprising that innovation corresponds to size (defined in terms of capabilities). Innovation is both expensive and risky. It is both time consuming and uncertain in results. States of primary capabilities are more likely to have not just the resource base but, more important, the extra margin of safety necessary to incur these risks. Secondary states have neither. Even the occasional secondary state that may have the resources and skills base may not have the extra margin of safety to risk innovation as competition increases.

Far more problematic is determining *ex ante* who innovates among the states that are innovation capable, and the rate of their innovation. The capacity to innovate is a necessary but not sufficient condition. The rate of innovation varies with intensity of competition. It is as much a product of system dynamics as it is of the size of the actors.[69] As in the market system, innovation arises from an intricate interplay of factors such as size, technical and resource capacity, and intensity of competition. The intensity of competition means that there is no direct relationship between innovativeness and size. Despite the big role for relative size and endowment differentials in innovation, the mediating role of competition intensity means that the relationship between innovation and emulation is neither symmetrical nor linear.

In this light, the emulation behavior of great powers comes into clearer view. Even for the great powers of the system, innovation is a product of a delicate balance between potential risks and prospective gains. As competition increases, we expect all states to be more risk averse, and thus opt for the certain and immediate payoffs of emulation. Given the risks and uncertainty that attend innovation, intensifying competition will dampen innovativeness. The relationship between innovativeness and competition is an inverted-U curve, with a steeper downward slope at higher levels of competition (see Figure 2.1). Risks of relying on innovation alone increase, and states become more risk averse, as security competition stiffens. Under such

---

[68] Waltz, *Theory of International Politics*, 127. See also Waltz's treatment of military emulation in, Waltz, "The Emerging Structure of International Politics," *International Security* 18, no. 2 (Fall 1993): 44–79.

[69] Scherer, *Industrial Market Structure*; Maria Brouwer, *Schumpeterian Puzzles*. See also Paul Auerbach, *Competition: The Economics of Industrial Change* (Oxford: Basil Blackwell, 1988).

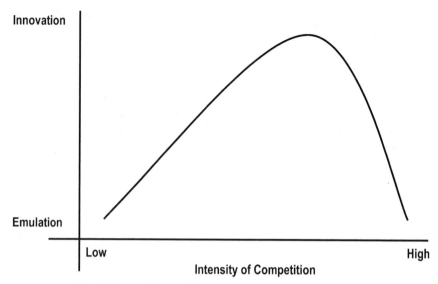

FIGURE 2.1. Emulation and Innovation.

conditions, innovation-capable states turn to emulation. As military competition increases, the extra margin of safety that their capabilities afford them dwindles accordingly. Emulation minimizes risks and maximizes the yield of security-enhancing efforts. As competition rises, all states put a greater value on proven effectiveness and on known results, which only emulation can bring.

The behavioral weight of uncertainty becomes more pronounced in the area of security and military capabilities. States place an even higher premium on the military components of competitive effectiveness as competition stiffens. In matters of military power and national security, states are more risk averse in their security-enhancing strategies. They are far less willing to gamble on untested practices. Proven effectiveness becomes the sole criterion in determining such strategies. States, like firms, are averse to basing their security on untested or unknown organizations and technologies, let alone on ones that have been shown to fail, or to be less effective. Where competitive pressures are especially harsh and the external environment becomes more adverse, states will shy away from trial and error attempts to contrive their own arrangements or technologies. Just as the risks of not keeping up are great when security competition intensifies, so are the risks of failed innovation or reliance on untested methods. This inherent risk aversion under uncertainty is an added stimulus to emulation behavior for states as it is for firms. In his seminal essay, Armen Alchian observes that, "in general, uncertainty provides an excellent reason for imitation of observed success. Likewise, it accounts for observed uniformity among the survivors."[70] The last part of his statement, regarding observed uniformity, echoes Waltz. I shall have more to say about this later.

Emulation carries its own risks. But these risks are lower than those that attend innovation at higher levels of competition. Indeed, the South Americans were quite wary of launching into full-scale military emulation. There were intensive studies and prolonged debates, even among advocates of military emulation, over the suitability of foreign practices in terms of producing improved military power. These were legitimate and expected debates. But they also betray just how risk averse states are in their decisions about security matters. Secondary states, in particular, worry about the suitability of foreign practices to their local conditions. These themes were repeated endlessly in the official documents and military journals in the cases studied.

The Virtues of Copying

Emulators have an enormous advantage that innovators do not – they already know the results. More important, emulators will reduce their uncertainty over the utility and results of borrowed practices by studying the experience of other emulators. The South Americans' reaction to Meiji Japan's military emulation is illustrative of how states evaluate and manage risks under uncertainty. What is striking in the documents is the regularity with which proponents of emulation pointed to Japan (and their own pioneering neighbors in South America) to allay concerns about the feasibility and suitability of adopting foreign military practices. The Japanese model was a favorite of Brazilian reformers. Successful emulation generates its own demonstration effect. Early emulators lessen the uncertainty over the viability of foreign models that follow-on emulators have. Japan's meteoric rise from the periphery to first-power rank, and its string of military successes, boosted considerably the level of confidence of the South Americans and other would-be emulators in the viability of military emulation. Emulators, therefore, enjoy two kinds of late-modernizer advantages, especially the second wave of emulators who are able to observe and learn from the efforts of earlier emulators. These early emulators further reduce the practical uncertainties future emulators have regarding the applicability and effectiveness of the military system.

For its advocates everywhere, the benefits of emulation were as great as they were obvious. In all the cases examined here, frustration, even anger, on the part of reformers was a common thread in historical records, for they were puzzled as to why others could not see the obvious benefits of emulation. We expect emulation to be more strongly displayed in anarchic systems irrespective of system polarity. Emulating proven best practice

---

[70] Alchian, "Uncertainty."

is a time-saving, risk-minimizing strategy in competitive realms. It allows states to maximize the returns on their security-enhancing efforts.[71] Emulation is not only the more reliable strategy under conditions of intensifying competition, but it also has practical payoffs. As Gerschenkron first reminded us, late modernizers have certain advantages that come with lateness. Emulation is a cheap and time-saving catch-up strategy. It allows states – like firms – to jump directly into the leading stages of technological and organizational practice, and to do so while minimizing risks and costs. Large-scale emulation, of course, is itself an expensive and long-lasting undertaking, but it is quicker and cheaper compared to innovation.

CONVERGING ON SUCCESS

Waltz argues that convergence in the international system occurs through two linked mechanisms – competition and socialization.[72] The anarchic structure of the international system, according to Waltz, produces uniformity in the behavior of states and the political outcomes of their interactions. Yet, the theory of emulation suggests that anarchic structure also shapes and molds the organizational attributes of states and pushes them toward similar outcomes over time. Structure has dual organizational effects on states: molding their development in response to the requirements of competition and pushing these organizational-technological responses toward convergence. States are like units, not just in terms of the absence of functional differentiation among them or the inescapable behavioral regularity imposed by the anarchy. Over time and as a result of their competition, they become more and more alike in their organizational attributes.

Crossnational emulation is one of the major avenues through which interstate convergence occurs in the system. Crossnational convergence is a product of international competition, not culture or other factors. Claims of international isomorphism and mimicry are long-standing in the literature. In the area of cross-national convergence, organizational sociology, especially the Stanford School, and the transdisciplinary new institutionalism literature, have been the most dynamic and pioneering. Postcolonial critical literature, working in the humanities, has been the most interesting and thought-provoking. Today it is commonplace to claim that the forces

[71] Sean Lynn-Jones, "Offense-Defense Theory and Its Critics," *Security Studies* 4, no. 4 (Summer 1995): 660–91, 664–65, fn. 10. See also Waltz, *Theory of International Politics*, 126; Zakaria, "Realism and Domestic Politics"; Taliaferro, "Security Seeking."

[72] Frantz Fanon, *The Wretched of the Earth* (New York: Grove Press, 1968); Derek Walcott, *Dream on Monkey Mountain and Other Plays* (New York: Farrar, Straus and Giroux, 1970); Amílcar Cabral, *Revolution in Guinea: Selected Texts of Amílcar Cabral*, trans., ed. Richard Handyside (New York: Monthly Review Press, 1969). Revolutionary leaders like Amílcar Cabral, Malcolm X, and Steve Biko devoted a lifetime of thought and struggle to cultural liberation.

of globalization, cultural as well as economic, are the prime engines of global convergence. The neorealist theory of emulation cannot claim that all convergence in the system is the byproduct of security competition, or the result of only emulation. As noted previously, coercion and imposition have been equally pervasive. This does suggest, however, that much of cross-national convergence accords with realist emphasis on the role of power and competition.

Strategic competition engenders convergence by promoting the spread of best practices as well as by winnowing variety. Structure selects best practices, and promotes their spread, and it also selects out bad practices through punishment and elimination. The international system can be treated as a dynamic, evolutionary realm, with a selection mechanism, selection criteria, and sources of continual variety.[73] Emulation is one of four competition-based mechanisms in anarchic systems that generate a dynamic tendency toward convergence. The four mechanisms of convergence in the international system (aside from pure chance) are: emulation, coercion, imposition, and selection. Here I concentrate on the last. Waltz conceives the international system as a realm of selection, although he fails to elaborate on the point.[74] In large measure, it may be more useful to view the first three mechanisms as simply different forms of selection, broadly defined. Irrespective of the form selection takes, its essence remains unchanged – power relations.

Selection inheres in all anarchically ordered, competitive realms. Structural selection, or system punishment, is most commonly interpreted to mean physical elimination of the entire state. The connotation is unavoidable in Waltz. Selection takes place according to a logic of consequence. In Waltz's famous phrase, states that behave foolishly and irresponsibly can expect to pay a price for their misbehavior. States that are poorly organized and equipped, or that behave in ways that contravene structural imperatives, will fall by the wayside. States may behave or internally organize any way they wish. They pay a price if they organize in ways that reduce their power and safety. Those better equipped and organized in ways that give them competitive advantage prosper. Physical elimination, either through defeat in war, conquest, imposition, or implosion as with the Soviet Union, is the most obvious form of selection. There were a myriad of immediate and mediating causes for the former Soviet Union's collapse, many of which were unit-level,

---

73 On evolutionary realms in political, biological, and economic realms, see Jack Hirshleifer, "Economics from a Biological Viewpoint," *Journal of Law and Economics* 20, no. 1 (April 1977): 1–52; Richard R. Nelson and Sidney G. Winter, *An Evolutionary Theory of Economic Change* (Cambridge: Belknap Press/Harvard University Press, 1982); Hodgson, *Economics and Evolution.*

74 The concept must be developed since it is a key causal mechanism, as noted by Peter Feaver, "Brother Can You Spare a Paradigm? (Or Was Anybody Ever a Realist?)," *International Security* 25, no. 1 (Summer 2000): 165–193.

but the deep cause of its implosion was the pressure of international competition. Skocpol had it right, so did Kennan.[75] States may, and often do, behave and internally organize as they please, or as dictated by ideological and other factors. Few and far between are states, like post–Cold War United States, with the surplus power and extra margin of security to engage in extravagance or indulge their whimsical adolescent impulses.

Selection should be thought of more broadly. First, structure punishes as well as rewards. Structure punishes misbehavior and uncompetitive practices, but it also rewards ways and practices that prove more effective. It rewards more effective practices with enhanced power and security as well as promotes their spread through emulation. Put differently, structure selects winners and losers. Selection is both a process of destruction as well as creation. The determination of winning and losing, growth and contraction occurs at the level of structure, and not the properties of the contending units. Structure selects both by reducing variety through elimination as well as promoting best practices through emulation.

Second, selection as punishment does not always, or mainly, consist of physical elimination of the entire entity. Selection also operates at the level of organizational attributes and internal arrangements of the state. Indeed, the rate of selection at the organizational design level is far greater than at the level of the entire state. Crossnational convergence results from both elimination (which reduces variety) as well as emulation. Such selection and convergence can occur at the level of the state or specific institutions, though internationally it is more accurate to say that the units of competition are states rather than military systems per se. Whether as reward or punishment, the rate of selection will correspond to the intensity of competition. Since intense competition is not always nor everywhere present in the system, selection works imperfectly and unevenly. More still, selection as punishment may work its effects immediately or over the long term.

The international system today is dominated by a specific organizational form of state – the nation-state – because this form proved to be stronger, more effective, than other competing forms in the system.[76] As Tilly and others remind us, the political-organizational form of the nation-state, like all its predecessors, unfolded according to a logic that met both internal as well as external requirements. Many of these internal requirements however had the purpose of serving external ones. The nation-state simply proved stronger than its competitors and its emulation more widespread. Spruyt and a number of others' works in social theory argue that the nation-state became dominant, not because of its competitive effectiveness, but because

---

[75] Theda Skocpol, *States and Social Revolutions: A Comparative Analysis of France, Russia, and China* (Cambridge: Cambridge University Press, 1979).
[76] Tilly, *Capital, Coercion and European States*.

it was more legitimate and credible.[77] Credibility and legitimacy did not seem to help the many nation-states that have come and gone since; that shrunk, expanded, rose to primary rank or fell under the shadow of others. Nor does it explain why some specific versions of the nation-state, or their specific organizational-technological attributes, are emulated and not others.

The death rate among states in the modern system may be low, as some have argued. It is quite high when we take into account all states, modern and premodern, since the first proto states appeared some eight thousand years ago in Mesopotamia. Assertions that selection is not a central feature of the system because the death rate of states is very low ignore the fate of political units across historical time, as it does the many ways, short of extinction, their fortunes rise and fall. They ignore the many ways units adjust internally and externally as a result of the pressures, coercion, and intimidation the weak suffer at the hands of the strong.

Structure acts as the selection mechanism, and the selection criterion is competitive effectiveness. The determination of competitive effectiveness – survival, viability, safety, and prosperity – is located at the level of system structure, not the characteristics, will, or aims of states. Structure establishes the minimum requirements, or threshold, of competitive effectiveness. In the market system, the market (industry structure) determines which firms are profitable and which are not, since it sets the minimum requirements of viability and profitability. The market determines which techniques, products, or practices are successful and effective. This minimum criteria for survival, autonomy, and prosperity will be determined, and will operate, whether or not the firms or states are ignorant, intelligent, skillful, or stupid and whether or not they are aware of it and desire it.[78]

The anarchic structure of the international system selects and, because it does so, convergence is generated. Two additional points regarding this convergence are worth highlighting. First, convergence through selection results indirectly from reduction of variety, as noted above. Second, this convergence is a dynamic tendency, and the similarity produced is likely to be a rough one. Competition ensures that the system is never at rest. It ensures that innovation is continual, giving birth to new ways and practices and altering the minimum requirements for successful competition. Moreover, the security dilemma means that not all states are simultaneously affected by the same levels of competition, thus convergence is always jagged, uneven, and partial. Convergence in the international system is likely to display a clustering tendency that is more strongly displayed in arenas of close competition.

---

[77] Hendrik Spruyt, *The Sovereign State and Its Competitors: An Analysis of Systems Change* (Princeton: Princeton University Press, 1994); Strayer, *On the Medieval Origins of the Modern State*.

[78] Alchian, "Uncertainty"; Moe, "The New Economics."

Just as innovation and emulation are clustered in arenas of competition, so too is crossnational convergence.

The convergence that takes place in the system is dynamic, irregular, and inefficient. It is never complete or stationary. As long as the system remains anarchically competitive, variety will be generated by continuous innovation. Since emulation and direct selection are functions of security competition, which varies in intensity across states and over time, variety persists. Inferior practices may persist for long periods in the absence of an external corrective jolt. Like emulation, selection is episodic and uneven. Finally, selection neither operates on the basis of, nor results in, optimality. The practices, technologies, and institutions that survive may have done so only because they proved to be better than synchronic alternatives.[79]

The Role of War in Competitive Emulation

How exactly does structure select best practices, and how are these spread in the system? The most direct mechanism by which convergence takes place is direct selection through physical elimination. Conquest, defeat in war, or self-directed purging of existing practices and their replacement by new ones, are typically the most common modes of variety-reducing selection. Through war, structure tests and selects which military institutions, practices, or technologies are more effective. War determines the relative military utility (success) of weapons technology and military systems, aside from determining the relative military prowess of the contending states. War is the primary test and determinant of relative competitive effectiveness, even though it may often be an imperfect one. Success in war is not always the product of technical superiority.

Proven success in war, in turn, determines emulation appeal and spread. In the military sphere, it is the victorious military system of every great war that sets the standard by which all others measure themselves and which acts as the model imitated by all. Large-scale military reorganization and emulation tend to follow major wars.[80] War reduces the need for states to make aggregate calculations regarding which state is the most powerful or which military system is most effective. War eliminates the need to make detailed but uncertain measurements about which military system would prove most effective.

It is the great power wars of every era that determine which military system is the most successful. In general, short of the test of battle, the performance of a particular organizational or technological innovation cannot

---

[79] Douglass North, *Institutions, Institutional Change, and Economic Performance* (Cambridge: Cambridge University Press, 1991), and others remind us that a variety of forces, and not just external competition, are at work shaping the structures and institutional makeup of states.
[80] Posen, "Nationalism."

be accurately compared or estimated.[81] Because the military cannot satisfactorily practice or test its innovations short of actual combat, indirect practical experience, the experience of others, becomes highly valued.[82] Major wars play another significant role in crossnational emulation. They are both the primary structural mechanism for determining proven effectiveness; also they act as a system-wide signaling device for what works and what does not. Major wars become a heuristic shortcut for states when making decisions about best practices. For both the participants and onlookers, major wars reveal the flaws and weaknesses of the competing military systems. Likewise, such wars demonstrate the effectiveness and superiority of alternative organizations, strategies, and technologies.[83] States exist in a realm in which they are continuously monitoring, assessing, and gathering information about the ways and practices of one another. That they study and monitor need not imply some complex learning or social construction.

There is no suggestion here that states learn the right lessons. The proverbial fog that surrounds every war – every victory, the performance of every weapons systems, the utility of every new invention, and every harbinger of future trends in war – cannot be lifted entirely. Yet the kinds of signals (information) states observe and evaluate – victory and defeat, overall combat performance, quantifiable indicators – are as clear and objective as possible under conditions of structural uncertainty. States have no other substitute measures or indicators. Even if states misinterpret the underlying factors on which victory or combat performance is based – the moral and skills factors that Creveld and Biddle speak of – what is structurally important is not whether they accurately understand the causes of the best practice they emulate but the competitive logic and effects of their emulation choices. In a realm of uncertainty, victory is the closest approximation to successful security-enhancing practices.

Later, I discuss the reasons why states engage in military emulation at different rates and scope, but intuitively it is understandable why the losing side in a war will move quickly to reorganize and improve its military system. Defeated armies will reform more quickly and extensively. Victors will usually lack the incentives to reorganize and reform.[84] This is especially true if victory propels them to a dominant or hegemonic position as a result of the defeat or collapse of nearest rivals and the general power vacuum that mark the immediate postwar period. War may also reveal flaws in the victors' military organization, technology, or tactics that demand reform. Moreover, major war is likely to be marked by a great deal of innovation, experimentation, and improvisation by both sides, and these new methods and practices

[81] Gray, "New Weapons," 249.
[82] B. H. Liddell Hart, *Strategy*, 2nd (New York: Merridian Books, 1991).
[83] Posen, "Nationalism."
[84] Posen, "Nationalism," 113.

will be incorporated after the war.[85] Victors may also be spurred to reform if the postwar period brings new security demands as a result of its own expansion, the intrusion of other powers, unsettled wartime issues, or the general hostility and counterbalancing that its victory triggers among its neighbors.

Finally, when sufficiently large scale in terms of intensity and duration, major wars will similarly reveal flaws and weaknesses in other parts and arrangements of the state apparatus, while also demonstrating the superiority of alternative arrangements. Large-scale armed conflict generates a much deeper and extensive organizational, fiscal, and mobilizational requirements for the state and society as a whole than wars of lesser scale and intensity.[86] In such instances, we should expect modernization and emulation processes to extend beyond the military system to other parts of the state apparatus directly and indirectly tied to the mustering of military power.

The rankings of states, based on their aggregate capabilities or resources, shift continuously as a result of changes in the underlying bases of national power.[87] The appeal of any one great power and its military system will wax and wane only with its fortunes in great-power war, not with shifts in its aggregate capabilities. (In the absence of a great war, states may emulate the institutions and practices of the most powerful in their numbers as the best bet). In the absence of a great-power war, states will continue to emulate the military system of a particular great power even after shifts in relative position have reduced it from the top rank or when an objectively superior military system is introduced by a rising challenger. After the Crimean War, the French army established itself internationally as the most successful and the one of greatest appeal for would-be emulators. But nothing substitutes for performance and victory in war. States will emulate the victorious system even if the system (its technology, organization, or doctrine) is ultimately shown inferior. In retrospect, by the early 1860s, the French army could no

---

[85] Many scholars have noted that some wartime innovations are never pursued, adopted, sustained, or recognized as such. See Edward L. Katzenbach, Jr., "The Horse Cavalry in the Twentieth Century," in *The Use of Force: Military Power and International Politics*, 4th ed., ed. Robert J. Art and Kenneth N. Waltz (Lanham: University Press of America, 1993): 161–80. On military revolutions see Michael E. Howard, *War in European Society* (London: Oxford University Press, 1976); Peter Paret, "Revolutions in Warfare: An Earlier Generation of Interpreters," in *National Security and International Stability*, ed. Bernard Brodie, Michael D. Intriligator, and Roman Kolkowicz (Cambridge: OG&H, 1983): 157–70; Posen, "Nationalism." See also Barry Buzan, *An Introduction to Strategic Studies: Military Technology and International Relations* (New York: St. Martin's Press, 1987); Clifford J. Rogers, "The Military Revolution in History and Historiography," in *The Military Revolution Debate: Readings on the Military Transformations of Early Modern Europe*, ed. Clifford J. Rogers (Boulder: Westview, 1995): 1–10; Geoffrey Parker, *The Military Revolution: Military Innovation and the Rise of the West* (Cambridge: Cambridge University Press, 1988).

[86] Rassler and Thompson, *War and State Making*; Tilly, *Coercion, Capital, and European States*.

[87] Kennedy, *The Rise and Fall of the Great Powers*.

longer be considered the best in the world by an objective measurement, given the profound innovations and restructuring that the rival Prussian army was undergoing while France's stagnated. Scholars have noted that the pre-1870 French army had crippling organizational and technological defects.[88] But up until 1870, France continued to generate widespread appeal in Latin America, the Far East, and elsewhere.

Convergence and "Socialization" in the International System

Among the more peculiar and ambiguous areas in *Theory of International Politics* are the last two sections of Chapter 4, where Waltz introduces the concept of socialization. Waltz argues that anarchic structure works its effects indirectly through competition and socialization.[89] What could socialization possibly mean – a social concept in a theory widely viewed as asocial in content and explanatory variables? In contrast to social theory, neorealism is at a distinct disadvantage in dealing with such a concept as it is commonly defined in IR theory.[90]

Waltz's language and some of his examples further complicate matters. His definition of socialization is elusive, but at times reads more like that of social theory. Socialization in social theory denotes social – nonmaterial – processes and causal forces. It is the conceptual master key in social theory's explanatory framework. The international system is both a socializing realm as well as a social product. For his part, Waltz's is a more sociological, or social psychological, definition; one that seems more consistent with cultural analysis than materialist theory.[91] Waltz inadvertently elevates socialization to the structural level, incorrectly implying that it has independent causal properties. He repeatedly notes that states are socialized by the system's structure, a claim that seemingly elevates socialization as a deep structural component on par with anarchy. Socialization, in his view, is a process whereby individuals internalize the norms of behavior and customs of the larger social system, and learn to behave within these accepted ranges.[92] Though he seems mainly concerned with the socialization of behavior, Waltz repeatedly refers to "socially most acceptable practices," "norms," "attributes," "rules of state behavior," and other such similar

---

[88] See, for example, Michael E. Howard, *The Franco-Prussian War: The German Invasion of France, 1870–1871* (London: Methuen, 1981), chap. 1, passim.

[89] Waltz, *Theory of International Politics*, 74.

[90] Alastair Iain Johnston, "Treating International Institutions as Social Environments," *International Studies Quarterly* 45, no. 4 (December 2001): 487–515.

[91] My own previous treatment of socialization in neorealist theory was likewise unclear and inconsistent. See João Resende-Santos, "Anarchy and the Emulation of Military Systems: Military Organization and Technology in South America, 1870–1914," *Security Studies* 5, no. 3 (Spring 1996): 193–260.

[92] Waltz, *Theory of International Politics*, 74–77.

phrases to describe socialization and its effects.[93] By way of illustration, he discusses how revolutionary, nonconformist states become socialized by the system, to accept the rules of state behavior, to conform to acceptable norms.[94] In this way, Waltz unwittingly seems to characterize the international system as a moral and normative realm, in which similarity among the units is a product of moral pressures, cultural assimilation, prescriptive norms, and social fitness in the context of a common moral framework. This apparent social conception in neorealism is, ironically, quite different from the stripped structuralism that so angered Ashley and other critics.[95]

Yet, socialization is not an independent variable in neorealism, and not intended to be by Waltz. It is not a social concept, even though Waltz's examples and analogies give it conceptual prominence and implied causal properties. As used in neorealism, the term socialization is an effect not a cause. At best, it is a poor word choice to describe structure's disciplining effects on the behavior and internal organization of states. The concept has no bearing on the essential logic of behavior in anarchic realms. The problem in this area of neorealism lies not with Waltz's theoretical intent but with his language, which confuses more than illuminates. Indeed, Waltz's real intention is to reinforce his argument about the predominance of material structural forces, and structural selection, in the behavior of states.[96] The real point he tries to make is not about internalizing norms and rules but about rational behavioral adjustments and adaptation to external constraints and inducements. In other words, structure socializes states with regard to behavior only in the limited and indirect sense that structure acts as a disciplining selection mechanism.[97] Waltz's example of the early Soviet Union's external behavior illustrates his real intention in using socialization to describe how anarchic structure eventually trumps ideology and other factors that push states to behave internationally in ways that prove costly.

Despite the undeserved attention it has drawn, socialization is more properly understood as a descriptive term in neorealism. Unlike its conception in critical theory, where socialization processes are anarchy-transcending and connote social-cultural bases of action, it plainly has no such properties in

---

[93] Waltz, *Theory of International Politics*, 75–77, 92, 127, 128. For a similar interpretation of this version of Waltz's definition, see Fred Halliday, *Rethinking International Relations* (Vancouver: University of British Columbia Press, 1994): 37.

[94] Waltz, *Theory of International Politics*, 127–28.

[95] Richard K. Ashley, "The Poverty of Neorealism," in Keohane, ed., *Neorealism and Its Critics*, 255–300, and "Untying the Sovereign State: A Double Reading of the Anarchy Problematique," *Millennium* 17, no. 2 (1988): 227–62.

[96] Johnston, "Treating International Institutions," makes a similar point.

[97] Waltz, *Theory of International Politics*, 73–74, notes that "structures select by rewarding some behaviors and punishing others."

neorealism. Homogenizing tendencies in the system are products of strategic competition, not social construction or social fitness-seeking behavior. Competitive pressures spur behavioral conformity, even among revolutionary states, and encourages similarities of attributes. This use of socialization describes, not explains, the process of competition-driven convergence and conformity to minimum structural standards. States adjust, rationally and instrumentally, their wayward behavior and practices because of the disadvantages and adverse consequences that arise from failing to comply with structural imperatives.

CHANGING LEVELS OF THREAT AND MILITARY EMULATION

The military emulation of the three major South American republics varied widely in terms of the timing, scale, and intensity of each country's efforts. Chile's decision in 1885 to import the German mass army drastically altered the terms of military competition in the region, making obsolete the methods and traditions of the past. Moreover, Chile's military emulation unfolded at a feverish pace. Argentina's emulation is rapid and vast like Chile's, but it does not launch its program until a decade afterwards. At the other end of the spectrum was Brazil, which did not begin its modernization until almost two decades later with its fumbling efforts to emulate the Germany system. Military emulation does not begin in earnest until 1919, when it hired a large French military-training mission. Unlike Chile, Brazil's efforts were slow, uncertain, and halting.

What explains this variance? What accounts for this wave-like but jagged pattern? A third-image cultural analysis would predict a regional pattern of emulation that is more uniform in timing and scale, rather than spread out and uneven. States, after all, should be equally motivated to pursue social fitness and, thus, adopt the latest symbols and practices of statehood. Only the neorealist theory of emulation can explain this regional pattern of military emulation. It offers a clean and economical set of testable predictions about emulation.

All states emulate. When, how fast and how extensively they do so will vary. The one obstacle we face in a neorealist account of the variance in emulation is that Waltz's formulation does not specify the immediate security situation of states. Waltz relies on shifts in the system's distribution of capabilities as the sole explanatory variable to account for patterns of behavior and international political outcomes. Given his explanatory aims, such a focus makes sense. However, the core logic of the theory is the security dilemma. Neorealism is, like its realist antecedents, a theory about security competition and its behavioral implications. I add that this competition will often entail organizational effects as well. We can, therefore, move down the ladder of generality (of the dependent variable) to explain these implications across individual states. Waltz's caution that the behavior of states is also determined by their internal conditions is practical, and stands as a humbling reminder of the limitations of structural explanations. He also insists that we cannot understand the behavior of states by looking only inside them, but also must take into account the pressures and opportunities they face externally. This book is an application of this latter injunction. We need to explicate more precisely these pressures and opportunities across states. I intend to incorporate other realist explanatory factors that emphasize power and security competition and that are consistent with neorealism's structural logic.

A state's military emulation varies with the timing, intensity, and scale of adverse changes in its external security environment or, generically, levels of threat. The magnitude of such shifts are themselves a function of a number of geostrategic factors, important among which are the state's relative military power, its geographic assets and liabilities, the offensive capabilities of the adversary, and the availability of external balancing options. I use these explanatory variables to operationalize levels of threat. As I noted in the previous chapter, these variables are prominent and familiar in the realist tradition, and are central to balance-of-threat and offense-defense theories. I leave out variables from these two theories that I find incompatible with Waltzian structuralism, variables that focus on perceptions, learning, and other cognitive factors. The basic idea behind balance-of-threat theory is that states are more sensitive to military-strategic conditions that are geographically proximate (where geographic proximity is also a relationship to existing technology). In an anarchic system, states face multiple types and sources of threats, but some are far more immediate and serious (survival threatening) than others.[98] States prioritize threats, responding more promptly and vigorously to the most serious and urgent. The security dilemma means that states always face some irreducible minimum of threats to their security and safety but, as Jervis reminds us in his classic essay, the security dilemma is not always intense.[99] Shifts in the aggregate power balance matter, but it is not the only variable determining level of threat. The kind of military capabilities states have – offensive or defensive – or the geographic advantages and liabilities they have, all matter in their security calculations. In operationalizing levels of threat my analysis is based primarily on the archival assessments of key military and political leaders in the three republics, the assessment of foreign diplomats, and collective judgments in the secondary diplomatic history literature.

[98] On this point, see Walt, *The Origins of Alliances*, especially chaps. 1 and 5. See also, Barry Buzan, "Security Complexes in Structural and Historical Perspectives," in *The Insecurity Dilemma: National Security in the Third World*, ed. Brian L. Job (Boulder: Lynne Reinner, 1990): 167–90.

[99] Jervis, "Cooperation Under the Security Dilemma."

Balance-of-threat and offense-defense theories are two widely used theories that realists have devised to capture the nature and changes in a state's local security environment. I borrow liberally elements of both. Both begin from the premise that aggregate capabilities alone are not the only factors behind balancing behavior. Both emphasize a number of strategic factors in common, such as technology, aggregate power, offensive military capabilities, and geography. There is an extensive literature on balance-of-threat theory and the offense-defense balance, none of which we need rehearse here. Balance-of-threat theory, like offense-defense balance theory, has its shortcomings.[100]

To reiterate, only those elements, or propositions that are internally consistent with structural realism are incorporated. I emphasize variables that are omitted (external balancing options) and deemphasize variables (perceptions) that are inconsistent or superfluous. Intentions matter insofar as capabilities matter. Walt's framework suffers from a certain degree of multicollinearity. It is not evident that intentions are ever separate from or independent of capabilities.[101] States are unlikely to feel threatened by the aggressive intentions of others if those intentions are not coupled with capabilities, a point Walt recognizes.[102] While Walt develops balance-of-threat theory to explain alignment behavior, I argue that the prior availability of direct and indirect external-balancing options also factors in threat levels. I also use external balancing much broader conceptually, encompassing much more than formal alliance making. Last, I expand on some of Walt's variables, such as geography. I do so for the practical reason that geography still loomed large in the era of premechanized, pre-aerial warfare that I examine.

As noted, the first three components are functions of an implicit master variable: military technology. They are functions of the lethality, speed, and volume of the instruments of violence. For example, geography and geographic terrain matter a great deal more in a premechanized, pre–air-power stage of warfare than they do in the age of mechanized warfare. Offensive capabilities and external alliances matter a great deal in a conventional world, but are meaningless in a nuclear world. For turn-of-the-century South America, changes in military technology introduced by emulation rapidly changed the geostrategic landscape. States now acquired the capability to project their power across great expanse of ocean and terrain.

There are two last points regarding threat levels. First, threat level is a dynamic continuum, rather than a dichotomous variable.[103] What matters

---

[100] Snyder, "Alliances"; Macdonald, "Origins of Alliances."

[101] Snyder, "Alliances," 126.

[102] Classical realist George Kennan made a similar point in his wide-ranging prescriptions for limited containment. George F. Kennan, *Memoirs* (Boston: Little Brown & Co., 1967); Walt, *Origins of Alliances*, 25.

[103] Lynn-Jones, "Offense-Defense Theory," 666–67.

most to states is the magnitude and speed of adverse shifts in their external-security situation. Last, as a qualitative measure, it has its limitations, as explained in the last section of the previous chapter.

Walt emphasizes four major components of threat: aggregate power, offensive military capabilities, geographic proximity, and aggressive intentions. I incorporate the first three. A state's aggregate power is the sum of its total material and human resources, especially as they pertain to generating military capabilities. As the realist tradition reminds us, national power consists of raw resources such as population, economy, technological prowess, and territorial size but also intangibles such as human capital, leadership, and political organization.[104] For our purposes, aggregate military power includes such factors as the overall size, quality, firepower, mobility, leadership, and organization of the country's military forces. Aggregate power and offensive military capabilities are closely related, since the latter is the ability to convert the former into large, mobile, rapidly deployable military forces. More precisely, as a variable, offensive military capability is a cost function. It is the ability to amass armed force to threaten, penetrate, and overrun the territory of others at an acceptable cost. Offensive capability is affected by a number of factors that determine the advantage of offensive over defensive military operations, primarily the technology of delivery, lethality, mobility, force protection, and communications. Organizational and doctrinal factors, which dictate force employment, are also important.[105]

All else being equal, offensive military capabilities intensify the security dilemma because states feel more vulnerable to attack and conquest. Offense dominance by one or more states will heighten the insecurity of all states in the local arena and intensify their military-security competition.[106] A state may acquire offensive capabilities for a number of reasons, some aggressive, others defensive. Like Germany, Chile favored offensive capabilities because historically it faced a multifront-war problem. Encircled by enemies, its territory small and narrow and vulnerable from land and sea, Chile's only option was to take the fight to its enemies. To its neighbors, however, Chile's offensive capabilities were aimed at conquest and territorial expansion. Chile's offensive power set in motion a chain-reaction throughout the rest of the region.

---

[104] Waltz, *Theory of International Politics*, 131.

[105] On this point see Stephen Biddle, "Rebuilding the Foundations of Offense-Defense Theory," *Journal of Politics* 63, no. 3 (August 2001): 741–74.

[106] Stephen Van Evera, "The Cult of the Offensive and the Origins of the First World War," *International Security* 9, no. 1 (Summer 1984): 58–107; Posen, *The Sources of Military Doctrine*, chap. 1; Jack Levy, "The Offensive/Defensive Balance of Military Technology: A Theoretical and Historical Analysis," *International Studies Quarterly* 38, no. 2 (June 1984): 219–38; Biddle, "Rebuilding."

Geography could either be an asset or a liability, holding technology constant.[107] Chile's geography made it easily conquerable, not-withstanding the impressive heights of the Andes. Brazil's continental size and ample natural barriers, in contrast, constituted defensive advantages whose effect was to help dampen its vulnerability. Large territorial size can be a defensive advantage, since it is much harder to conquer and occupy such states; the smaller and more compact the state, the greater its geographic liabilities because it is easily conquered and occupied.[108] Walt mainly emphasizes geographic proximity, but I expand geography as a variable to include size, terrain, and overall characteristics pertaining to natural features that, from a military operational standpoint, either translate into a defensive advantage or liability. I also use it to refer to the relative dispersion or concentration of vital economic-population administrative centers, which itself closely relates to the other geographic factors. Depending on prevailing military technology, geography can encourage or discourage attack, make defense easy or difficult.[109]

The Availability of External Balancing Options

Emulation is an expression of balancing behavior through internal means. States also balance through external means. The availability of external balancing options will also help determine a state's threat levels. External balancing can range from the formal and direct to the tacit and indirect; from military alliance to free riding. External balancing can never substitute as the only form of balancing; and questions of reliability plague external balancing whether direct or indirect. Direct or indirect, what matters is the strategic effect of external balancing on the behavior of contending states, whether or not it involves formal alliances. Indeed, the possibility of common cause or joint action among others could have the same behavioral effects on a common adversary as would a formal alliance among them. A state may benefit indirectly from external balancing among third parties if the result is to divert the attention of its adversaries to more threatening competitors. The idea is ancient – my neighbor's neighbors are my friends – and it frequently manifests in the form of tacit alignment among countries sharing a common foe. I emphasize this dimension of external balancing because it played a pivotal role in the power balancing of the South American subsystem.

---

[107] Waltz, *Theory of International Politics*, 144–45; Jervis, "Cooperation under the Security Dilemma," 173. Both argue that relative territorial size affects levels of vulnerability.

[108] Jervis, "Cooperation Under the Security Dilemma," 173.

[109] Jervis, "Cooperation Under the Security Dilemma," 194. Posen, *The Sources of Military Doctrine*, discusses the effects of geography and technology on the security dilemma. See also Deudney, "Dividing Realism."

The availability of external balancing dampens threat levels and therefore dampens the timing, pace, and scale of military emulation. States that have external balancing options, directly or indirectly, are more secure in the short run, though such options will not nullify or indefinitely delay its internal balancing. The extra margin of safety may be temporary or uncertain, but its general effect is to delay and slow military emulation. Thus, we expect to see a much bigger gap between the surfacing of major threats and the timing of emulation for states that benefit from external balancing. Conversely, the absence of external balancing options will spur threatened states to move with alacrity in their internal-balancing efforts. We expect to see large-scale military emulation taking place, given the other conditions under which we expect to observe it, even for states with external-balancing options. What is indeterminate is exactly how much of the timing, pace, and scale is affected. We cannot establish *ex ante* precisely how or how much the availability of external balancing options reduces internal-balancing efforts, since there are so many other contingent strategic factors. For severely exposed and vulnerable states, such as Chile, the availability of external balancing may not have any discernible impact on their military emulation. States with dire security problems – encirclement by hostile powers, small size, and geographic exposure – find no relief or safety in alliances or free riding.

In summary, I deduce a number of falsifiable hypotheses on military emulation and its variance across states. Military emulation is a security-enhancing strategy that states adopt when confronted with threats. The scale of emulation will vary along a continuum. Confronted with deep and lasting adverse shifts in its strategic environment, I expect even innovation-capable states to emulate. The higher the level of threat a state faces, the more prompt, rapid, and extensive will be its military emulation. Highly vulnerable states will react more promptly and more extensively to changes in its external-security situation. The less vulnerable the state is to changes in its external-security situation, the more slowly it will respond to such changes and the more limited the pace and scale of its military emulation.

At the regional strategic level, we expect to see certain patterns of behavior associated with the changing levels of threat.[110] Whether it is the local regional system or the global system, the direction and magnitude of shifts in the levels of threat will affect the character of international politics in the system. The less vulnerable the contending states are to each other's power, the more tempered their military competition. Where technology, geography, or other factors shift toward defense and defensive advantages, there will be a corresponding dampening of competition, a decrease in the rapidity and scale of arms acquisition and buildup, and perhaps more cooperative

---

[110] On this point, see Van Evera, "The Cult of the Offensive."

diplomatic strategies and conflict resolution.[111] Where the shift is toward the offense and offensive advantages, international politics becomes more competitive, arms races more frequent and extensive, balancing more rapid and vigorous, armed conflicts more likely, crises more frequent, external policies more confrontational, and an overall much greater sensitivity to the capabilities-enhancing efforts of others.[112]

Military emulation is only one of several internal balancing strategies that states adopt, and is nearly always accompanied by some of these other strategies. That states may turn to other internal mobilization measures, such as quantitative increases in military strength, as their initial responses to external threats is perfectly consistent with the theory. The theory is weakened only if, given the conditions under which we expect to see large-scale military emulation, none takes place at any point. For the theory, a true but nonfatal anomaly would be a case where large scale emulation does not take place as predicted, but the state engages in other forms of large-scale balancing. Failure to undertake large-scale emulation (or any form of balancing) in the presence of such adverse shifts, and lacking external-balancing options, fatally undermines the theory. It follows that in the absence of adverse shifts, we will not see military emulation.

Equally crucial to the debate with social theory is the question of timing. The timing of military emulation is related to the timing of adverse shifts. We expect a reasonably close temporal association. Timing will be affected by the availability of external balancing. The theory of emulation cannot establish *ex ante* the precise day and time. No theory can. Large-scale emulation is a big undertaking, involving a number of practical matters as well as domestic and international political issues. How much of a time delay is reasonable? A delay measured in single digit years is not a problem for the theory, but the question is far more complex. First, emulation is only one of a number of internal- and external-balancing strategies a state may adopt in response to external threats, with states often engaging in multiple, mixed strategies. Any one of these strategies may delay the launching of military emulation. Second, the availability of external-balancing options must be taken into account.

The question of the timing, or start, of military emulation is, empirically, more challenging to establish than might first appear. The South Americans hired official-military-training missions from Germany and France (see Table 1.1). As a matter of convenience, I use the dates when the missions are hired to designate the start of emulation. However, this is methodologically and historically unsatisfactory. Needless to say, not all emulators will hire

---

[111] On these points, see Lynn-Jones, "Offense-Defense Theory," 670; Van Evera, "The Cult of the Offensive."

[112] Lynn-Jones, "Offense-Defense Theory," 670.

training missions or are able to get them. More important, it was often the case that a country would put in motion large scale military emulation on its own prior to contracting official missions. Using the date of missions, while convenient in our particular cases, is problematic for another important reason. These missions are the byproducts of often complex diplomacy, conflicting diplomatic and commercial objectives, and geopolitical maneuvers. Many factors determine the date of arrival or approval of formal missions, not the least of which are the regional and great-power politics involved. Argentina had been seeking a formal military mission from Germany as early as 1895, but Germany declined because it did not want to damage its lucrative relations with Argentina's chief rival, Chile, which already had a German mission.

3

Arms and States in Nineteenth-Century South America

This chapter addresses two important, if disparate, empirical matters. The first part of this chapter provides a general sketch of the Prussian/German and French military systems from the 1860s to the interwar period. The purpose of this sketch is to identify their distinguishing features in order to trace their reappearance in the emulation processes of the South American republics. As noted previously, since the South Americans hired French and German military-training missions to direct their modernization, we need not be too concerned about fidelity to the original model. The second section offers an analysis of the South American balance-of-power system and the regional militaries prior to large-scale military emulation.

THE GERMAN AND FRENCH MILITARY SYSTEMS, 1870–1930

This section summarizes the main features of the French and Prussian/ German military systems in the areas of conscription and training, officer recruitment and instruction, general staff organization, command structure, and territorial and reserve organization. I focus exclusively on army organization.[1] The summary centers on two aspects of these systems that

---

[1] My summaries of the French and Prussian/German militaries are based principally on the following works: Michael E. Howard, *The Franco-Prussian War: The German Invasion of France, 1870–1871* (London: Methuen, 1981); Richard D. Challener, *The French Theory of the Nation In Arms, 1866–1939* (New York: Russell & Russell, 1965); Gordon A. Craig, *The Politics of the Prussian Army, 1640–1945* (New York: Oxford University Press, 1964); Martin Kitchen, *The Military History of Germany: From the Eighteenth Century to the Present Day* (Bloomington: Indiana University Press, 1975) and *The German Officer Corps, 1890–1914* (Oxford: Clarendon, 1968); Christian O. E. Millotat, *Understanding the Prussian-German General Staff System* (Carlisle: U.S. Army War College, 1992); David B. Ralston, *The Army of the Republic: The Place of the Military in the Political Evolution of France, 1871–1914* (Cambridge: MIT Press, 1967); Herbert Rosinski, *The German Army* (New York: Praeger, 1966); Wilbur E. Gray, *Prussia and the Evolution of the Reserve Army: A Forgotten Lesson of History* (Carlisle: Strategic Studies Institute, 1992). For a general survey of warfare

distinguished them most: their conscription system and their general staff organization.

The German and French systems shared a long history of armed competition as well as mutual imitation, such that by the 1880s they shared in common a number of organizational elements. In the wake of devastating defeats at Jena and Auerstädt, Prussia borrowed heavily from the innovations of Napoleon. After the embarrassment of 1870, France emulated the Prussian system. As a result of this overlap, isolating their unique features is challenging. My summary is a snapshot of these militaries. It is important to bear in mind that both military systems were undergoing rapid changes during this period under study as the entire European continent prepared for war. (Of course, this raises the interesting question of what exactly emulators do copy, or whether they adjust as what they are copying mutates.) Since the South Americans emulate each of the systems at different times, I devote more attention to the corresponding time periods when the German (1870 and 1914) and French (1918 and 1940) armies were being emulated.

Emulation of the French and German armies transformed the regional military establishments into permanent professional organizations. For the first time, the hallmarks of the modern military appeared in the region. First, the three big regional powers institutionalized a system of officer formation and advancement. Second, for the first time in the region there appeared within the military a permanent organ devoted to war planning, study, and execution. Third, all three big powers adopted universal military obligation – a military policy that many in the region viewed through the prism of nation-building and human capital formation.

To varying degrees of scale and success, the South Americans emulated both the hardware and software of the main European armies. Insofar as the mass army was a revolution not simply or primarily in organization but an intellectual transformation in how countries think about, plan, mobilize, and fight wars, the true outcome of large-scale military emulation in the region was also intellectual. One of the changes was the emphasis on, and emergence of, officership as a profession formed through specialized study, training, and merit. The South Americans became avid consumers of French and German military ideas. They imported large training missions. These missions, in turn, established and staffed the higher military academies, which by World War I were rapidly becoming the primary avenue to high command. South American officers, many of whom would later lead both the military as well as the nation, were pupils at home as well as in the training camps and academies of France and Germany. These foreign-trained officers, in

during the period see: Michael Howard, *War in European History* (London: Oxford University Press, 1976); Gunther E. Rothenberg, *The Art of Warfare in the Age of Napoleon* (Bloomington: Indiana University Press, 1978); Robert M. Epstein, *Napoleon's Last Victory and the Emergence of Modern War* (Lawrence: University Press of Kansas, 1994).

collaboration with the missions, rewrote the main internal regulations, field manuals, combat tactics, and war doctrine.

The practical result of the South Americans' emulation attempt was to import the European mass army. The mass army was characterized by certain defining features.[2] The essence of the modern mass army format innovated during the Napoleonic wars was the coupling of a highly trained and expandable core standing army, officered by professionally trained commanders; and a mass conscript army based on short-term universal military obligation, trained in peacetime, prepared and organized for rapid mobilization at the start of war. These two dominant features gave rise to a third: new forms of higher command organization and planning. Millis refers to a managerial revolution in mass warfare.[3] In response to the command, administrative, and control problems created by great size, a more consequential general staff system came into being to replace the long-standing but marginal quartermaster system or other ad hoc administrative bodies. These new requirements of command, control, and planning, in addition to the operational challenges posed by mass armies fighting on extended fronts, put greater demands on the quality and doctrinal unity of officers. The mass army could no longer be captained under the old patterns of officer recruitment, training, and advancement.

There were various permutations of these main features of the mass army across Europe. In fact, despite the early development and spread of the mass army during the Napoleonic wars, much of Europe slid back to traditional practices of the small, long-serving professional army format or combinations of the two formats.[4] However, important differences existed between the French and German versions of the mass army, both in terms of their organization and the doctrinal precepts.

The German Military System

The basic organization and guiding principles of the Prussian/German military system had been laid during the 1806–14 restructuring in the wake of defeat during the Napoleonic wars, though some measures (such as full universal conscription) were not fully implemented until the 1850s. The Prussian system was extended to the other armies of the German states with the

---

[2] Posen, "Nationalism, the Mass Army, and Military Power," *International Security* 18, no. 2 (Fall 1993): 80-124;" Peter Paret, "Revolution in Warfare: An Earlier Generation of Interpreters," in *National Security and International Stability*, ed. Bernard Brodie, Michael D. Intriligator, and Roman Kolkowicz (Cambridge: OG &H, 1983): 157-70; Howard, *War in European History*; Rothenberg, *The Art of Warfare*; Epstein, *Napoleon's Last Victory*.

[3] Walter Millis, *Arms and Men: A Study in American Military History* (New York: Putnam's Sons, 1956).

[4] On the spread of Napoleon's organizational and strategic innovations, see Epstein, *Napoleon's Last Victory*.

creation of the North German Federation (Prussia, Bavaria, Wurttemberg, and Saxony) and the final unification of Germany.[5] The German military system was in constant motion as a result of continual adjustments and improvements, though its basic architecture remained in place. As a moving target, its emulation proved challenging for the South Americans, who also tinkered and adjusted accordingly. Challenging also were the many constitutional issues involved in emulating the German system. The Prussian/German military system was characterized by great institutional autonomy and authority over its own affairs – an autonomy that was difficult to reproduce. The Prussian military was often described as a veritable state within a state.[6] It was highly autonomous and centralized, reflecting the overall concentration of political power in the monarchy. The military was responsible solely to the Emperor. Legislative bodies had little power of oversight or jurisdiction. The military also achieved great influence in domestic as well as foreign affairs. Some of this power and autonomy was informal. The high degree of centralization in the German system, with the powerful general staff as the coordinating organ, made possible common training, unity in arms and planning, and doctrinal uniformity. However, the German system never fully resolved the fundamental constitutional issues and political struggles provoked by this autonomy.[7] Nor was military command structure as efficient and perfected as its admirers presumed, for confusion persisted in the chain of command.[8]

The combat power and effectiveness of the Prussian/German army rested on three organizational pillars: an efficient conscription system that gave it superior mobilizational capacity, the excellence of its officer corps, and its superb general staff system.[9] The efficiency and strength of the organization, in turn, exacted at all levels continuous and uniform training, instruction, and study. Perhaps the true legacy of the Prussian/German system, and the inheritance of the South Americans, was the idea of continuous preparation, improvement, and training of the entire military machinery in peacetime. Emulators everywhere cited this particular aspect of the German system as the core principle their countries should embrace.

Rosinski and Creveld note that much of Germany's combat power was due to the immeasurable (and inimitable) moral and intellectual excellence

---

[5] Some of the German states initially retained nominal autonomy in some military matters, though the Emperor was commander in chief of all German armies. The German armies remained de jure separate (for example, there was no imperial war ministry), but in practice were simply integrated into the Prussian system.

[6] Craig, *The Politics of the Prussian Army*.

[7] Ibid.

[8] Holger H. Herwig, "The Dynamics of Necessity: German Military Policy during the First World War," in *Military Effectiveness*, ed. Allan R. Millet and Williamson Murray (Boston: Allen and Unwin, 1988): 80–115.

[9] Rosinski, *The German Army*, 104.

of the military's leadership, rather than the organizational hardware alone.[10] But the excellence and efficiency of organization cannot be underestimated either, for much of this combat power also depended on an efficient military organization to handle such great numbers and administer a large, complex standing army. The system produced excellence. It institutionalized genius.[11]

The appeal of the German system in South America did not rest on the South Americans fully understanding the ingredients behind its victories. Its battlefield performance, its victories, attracted them. Victory was the basis for their confidence that emulating the Imperial army was an effective strategy to bolster their own military power and enhance their security. Prussia's victories in the 1860s and 1870s were made possible by the continuous organizational-technological improvements and innovations it had been making since it was defeated at Jena and Auerstädt in 1806.[12] The early founding reforms were essentially an integral part of a much larger process of reform and modernization of the entire state and not just its military system.[13] This fact was not lost on the South Americans. Major reform measures were taken in the late 1850s and early 1860s, giving Prussia the ability to capitalize on the technological innovations of the Industrial Revolution and turned the Prussian army into the most efficient and powerful in the world.

Given its geographic exposure, compact size, and encirclement by larger, hostile great powers, Prussian/German doctrine emphasized speed, mobility, and size, all geared toward quick, decisive battles of annihilation.[14] As elaborated and institutionalized by Helmut von Moltke, the celebrated chief

---

[10] Rosinski, *The German Army*; Martin van Creveld, *Fighting Power: German and U.S. Army Performance, 1939–1945* (Westport: Greenwood Press, 1982).

[11] Rosinski, *The German Army*, 24.

[12] Walter Görlitz, *The German General Staff: Its History and Structure, 1657–1945* (London: Hollis and Carter, 1953); Trevor N. Dupuy, *A Genius for War: The German Army and General Staff, 1807–1945* (Englewood Cliffs: Prentice-Hall, 1977).

[13] On the broader aspects of Prussian military reforms in the early 1800s see Rosinski, *The German Army*, chap. 1, passim.

[14] Dupuy, *A Genius for War*; Hajo Holborn, "Moltke and Schlieffen: The Prussian-German School," *The Makers of Modern Strategy: Military Thought from Machiavelli to Hitler* in Edward M. Earle, ed., (Princeton: Princeton University Press, 1952); *Moltke: On the Art of War, Selected Writings*, ed. Daniel J. Hughes (Novato: Presidio Press, 1993); Barry R. Posen, *The Sources of Military Doctrine: France, Britain, and Germany Between the World Wars* (Ithaca: Cornell University Press, 1984); Dennis E. Showalter, "Total War for Limited Objectives: An Interpretation of German Grand Strategy," *Grand Strategies in War and Peace* Paul Kennedy, ed., (New Haven: Yale University Press, 1991): 105–24; Rothenberg, "Moltke, Schlieffen, and the Doctrine of Strategic Envelopment," in *Makers of Modern Strategy: From Machiavelli to the Nuclear Age*, ed. Peter Paret (Princeton: Princeton University Press, 1986): 296–325; Arden Bucholz, *Hans Delbruch and the German Military Establishment: War Images in Conflict* (Iowa City: University of Iowa Press, 1985).

of staff between 1857 and 1887, Prussian tactical and strategic doctrine stressed flanking and envelopment tactics as well as the concentration of numerically superior forces on the battlefield. Moltke's famous dictum to his armies was, "march separately, fight together." Nearly every aspect of the military system was geared toward rapid mobilization, transportation, and deployment for the purpose of force concentration; great importance was attached to the massing of trained reserves, preparation, mobilization, and especially transportation, to which an entire department in the general staff was devoted.

At the level of both operational command and military organization, the Prussian system emphasized flexibility and decentralization. The military was organized into independent corps, each of which were largely self-sufficient and responsible for conscription, training, and mobilization. Armies were organized as separate units capable of marching and functioning separately. At the operational-tactical level, decentralization took the form of what became know as Auftragstaktik, or mission-oriented command and control.[15] This long-standing philosophy and practice in the German army gave ample freedom of action to subordinate commanders in the execution of military missions within the general guidelines and objectives laid out by high command.[16] Though ensuring uniformity of doctrine and coordination, the German military substituted general directives for detailed orders at the level of operations and execution. Last, continuous training was emphasized at all levels of the military, beginning with conscripts and reserves.

The Prussian/German military system had a number of defining organizational features. The first was its conscription system, which dated back to the original reforms of August Gneisennau and Gerhard von Scharnhorst. Its conscription system had two distinguishing qualities: short-term service in the first line and the consequent buildup of trained reserves, and decentralization. In contrast to France where the concept originated, it was Prussia that came closest to putting into practice the principle of the nation-in-arms. The army was composed of a large regular army and a trained organized reserve. The 1859 reorganization reforms provided for three years in the line forces, four in the active reserves, and then five in the Landwehr, or territorial militia. Reserve officers followed the same pattern. On the whole, service in active duty and in the reserves was all done in the local district of enlistment. Germany's was a short-term service-conscript army, with a multitiered trained reserve system. The mass of trained and organized reserves gave Prussia the capacity to mobilize and amass an army of over one million by 1870, a size unheard of in warfare up to that point.[17] Recruitment, training, and mobilization were decentralized into separate military regions.

---

[15] Rothenberg, "Moltke," 296.
[16] Millotat, *Understanding the Prussian-German General Staff System*, 23.
[17] Howard, *The Franco-Prussian War*, 22–23.

Enlistment was regional. Local draftees trained and served in their home-town regiment for all three years, and were then placed in the local regiment's reserve pool for four years (and, if called up into service again, would likely rejoin the same company served in while on active duty).[18] The regiments of each conscription district were responsible for training the new recruits in the district. The same regional and decentralized principle applied to the Landwehr.

The second most important distinguishing feature of the Prussian/German military system was its system of officer recruitment and instruction. Long prior to professionalization among the other great powers, the German Offizier Korps was formed through rigorous instruction, training, and selection. The hallmark of the German system was the excellence of its offi-cer corps, an excellence produced through rigorous instruction and selec-tion. The German system of officer formation was selective and demanding; it emphasized competitive examination and merit every step of the way. We should note that officer formation in the German system instilled and rewarded personal and moral qualities in officers, and not just their tech-nical training and professional skill. While merit and stringent examination marked the recruitment, training, and advancement of officers, they should not be exaggerated. Particularistic and exclusionary practices barred Jews, middle classes, and individuals with unorthodox ideas and gave the officer corps an aristocratic, conservative bent.[19]

The famed Kriegsakademie by the 1870s had changed from an institution of general military instruction to a school for general staff service. It was formally placed under the supervision of the general staff. Its instructors were general staff officers. Admission into the academy was highly selec-tive by examination. At the end of the three years curriculum student cadets took another exam before proceeding to general staff service. The general staff itself became the focal point in the formation and advancement of the German officer corps by the 1880s, with service in the general staff becom-ing the normal road for all high command leadership.[20] The war academy became the only access point to the general staff, with only the best and brightest graduates selected through rigorous exam. Admitted officers were placed on a three-year probation, at the end of which was another rigorous examination and evaluation.

The German system placed great emphasis on intensive study and instruc-tion, early on instituting competitive examinations for all military schools, promotions, and command title. The training and instruction of officers in the general staff, as well as the top military academies, were based on the case study method of instruction. The case study method of training

[18] Gray, *Prussia and the Evolution of the Reserve Army.*
[19] Craig, *The Politics of the Prussian Army,* 218.
[20] Rosinski, *The German Army,* 119.

and war gaming were geared toward preparing officers to be able to lead large formations, such as an army corps, that could move and fight independently and be able to converge with others at the point of decisive battles.[21] In both the military academies and the general staff, German military instruction emphasized the study of military history in combination with practical training (or historical exercises) around field maneuvers and field trips to battle fields. Indeed, military history became institutionalized in the German army, as an entire department in the general staff was devoted to military history. In the decade prior to the Great War in Europe, military history consumed three to four hours per course every week at the war academy.

The German system is best known for the third distinguishing feature, its general staff organization. Of all the innovations that Prussia introduced to industrial warfare, none inspired the rest of the world more than its general staff system. Germany innovated mass warfare management. The German general staff became the brain of the army, the nervous system that singularly made it an effective and efficient military force.[22] Germany's Grosser Generalstab was widely credited by other states as the key to its impressive victories over Denmark, Austria, and France during the 1860s and 1870s. It was an organ *sine pares,* combining in a single instrument all the principal requirements of modern mass warfare. It was one part a management organ; one part school for scientific study; one part leadership training ground; one part command; one part war planning. As with everything else in the German system, service in the general staff involved a rigorous and competitive process of recruitment, instruction, and advancement. Doctrinal uniformity was ensured by preparation for and service in the general staff.

The institutional and operational design of the Prussian/German general staff was mission-oriented, whereby the functions of the staff were carried out through a highly articulated division of labor among its departmental divisions. Though the specific departmental arrangements and matrix were reorganized on occasion, the functions of the general staff continued to be organized around functional groupings. Among all its many roles and functions, the general staff's defining job was to think and plan. In 1867 the general staff was reorganized to consist of two major divisions, a main establishment in charge of the three main theatre departments, and a supporting establishment in charge of five specialized sections, which included sections on military history, geographical and statistical study, and topography-cartography. The general staff was put in charge of armaments and equipment as well as the major military schools. In 1872 the Kriegsakademie was formally placed under the control of the general staff. Aside from the occasional minor reorganization of the departmental divisions and the reforms

---

[21] Kennedy, *The Rise and Fall of the Great Powers,* 184–85.
[22] Howard, *The Franco-Prussian War,* chap. 1.

measures of the 1880s aimed at clarifying the command hierarchy and giving greater autonomy to the general staff, the basic organization and functions of the German general staff remained unchanged between 1870 and 1914.

The general staff was divided into the Great General Staff, Grosser Generalstab, and the Truppengeneralstab, the field general staffs attached to each corps and division. The Great General Staff itself was divided into four major departments in the 1890s, three strategic theatre departments (one responsible for overall strategic planning, mobilization, fortifications, armaments, and railways; a second devoted to training, maneuvers, and reconnaissance; and the third devoted to the French strategic theatre). A fourth department was devoted to military history, topography, and cartography. A separate railways department was added. The German general staff performed both collective (centralized) and decentralized functions.[23] It was a rare combination of doctrinal uniformity and central direction with flexibility and initiative at lower levels of command.[24] It was an open staff system, with staff officers having to perform regimental duty at each stage of their advancement. The general staff was responsible for strategic planning, mobilization, training, instructions, intelligence, transportation, and communications.

The Truppengeneralstab were responsible directly to the main staff in Berlin. These field staffs, ordinarily divided into three major sections, were responsible for operations and mobilization plans, exercises and maneuvers, railways and supply, and intelligence for their respective corps and divisions. Another distinctive feature of the German system was the authority and role of the field staffs in peacetime and wartime command. Regimental command was collectively shared between the corps or divisional commander and the chief of field staff. The field staff officer was to act as more than a subordinate, adviser, or technical planner. The practice of joint command was unique and informal, and facilitated by the high level of doctrinal uniformity among the officer corps, with most field commanders having gone through general staff service and personal training by Moltke.[25] This relationship of collaboration and coordination was undefined, though officially the field staff was supposed to act only in an advisory capacity. These ill-defined features, or inimitable informal practices, proved difficult for emulators everywhere.

The other attribute of the German general staff that separated it from all others was its power and authority. The great authority and autonomy proved both difficult and contentious for its advocates in South America. The resistance in the region to such a powerful general staff was stiff inside and outside the military. In the period after the war with Austria in 1866

[23] Rothenberg, "Moltke," 301.
[24] Ibid.
[25] Howard, *The Franco-Prussian War*, 22–25.

(and formalized in the 1883 reforms), the general staff was endowed with command authority in wartime.[26] The military chain of command went directly from the chief of the general staff to the King himself, whereby the general staff chief exercised more planning and command authority than the war minister or the head of the military cabinet. Up until the 1850s, the Great General Staff was a quasiautonomous organ in the war ministry and, though its functions were traditionally extensive, it played a relatively insignificant role in military affairs. It was not until the reforms and initiatives taken in the time of Moltke that it rose to its preeminent position in the chain of command and came to have near total control over every aspect of the military system.[27]

The reform measures of 1883 gave the general staff greater institutional independence from the war ministry and every other administrative or legislative organ of the state. The war ministry became largely an administrative organ and liaison to parliament.[28] It effectively lost its role in military command and essential military matters, which now came to be shared uneasily between the general staff and the military cabinet. The chief of the general staff formally was made the commander in chief of the army in wartime and peacetime. But these reforms did not fully solve the chaotic and redundant character of Germany's higher command organization, and the confusing division of labor among the general staff, the war ministry, and the military cabinet, and later a fourth organ, the Kaiser's own military headquarters.[29] All four organs had direct access to the Kaiser. The period of the 1880s to World War I was marked by frequent clashes among the three semi-independent bodies.[30] While the rest of the world may have perceived a monolithic, streamlined command organization in the German army, it suffered from a good deal of disunity, confusion, and rivalry, which often hurt military effectiveness and war planning.[31]

Stringent selection and hard training characterized service in the German staff system. The Kriegsakademie became the only route to general staff service, and only its top graduates were selected and admitted – but only after passing an entrance examination. The relationship between the academy and the general staff evolved into greater coordination, and much of the instruction was done by general staff officers. Admitted candidates were placed on a two-year probation, during which time they would be repeatedly tested and trained. Candidates were normally distributed among the various sections, attended weekly map exercises and annual strategic exercises, and

---

[26] Göerlitz, *The German General Staff*, 90.
[27] Göerlitz, *The German General Staff*, 82; Dupuy, *A Genius for War*, 112.
[28] See Craig, *Politics of the Prussian Army*, for a discussion.
[29] On the political and command problems created by this arrangement, see Rosinski, *The German Army*, chap. 4; Craig, *Politics of the Prussian Army*, 218–30.
[30] Craig, *Politics of the Prussian Army*, 230.
[31] Kitchen, *The German Officer Corps*, 15, 225; Craig, *The Politics of the Prussian Army*, 251.

had a third and final exam awaiting them at the end of the probationary period. Advancement in the service and in the general staff, in particular, was based on personal factors (intellect, character, manners, and decision-making skills) and not just technical military merit. After the probationary period, general staff officers would then begin the normal cycle of service, first transferring to the Truppengeneralstab and then alternating between field staff service, regimental command service, and spells in the Great General Staff itself.

The French Military System, 1919–1940

In the decades prior to 1870 the French military system stagnated.[32] Whereas Germany kept pace with the technological and industrial changes of the time, France did not. The closing three decades of the nineteenth century was a time of considerable turmoil and upheaval in the politics and military of France. Napoleon had revolutionized warfare, both at the tactical and organizational level, but between 1815 and 1870 the French military system languished in intellectual and organizational stagnation.[33] Despite the mass army, or grande guerre, format inaugurated by Napoleon, France continued its ardent attachment to the small, experienced, battle hardened, professional army.[34] Whereas Germany emphasized institutionalized training and instruction, France emphasized personal bravery, battlefield experience, and individual talent in the formation of its officers and soldiers. In the summer of 1870 France found itself unprepared, poorly organized, and poorly equipped for the new age of warfare.[35]

The French system underwent changes during the last quarter of the century. Moreover, many of these changes were in the direction of greater overlap with the German system after 1870. As such, it is difficult to capture its distinguishing features. The pre-1870 French military system was built around a small, long-term service army. Because the French believed that the most effective army was one that stressed long-term (seven years or more) service, conscription was not truly universal, obligatory, or personal. Conscription was by ballot, with only the necessary number of men who were needed called up to serve, with the rest remaining as an untrained, hypothetical reserve. Conscription laws provided ample exemptions and opportunities to avoid service, such as allowing for personal substitutions or the payment of a fee. French conscription practice, along with its abuses, was widespread throughout South America, and exhibited the same social inequalities and

---

[32] Howard, *The Franco-Prussian War*; Richard Holmes, *The Road to Sedan: The French Army, 1866–1870* (London: The Royal Historical Society, 1984).

[33] Ralston, *Army of the Republic*, chap. 1, passim.

[34] Howard, *The Franco-Prussian War*, 13.

[35] Howard, *The Franco-Prussian War*, chap. 1.

military inadequacies. Up until 1868, the legal length of service was seven years. France did not have a trained reserve.

Prior to 1870, there existed no department responsible for peacetime strategic planning and mobilization. The nominal general staff that existed was largely bureaucratic, without planning, preparation, command, or other functions. Moreover, there were no specific staff service requirements. The staff itself was a closed system, whereby regimental service was not required either for admission or promotion of staff officers. The military schools and the instructional level of the officer corps were, on the whole, of poor quality and stagnant.[36] Instructional and educational requirements for officers, in the hierarchy and in field command, were lax. Not all officers went through the military schools, a practice widespread in South America. The full inadequacies of the military system became evident only in 1870. These inadequacies were overlooked prior to 1870, as Howard observes, since victory (and the more severe inadequacies of France's opponents) provided ample justification for preserving the existing system.[37]

Prussia's victory over Austria in 1866, laid bare the full extent of Prussia's organizational and technological prowess, and spurred France to undertake several reforms during 1866–70. The government of Louis Napoleon Bonaparte favored an extensive overhaul and modernization of the military, but his reform program encountered strong opposition within the military and the national assembly. The watered-down reforms that were eventually implemented included a new military service law requiring five years of line service and four in the reserves; a portion of the annual contingent was required to serve only five months. A *garde mobile* was created, and consisted of men who were not called up and who had to serve for five years, but received only two weeks of training and drill.[38] It was not until its embarrassing defeat in 1870 that France overhauled its military system, and in the process used the Prussian system as both a standard and a model to emulate.[39] Post-1870 French military reorganization was both rapid and extensive. Throughout much of the 1870s the debate in France came down to how much of the German model France should emulate.[40] One of the first areas of reform was conscription.

With much difficulty and debate, France moved to adopt personal, universal military obligation. The new conscription law of 1872 stipulated a

---

[36] Ralston, *The Army of the Republic*, 19–21; Howard, *The Franco-Prussian War*, 16.

[37] Howard, *The Franco-Prussian War*.

[38] Howard, *The Franco-Prussian War*, 35.

[39] Alan Mitchell, "'A Situation of Inferiority': French Military Reorganization After the Defeat of 1870," *American Historical Review* 86, no. 1 (February 1981): 49–62, and *Victors and Vanquished: The German Influence on Army and Church in France after 1870* (Chapel Hill: University of North Carolina Press, 1984); see also Ralston, *The Army of the Republic*; Posen, "Nationalism."

[40] Mitchell, *Victors and Vanquished*, 15.

five-year personal and obligatory service. Germany's one-year volunteer system for reserve officer training was introduced. In 1889 France adopted a new conscription law, requiring three years of personal obligatory service. Exemptions and loopholes were tightened, though the law was modified again to two years and eighteen months. The military reorganization commission had recommended the adoption in full of Prussia's conscription system, though without its regional recruitment and mobilization arrangements.[41] Like its South American devotees, France wavered continually on the shape and length of military service. The military was heavily decentralized. Individual regiments formed their own reserves and territorial guard. Conscripts received training at special centers rather than in line units.

As war appeared imminent in Europe, France increased the length of service from two to three years in 1913. The 1926 reforms reintroduced the eighteen months length of service, later reduced to one year. After the trauma of World War I, France became a much firmer believer in the nation-in-arms principle and finally abandoned its attachment to the long-term-service professional army. But France continued to vacillate among different lengths of service, from two years in 1921, eighteen months in 1923, and one year in 1928.[42] Those who served moved into the category of *disponibilité*, the inactive list, subject to immediate recall for two years. The 1927–28 law also made provisions for the recruitment of career soldiers aside from the development of a large short-term-service reserve army.

In 1935 France returned to a two-year length of service, after which the conscript moved on to three years in the ready reserve service (with a maximum of a three-week period of active training, however) and sixteen years in the first inactive reserve and eight years in the second inactive reserve. During mobilization, the active army was broken up to form the newly mobilized army, creating a situation where France lacked both a ready-made expeditionary force at the start of hostilities and a force capable of limited or small-scale wars. The peacetime army would be comprised of units no larger than a division, with regional divisions organized into corps armies during wartime.[43] The French reserve system suffered from woeful training because of the restrictions put on the training of reserve forces.

In essence, the French army consisted of a small nucleus of active forces around which the national mobilized army was constituted at mobilization time. The French army became essentially a training organization, with the real army consisting of a large trained reserve rather than combat-ready

---

[41] Ralston, *The Army of the Republic*: 39.

[42] Robert Allan Doughty, *The Seeds of Disaster: The Development of French Army Doctrine, 1919–1939* (Hamden: Archon Books, 1985): 19.

[43] On these points see, Doughty, *The Seeds of Disaster*: chap. 1.

units.[44] Nor was it an army organized and trained to conduct limited, offensive war. Rather it was an army to fight the total, costly, drawn-out war that it believed World War I heralded. Finally, France had a different kind of decentralized system for conscript training than Germany. Training and mobilization were decentralized, performed by special local training centers rather than in individual line regiments. Prior to World War I, regimental units were responsible for the training, administration, and mobilization of reserve officers and soldiers. The 1927–28 reorganization established the special training centers, with units constituted solely for the training period, and no provision allowing reserve units to train in peacetime with their wartime units.[45]

France's higher command and staff organization differed markedly from German practice. The French general staff did not achieve the institutional supremacy of its counterpart. Both before and after its defeat in 1870, the French military system was marked by a more fractured, decentralized, and civilian-dominated hierarchy than Germany's. The organization of the high command was poorly delineated. Corps and divisional commanders remained the highest ranking officers. Unlike Germany, republican France abhorred the idea of concentrating peacetime and wartime command under one organ or individual. It was not until the reforms of 1911 that there was unity in peacetime and wartime command. Military hierarchy continued to be subordinate to the war minister.

The German model was a topic of frequent debate inside the French military, but France consistently rejected German staff practice. The French staff remained a subordinate institution; its chief occupied a second-rank position in the military hierarchy up until the late 1930s. The chief's wartime role and relation to the top and operational command were ill defined. Reforms in the late 1890s and in 1911 gave the chief more power and authority over military affairs and brought the functions of the general staff into closer correspondence with those of its Prussian counterpart.

Post-1870 French practice favored a civilian-military organ as the supreme body in charge of military affairs in peacetime and wartime. After 1918, the Brazilians would experiment with French practice. Accordingly, in 1872 a Superior War Council, the Conseil Supérieur de la Guerre (CSG) was created. The CSG was the organ responsible for postwar reorganization. It was composed of leading military officers and top executive branch leadership, with the state president (or minister of war in his stead) as the president of the council. The vice president was the designated commander of the army in wartime. The council did not possess actual command and control, but acted as an advisory and consultative body across nearly all military matters

---

[44] Challener, *The French Theory of the Nation In Arms*: 180.
[45] Doughty, *The Seeds of Disaster*, 30.

except strategic planning. The council acted as the principal forum in which reform measures were discussed. It became a de facto general staff.

Historically, French preference was for a closed general staff, an elite body of officers trained exclusively for staff service, rather than officers drawn from various branches of service or rotated between staff and regimental service.[46] In the 1880s the French partially adopted Prussia's open staff system, where staff officers alternated between regimental and staff service. But unlike the German practice, field staffs in France were strictly subordinate to the regimental command and did not share in command functions. Admission to general staff service was based on competitive examinations and graduation from the École Supérieur de Guerre, which was created in 1880 and patterned after the Kriegsakademie in Berlin. Unlike in Germany, graduates of the academy were sent directly to field service, rather than further training and instruction in the main general staff. The famed Saint Cyr trained infantry and cavalry officers, while the École Polytechnique served the artillery.

France moved slowly and haltingly during the interwar years to reorganize its military system in light of the lessons and experience of the great war. The emasculation of German military power after 1918 had a dampening effect of French postwar military reforms. A major participant in the interwar reform debates and formulation would be General Maurice Gamelin, future chief of staff and commander of the French army, who would head the French military mission in charge of reorganizing the Brazilian army in 1920.

France adopted several major initiatives between 1919 and 1928, with another major spurt in the mid-1930s, though on the whole the pace of reform was slow and discontinuous.[47] At the doctrinal and grand strategic level, a change occurred in the direction of emphasizing the importance of the defense and the total mobilization of the material resources of the nation for war.[48] French war doctrine, as laid out in the Provisional Instructions on the Tactical Employment of Large Units of 1921 and the Instructions on the Tactical Employment of Large Units of 1936, emphasized the increasing deadliness and preponderance of firepower in modern combat. These factors, the French believed, not only created a situation of defensive dominance but also created an immense problem for central command.

In the interwar period France also moved toward greater centralized command and control, though peacetime command continued to be divided. The principal lesson the French drew from World War I was that modern warfare required even greater control and coordination from the center, and that modern combat could only be conducted through step-by-step

---

[46] Mitchell, "A Situation of Inferiority," 59.
[47] Challener, *The French Theory of the Nation in Arms*, 137.
[48] Doughty, *The Seeds of Disaster*; Posen, *The Sources of Military Doctrine*.

methodological battles that made effective use of firepower and vast numbers. Doctrine and practice emphasized rigid control of operations and the coordination of subordinate units, as opposed to German practice of fostering subordinate initiative.[49] Military potential was based on the capacity to mobilize resources beyond military resources. The state had to be more active in fostering and intervening in all areas related to economic development and industrial organization. A new Superior Council of National Defense was created in 1921, to oversee interministerial coordination on all questions relating to national defense.[50] The council was the highest defense policy organ.

France did not have a specific body or individual charged with coordinating military activities.[51] Despite the greater centralization of command and control after 1918, the army high command was not organized around a specific individual or organ. A great deal of military planning and work was organized around councils, committees, and bureaucratized routines. In the interwar period France unsuccessfully experimented with several interservice and interministerial bodies created to address general military matters, though none served as central organs of command nor dealt with strategic planning, doctrine, or operations. The postwar hierarchy was divided among the war minister, the chief of the general staff, and the Superior War Council, with the latter two formally subordinate to the minister.

STATES, ARMIES, AND WAR IN SOUTH AMERICA

Latin America is missing as a source of empirical cases in the main security studies literature. Its absence has little to do with the reality of its diplomatic history or contemporary interstate relations in the region. Rather, it is rooted in a widely shared misconception of the region as conflict free, and void of the kinds of military-security dynamics so familiar to students of European history. Consequently, one of the big challenges for this study is to break through this misperception, and show that the South American regional system has been an arena of security competition. The presumption has been that the region has not experienced bouts of warfare and other forms of military competition.[52] In many ways we can trace this idea of pacific union among Latin American countries to the region's great liberator, Simón Bolívar, whose effort to create political union among the newly

---

[49] Doughty, *The Seeds of Disaster*, 34–35.
[50] Challener, *The French Theory of the Nation In Arms*, 191.
[51] Doughty, *The Seeds of Disaster*, 115.
[52] The most coherent recent statement of this view is Miguel Angel Centeno, *Blood and Debt: War and the Nation-State in Latin America* (University Park: Pennsylvania State University Press, 2002).

independent countries was stillborn. He too presumed a special bond, traits unique to their cultural-historical makeup, that supersede anarchy's effects in the region. The historical cases examined here will show otherwise. The presumption, nonetheless, has persisted that the region has been conflict free, despite the superb works of people inside and outside the region like David Mares.[53]

The reasons are numerous for this misconception, even if not always explicitly articulated in the wider literature. The region's perceived cultural-historical affinities, it is implied, override the usual antagonisms that lead to war among other states. Alternatively, the region's geographic misfortune of living in the shadow of the United States is viewed as favoring pacific intraregional relations. Hegemonic management by the United States is presumed to have dual effects, one positive and one negative, that eliminate the sources of conflict: the United States provides public goods in the form of extended security and institutionalized conflict mediation, or it simply relies on hegemonic power to suppress intraregional conflict.[54] Recent decades, moreover, have witnessed deep transformations in the region's politics and economics that reinforce the presumption of pacific union. Since the 1980s, the region has experienced a sustained dual transition toward freer politics and freer markets, accompanied by meaningful economic integration.[55] No less significant have been the many changes that have taken place in intraregional relations, particularly in the security arena. The internationalized civil wars, cross-border violence, armed clashes, and even nuclear competition that characterized much of the region's postwar history came to an end. The primary axes of military-security competition, which dominated the region's diplomatic history since colonial times, gave way to elements of institutionalized security cooperation.[56] The combination of democratization and regional economic integration, in addition to security cooperation, reinforced the view of the region as pacific.

The view of South America as a region free of conflict and security competition is mistaken.[57] Nineteenth-century South America was anything but

---

[53] David R. Mares, *Violent Peace: Militarized Interstate Bargaining in Latin America* (New York: Columbia University Press, 2001).

[54] On this hegemonic management argument, see Mares, *Violent Peace.*

[55] *Technopols: Freeing Politics and Markets in Latin America in the 1990s,* ed. Jorge I. Domínguez (University Park: Pennsylvania State University Press, 1997).

[56] On this question see João Resende-Santos, "The Origins of Security Cooperation in South America," *Latin American Politics and Society* (Winter 2003): 89–126.

[57] This point is also made by Walter Little, "International Conflict in Latin America," *International Affairs* 63, no. 4 (Autumn 1987): 589–602. See also Mares, *Violent Peace*; Frederick M. Nunn, *The Military in Chilean History: Essays in Civil-Military Relations, 1810–1973* (Albuquerque: University of New Mexico Press, 1976), chap. 1; Arthur P. Whittaker, *The United States and the Southern Cone: Argentina, Chile, Uruguay* (Cambridge: Harvard University Press, 1976).

free of conflict and armed competition.[58] It was a time of war making and state making.[59] The region's twentieth century was no less violent. The century spanning the 1830s and the 1930s was characterized by interstate warfare and militarized competition. While militarized rivalries and border tensions have been common features of Latin American diplomatic history, as the recent Peru–Ecuador skirmishes remind us, late-nineteenth-century South America was set apart for both the frequency of major warfare and intense militarized competition.

Interstate violence and conflict in the region came in all forms and scale: major wars that resulted in both great human and material destruction as well as reconfigured power balance; militarized interstate disputes (MID), border clashes, arms racing, and enduring rivalries. Mares lists twenty regional wars between 1825 and 1995, using the standard coding in the literature.[60] No claim is made here that Latin America replicated Europe's experience of frequent, large-scale, sustained organized violence. In comparison, the region's wars might appear limited and infrequent, but it has been just as violent as any other region when measured by militarized disputes.[61] Regional wars created states (Uruguay), dismembered states (Peru, Bolivia), deposed states from the top rank (Paraguay), and nearly erased some from the map (Paraguay). As any Mexican might readily point out, this is just in South America. In some wars, the level of destruction, in proportion to the population, was enormous. Mares points out that interstate relations in Latin America have been violence prone when we look at the entire spectrum of conflict. The twentieth century alone witnessed over two hundred militarized disputes.[62] As this study shows, historic rivalries

---

[58] Works in English that systematically examine diplomatic relations of the South American states are few in number. To date the best diplomatic history work remains Robert N. Burr, *By Reason or Force: Chile and the Balancing of Power in South America* (Berkeley: University of California Press, 1965). Burr explicitly applies versions of the balance of power theory; he focuses mainly on Chile. See, also, *Latin American Diplomatic History: An Introduction*, ed. Harold E. Davies et al. (Baton Rouge: Louisiana State University Press, 1977). For a more contemporary analysis of interstate relations in the region, see G. Pope Atkins, *Latin America in the International Political System*, 3rd ed. (Boulder: *Westview Press*, 1995).

[59] The most comprehensive work in English on the question is Centeno, *Blood and Debt*. Another useful study, dissenting from Centeno's is Fernando López-Alves, *State Formation and Democracy in Latin America, 1810–1900* (Durham: Duke University Press, 2000). Good studies exist on individual states. See, for example, Oscar Oszlak, *La formación del estado argentine* (Buenos Aires: Editorial Belgrano, 1985). This area is fertile ground for research, despite Centeno's conclusions.

[60] Mares, *Violent Peace*, 33.

[61] On this point, see Centeno, *Blood and Debt*; Mares, *Violent Peace*, 38.

[62] Mares, *Violent Peace*, 38.

FIGURE 3.1. The Wars of South America, 1810–1940.

and sustained military competition were permanent fixtures in the two centuries following independence. The Argentine–Chilean rivalry, for instance, sparked several near-war crises, the two most serious being those in 1898–1902 and in 1978. Chile still keeps a suspicious eye on Bolivia, which has never given up hope of recouping its seacoast. This study shows that sustained competition also transformed significant parts of the state's apparatus in the countries examined.

Centeno's assessment that the region's wars were limited and often irregular is generally accurate, although not his conclusions that little or no state making resulted.[63] The region also underwent system-transforming wars. Leaving aside ambiguities over the dependent variable and shifting criteria for what constitutes state making, Centeno's study does not consider that hot as well cold wars could generate state-making effects in some countries. War preparation and militarized competition have organizational effects, and neither was in short supply in nineteenth-century South America. Be that as it may, the basic point stands that the region did not experience wars of the scale and impact of the Thirty Years' War or the two world wars. Like the political history of most regions, the bulk of organized political violence was internal and unconventional. In many cases, participation in war was confined to a small segment of the population (the poor and marginalized) on long-term service. Brazil fought the lengthy and destructive Paraguayan, or Triple Alliance, war with a slave army. Whether we measure state-making effects or level of destruction, there was a good deal of cross-regional variation among the different countries, a corrective noted by López-Alves.[64] As Rasler and Thompson note, not all wars produce the same state-making effects.[65] Military competition remained intense, along with the accompanying arms races, militarized disputes, and near-war crises. This is especially true for the three countries examined here. Since the immediate post-independence period – and some might claim even during colonial times – the region was characterized by deep, cross-cutting animosities and armed competition. In other words, the region was marked by enduring rivalries.[66] The large-scale military emulation and buildup of the last quarter of the century only intensified an already competitive, war-prone regional system.

---

[63] Centeno, *Blood and Debt*, 20–21.

[64] López-Alves, *State Formation*.

[65] Karen Rasler and William R. Thompson, *War and State Making: The Shaping of the Global Powers* (Boston: Unwin Hyman, 1989), and "War Making and State Making: Governmental Expenditures, Tax Revenues, and Global Wars," *American Political Science Review* 79, no. 2 (June 1985): 491–507.

[66] *Dynamics of Enduring Rivalries*, ed. Paul Diehl (Urbana: University of Illinois Press, 1998); Gary Goertz and Paul Diehl, "Enduring Rivalries: Theoretical Constructs and Empirical Patterns," *International Studies Quarterly* no. 37 (June 1993): 147–72.

ENDURING RIVALRIES AND THE REGIONAL
BALANCE-OF-POWER SYSTEM

Can we treat South America as a self-contained arena of competition rather than a mere extension of the European balance-of-power system? Notwithstanding Waltz's focus on the global distribution of power, nineteenth-century South America can be treated as a self-contained regional subsystem of power balancing, what Buzan and others have termed a security complex.[67] Waltz notes that neorealist theory can be applied to nongreat powers insofar as their relations are insulated from great-power politics.[68]

South America's geographic remoteness and relative insularity allow us to treat it as a self-contained arena of competition, one whose dynamics were relatively separate from the global great-power system.[69] By the latter half of the nineteenth century, Mexico and the Central American republics were firmly under the informal U.S. empire. This was not the case for South America, where prior to the 1920s the United States lacked power projection capabilities and its presence was thin. Even with the consolidation of U.S. hemispheric hegemony after 1945 and the many episodes of Cold War confrontations in the region, the historic rivalries and subsystems of competition remained unaltered and largely insulated. The tripolar competition involving Argentina, Brazil, and Chile, the so-called ABC powers, retained its peculiar essence from the border disputes of the early postcolonial years to the nuclear proliferation of the 1970s. This is not to say that security competition in the region, let alone among the ABC powers, remained uncontaminated by great-power meddling and armed intervention. In fact, as the historical cases will show, great-power meddling became both a source of vulnerability and insecurity as well as presenting external balancing options.

Ironically, the United States's presumptive claim to an exclusive hemispheric backyard may have actually have helped to keep the region self-contained. The 1823 Monroe Doctrine warned off the European great powers, even though it was really the might of the British Royal Navy that kept the other European powers at bay. More often than not, the great powers tended to neutralize each other, all to the benefit of the region's self-enclosure. Great-power presence and ties, mainly commercial and primarily British and later the United States, did not significantly alter the dynamics of the local system of balancing. The British held commercial sway in the region, and this translated in political influence in places like Argentina. Great-power intrigue

---

[67] Barry Buzan, "Security Complexes in Structural and Historical Perspective," *The Insecurity Dilemma: National Security of Third World States*; Brian L. Job, ed., (Boulder: Lynne Reinner, 1992): 167–90.

[68] Kenneth N. Waltz, *Theory of International Politics* (Reading, PA: Addison-Wesley, 1979), 72–73.

[69] Buzan, "Security Complexes."

and commercial greed were frequently alleged to be behind the major wars on the continent, as well may be the case, but more likely only added a layer to the underlying power competition. European interests in the region were as heterogeneous as they were conflicting, thus the leverage Europe derived from the region's dependence did not cut clearly and predictably.

Nevertheless, regional balance-of-power politics was never immune from great power intervention. The United States was a critical, if periodic, player in ABC power competition. Aside from infrequent episodes when a great power represented an immediate and credible military threat, as in Chile's case in 1892, the overall effect of great-power meddling on the security behavior of the regional states occurred both in subtle and irregular ways or confined to isolated episodes. Like all peripheral states then and now, these states were highly dependent on Europe as a source of trade, capital, and technology. This dependence gave the European great powers not only certain leverage and prerogatives when it came to regional diplomacy, but it also gave them an important political instrument to which the regional countries were sensitive. In addition, the great powers (mainly the United States and Britain) occasionally acted as mediators in regional disputes, as did the British Crown in 1902 to avert war between Chile and Argentina.

There were occasions when the United States and European great powers (Britain and France mainly, Spain and Germany marginally) intervened militarily in the region, as Britain did in the 1820s and later in the 1840s and 1850s when the Royal Navy turned its guns on Buenos Aires. The Argentine confederation between the 1830s and the 1850s was subject to repeated armed intervention and attack by the European powers, mainly France and Britain. The Spanish fleet razed Chile's second largest city and commercial center in 1865. The United States, Britain, France, and Italy contemplated joint military intervention during the Second War of the Pacific to forestall Chilean victory. Turn-of-the-century Venezuela and Colombia provide even starker examples of great-power coercion, armed attack, and imperialism. Most of these interventions were punitive and retaliatory, thus confined to issues of the day rather than to a sustained pattern or component of regional security dynamics.

Occasional great-power meddling aside, South America developed a dense, mature, and relatively insulated regional system of power balancing, one with a lengthy historical span, in contrast to Asia and even the Middle East. Robert Burr, in his classic study on Chilean diplomatic history and the balance of power in South America, argues that international politics in the region can be analyzed in terms of a balance-of-power system since the early days of independence.[70] This system of balancing did not encompass

---

[70] Burr, *By Reason or Force.*

the entire continent until the middle of the nineteenth century.[71] Burr argues that it was not until the 1860s that a truly continental system can be said to have emerged.[72]

Geography, technology, and internal disunion all conspired to inhibit the early and uniform operation of a continental balance-of-power system. The emergence of centralized states, even if defined minimally in terms of Weberian monopoly of violence, was both delayed and uneven. Many of the regional states did not achieve national consolidation and centralized rule until several decades after independence. The region's tortured geography posed national consolidation problems for individual countries like Bolivia. The process of national political consolidation was prolonged and violent in most states. It was not until 1880, for example, that an effectively unified Argentine state can be said to exist. As a result of low technology and weak national capabilities of the individual states, the South American region did not have the sufficient level interaction capacity to sustain a region-wide structure of security competition.[73]

Like Europe, South America was a tightly confined geographic area of crosscutting enduring rivalries, mutual antagonisms, and intractable territorial disputes. The many disputes and rivalries that poisoned interstate relations had their origins in colonial days and the chaotic breakup of the Iberian (mainly Spanish) empire. Territorial dispute was the primary fuel for interstate animosity and armed competition. Diplomatic relations of the newly independent states turned immediately to border demarcations and conflicting territorial claims. No state escaped this issue, and it was rarely just a bilateral affair. Territorial disputes were so pervasive that each could always find common cause for balancing with enemies of its enemy. There was, then, considerable strategic and political spillover among the principal subsystems of the region, as discussed below. Some countries, like Argentina, laid claim to the same borders as the colonial vice royalties, which meant that for decades Paraguay was treated like a runaway province. Others, like Peru and Bolivia, favored union, which struck fear in neighbors like Chile because such combined power was seen as menacing to their security. Everywhere border disputes festered, so did an intricate interplay of alignment and shifting coalitions.

---

[71] Burr, *By Reason or Force*, chap. 1, passim.

[72] See also Ron L. Seckinger, "South American Power Politics during the 1820s," *Hispanic American Historical Review* 56, no. 2 (May 1976): 241–67.

[73] I agree with Deudney that the capacity to interact violently is an important, and overlooked, structural variable in realism. This interplay between geography and technology is likely to be a crucial variable in explaining state making (or lack thereof) in the region. On interaction capacity and the operation of structural balancing logic, see Barry Buzan, Charles Jones, and Richard Little, *The Logic of Anarchy: Neorealism to Structural Realism* (New York: Columbia University Press, 1993); Daniel H. Deudney, "Regrounding Realism: Anarchy, Security, and Changing Material Contexts," *Security Studies* 10, no. 1 (Autumn 2000): 1–42.

Given this colonial legacy of intractable territorial disputes – further complicated by the territorial dismemberment from succeeding wars – regional states became sensitive to the balance of military capabilities. Real power gains (and losses) were at stake, for the disputed territories were often not only sizable but also resource rich. They were of substantial military-strategic value. What all this meant is that the fear of the relative power and capabilities enhancing efforts of neighbors was real. Since the disputes involved substantial power gains and losses, small changes in relative military capabilities made big differences – let alone the large-scale modernization of the late 1800s. Each state feared the military power of neighbors not just out of the real consequences for their physical security and territorial claims, but also for the enhanced bargaining position it gave those neighbors. None could afford to permit an opponent to set the terms of negotiations. In 1906, Brazil's formidable foreign minister, the Baron Rio Branco, warned that the "great extension of our coast and our interior territory, [in view] of our neighbors who continue to arm themselves, commands us to organize the elements of our security [in order] to guarantee our rights which at times can be established only by force."[74] The head of Argentina's congressional military commission, General Francisco Bosch, argued in favor of military emulation by observing that "noticeable are the efforts that [Chilean] leaders undertake to bring their army to a high state of preparation capable of positioning [Chile] in conditions to settle by force disputes which reason dictates be resolved by diplomacy. It is our duty to follow this evolution, to put ourselves in a position to prevent such developments from taking place."[75]

Historically, the major continental powers, Argentina, Brazil, Chile, Paraguay, and to a lesser extent Peru, Bolivia, and Ecuador represented the principal axes of competition and armed conflict. Each of the four major powers made separate bids for continental primacy in the last two centuries; and each attempt was resisted by coalition and individual balancing efforts to prevent hegemony. After the fall of Paraguay, the South American balance of power pivoted on three major axes of militarized competition: the Pacific subsystem comprising Chile, Peru, and Bolivia; an Andean subsystem comprising mainly archrivals Chile and Argentina, with Peru and Bolivia as victims and pawns more than protagonists following the Second Pacific War; and the La Plata River Basin system of Brazil and Argentina, with postwar Paraguay and Uruguay as pawns and natural buffers.

[74] José Maria da Silva Paranhos, the Barão do Rio Branco, "Homenagen do Exército nacional," November 10, 1906, in *Obras do Barão do Rio Branco*, vol. 1, *Questões de limites entre o Brasíl e a República Argentina* (Rio de Janeiro: Ministério de Relações Exteriores, 1948), 104.

[75] General Francisco Bosch, in Argentina, Congreso Nacional, *Diario de Sessiones de la Cámara de Diputados* (Buenos Aires: Congreso de la Nación, 1900): 966.

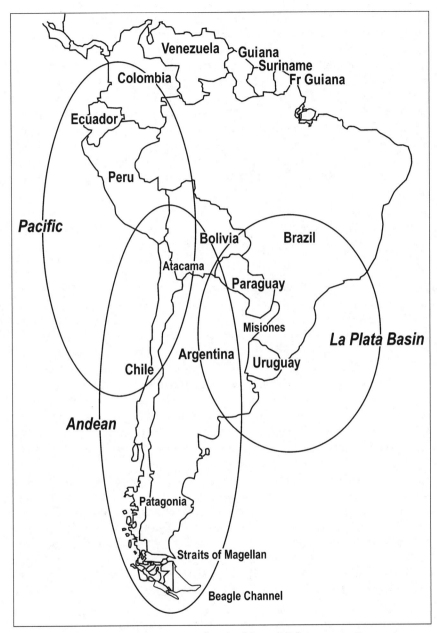

FIGURE 3.2. South America's Main Balance-of-Power Subsystems, 1870–1930.

After the Second War of the Pacific (1879–83), the epicenters of continental balancing were the Andean and La Plata subsystems. By the last quarter of the century, the two subsystems were interpenetrating, more or less functioning as one single arena of competition covering the greater Southern Cone. The two subsystems had always crosscut since the early postcolonial years, a natural and expected outcome of balance-of-power politics. Argentina was the common bridge. It was encircled by its two greatest enemies, who naturally found common cause as enemies of their common enemy. Brazil and Chile developed an "unwritten alliance," as it came to be called in diplomatic circles. Since relations between Brazil and Chile, who did not share common borders, were cordial, balancing in the region generally had a chain-reaction dynamic.

The Major Regional Wars

Absent in South America was the kind of frequent, long-lasting, and dynastic warfare that marked much of Europe's history, the same kinds of warfare that drove technological and political development. Yet, as in Europe, South America experienced system-transforming wars that reconfigured the regional distribution of capabilities. Up to the time of large scale military emulation the region had gone through a period of four to five decades of nearly continuous interstate warfare – in addition to the uninterrupted stretch of civil wars and internal political violence that nearly every country experienced.[76] The period was marked by territorial adjustments by force, recurring border clashes, arms racing, armed posturing, and frequent military mobilizations. Burr lists eight wars, not including the wars of independence, involving the major powers in the nineteenth century.[77] It was, however, the two big wars of the century's second half that transformed the regional system.

The Pacific, Andean, and La Plata subsystems experienced three major wars that changed the strategic landscape on the eve of large scale military emulation: the First War of the Pacific (also known as the war of the Bolivian–Peruvian Confederation, 1836–39), the Paraguayan, or Triple Alliance, war (1865–70), and the Second War of the Pacific (1879–83). Two of South America's biggest wars, the bloody and protracted Paraguayan war (1865–70) and the Second War of the Pacific (1879–83), reconfigured the geographic-political map of the region and altered the balance.[78] The Paraguayan and

---

[76] On the wars and conflicts of the nineteenth century, see Burr, *By Reason or Force*; also, Davies, ed., *Latin American Diplomatic History*.

[77] Burr, *By Reason or Force*, chap. 1, passim.

[78] The Paraguayan war, also known as the war of the Triple Alliance, brought together a loose, defensive alliance among Argentina, Brazil, and Uruguay against Paraguay, which in 1865 was considered to be the strongest power in the River Plate Basin. The long-standing jostling for control over Uruguay by the three major River Plate powers, and Paraguay's historical

Pacific wars were major wars in terms of scale, duration, and severity.[79] The severity of the Paraguayan war, pitting then feared Paraguay against an uneasy alliance of Argentina, Brazil, and Uruguay, rivaled that of the Franco-Prussian war and the Crimean war.[80] There are no reliable figures on the total human and material costs of the war. The battlefield deaths of Brazil alone were well over 100,000; a U.S. diplomat put the figure at 168,000.[81] Argentina's figure is estimated to be twenty thousand. Paraguay's losses were staggering. As a result of battlefield deaths and war-related famine and disease (the results of what appeared to be genocidal intent of its enemies), Paraguay lost about a half of its national population, which is estimated to have been anywhere between 300,000 to 800,000.[82] Prior to the war Paraguay was widely considered the continent's premier military power, with a productive economy and a precursor to the welfare state. By 1870 Paraguay was on the brink of extinction. It never recovered.

The Paraguayan and Pacific wars were system-transforming wars in that victory and defeat promoted and eliminated states in the top ranks in the regional system. The two wars reduced the system from five major powers (Chile, Argentina, Brazil, Peru, and Paraguay), to one of only three real major powers, (Argentina, Brazil, and Chile). A multipolar continental system was transformed into a tripolar system, with all it implies in terms of the stability of tripolarity. Peru, the dominant naval power on the eve of 1879, only partially recovered from its defeat and postwar internal collapse. Paraguay, nearly scratched out of existence by the war, would never recover the position and national viability it once possessed.[83] Of more significance was the rise of

---

search for an outlet to the sea, provided the background to the war. The third major regional war was the Chaco war between Bolivia and Paraguay in 1932–35. The Second Pacific War is frequently dated as ending in 1884, mainly because it is when Bolivia and Chile finally agree to a truce, but did not sign a peace treaty until 1904.

79 Severity refers to battlefield deaths of military personnel.

80 Jack S. Levy, *War in the Modern Great Power System* (Lexington: University of Kentucky Press, 1983); Kennedy, *The Rise and Fall of the Great Powers*. For estimates on the two wars in South America, see Michael Clodfelter, *Warfare and Armed Conflict: A Statistical Reference to Casualty and Other Figures, 1618–1991*, 2 vols., A Note on the Statistics, Introduction, vol. 1, 1618–1899 (Jefferson: McFarland, 1992).

81 Harry Gaylord Warren, *Paraguay and the Triple Alliance: The Postwar Decade, 1869–1878* (Austin: University of Texas Press, 1978), 30.

82 On this issue, see Warren, *Paraguay and the Triple Alliance*; John Hoyt Williams, *The Rise and Fall of the Paraguayan Republic, 1800–1870* (Austin: University of Texas Press, 1979); Vera B. Reber, "The Demographics of Paraguay: A Reinterpretation of the Great War, 1864–70," *Hispanic American Historical Review* 68, no. 2 (May 1988): 289–320.

83 On Paraguay's decline and emasculation, see Warren, *Paraguay and the Triple Alliance*; Paul H. Lewis, "Paraguay: From the War of the Triple Alliance to the Chaco War, 1870–1932," *The Cambridge History of Latin America*, vol. 5, Leslie Bethell, ed., (Cambridge: Cambridge University Press, 1994).

a unified and prospering Argentina following the Paraguayan war.[84] The rise of a larger, unified Argentina presented for both of its principal neighbors a qualitatively different strategic environment. Argentina came to embody the relationship between national wealth and military power, and how uneven rates of growth promote and demote states in the top ranks.

The two major regional wars not only altered the strategic landscape in the region, they engendered qualitatively different demands on the machinery of the state and its mobilizational capacity. The two big regional wars revealed organizational shortcomings of the state apparatus as well as the weakness of the material and human bases of national power. The Paraguayan and Pacific wars, because of their scale and duration, revealed for all the participants the glaring organizational and technical weaknesses of their land and naval forces.

In terms of the large-scale military emulation begun in the 1880s, no other war had greater impact in the region than the War of the Pacific in 1879. For the victor, the vanquished, and nonparticipants alike, the war drastically altered the military-strategic landscape. While the war itself was confined to the immediate subsystem, its consequences rippled through the region because the main axes of competition were interlaced. The strategic-diplomatic fallout of the war elevated the scale and intensity of the security competition in the region. Chile vanquished its longtime rivals Peru and Bolivia, and annexed their mineral-rich provinces. Its annexation of Bolivia's Antofagasta province alone added nearly 60,000 square miles of resource-rich territory and nearly two hundred miles of coastline. Victory brought gains but also new security challenges for Chile, including near-war with a United States intent on rolling back Chilean gains. Chile's military buildup rippled throughout the region, as its erstwhile enemies, its rivals, and the enemies of its enemies all chain-ganged into a spiraling arms race. Chile in 1885 set in motion a process of large-scale military modernization that lasted for the next four decades.

The Pre-Reform Armies of South America

Prior to large-scale military emulation, the contending states of South America fought their many internal and interstate wars with improvised, temporary armies. Each war revealed their utter inadequacy. South America's wars revealed, among other things, the severe lack of a technically competent officer corps, trained soldiers, the chaotic and improvised nature of logistical support services, the absence of adequate means of communications and transportation, and the absence of a technical body dedicated to strategic planning, peacetime preparation, and mobilization. Even victorious Chile

---

[84] Juan Bautista Alberdi, *La guerra del Paraguay* (Buenos Aires: Hyspamérica Ediciones, SA, 1988; originally published 1869).

was forced to grapple with serious flaws in its military organization, as the many wartime setbacks demonstrated.

With the partial exceptions of Chile and Paraguay, the militaries that participated in these wars were essentially rag-tag militia forces, haphazardly assembled in wartime, rather than regular, standing national forces.[85] In many cases, permanent standing militaries did not exist. For instance, a permanent national army did not exist in Argentina until the early 1880s; the national forces that existed previously were either temporary or privatized by whichever dominant faction or warlord held sway. In Brazil what passed for a national army was a skeletal federal force stationed in the capital, Rio de Janeiro, with units conscripted and stationed in the provinces and nominally attached to the federal units. National armies, in general, tended to be a collection of regional *caudillo* armies and provincially based national guard units and militias.

South America's armies were preprofessional, in Huntington's definition.[86] Throughout much of the nineteenth century they were plagued by deficiencies in bureaucratic-administrative structure, conscription, professional officer formation, military training and education, high command and staff organization, as well as supply and other service organs. To varying degrees, all the regional militaries suffered from problems of enlistment and quality of soldiers. The rank and file consisted mostly of illiterates, slaves, convicts, and vagrants impressed into service.[87] Universal obligatory service did not exist. Prior to the 1880s, none of the regional militaries had a standardized system of enlistment, training, and reserves. Military service was accomplished by forced recruitment and legal punishment. Naturally, the armies suffered high rates of desertion, and none were able to meet their legal or desired size.

The armies were poorly organized and poorly equipped. In general, the bigger regional armies were occasionally equipped with the latest weapons technology, but general equipment and supplies were poor in quality and quantity and individual armies often found themselves with outdated armaments. These armies lacked solid bureaucratic structure and standardized

---

[85] Alain Rouquié, *The Military and the State in Latin America* (Berkeley: University of California Press, 1981); Frederick M. Nunn, *Yesterday's Soldiers: European Military Professionalism in South America, 1890–1940* (Lincoln: University of Nebraska Press, 1983); *The Latin American Military Institution*; Robert Wesson, ed., (New York: Praeger, 1986); Edwin Lieuwen, *Arms and Politics in Latin America* (New York: Praeger, 1961); Liisa North, *Civil-Military Relations in Argentina, Chile, and Peru* (Berkeley: University of California Press, 1966); John J. Johnson, *The Military and Society in Latin America* (Stanford: Stanford University Press, 1964).

[86] Samuel P. Huntington, *The Soldier and the State: The Theory and Politics of Civil-Military Relations* (Cambridge: Belknap Press, 1957). See also North, *Civil-Military Relations*.

[87] Alain Rouquié, *The Military and the State*. See also Alain Rouquié, *Poder military sociedad política en la Argentina, hasta 1943*, vol. 1 (Buenos Aires: EMECE, 1981).

systems of administration. War ministries that existed did so without much internal functional specialization. A specialized department devoted to war planning and preparation did not exist, let alone one endowed with command functions and officer formation responsibilities.

The most glaring deficiency of the regional armies was the absence of professional officer formation. Like their European counterparts of earlier times, the regional armies were also small, long serving armies. At both the command level and the rank and file, these armies lacked basic, standardized training and technical expertise. The result was that the officer corps often comprised officers with little or no formal education beyond elementary levels, let alone specialized military instruction. Argentina's War Ministry reported in 1893 that of the roughly 1,400 army officers, only thirty had any advanced technical training or graduated from a military academy. Specialized military schools either did not exist, functioned intermittently, or did not reach the entire corps. The few military academies that did exist tended to be small, understaffed, largely civilian institutions that functioned intermittently in places like Brazil. The curriculum consisted of, what Huntington termed, "technicism" and civilian disciplines. The military schools essentially became places where well-to-do young men received a baccalaureate education to pursue civilian careers. In exceptional cases like Chile, a handful of officers were sent to Europe (France, Belgium, and Britain primarily) for advanced training.

By and large, these armies also tended to be top-heavy, staffed by political appointees, landed aristocrats, and family members of the elite. The officer corps was governed by particularism, rather than a standardized system of recruitment, formation, and advancement. Officer recruitment and advancement did not rest on even minimum standards of general education. A system of advancement based on merit and expertise emerged only after military emulation. Particularistic, subjective criteria predominated. Recruitment and promotions were done largely on the basis of patronage politics, personal connections, class privileges, cronyism, or regional favoritism. Most officers were civilians who received their commission by executive decree or provincial appointment. Politicians often held military ranks and posts. In general, the military did not constitute a true profession for the officers; many were engaged in civilian political and economic activities while on active duty.

Similarly, civil-military relations in most of the regional countries were characterized by subjective control.[88] Again with the partial exception of Chile, the harshness of military service, brutal corporal punishment, and the low remuneration meant that the military had low social standing. Unlike in most parts of Europe, military officers did not receive special privileges or social recognition nor was officership an esteemed career.

---

[88] North, *Civil-Military Relations*.

Chile was an early exception among the major powers in terms of military organization. Since the 1830s, Chile possessed a regular national army and navy, with a relatively solid structure, standardized training and recruitment, and competent officer corps. To be sure, its military suffered from organizational defects, and particularistic criteria were rampant in officer recruitment and advancement. But its defects were less severe than the regional norm. Chilean exceptionalism derives principally from the fact that the country was engaged in nearly continuous warfare in the post-independence period. Aside from the hostility and security competition with its neighbors, Chile fought a major international war early on (the first War of the Pacific, 1836–39 against the Peruvian–Bolivian confederation). This condition of encirclement and active external threats also partly explains the development of solid military organization in Paraguay, whose political independence and territorial integrity were challenged by neighboring Argentina and Brazil.

Argentina represents an extreme case of the virtual absence of a permanent national army for much of the post-independence period. The Argentine confederation plunged into protracted civil wars and interprovincial violence. By and large, no central authority governed. The thirteen provinces governed themselves independently. Consistent with the high degree of federalism and interprovincial strife, what existed in Argentina were individual provincial armies alongside various collections of private, *caudillo* armies and *gaucho* forces. These forces were used mainly for internal policing functions and provincial power grabs.[89] Throughout much of the 1830s–50s period, Argentine politics was dominated by the dictator Rosas, who lay claim to central authority and managed to organize a large army. Rosas's army at first was an irregular collection of rural *gaucho* and provincial militias, but he later put his army under more regular organization. Rosas's self-proclaimed federal army was an instrument of his rule, an instrument of internal repression, and a pillar to his governing coalition of provincial landowners. After several bloody civil wars in the 1850s, national unification was formally declared under the presidency of Bartolemeo Mitre. Attempts to organize a more permanent and professional national army were taken in the 1860s and 1870s, when a permanent national army was legally enacted and the Colégio Militar created. The Colégio, intended as a military preparatory school and having a three-year course of study, did not begin operating in earnest until the early 1870s. Graduation from the Colégio was not a prerequisite for commission. Despite the founding of a military academy, the officer corps remained preprofessional and without standardized formal instruction. Some officers could be considered professional in the sense that many were long serving. The careers of many dated from

---

[89] For a discussion on provincial politics and the development of centralization, *Argentina Since Independence*, see Leslie Bethell, ed., (Cambridge: Cambridge University Press, 1993).

the time of the independent regional armies.[90] The soldiery was comprised of long-serving *destinados* and *enganchados*, typically the dregs of society pressed into service or sentenced to the barracks instead of prison. Finally, the absence of a solid military organization in Argentina was worse for its naval forces. Argentina did not have a navy, save for a loosely organized riverine coast guard. The early 1890s, centralization was fictional. It would take another two decades for the consolidation of the national state and central rule.[91]

Brazil was very much in line with the regional pattern of small, preprofessional, poorly organized national armies. Brazil escaped the internal anarchy, centrifugal warfare, and caudillist violence that plagued many of its neighbors, at least prior to the 1890s. Its transition from colonial rule to independent empire was a peaceful one. Its army and navy were small and poorly organized. It fought the Paraguayan war with an army of slaves commanded by officers who could barely read and write. Military academies were established early on, but there was no uniform regulation governing the recruitment and formation of officers. In Brazil the problems of technicism and popularism were much more severe than among its neighbors, especially in the period after the Paraguayan war. Brazil also experienced severe enlistment problems, much more so than Argentina and Chile. The rank and file consisted mostly of criminals, slaves, vagabonds, and lower-class individuals pressed into service. Problems with discipline and desertion were rampant.

Brazil's biggest political, and thus military, problem was its hyperfederalism. Regionalism was strong in Brazil, and this was reflected in the weakness of the federal army. Brazil's states, especially the large and powerful ones like São Paulo and Minas Gerais, resisted efforts to create a large federal force, though there is some indication that the monarchy itself preferred a weak, negligible force. In sharp contrast to the national army, many of the provincial armies, especially those of the states of São Paulo and Minas Gerais, were larger, better trained, better equipped, and better organized than the federal forces. São Paulo staunchly defended provincial autonomy and prerogatives by maintaining and modernizing a large, powerful state militia.[92] In sharp contrast to the stagnation of the national army, São Paulo's state militia was first to undertake large-scale military emulation and professionalization

---

[90] Rouquié, *Poder militar y sociedad política*, 75, argues that many of the officers in the federal army can be considered professional in the Huntingtonian sense.

[91] Oscar Oszlak, *La formación del estado argentino* (Buenos Aires: Editorial de Belgrano, 1982).

[92] See essays in *Perspectives on the Armed Forces in Brazil*; Keith H. Henry and Robert A. Hayes, eds., (Tempe: Arizona State University Press, 1976); Joseph Love, "Autonomia e interdependência: São Paulo e a federação brasileira, 1889–1937," *Historia geral da civilização brasileira: Brasíl republicano*, tome 3, vol. 1, Boris Fausto, ed., *Estrutura de poder e economia, 1889–1930* (Rio de Janeiro: DIEFEL, 1977).

when the state contracted a French military mission in 1906.[93] The modernized São Paulo militia would repeatedly defeat federal forces during the various civil wars and rebellions of the 1920s and 1930s.

EARLY EPISODES OF MILITARY EMULATION

The South Americans were not the only ones to engage in military emulation during this time.[94] Nor was the large-scale military emulation analyzed here the first or only time the South Americans borrowed military best practices from Europe. Post-colonial South American armies have gone through three successive waves of external military influence: French, German, and United States. Importing foreign military influence has a long history in South America. Since the time of their independence, the South Americans had been imitating various aspects of European military systems.[95] In countries with strong marshal traditions like Chile, the major avenues and statutes of war heroes have names like O'Higgins, Williams, Lynch, and Cochrane. The regional navies were, more often than not, offsprings of the British Royal Navy, the predominant influence into the 1920s.[96] The South American

---

[93] Dalmo de Abreu Dallari, *O pequeno exército paulista* (São Paulo: Editôra Perspectiva, 1977); Euclides Andrade, *A Força Pública de São Paulo: esboço histórico, 1831–1931* (São Paulo: Imprensa Oficial do Estado, 1982); Heloisa Rodrígues Fernandes, *Política e segurança: Força Pública do estado de São Paulo, fundamentos históricos-sociais* (São Paulo: Editôra Alfa-Omega, 1974); General Alfredo Souto Malan, *Missão militar françesa de instrução junto ao Exército brasileiro* (Rio de Janeiro: Biblioteca do Exército, 1988).

[94] Most scholars have studied military emulation, and professionalization more broadly, in South America from the standpoint of civil-military relations and the military's intervention in politics. These are important questions – though I believe unrelated to foreign influence – but I am more concerned with the why and how of military emulation per se, not its sociopolitical consequences. See the works of Frederick M. Nunn, *Yesterday's Soldiers*; "Effects of European Military Training in Latin America: The Origins and Nature of Professional Militarism in Argentina, Brazil, Chile, and Peru, 1890–1940," *Military Affairs* 39, no. 1 (February 1975): 1–7; "Military Professionalism and Professional Militarism in Brazil, 1870–1970: Historical Perspectives and Political Implications," *Journal of Latin American Studies* 4, no. 1 (Summer 1972): 29–54. See also Alain Rouquié, *The Military and the State*; Edwin Lieuwen, *Arms and Politics in Latin America* (New York: Council on Foreign Relations, 1960).

[95] In addition to the works of Nunn, see also Efraín Cobas, *Fuerzas Armadas, missiones militares, y dependencia en el Peru* (Lima: Editorial Horizonte, 1982); *The Latin American Military Institution*; Robert Wesson, et al. eds. (New York: Praeger, 1986).

[96] There is scholarly disagreement on the extent of British influence in individual navies. For a good discussion, see Varun Sahni, "Not Quite British: A Study of External Influences on the Argentine Navy," *Journal of Latin American Studies* 25, no. 3 (October 1993): 489–514; Adrian J. English, *The Armed Forces of Latin America: Their Histories, Development, Present Strength, and Military Potential* (London: Jane's, 1984). On the United States as a model, see David Healy, "William B. Caperton and United States Naval Diplomacy in South America, 1917–1919," *Journal of Latin American Studies* 8, no. 2 (November 1976): 297–323; Joseph Smith, *Unequal Giants: Diplomatic Relations between the United States and*

powers borrowed heavily and consistently from France (army) and Britain (navy) in the period before 1870.

The best example of early large-scale military emulation is provided by the regional navies, which, relative to land forces, tended to be better organized and marked by greater professionalism than the armies. The navies of Chile, Argentina, and Brazil were direct creations of British naval officers.[97] Several of the navies of the independence wars were organized and led by active and inactive British naval officers. The navies of both Chile and Brazil were led by British admirals during and immediately after independence. In addition, there were numerous British and other European military officers and advisers in the armies of independence. The armies, by and large, remained holdovers from the colonial royal armies as far as organization, doctrine, field tactics, and internal regulations were concerned. Emulation was sporadic and largely superficial, not the sustained and thorough remolding that came later.

In the period before 1870, as the theory predicts, the French army generated the greatest emulation appeal among the regional powers. Various aspects of the French military system were adopted all over the region, especially after the Crimean war. French influence seemed to be deepest at the intellectual level, especially in Brazil and Chile. Like France, the South Americans favored the small long-serving professional army. French armaments predominated throughout the region. As with the French army itself, the South American armies continued to neglect the formation of a general staff service. Argentina and Chile, who would later become the most extensive emulators of Germany, were heavy imitators of the French military system during this period. In 1858, Chile hired a small French military mission, composed of four officers, to act as instructors in infantry, cavalry, engineering, and artillery.[98] In addition, Chile adopted French regulations as part of its ongoing efforts to reorganize and professionalize its military in the period after the First War of the Pacific. Up to this point Chile, like the rest of the Spanish American states, had been using the archaic, rigid *Ordenanza General* of Charles III of Spain. Finally, an important aspect of Chile's emulation of the French system was an agreement with France to send Chilean officers to French military academies for instruction.

Brazil, 1889–1930 (Pittsburgh: University of Pittsburgh Press, 1991), and "American Diplomacy and the Naval Mission to Brazil, 1917–1930," *Inter-American Economic Affairs* 35, no. 1 (Summer 1981): 72–91; Stetson Conn and Byron Fairchild, *The Western Hemisphere: The Framework of Hemisphere Defense* (Washington, DC: Department of the Army, 1960); Robert L. Scheina, *Latin America: A Naval History, 1810–1987* (Annapolis: Naval Institute Press, 1987).

[97] On the early histories of regional navies, see Scheinna, *Latin America*; English, *The Armed Forces of Latin America*.

[98] Hernan Ramírez Necochea, *Fuerzas Armadas y política en Chile, 1810–1970: antecedentes para una historia* (Havana: Casa de las Americas, 1985): chap. 2.

Even while it struggled to find a workable national union, Argentina emulated superficial aspects of the French system. During the post-independence decades, Argentina borrowed from a mixture of great-power armies, especially in the area of armaments. There were organizational and doctrinal influences from France, especially after the 1850s. In 1852 the national guard was reorganized, with the intention of serving as the main reserve force, and explicitly based on the French model. After the creation of a nominal national army, Argentina turned to France for weapons and an organizational model. Argentine cavalry and artillery regulations were directly translated from the French, as well as other regulations and doctrinal literature.[99] In 1864 the first contingent of Argentine officers was sent to St. Cyr for training and instruction under a special agreement with France.[100] Brazil too looked to the French. I have noted above that the state militia of São Paulo undertook the extensive emulation of the French. French influence was deep in the areas of conscription and military education in the federal army.

[99] Colonel Augusto G. Rodriguez, *Reseña Histórica del Ejército argentino, 1862–1930* (Buenos Aires: Secretaria de Guerra, 1964), discusses these early influences.
[100] Rodriguez, *Reseña histórica*, 30.

4

Military Emulation in Chile, 1885–1914

Today, as in the past, Chile is exceptional among Latin American countries. In good and bad ways, Chile has usually bucked the regional trend. It has been both pioneer and pariah. It was first to achieve effective national unification after independence when the rest of the region plunged into internecine warfare. It was first to experiment with constitutional government at a time when dictatorship was the norm in the region. Much later, as the rest of the region worshiped the virtues of *dirigisme* and import substitution industrialization, it championed neoliberal fundamentalism two decades before it became international gospel. Whereas the rest of the region embraced democracy in the 1980s, Chile clung to its modernizing but brutal military dictatorship. Over a century earlier, Chile was first to undertake a root and branch remaking of its military system by importing wholesale Prussia's renowned Imperial army. Chile's bold decision, and its successful emulation, altered the regional strategic landscape, setting a standard by which all others had to measure and adjust. That large-scale military emulation in the region began with Chile is not surprising from the standpoint of the theory of emulation.

This chapter examines the nature and causes of military emulation in late-nineteenth-century Chile. The first section narrates Chile's process of large-scale military emulation. It provides a comprehensive examination of its military emulation during the principal years of the process, 1885 to 1914. It details emulation in the areas of military armaments, conscription system, officer formation, and general staff organization. This section highlights carefully the timing, pace, and scope of Chile's military emulation. Military emulation in Chile unfolded in three historical phases: 1885–91, the post–civil-war phase, and the 1906 reorganization. The discussion flows accordingly. The second section analyzes the causes of Chile's military emulation. It examines the relationship between Chile's external security situation and the timing, pace, and scope of its military emulation. My findings are consistent with the neorealist theory of emulation. Chile's massive undertaking was a response to adverse changes occurring in its external security during the period under study. The timing, intensity, and scale of Chile's military modernization correlated with the timing, proximity, and scale of security threats. As equally predicted by the theory, regional insecurities (local threats) prompted Chile to look for, and emulate, global best practices, as embodied by Germany's Imperial Army.

MILITARY MODERNIZATION IN CHILE, 1885–1914

Large-scale military emulation in Chile, based on the German model, presents us with several puzzles. Chile is a small country in the periphery of the global system that copies the best practices of a great power with whom it shares no cultural, economic, or diplomatic ties. Chile previously had been a devotee of the French military, having contracted a French training mission in 1858. Why switch? The more immediate puzzle is that, despite conquering its enemies in 1883, Chile moved quickly to restructure its military system.

The first phase of Chile's military emulation, 1885–91, was in motion even while the Second War of the Pacific (1879–83) was still being prosecuted. The initial push to modernize Chile's armed forces started under the presidency of Domingo Santa Maria González (1881–86) and sustained (if not expanded and accelerated) under his successor, José Manuel Balmaceda (1886–91).[1] The decision to undertake a complete modernization of the army, based on the German model, occurred in the midst of the Second War of the Pacific. Two years after the war's conclusion, in 1885, Chile entrusted its military modernization to German officers.

Details are scant as to the process leading to the decision to contract a German military mission. What is known is that Chile attempted to hire a German military mission sometime before the close of the Second War of the Pacific and as early as 1881.[2] What is also indisputable is that the initiative

---

[1] For a detailed survey of military reforms, see Gonzalo Vial Correa, "Fuerzas Armadas e Iglesia," in *Historia de Chile, 1891–1973*, vol. 2, tome 1, *Triumfo y decadencia de la oligarquía, 1891–1920* (Santiago: Santilla del Pacífico, S.A., 1982); Vial, "Las Fuerzas Armadas," in *Historia de Chile*, vol. 1, tome 2, *La sociedad chilena en el cambio de siglo, 1891–1920* (Santiago: Santilla del Pacífico, 1981). I rely extensively on the official military history in Ministerio de Guerra y Marina, Estado Maior General del Ejército (EMGE), *Historia del Ejército de Chile*, 10 vols. (Santiago: EMGE, 1980), especially vol. 7, *Reorganizacíon del Ejército y la influencia alemana, 1885–1914*. Also used extensively are the annual reports of the war ministry during 1882 to 1908: Chile, Ministerio de Guerra y Marina, *Memoria del Ministro de la Guerra presentada al Congreso Nacional de Chile* (Santiago: Imprenta Nacional). Note that the complete title of the *Memoria* series changed over time, as did the ministry's name.

[2] Patrício Quiroga Zamora and Carlos Maldonado, *El prusianismo en las fuerzas armadas chilenas: un estudio historico, 1885–1945* (Santiago: Ediciones Documentas, 1988): 38.

to contract a German military mission was Chile's and not the result of Germany's prompting, which at the time had only negligible diplomatic and economic ties with Chile and the rest of the region.[3] In 1881 the Chilean legation in Berlin was instructed to find a suitable officer to lead a training mission.[4] Chile's representative in Berlin, Guillermo Matta, was instructed to request a military mission from the German government. In late 1883, he cabled his home government that "the army in Germany is the best there is in terms of organization."[5] Chile's request for a formal training mission was just the beginning of several such requests to Germany from Latin America, among them Chile's very own enemies.

Matta and the Chilean delegation first attempted to contract Jacob Clemens Meckel, who instead went to Japan to lead the successful modernization program there.[6] Matta also attempted unsuccessfully to hire a Captain Halder, who spoke Spanish.[7] In mid-1885 Matta approached German War Minister Bronsart von Schellendorf, who recommended Captain Emile Körner Henze as chief of the first German military mission to Chile.[8] Körner, a graduate of the renowned Kriegsakademie in Berlin, was an instructor of tactics and military engineering at the School of Artillery and Engineering in Charlottenburg. He participated in the battles of 1870, including Sedan, and was considered an expert in tactics. His contract was for five years and renewable for more. His specific duties revolved around instruction at the military school and the creation of an academy for superior and general staff instruction.

Emile Körner would become one of the most controversial figures in the entire span of foreign military influence in Latin America. Körner, who would adopt Chilean citizenship after 1891, came to occupy the highest positions in the military hierarchy. He headed an initially modest size German military mission that arrived in Santiago in early 1886. A key member of the Chilean delegation that hired Körner was Belgian-educated Jorge Boonen Rivera, who had firsthand knowledge of German regulations and military literature. Körner and Boonen would form a partnership that spanned nearly three decades. Boonen became Körner's right-hand man and most ardent backer in military and political circles.

---

[3] For arguments that give more primacy to Germany's economic and strategic interests in military emulation in the region, see Elizabeth B. White, *The German Influence in the Argentine Army, 1900–1945* (New York: Garland, 1991).

[4] Quiroga and Maldonado, *El prusianismo*, 38.

[5] Quiroga and Maldonado, *El prusianismo*, 39.

[6] Frederick M. Nunn, *Yesterday's Soldiers: European Military Professionalism in South America, 1890–1945* (Lincoln: University of Nebraska Press, 1983): 51.

[7] Estado Mayor General del Ejército (EMGE), *Reorganización del Ejército*, 29.

[8] Frederick M. Nunn, "Emil Körner and the Prussianization of the Chilean Army: Origins, Process, and Consequences, 1885–1920," *Hispanic American Historical Review* 50, no. 2 (May 1970): 300–22, provides an elaborate biography.

The German Military Model and Reformers

Military emulation in Chile, based on the German system, had powerful political backers. Indeed, political support for military reforms was strong throughout the so-called Liberal Republic decades (1860s, 1870s, and 1880s). President Federico Errázuriz Zañartu (1871–76) undertook military buildup during his tenure, giving special attention to Chile's principal arm of defense, the navy. Both Santa Maria and his foreign minister, Balmaceda, supported the wholesale modernizing of the armed forces.[9] Having served as foreign minister during the war, Balmaceda was uniquely sensitive to Chile's postwar security situation. During his presidency, military emulation was at the heart of a national project of social, infrastructural, and economic modernization, made possible by the enormous wealth generated from the conquered mineral-rich territories. Indeed, Chilean society as a whole underwent dramatic changes during the Liberal Republic years, including separation of church and state. The state apparatus itself also underwent organizational expansion and restructuring, including the creation of new ministries such as public works.

As in Brazil and Argentina, the earliest and strongest advocates of military modernization emerged within the military establishment. A modicum of opposition is always present in any deep organizational change, however, and Chile's military emulation was no exception. Intramilitary opposition to reforms in Chile was not as intense as it was in Brazil, but it did exist and it split the military along generational lines.[10] The war ministry in 1888 made a passing reference to the fact that "naturally this reform will encounter resistance and will present difficulties."[11] The idea of thorough reform was not uniformly shared or accepted. General Francisco Javier Diaz argues that victory in 1883 led the majority of civil and military leaders to believe Chile's military organization, strategy, and tactics were the best possible. Victory "caused the great majority of the officers to lose sight of the need to modify, to rejuvenate the methods of warfare that had been tested previously in the Franco–Prussian War."[12]

The push for thorough reform was irresistable. Modernization was backed by a potent coalition of civil-military leaders. A prominent advocate was Admiral Patrício Lynch, one of the most prestigious and politically influential senior officers. Lynch was a war hero, notwithstanding some controversial actions during the war. Notably, Lynch had also commanded

---

[9] Vial, *La sociedad chilena*, 786.

[10] Vial, *La sociedad chilena*, 789–92; Nunn, *The Military in Chilean History*, and "Emil Körner."

[11] Ministerio de Guerra y Marina, *Memória del Ministerio de Guerra y Marina presentada al Congreso Nacional* (Santiago: Imprenta Nacional, 1888):9. Hereafter *Memória*.

[12] General Francisco Javier Díaz, *La guerra civil de 1891: relación historica militar*, 2 vols., vol. 1, *La campaña del norte* (Santiago: Imprenta La Sud América, 1942):15.

army divisions on the final assault on Peru's capital, Lima, and subsequently served as a successful military governor of conquered Peru. This experience gave him valuable insights into the state of the army, and not just the overall grand strategic needs of the country. The Admiral was well aware that the armed forces required rebuilding. Though victorious, both the army and navy suffered terrible losses and material destruction in the war. Observing that the army suffered from organizational flaws, particularly with respect to strategic planning, officer formation, and the artillery combat arm, Lynch argued that Chile needed good military schools and technical departments.[13] Lynch approached President Santa Maria with a set of reform proposals. Another key proponent of modernization was the director of the Escuela Militar, Emilio Sotomayor. A war hero who led the successful campaign to conquer Antofagasta, Sotomayor was also a major proponent of hiring foreign instructors to teach modern tactics.[14] General Francisco Javier Díaz, one of Chile's most prolific and insightful military historians, credits Sotomayor as responsible for proposing an ample reorganization program, including his proposal to the war minister in 1882 to contract German military instructors.[15]

The principal reformist bloc within the military consisted of several senior officers, field commanders, and young officers, who believed Chile's future military security depended on a thorough reorganization and professionalization of the military. Future war minister and prominent military historian, Carlos Saez Morales, notes in his memoirs that "the new generation of officers represented a material that was easy to mold. On the other hand, *the danger of war with Argentina* had made government understand the necessity of reconstituting, rapidly, an army whose efficiency would be the guarantee of international security, a task entrusted to General Körner [head of the proposed German military mission]."[16] Saez Morales himself was one of the first young officers to be molded by the German mission. Proponents of modernization were motivated by concerns over organizational and technological flaws as well as the array of strategic problems facing the country. As the Second Pacific War drew to a close there was a widely shared belief among Chilean military and political leaders that a war with Argentina was likely soon.[17] Admiral Lynch asked the government whether Chile could fight and win a third war, this time with Argentina's participation, with the

---

[13] Vial, *La sociedad chilena*, 786.
[14] Estado Maior General del Ejército, *Reorganización del Ejército*, 29. On Sotomayor's support for a foreign military mission, see also Quiroga and Maldonado, *El prusianismo*, 36–39.
[15] Díaz, *La campaña del norte*, 15–16.
[16] Generel Carlos Saez Morales, *Recuerdos de un Soldado*, 3 vols., vol. 1, *El Ejército y la política* (Santiago: Biblioteca Ercilla, 1934): 22. Emphasis added.
[17] Vial, *La sociedad chilena*, 785–86; Quiroga and Maldonando, *El prusianismo*, 36.

same improvisations and defects evident in its military system during the previous wars.[18]

The defeat of France in 1870 had left the Prussian/German army without equals and the undisputed model for the Chileans. Germany's spectacular victory inspired a generation of admirers all over the region. Chile remained doggedly tied to the British Royal Navy before and long after its extensive emulation of the German army. Its diplomatic and commercial relations with Germany were thin. Germany's favorable conduct during Second the War of the Pacific helped, but it was the proven strength of Germany's arms that prompted the Chilean decision. A decade into the process, the war ministry pronounced that "in a short time to come the Republic will be able to count on an army organized, equipped and armed in accordance with the models of the best armies of the European continent."[19]

As in the other cases of military emulation that followed, Chile's modernization efforts were concentrated in four major areas: armaments, conscription, officer recruitment and instruction, and general staff organization. Emulation in Chile extended into military logistics and medical services, promotions, retirement, salary regulation and even into superficial matters such as uniforms, marching styles, helmets, parades, and military music.[20] Although this study does not examine it, another area of extensive emulation was military doctrine.[21] Modernization also involved the navy, Chile's pivotal combat arm, even though it receives no attention in this study. More so than in Argentina or Brazil, army military emulation was so extensive in Chile that its imprint was visible in the organization long after the process came to a close.

ARMAMENTS

Prior to 1883 Chile relied mainly on French light armaments, though even before the war the army's artillery were mainly German.[22] The army was equipped with a variety of rifles (mostly French and Belgian), including the 1873 model of the Comblain, Grass, and Chassepot as well as the U.S.-made Winchester. After 1885 and the arrival of the military mission, Germany

---

[18] Cited in Vial, *La sociedad chilena*, 786.

[19] Ministério de Guerra, *Memória*, 1895, 5.

[20] Frederick M. Nunn, *The Military in Chilean History: Essays on Civil-Military Relations, 1810–1973* (Albuquerque: University of New Mexico Press, 1976).

[21] On German doctrinal influences see Genaro Arriagada Herrera, *El pensamiento politico de los militares* (Santiago: Editorial Aconcagua, 1986). See also Quiroga and Maldonado, *El prusianismo*.

[22] Estado Maior General del Ejército, *Historia del Ejército*, 10 vols., vol. 5, *El Ejército en la Guerra del Pacífico: Ocupación de Antofagasta y campaña de Tarapacá, 1879* (Santiago: Estado Maior General del Ejército, 1980):chap. 2.

became the exclusive supplier of arms and equipment for the military up until 1914. There is no evidence to suggest that preference for German arms was a condition or stipulation of the original contract for the military mission, as was the case later in Brazil's dealing with the French. Like all successful arms traders, Germany actively promoted the sale of its arms. It partially financed Chile's arms purchases through German loans – although this occurred long after their military and commercial relationship was well established. Chile's large arms purchases of 1889 and 1890 were also financed by German loans.[23]

An arms purchasing and testing commission, headed by Körner himself, was set up early in the modernization process, with the ostensible purpose of testing and reviewing the quality of arms from different sources and their suitability for the army's needs. Another commission in Europe, was headed by General Estanislao del Canto in 1894, who was in Germany at the same as Argentina's own purchasing commission. The period 1892–1902 marked the peak of Chile's large-scale armaments acquisition and buildup, for both land and naval forces. As discussed later, this was also the time of its historic near-war confrontation and arms race with Argentina. The period, coinciding with a near-war clash with the United States, began with the purchase of one hundred thousand Mauser rifles, in addition to a major acquisition of new Krupp artillery.[24] Over three million Deustche Marks (DM) were spent in 1893 on arms just for the army.[25] By 1895 two million DM were budgeted for arms purchases, and during the 1898 war scare the government approved an emergency budget to equip a standing force of 150,000 men. By the end of the year Chile had contracted 15 million DM in weapons.[26] During this time Chile also began to establish munitions factories and state-owned small-arms manufacturing plants, all with either the technical advice or direction of members of the German mission.

A large fraction of the money spent on armaments during this time period went to purchase new warships for the navy. Chile's naval forces experienced a rapid and extensive expansion between 1890 and 1902, expanding from seventeen warships and two thousand sailors to twenty-nine warships and seven thousand men.[27] For a brief moment in the years prior to the century's

[23] Quiroga, *El prusianismo*, 74; Estado Maior General del Ejército, *Reorganización del Ejército*, 70. Data on the terms of these loans is not available.

[24] Estado Maior General del Ejército, *Reorganización del Ejército*, 213.

[25] Quiroga and Maldonado, *El prusianismo*, 74.

[26] Estado Maior General del Ejército, *Reorganización del Ejército*, 219.

[27] Emílio Meneses Ciuffardi, "Los límites del equilíbrio de poder: la política exterior chilena a fines del siglo pasado, 1891–1902," *Opciones* 9 (May–September 1986): 97. These figures represent all vessels, not just capital warships. See also Emilio Meneses Ciuffardi, *El factor naval en las relaciones entre Chile and los Estados Unidos, 1881–1951* (Santiago: Ediciónes Pedagógicas Chilenas, 1989): especially chap. 3, 78, 104. Meneses, for example, lists Chile as possessing eight capital warships in 1891–02, and nine in 1903–04.

turn, Chile quickly rose as the unrivalred naval power in the hemisphere. By 1908 the three big South American powers rushed to acquire the revolutionary dreadnought warships. But this time Chile's weak, crisis-ridden economy and financial system could no longer support the massive arms purchases, the arms racing of the past.

That Chile equipped its army with German arms may not be surprising in view of the fact that it wanted to modernize its army on the German model, and a German military mission directed this modernization. This makes sense in terms of doctrinal and tactical compatibility, interoperability, training, and instructions. That is to say, that Chile adopts German arms – in the context of hiring a German mission – does not, by itself, constitute persuasive confirmation for the theory of emulation. Yet two points need to be emphasized with respect to Chile's arms acquisition. First, all available evidence suggests that Chile's choice of armaments supplier was not a condition for the military mission. (Though presumably a country's decision to model its military after another presupposes a prior evaluation of the quality of the latter's armaments as well.) Second and more important, Chile's choice of supplier for its naval arms was exclusively Great Britain, not Germany.

The First World War had a tremendous impact on Chile, as it did with all the South American states, because they had become so dependent on Europe, mainly Germany, as the exclusive source of weapons and equipment. The defeat of Germany and the restrictions of the Versailles treaty effectively shut off Chile's principal supplier up until the late 1920s. In the meantime, Chile either experimented with French and United States arms and equipment, or it continued to rely on the now-outdated German weapons it had acquired prior to 1914.

CONSCRIPTION

Chile, like the rest of South America, had adopted the French practice of a small army composed of long-term service officers and conscripts. This system suffered from all the defects and problems that plagued France and everyone else when war came. Chile appears to have been more successful with its prereform rank-and-file recruitment, in contrast to its neighbors. Conscription problems were less grave in Chile. As in Brazil and Argentina, however, the effective size of the army during peacetime fluctuated, and usually remained below the legislated size. Like its neighbors, Chile relied on a combination of volunteers and forced recruitment (*enganche*). Volunteers usually served two to three years, while *enganchados* served five.[28]

In 1900 Chile became the first country in Latin America to adopt a system of universal personal obligatory military service. Chile replicated Germany's decentralized system, whereby recruitment and training took place in zones

[28] Estado Maior General del Ejército, *El Ejército en la Guerra del Pacífico*, 21-22.

of divisional organization. Save for a brief period, the general staff retained full control of conscription. In modeling conscription after the German example, Chile's objective was to create a solid military structure that could be easily and quickly expanded or doubled. Much as in Argentina and Brazil, universal obligatory service was seen as an instrument of nation building, and Prussia was regarded as providing the "enviable splendor" of this example, as the general staff's *Revista Mensual* noted.[29] Yet it was military necessity that led to its adoption.

Reformers within the military had been advocating obligatory service since the early 1890s. Foremost among them was Körner, who understood from the start that modernization was not possible without universal compulsory service. As early as 1891, Körner proposed obligatory service, but one that went beyond the superficial obligatory service practiced in the national guard and militias. He had in mind Germany's long-standing practice, where young males would be incorporated and trained for a fixed, continuous period in the army and its reserves.[30]

The German mission, as a whole, constantly stressed the importance of peacetime preparation and mobilization, all of which depended on having well-trained, combat-ready reserve forces. By the late 1890s it was becoming clear to reformers that modernization was producing "an army without troops," given that the number of volunteers and forced recruits was not keeping up with the rate of organizational and force structure expansion.[31] During the 1898 crisis with Argentina, when the armed forces were mobilized and placed on alert, the need for compulsory military service became more urgent. Körner was able to mobilize some 60,000 conscripts in three phases in the general mobilization of 1898, though he informed the political leadership that the army was not prepared or trained for an immediate armed conflict.[32]

The drafting of the service law began immediately under Körner's direction. Körner, as chief of the general staff, headed a commission that traveled to Europe to study the conscription systems of various countries.[33] The Law of Recruitment and Reserves (Lei de Reemplazos) was submitted to congress in 1899 and approved in early 1900. Chile's conscription system was modeled closely on Germany's, which the general staff's *Memorial del Estado Maior General del Ejército* considered the most "perfected" in the world and "imitated by other countries."[34] It was a decentralized system, whereby

[29] Ministério de Guerra, Estado Maior General del Ejército (EMGE), "El Servicio Obligatorio," *Revista Mensual* 1, no. 3 (April 1899): 65–66.

[30] Vial, *La sociedad chilena*, 794.

[31] Vial, *La sociedad chilena*, 797.

[32] Vial, *La sociedad chilena*, 793.

[33] Ministério de Guerra y Marina, *Memória* (1900), 6.

[34] Chile, Ministério de Guerra, Estado Maior General del Ejército, *Memórial del Estado Maior General del Ejército* 1, no. 5 (June 1899): 130.

the recruitment, incorporation, and training of new conscripts were carried out by each regional military division or zone.[35] There were four such zones of recruitment and instruction initially. As in Germany, conscription came under the jurisdiction of the general staff and was administered at the regional-district level by the divisional field staffs. It was placed under the general war department of the war ministry briefly, but returned to the general staff under the 1906 reorganization. The first class convoked nearly 12,000 recruits. The following year, 1902, nearly 10,000 were incorporated, out of 400,000 registered.

One important difference between the Chilean and German conscription systems is that the latter required a three-year length of service, while Chile experimented with five to eighteen months initially. Military leaders complained about the short period of service, most favoring a two-year length of service.[36] The 1903 class was incorporated for only five months. This, in part, may have been due to the desire to build up as quickly as possible a reserve. Chile also differed in that, in practice, service was not fully obligatory and personal, for it fell disproportionately on the lower classes.[37] Financial restrictions also limited the impact of the law.[38] Rarely did the budget allow for the incorporation of more than 20 percent of the eligible annual contingent, with only an estimated seven to eight thousand men incorporated.[39] Budgetary restrictions also prevented the periodic retraining of enlistees who moved to first- and second-line reserves, as originally envisioned.

The organization of reserve forces closely resembled German practice. Chile adopted Germany's two-tier reserve army system. Service in the line was followed by nine years of service in the first-line reserve forces. The national guard, historically the de facto reserve, was dissolved in 1900. It was replaced by a territorial guard that was modeled after Germany's Landwehr. The territorial guard was to serve as the first-line army's second reserve pool, and was placed under the jurisdiction of the war ministry – as opposed to the justice ministry, which had controlled the national guard. Service in the first-line reserves was followed by fifteen years of service in the territorial guard. Individuals in both categories were required to attend periodic exercises and training sessions. The new conscription system was accompanied by a renewed emphasis on primary instruction in the barracks. For those

---

[35] For a more elaborate discussion on the new conscription system, see Estado Mayor General del Ejército, *Historia del Ejército*, vol. 8, *La Primera Guerra Mundial y su influencia en al Ejército, 1914–1940* (Santiago: EMGE, 1980).

[36] Vial, *La sociedad chilena*, 797.

[37] Nunn, "Emil Körner," 312.

[38] In 1902, out of the 400,000 eligible who registered, only 9,300 were called up for service. The totals for 1902 and 1903 are 4,000 and 6,000 respectively. Source: Estado Maior General del Ejército, *Reorganización del Ejército*, 254.

[39] Vial, *La sociedad chilena*, 794.

individuals not incorporated at all, Chile imitated Germany's national system of *sociedades de tiro* (shooting clubs) where individuals received basic training in shooting and weapons handling.

OFFICER FORMATION AND TRAINING

The war experience revealed not only the shortage of officers, but more important it exposed the near absence of qualified, technically trained officers at all levels. This was particularly true among the middle ranks and noncommissioned officers, namely those officers needed to command the smaller units in battle.[40] Naval commander and war hero, Patrício Lynch, had pointed out these same deficiencies and lamented the overall poor technical competence of the officer corps.[41]

For Chile, much as in Argentina and Brazil, at the heart of the idea to modernize the armed forces and contract a foreign military mission was a call to professionalize the officer corps. The first few years of the German mission were devoted almost exclusively to officer instruction and the organization of a standardized, technically oriented military education system. The German mission inculcated in the Chilean military what was perhaps the essence of Moltke's German military system: continuous study. The members of the original mission were hired primarily as instructors in artillery, infantry, cartography, military history, and tactics. The mission's charge was to create a modern, professional, technically trained officer corps. Körner was appointed subdirector of the Escuela Militar (Military School), then under the direction of the reformer and war veteran, General Emílio Sotomayor. Sotomayor was a major supporter of military emulation and the German mission. Körner's assistant was Major Jorge Boonen Rivera. Boonen Rivera and Körner coauthored several studies and reform proposals, including a compendium on military history. The Escuela Militar, first opened in 1863, was the main officer training school, but many in the hierarchy were not graduates.

Körner and the other German instructors immediately began to revamp the outdated, lengthy curriculum at the school. The extant six-year plan of study contained many nonmilitary courses, described as "encyclopedic" by the general staff.[42] The new, four-year plan of study included more technical instruction for officers of the different combat arms. Körner modernized and expanded the specialized courses for officers in the infantry, engineering, artillery, and cavalry.[43] But he was also critical of overspecialization in the school's curriculum, and insisted that cadets receive training in all

---

[40] Estado Maior General del Ejército, *El Ejército en la Guerra del Pacífico*, 44.
[41] Vial, *La sociedad chilena*, 786.
[42] Estado Maior General del Ejército, *Reorganización del Ejército*, 31.
[43] Vial, *La sociedad chilena*, 788.

three major combat arms.[44] Reflecting his own training in Moltke's philosophy, he favored the formation of well-rounded officers, particularly general staff officers who should have a basic knowledge of the major combat arms. Courses on combined-arms tactics were introduced after 1892. The new plan of study also included courses in tactics, logistics, cartography, and topography, as well as practical training in arms firing and physical fitness.[45]

While continuing his duties at the Escuela Militar, Körner was laying the groundwork for organizing a school for advanced officer instruction, the Academia de Guerra (War Academy). In 1886 the Academia was opened, admitting its first class a year later. The decree authorizing the academy noted that the purpose of the school was "to elevate the level of technical and scientific instruction of army officers, in order that they be able, in case of war, to utilize the advantages of new methods of combat and modern armaments."[46] The principal goal of the War Academy was training captains and lieutenants for service in the general staff. It became the first battleground between the reformers (mostly junior officers) and the old guard of the military, the so-called *viejos tércios*.[47] Körner served as professor of military history and strategy. The teaching staff in 1888 consisted of nine professors, five of whom were German officers. His influence, however, reached far beyond his official duties. He modeled the academy after the Kriegsakademie in Berlin. Like its Berlin counterpart, the war academy had a three-year curriculum, with the third year reserved for only the top students. From this top tier came candidates for general staff service after passing a grueling exam.

Another element of the Prussian/German system that the mission introduced to Chile was thorough examinations at every stage of the officer formation process. This was particularly true in the war academy, where admission, advancement, and graduation involved a series of examinations (usually written by the German staff). The instructional texts at the academy were imported from Germany and translated into Spanish. As in the Kriegsakademie, war games, military history, and the study of specific wars became an integral part of the curriculum. The Franco–Prussian war received extensive study. The general staff would later comment that the "Franco–Prussian War was being analyzed by officers from both nations to draw its lessons and implications that had changed tactical operations."[48]

Körner was critical of the poor level of officer training as well as the lack of primary education for conscripts. By the mid-1890s he turned his

44 Nunn, *The Military in Chilean History*, 76.
45 For an outline of the four-year plan of study see, Estado Maior General del Ejército, *Reorganización del Ejército*, 32–36.
46 Quote cited in Nunn, *Yesterday's Soldiers*, 101.
47 Vial, *La sociedad chilena*, 789.
48 Estado Maior General del Ejército, *Reorganización del Ejército*, 41.

attention to training and instructing the rank and file.[49] Additional schools
and specialized courses of study were organized by Körner and the other
German officers. A year after the War Academy opened, the Escuela de
Clases (School for Non-commissioned Officers) was founded. It offered an
eight-month-long plan of study for sergeants and corporals in artillery and
infantry. Admission was based on an entrance examination. In 1903 specialized schools for the cavalry, engineering, and infantry were opened. By this
time a system of primary education in army-run schools was implemented
throughout the army.[50] A position of inspector general of primary instruction was created to oversee the regimental schools (*Escuelas Primárias*) that
operated in the barracks of every unit.[51]

By the turn of the century, the various military schools had become fully
Prussianized.[52] German was added to the curriculum as a mandatory language. The core teaching staff at the schools, including their directors, consisted mostly of German officers, especially after 1894 when a new, large
mission of thirty-six officers arrived from Germany.[53] In addition, former
students and protégés of Körner were also taking up position in the faculty.
Already by 1891 the Military School was under the control of former students of Körner; by 1895 both the director and subdirector were German
officers.[54] Future directors were either German or graduates of Körner's War
Academy.[55] The various military schools had touches of Prussianism in every
aspect of the operation, particularly with respect to their internal discipline
and curriculum emphasis on practice. Even the uniforms of cadets at military schools were patterned after their German counterparts. Despite the
Germanizing professionalization, flaws in officer recruitment and instruction inevitably persisted well into the new century. One of the top graduates
of the German mission's courses and future war minister, General Carlos Saez
Morales, noted that favoritism in recruitment and admissions persisted. He
criticized the fixation with dress, reviews, and other superficial matters rather
than course work.[56]

Another key element in the Prussianization of the officer corps, and an
integral part of Körner's goal of creating a uniform, professional officer class,

---

[49] See Nunn, "Emil Körner."

[50] The Chilean army had been offering primary instruction to its recruits since the 1840s but
operated irregularly and reached only a fraction of the conscripts. See Estado Maior General
del Ejército, *Reorganización del Ejército*, 83–85.

[51] Estado Maior General del Ejército, *Reorganización del Ejército*, 207–208.

[52] Vial, *La sociedad chilena*, 788.

[53] The German missions after 1895 were not only larger than the original missions, but were
also composed of more senior military officers (captains and lieutenant colonels), and usually
members of the German general staff. On this point, see Vial, *La sociedad chilena*, 790.

[54] Vial, *La sociedad chilena*, 788.

[55] On the extent of Prussianization at the military school, see Vial, *La sociedad chilena*, 788.

[56] Saez Morales, *El Ejército y la política*, 14–15.

was sending Chilean officers to Germany for further instruction and training. These officers were usually top graduates of the Academia de Guerra. Most were incorporated into various regiments of the German Imperial Army for an eighteen-month tour of duty. Others served as military attachés or were members of various commissions. Körner was personally instrumental in securing permission from the Imperial court and Grosser Generalstab to allow Chilean officers to serve in the Imperial Army and attend its military schools. Germany had always been reluctant to permit foreigners into its military schools.

In 1889 the first contingent of Chilean officers left for Germany.[57] As the 1906 reform phase got underway, the largest group of Chilean officers (twenty-seven in all) was sent to Germany. (In 1895, the war department reported Chilean officers being sent to Italy, as well, for instruction.) Between 1895 and 1913 some 130 Chilean officers served in Germany in one capacity or other.[58] They represented the cream of the crop in the Chilean officer corps, and service in Germany usually resulted in faster advancement. Much of the military hierarchy in the 1920s through 1940s was composed of officers who had served in Germany. Coincidently, the majority of officers involved in the political turmoil and military intervention of the mid-1920s had also trained and served in Germany – though no causal implication is intended here since their involvement came by virtue of their position rather than training.[59] The practice of sending officers to Germany for instruction and training came to an end with World War I (though German officers continued to arrive in Chile up to the Second World War).

By 1891 the foundation of a modern army had already been set in critical areas such as officer formation. More significant, the professional and intellectual groundwork was in place for creating a modern high command, but very little was done to organize a modern general staff. The creation of a powerful directing agency would come only after the civil war of 1891.

Military Emulation and the Civil War of 1891

Post-independence Chile distinguished itself from the rest of South America by its long stretch of uninterrupted, stable constitutional rule. This stability was abruptly shattered in 1891. The civil war interrupted, but did not derail, the military emulation already under way. The origins and issues surrounding the civil war need not concern us here. They were partisan-constitutional in

---

[57] Vial, *La sociedad chilena*, 790. The general staff dates the first contingent to 1893, when five Chilean officers were sent to Germany for service and training. See Estado Maior General del Ejército, *Reorganización del Ejército*, 316.

[58] Vial, *La sociedad chilena*, 790.

[59] On this point, see Nunn, *The Military in Chilean History*, chap. 6. See also Nunn, "Emil Körner," 308–09.

nature, and revolved mostly around different interpretations of interbranch prerogatives.[60] The dispute originated in a climate of growing political rivalries, partisan ideological battles, and opposition politics – the same recipe that would haunt Chile nearly a hundred years later in 1973. Its causes, in other words, were unrelated to military emulation or the German mission. The civil war's impact on military modernization, nonetheless, was considerable. First, it divided the armed forces into loyal and rebel factions. Second, it temporarily halted the German mission and its work. Third, though its causes were unrelated to emulation, the civil war's outcome greatly affected the process.

The civil war divided the country into presidential and parliamentary forces; it divided the armed services accordingly. The bulk of the army, especially the hierarchy and old guard in the officer corps, remained loyal to President José Manuel Balmaceda. The navy, and the small contingent of rebel army officers, joined the congressional side, whose rebel forces operated out of the northern provinces. Most of the army officers who joined the congressional side were junior officers and followers of Körner.[61] Körner himself was sympathetic to the congressional cause, and was removed from duty by Balmaceda in early 1891 during a purge of officers considered disloyal.[62] Körner, known to criticize the pace and scope of military reforms, may have fallen victim to this purge.[63] Körner and his disciples, numbering about forty junior officers and cadets, subsequently set sail north to join the congressional forces at their headquarters in Iquique. As far as can be determined, the other members of the German mission remained neutral in the war.[64]

Körner's decision to become an active participant in the civil war – an unprecedented act by a foreign military adviser in the internal affairs of the

---

[60] There are varying interpretations of origins of the 1891 civil war. For a brief, informative review of the historiography, see John R. Bowman and Michael Wallerstein, "The Fall of Balmaceda and Public Finances in Chile: New Data for an Old Debate," *Journal of Inter-American Studies and World Affairs* 24, no. 4 (November 1982): 441–61. On the civil war see, also, Harold Blakemore, *British Nitrates and Chilean Politics, 1886–1896: Balmaceda and North* (London: The Athlone Press, 1974). See also Fernando Bravo Valdivieso, Francisco Bulnes Serrano, and Gonzalo Vial Correa, *Balmaceda y la guerra civil* (Santiago: Editorial Fundación, 1991); Harold Blakemore, "Chile: From the War of the Pacific to 1930," in *Chile since Independence*, ed. Leslie Bethell (Cambridge: Cambridge University Press, 1993): 33–86; Frederick B. Pike, *Chile and the United States, 1880–1962: The Emergence of Chile's Social Crisis and the Challenge to United States Diplomacy* (South Bend: University of Notre Dame Press, 1963): 77–79.

[61] Francisco A. Encina, *Historia de Chile: desde la prehistoria hasta 1891*, 20 vols., vol. 20 (Santiago: Editorial Nascimento, 1952): 230, who estimates that about forty army officers joined Körner. See also Nunn, "Emil Körner."

[62] Nunn, "Emil Körner"; Vial, *La sociedad chilena*; Bravo, Bulnes, and Vial, *Balmaceda y la guerra civil*; Blakemore, *British Nitrates and Chilean Politics*, 191.

[63] Nunn, "Emil Körner."

[64] Bravo, Bulnes, and Vial, *Balmaceda y la guerra civil*, 273.

host country matched only decades later by the actions of Hans Kundt in Bolivia – remains a matter of conjecture.[65] Nunn argues that Körner was "never popular" with Balmaceda, and that Körner perceived the president to be an obstacle to his reform ambitions.[66] In Nunn's view, Körner's decision was based on a cold calculation that a congressional victory would allow him full control over the modernization process.[67] Körner did favor an extensive, rapid modernization program, but it cannot be said that Balmaceda was an obstacle, since he fully supported military reforms.[68] The president, in fact, often acted as a protector and advocate of the reformist officers, who often clashed with the old guard in the military hierarchy.[69] Military modernization was not an issue in contention, though Körner had been critical of the state of affairs, the pace of reforms, and the availability of resources, as Nunn notes.[70] But there is nothing unusual about such disagreements and conflicting demands in any reform setting. Finally, Körner could not have known or predicted the outcome of the civil war. More still, most of the army he was trying to recreate had remained loyal. Modernization was already five years in the making, and would continue into the future even with a presidential victory.

We can outline two likely factors that motivated Körner to side with the rebel cause. First, his disciple and right-hand man in Chile, Boonen Rivera, joined the congressional forces and may have influenced Körner's own decision.[71] The second factor may have been Körner's own frustration and disappointment with the army's old guard, the *viejos tércios*, all of whom had remained loyal but who also opposed extensive, rapid reforms.[72]

Körner and the Rebel Army

The first several months of the civil war was a phony war. The numerically superior presidential forces had the manpower but neither the ships nor the transport infrastructure to bring the war to the north. The rebels, based

[65] Ibid., 273. The other members of the German mission assumed a neutral role in the civil war. Likewise, the German government remained neutral, though the United States suspected that it supported the rebel cause. Dispatches from the U.S. ambassador in Chile, however, claimed that Germany and Britain supported the rebel forces. See *Foreign Relations of the United States*, 1891, cables from Ambassador Patrick Eagan to State Department, especially cable from 14 April, 1891. Only Körner became a participant. Emperor Wilhelm II was perturbed by Körner's actions.

[66] Nunn, *Yesterday's Soldiers*, 103.

[67] Nunn, "Emil Körner," 305.

[68] On this point see, Vial, *La sociedad chilena*; Bravo et al., *Balmaceda y la guerra civil*.

[69] Bravo, Bulnes, and Vial, *Balmaceda y la guerra civil*, 345. See also Vial, *La sociedad chilena*, 789.

[70] Nunn, "Emil Körner," 304.

[71] Bravo, Bulnes, and Vial, *Balmaceda y la guerra civil*, 273.

[72] Vial, *La sociedad chilena*.

in newly annexed Tarapacá province, had the ships but not the force to challenge the south.[73] Körner, then only a lieutenant colonel, was named secretary of the general staff of the rebel forces. But once again his influence and activities reached far beyond his official duties.[74] He single-handedly created and trained a new army from scratch – one that became the skeleton of the post-civil-war national army. He was officially in charge of instruction and training of conscripts, but immediately became the chief architect of the new army's organization.[75] He concentrated first on putting together a solid structure, particularly the officer corps, which could then incorporate, train, and instruct new recruits.[76]

Körner was critical of the rebel army's initial organization into ten infantry battalions and five cavalry squadrons. He proposed a new organization based on three combined arms brigades, with three infantry regiments, an artillery group, an engineering company, and one sanitation group.[77] He introduced one of the signal innovations of the German system, whereby each brigade was to have a field general staff composed of Körner's former War Academy students. Körner instituted the practice of constant drill and rifle-shooting exercises, both new to Chile. Infantry and cavalry units were trained for offensive and defensive combat, with the latter also trained for reconnaissance.[78] He trained his 9,500 strong rebel army to employ open, or dispersed, formations, which proved effective during the civil war.[79] The rebels were successful at acquiring arms, much of it from Germany. They were also successful in pressuring Britain and other countries not to sell ships to the presidential forces.[80] Körner, veteran of the Franco–Prussian war and product of Moltke's system, understood the importance of repeating-rifle fire to battlefield tactics. One of his first measures was to outfit the army with Mannlicher rifles and Krupp cannons.[81] Körner was able to equip nearly half of his men with Mannlicher rifles by mid-1891, which became a decisive factor in the war.

Körner's measures and innovations were resisted by Colonel Estanislao del Canto, named chief of the rebel army.[82] Despite this, Körner was promoted

---

[73] Blakemore, *British Nitrates and Chilean Politics*, 193.
[74] On the rebel army and Körner's activities, see Encina, *Historia de Chile,* vol. 20, 226–35.
[75] Díaz, *La campaña del Norte.*
[76] Bravo, Bulnes, and Vial, *Balmaceda y la guerra civil,* 274.
[77] Encina, *Historia de Chile,* vol. 20, 230–31.
[78] Encina, *Historia de Chile,* vol. 20, 232.
[79] Bravo, Bulnes, and Vial, *Balmaceda y la guerra civil,* 275.
[80] On this point, see Harold Blakemore, "Chilean Revolutionary Agents in Europe, 1891," *Pacific Historical Review* 33, no. 4 (November 1964).
[81] See Blakemore, *British Nitrates and Chilean Politics.*
[82] Del Canto was a political opportunist and more a member of the *viejos tercios* than a reformer. He was named division general after the civil war and was soon after forced into retirement. His difficulties with Körner may also be attributed to his long running personal animosity with Boonen Rivera.

to chief of the general staff, and became one of the key planners and leaders of the rebel forces. Effective command and control of the rebel army and its operations were highly concentrated in his general staff, even though Del Canto was formally the commander in chief. It was Körner who led the rebel forces in the major clashes of the civil war. By August 1891, Körner had masterminded the complete rout of the presidential forces.[83] Aside from possessing a navy, the outnumbered rebels' other advantage were their superior armaments and their leadership.[84] The British minister in Santiago reported to the Foreign Office during the final stages of the civil war that the congressional forces led by Körner and Del Canto were "well-drilled by Körner" and had "routed" the presidential forces who suffered some five thousand casualties.[85] The pro-Balmaceda and opinionated United States ambassador, Patrick Eagan, grudgingly reported that the rebels owed their victory to "superior generalship" and the use of Mannlicher rifles.[86]

What did the rebel victory mean for military emulation? In many ways, the civil war was a mere intermission. Differences in the pace and scale of pre- and post-civil-war phases of military modernization were minimal. To be sure, military emulation benefited from far more favorable institutional and political conditions after the war.[87] Purges of the old guard and loyalist officers smoothed the way internally for reforms. Modernization benefited from the new constellation of political forces. Körner and the rebels were victorious. Reformers were in charge of the top ranks after the war. Körner himself amassed enormous institutional powers. Körner and the reformers now had a rare opportunity to create a national army from scratch and mold it to their own vision. The victorious navy, for its part, benefited most from the civil war's outcome.[88] It was bestowed with a greater degree of institutional autonomy with the creation of a separate ministry of the navy.

[83] On other differences between the two forces, see Blakemore, "Chilean Revolutionary Agents."

[84] Bravo, Bulnes, and Vial, *Balmaceda y la guerra civil*, 279.

[85] Cable from British Legation to the foreign office, 1 September 1891, in *British Documents on Foreign Affairs: Reports and Papers From the Foreign Office Confidential Print*, part I, series D, *Latin America, 1845–1914*, vol. 2, *Chile and Peru, 1865–1891*, ed. George Philip (Bethesda: University Publications of America, 1991).

[86] United States, Department of State, *Foreign Relations of the United States (FRUS) 1891* (Washington DC: Government Printing Office, 1891), 31 August 1891 cable from Eagan to State Department. Up until late August, Eagan had been reporting favorably on the presidential forces, which he predicted would win, often exaggerating their strength while downplaying the size and strength of the rebel forces. He strove to create an unfavorable opinion, in Washington, of the rebel forces, which he described as having "bitter feelings" against the United States, backed by Germany and Britain. See cables from Eagan to State Department, 3 June 1891; 14 April 1891; 31 August 1891, 17; September 1891, in *FRUS, 1891*.

[87] Between 1894 and 1896 alone, roughly 60% of the increase in national expenditures was accounted for by the military. See Bowman and Wallerstein, "The Fall of Balmaceda," 435.

[88] Bravo, Bulnes, and Vial, *Balmaceda y la guerra civil*, 344, 359.

Its officer class remained intact, unlike the army's, and came to be much better paid than army officers.[89] The new government was headed by rebel war hero and legendary naval commander, Jorge Montt.

Change was great in the army. A purge of the old guard was significant. It cleared the way for the German mission and the ambitious plans of the reformers.[90] The purging of the pro-Balmaceda officers, to a limited extent, was a double-edged sword. It created a severe shortage of officers. This, in turn, was a serious obstacle to modernization and expansion. In the immediate post-civil-war period, therefore, there was a renewed emphasis on officer recruitment and instruction.

Körner and the German military mission resumed their work right after the civil war came to an end. The size of the German mission increased. Körner returned to Germany in 1895, and brought back with him a new mission of thirty-six officers – the largest contingent of foreign military officers to come to Chile.[91] Two years later, twenty-seven more German officers arrived. These new missions were key in the full emulation of the German military system.[92] German officers were serving in different advisory and supervisory positions throughout the military, including supervision of military arsenals and factories, supervision of coastal artillery service, and advisory capacity within the war ministry, general staff, and the many reform and armaments commissions. These functions were in addition to their service as instructors, organizers, and directors of the various military academies and specialized schools. Körner – now a Chilean citizen – was promoted to brigadier general and continued as chief of the general staff of the army. He also resumed his teaching functions at the War Academy. Körner's elevated position in the military hierarchy permitted him near-total control of military affairs. This is particularly true because between 1892 and 1906 there was a high degree of centralization of military authority in the general staff.

ORGANIZATION

The post-civil-war period marked the high point of Chile's adoption and consolidation of nearly every aspect of the Prussia/Germany's military organization, doctrine, and technology – from adopting German uniform for the entire army in 1904 to the formal adoption of German war doctrine in 1906. Chile's general staff reported, in 1906, that the country had "resolved to give the army, especially its upper echelons, an organization based on the

---

[89] Bravo, Bulnes, and Vial, *Balmaceda y la guerra civil*, 359. The naval officer corps remained intact also in terms of social class (aristocracy).

[90] Nunn, "Emil Körner," 307. See also, Vial, *La sociedad chilena*, 792; Saez Morales, *Recuerdos de un soldado*, vol. 1, 22.

[91] Nunn, *Yesterday's Soldiers*, 104–06. Nunn provides the names and duties of the German officers who arrived in 1895. Among the officers were individual Danes, Irish, and Swedes.

[92] Nunn, "Emil Körner," 308.

German model."[93] Much later the general staff itself applauded that Chile "copied virtually the entire organization of the Prussian army."[94] The pace and scope of military emulation post-civil-war did not dampen because, as discussed in the next section, new threats emerged.

The post-civil-war period was the high point of Körner's influence, which Saez Morales describes as "indisputable" after the civil war.[95] Körner was looked upon as the guarantor of Chilean victory; his was for the Chileans a "magical name, the guarantor and pillar of the future victory."[96] It is no coincidence that Körner's influence waned after the nonaggression accords between Chile and Argentina in 1902.[97] For the present, he was the most important, almost mythical, figure in the Chilean army. He was occupying its highest rank as chief of the army general staff. Significantly, as in the past, he continued to head all military reform commissions.[98]

During the second and third phases of military emulation, Chile adopted the German system virtually without significant modification.[99] Modernizing emulation reached deeper and farther. The creation and reorganization of the various service departments, especially logistical and health services, were resumed or started anew. Reforms were targeted at the army's internal and combat regulations as well as its territorial organization. Modernization also reached salary, promotions, and retirement regulations. Yet the central focus of reforms during this phase was the restructuring and streamlining of military command and administration and the creation of the all-important general staff.[100] Right after the rebel victory, Körner and the German mission immediately set about to give the army a new command and administrative structure and territorial organization. They began with reorganizing the war ministry in 1893.

The initial step in creating a permanent, more powerful general staff was the 1893–94 military reorganization. Much as in Germany at the time, the intention was to give the general staff control over military affairs in peacetime and wartime, but this was never spelled out formally. The new general staff replaced the powerful inspector general of the army. It was given four main sections: the first was in charge of instruction and discipline, performing essentially the functions of the old inspector general; the second section was in charge of the military schools; the third section was responsible for

[93] Ministério de Guerra, *Memória*, 1906, 5.
[94] Estado Maior General del Ejército, *Reorganización del Ejército*, 337.
[95] Saez Morales, *Recuerdos de un soldado*, vol. 1, *El Ejército y a política*, 22.
[96] Vial, *La sociedad chilena*, 793.
[97] Both Vial and Nunn make this point. Vial, *La sociedad chilena*, 793.
[98] Estado Maior General del Ejército, *Reorganización del Ejército*, 176.
[99] Arriagada Herrera, *El pensamiento*, 74.
[100] On the history of the Chilean general staff, see Pablo Barrientos Gutierrez, *Historia del Estado Maior General del Ejército, 1811–1944* (Santiago: Instituto Geográfico Militar, 1947).

scientific works, including strategic and operational planning and cartography; the fourth was administrative. The field staffs were in the process of being set up.

The new general staff was endowed with much authority and control over military affairs under the 1894 reorganization. But at this stage it was still only a poor copy of Germany's staff system. Its functions and jurisdiction were poorly delineated. It did not, and never would, reach the same level of institutional autonomy and constitutional prerogative over military affairs as did its counterpart. Nonetheless, it was becoming the true brain of the army in terms of being the source of strategic planning, study, and reform proposals. In practice, the general staff (or, more accurately, its chief) enjoyed enormous authority and influence over military affairs between 1892 and 1906. This was the high point of Körner's prestige and acclamation.[101] The general staff became his idea factory.

After the civil war, Chile adopted German organization of the army's higher (divisions and corps) combat formations and force structure. Körner had been critical of the military's existing force structure and territorial distribution. The army was not organized at the level of division or higher. Many units existed in isolation. There was little integration among the combat arms. The exact chain of command in the field was poorly specified. All of this, combined with the fact that the country still did not possess an adequate rail network, made mobilization and uniform preparation difficult. In 1895 the country was organized into five military zones, each consisting of a brigade composed of the three combat arms and a field general staff. The field staffs and the zone commanders were responsible directly to the main staff in Santiago. This system, though, was highly centralized, unlike Germany's which combined central coordination and direction under the Great General Staff, with flexibility and independence of each corps and divisional formations.

Most of the administrative and territorial restructuring was completed by 1897. By this time Chile had begun its historic brinkmanship with neighboring Argentina. Körner's vision had been to create a well-organized military skeleton which would be expandable on short notice with trained, combat ready conscripts. The goal was to have a rapidly deployable force of a hundred thousand.[102] In a new round of reform measures in 1897, each battalion of infantry and regiment of cavalry and artillery was assigned four companies, only two of which were complete. The other two were assigned only officers, with conscripts to be called up in emergencies, the effect of which would be to double the size of Chile's first-line forces.[103] Among the other parts of this reform stage was the creation of coastal

[101] On this point, see Nunn, "Emil Körner." See also, Vial, *La sociedad chilena*, 793.
[102] Quiroga and Maldonado, *El prusianismo*, 46.
[103] Vial, *La sociedad chilena*, 794.

fortifications and the construction of an elaborate rail system geared toward rapid mobilization and concentration of forces. During the post-civil-war decade, rail expenditures accounted for an average of half of the Ministry of Industry's total expenditures.[104]

THE PRUSSIA OF SOUTH AMERICA AND THE THIRD REFORM PHASE

The reforms launched in 1906, the third phase of reforms, brought the Chilean military into closer correspondence with the German system.[105] The War Department declared in 1907 that all the services and aspects of army organization were "based on the German organization to the extent possible."[106] Once again the main targets of reforms were command, administrative and territorial organization, and general staff. Military zones were reorganized, as in Germany, into four highly independent and self-sufficient divisions. Each division had its own services and field staff, and acted independent of the authority or jurisdiction of the other divisions. A rail battalion, under the supervision of the general staff, was attached to each division. Divisional commanders were responsible directly to the war ministry.

The 1906 reforms were designed to approximate Germany's decentralized system. Criticism of the high degree of centralization in the post-civil-war period had been mounting for some time, despite Körner's personal popularity. Officers who favored decentralization argued that centralization was excessive in Chile. They pointed out that in Germany the corps and divisional formations as well as the field general staffs had much greater autonomy.[107] Decentralization was favored by young officers, "*ortodoxos*" as General Saez Morales calls them, who wanted a more exact and thorough emulation of the German system.[108] By 1906 in Chile there were many officers who had served in Germany, and who had come to see the divergence between the Chilean copy and the German original. Saez Morales recounts that "some of these officers studied, with great care, the organization and regulations of the German Army, and their study led them to see the enormous difference which, in this material, existed between our army and the chosen model."[109]

Despite these reforms, Chile's system was still only an imperfect copy of Germany's divisional and command organization. Decentralization went to the extreme. The 1906 reforms weakened central coordination and direction,

[104] Bowman and Wallerstein, "The Fall of Balmaceda," 437–38.
[105] On the 1906 reforms and their impact see firsthand account in Saez Morales, *Recuerdos de un soldado.*
[106] Ministério de Guerra, *Memória, 1907, i.*
[107] Vial, *La sociedad chilena,* 795–96.
[108] Saez Morales, *Recuerdos de un soldado,* 27.
[109] Ibid.

largely through the marginalization of the general staff. The position of inspector general of the army was reinstated in 1904. The reforms increased the power of the war minister. The inspector general became the highest ranking officer, subordinate only to the war minister. He became, in effect, the immediate field commander-in-chief, though Saez Morales notes that the inspector general's power was more limited.[110] "All that occurred in the military fell under the concern [of the inspector general]."[111] The new post was to be the outfit through which the war minister (and president) exercised actual command, though the relationship between the inspector general and the divisional commanders remained confused. Nominally, the military zones, the general staff, and the personnel department were to fall under the inspector general's jurisdiction.

Though its institutional autonomy was increased, the general staff's authority was reduced by the 1906 reforms, in favor of greater autonomy for the military zones and the inspector general.[112] The inspector general presided over the national war council, which consisted of the heads of the various departments of the war ministry including the general staff. Within the council's jurisdiction were military budget, acquisitions, promotions, war planning, maneuvers, and regulations – all functions that would have fallen under the purview of the general staff.[113] The general staff also lost control over weapons procurement, training, and the other military schools. Körner, now brigadier general, occupied the position of inspector general of the army during 1906–10, providing some continuity and central direction. Yet the general staff's organizational power, as measured by the German ideal, was weakened.

The general staff was itself reorganized at this time, "taking as its model the organization of [the general staff] of the German army."[114] General Saez Morales, then a young officer in the general staff, recounts that in 1906 the Chilean general staff "received an organization similar to that of the Great General Staff of Germany."[115] The new general staff replaced several other departments as the central planning organ within the military, including the sole responsibility for studying theatre operations and devising war plans. It now consisted of five departments, though now the essence of its functions was war planning and study. While it may have lost some authority over military affairs to the new inspector general position and national war council, it approximated the German ideal as the central war planning and

---

[110] Saez Morales, *Recuerdos de un soldado*, 28–29.

[111] Estado Maior General del Ejército, *Reorganización del Ejército*, 271.

[112] Nunn, *Yesterday's Soldiers*, 110; Vial, *La sociedad chilena*, 797.

[113] Estado Maior General del Ejército, *Reorganización del Ejército*, 184.

[114] Estado Maior General del Ejército, *Reorganización del Ejército*, 272.

[115] Saez Morales, *Recuerdos de un soldado*, 28.

study body. A rail transportation department was put under its jurisdiction, and it retained control of the war academy.[116] In addition, it was also in charge of conscription, maneuvers, mobilization, and the drafting of reform projects and military regulations. Chile also adopted Germany's two-year, open staff system, whereby regimental service was required at each stage of the advancement process in general staff service.

This phase also brought reforms into two other important areas. A new promotions system was implemented. Among its features was the setting of a maximum age limit that officers could remain in the same grade. This was one way to push out the remaining old guard and provide greater access and upward mobility to the German-trained junior officers.

A major overhaul of the military's internal and combat regulations was also initiated. A long-standing goal of the reformers within the military was to institute a uniform system of instruction and doctrine.[117] This was tackled on two fronts; first and most important through officer formation and second, through uniform internal regulations and war doctrine. The military's regulations were both outdated and eclectic as of 1906. A major push, headed by Körner and Boonen, had been launched after 1901 to translate German and other European military regulations. The process of translating and adopting German military regulations had been under way since the close of the civil war but in piecemeal fashion. Prior to 1897 the army lacked uniform regulations, relying mostly on manuals put together and translated by German-trained young officers, such as the regulations for troop command translated from the German.[118] Nearly all of the new regulations were adopted directly from the German. With the 1906 reforms, General Saez Morales recalls, "we undertook to apply to the letter the German regulations."[119] "The new regulations," observed the war ministry, "were made in conformity with those of the German Army [that we] adopted as a model for our own, adapting its provisions to the laws and decrees that govern us."[120] Chilean reformers kept up with changes introduced in Germany, and adjusted their own practices accordingly. In the case of military regulations, the War Ministry reported a year later that the regulations adopted in 1907 were updated "with the last modifications introduced in the German Army."[121]

---

[116] For a more elaborate discussion of the 1906 reorganization of the general staff, see Barrientos Gutierrez, *Historia del Estado Maior General del Ejército*. Barrientos was a general staff officer.

[117] On this point, see Ministério de Guerra, *Memória, 1901*, annex, 168. See also the *Memória 1907*.

[118] Saez Morales, *Recuerdos de un soldado*, 22.

[119] Saez Morales, *Recuerdos de un soldado*, 29.

[120] Ministério de Guerra, *Memória, 1907*, 6.

[121] Ministério de Guerra, *Memória, 1908*, 9.

The 1906 reorganization was impressive on paper. In reality the 1906 reforms fell far short of the German standard.[122] The reforms were never fully implemented. There were two key factors for its incomplete success. The first was financial. Budgetary constraints was already hampering the full implementation of the new conscription system, which itself was an obstacle to the 1906 reforms. The lack of resources was serious and had a lasting impact on the army's subsequent organizational and technological evolution. The second factor was a shortage of officers to make feasible reorganization and force structure expansion. Since the post-civil-war purges of the officer ranks, Chile had been experiencing a shortage of officers, particularly middle-level and Non-commissioned Officers. Many new combat units created under the 1906 reorganization could not be set up due to the lack of staff and line officers.[123] The entire army experienced a shortage of second lieutenants to fill training positions.[124] Körner himself complained in his 1907 *Memória* that "the lack of qualified officers prejudices in an extraordinary manner the job of the army."[125] His concern with the shortage of officers may in part explain Körner's disagreement with the 1906 reforms. Saez Morales notes that, despite the scope and speed of the military emulation, "it needs to be confessed that our military prestige in this period was based primarily on simple appearances than on real value."[126]

Finally, the 1906 reforms marked a transition of sorts within the military. First, it marked the end of Körner's authority and influence over military affairs. Körner, in fact, opposed much of the 1906 reforms. He argued against the rapid and complete emulation of the German system without modification, and without consideration for Chile's lack of the infrastructural, organizational, and human capacity to sustain such a complex system. In particular, Körner opposed the level of decentralization envisaged by the reform proponents as well as the full emulation of the German model.[127] Other high-ranking officers, though in the minority, opposed the full emulation of the German system and what they considered to be the "slavish emulation" of Germany. Saez Morales criticized the adoption of German

---

[122] Both Nunn and Vial share this assessment of the 1906 reforms. See Nunn, *Yesterday's Soldiers*, 109–11, and "Emil Körner"; Vial, *La sociedad chilena*, 797–98. See also: Saez Morales, *Recuerdos de un soldado*.

[123] Nunn, *Yesterday's Soldiers*, 109.

[124] Ibid.

[125] Quote cited in Nunn, *Yesterday's Soldiers*, 110–11. Körner added in 1909 that "The present complement of army officers, in terms of numbers, does not correspond to the service's needs. In the last few years a number of units have been created in order to provide for the new organization of the army [but] the officer corps has not been augmented in corresponding proportions."

[126] Saez Morales, *Recuerdos de un soldado*, 25.

[127] On Körner's opposition to the 1906 reorganization, see Saez Morales, *Recuerdos de un soldado*, 27–29.

divisional organization, which was too large and cumbersome given Chile's resources. General Indalecio Téllez, future chief of the army, complained that "what harmed us greatly was the reckless tendency that we have in slavishly copying what we believed to be good." He noted that Chileans adopted German regulations and practices "without considering whether or not there are aspects of them that we should or should not adopt. It was German and that's all that mattered. I protested hundreds of times, despairingly, but it was like shouting in a desert."[128]

Despite its inability to replicate fully Germany's Imperial army on South American soil, the imprint from Chile's military emulation was deep. Chile was among the handful of countries in the world to come closest to adopting the German system in entirety. Military historian Alain Rouquié, commenting on Chile's military modernization, noted that the 1906 "reform of the army's organization and internal regulations transformed the Chilean military into a veritable reflection of the German army."[129] Military emulation in Chile transformed it into the "Prussia of South America," as it was being referred to throughout the region. By the first half of the 1890s Chile had emerged as the undisputed dominant military and naval power on the continent. The respected *Army and Navy Journal* of the United States, in an article assessing the relative capabilities of Chile and Argentina during their near-war crisis in 1902, regarded Chile as having an army of a "high state of training," and whose arms and equipment made it "second to none on this side of the Atlantic."[130] Its navy possessed "ships of war of great power and enormous value," similarly having a high state of professional training and discipline that nullified Argentina's advantage in total tonnage.[131] The U.S. minister in Santiago reported to Washington that, "if war breaks out [between Chile and the larger Argentina], I am confident that Chile will find itself on equal footing, at least, with its antagonist. Its land forces are vastly superior in equipment and efficiency, and [with the new warships] it should be able to hold its own at sea."[132]

Victory and expansion in the Second War of the Pacific, together with the internal collapse and military weakness of its main neighbors north and east, had (largely by default) propelled Chile to the top rank on the continent. With large-scale military emulation Chile greatly widened the gap in relative standing and amassed the military power and offensive capabilities that

---

[128] General Indalecio Téllez, quote cited in Arriagada Herrera, *El pensamiento de los militares*, 75.

[129] Alain Rouquié, *The Military and the State in Latin America* (Berkeley: University of California Press, 1981): 78.

[130] "Chile and Argentina," *Army and Navy Journal* 39, no. 18 (4 January 1902): 446.

[131] Ibid. One of Chile's main warships, the *Esmeralda*, had more gun power per ton than any other ship in its class in the world.

[132] Quote cited in Meneses Ciuffardi, "Los limites," 114–15.

would allow it to conduct an offensive, multifront war. Chile managed to organize a large and impressive military system. In 1920 its army numbered 24,000 strong, giving it a ratio to population of 6 per 1,000.[133] The armed forces, however, accounted for a staggering 30 percent of the national budget.

EXPLAINING MILITARY EMULATION IN CHILE, 1885–1914

How can we explain why Chile adopted military emulation and why it imitated Germany? Additionally, how can we account for the timing, pace, and scale of its military emulation? This section's primary objective is to elaborate the neorealist explanation for Chile's military emulation. It dissects the various aspects of Chile's military emulation process – timing, pace, scale, and phases – during this time period, and assesses the degree to which the findings corroborate the predictions of the theory of emulation. I argue that only neorealism's theory of emulation can account for Chile's military emulation and its variance.

As discussed in Chapter 1, this study does not evaluate and compare competing explanations of military emulation. There are some aspects of Chile's military emulation process that give surface credence to social theory accounts of emulation as a cultural act. Chile conquered its neighbors and longtime foes in 1883. Despite its victory, it moved quickly to remake its military system by hiring a large German military training mission in 1885. At first this is puzzling. We do not expect victors to reform and remake their armed forces. Victors like Chile normally lack the incentive to modernize their armed forces. Victory creates internal incentives to stand pat, to preserve the prevailing institutions and practices that have proven effective. Yet, if emulation is culturally driven, we would expect continual emulation, unaffected by victory or defeat, as countries upgrade their practices and symbols of statehood to fit changing global norms. Why wait a decade and a half after the German model was proved superior? There is nothing in the words and actions of Chile's political and military leaders to support a cultural interpretation of military emulation. Variants of social theory cannot account for the timing, pace, and scope of Chile's emulation. Domestic explanations are equally incapable. External security considerations drove Chile's emulation.

Chile's victory was pyrrhic, for war and victory gave rise to new security challenges. Postwar Chile was less safe. War and victory set in motion a series of adverse events, and gave rise to an array of hostile forces, which it neither intended nor could control. Victory came at a high cost. The army and navy suffered extensive human and material losses. The Chilean fleet was battered, its main ironclad warships receiving extensive damage in several notable sea battles. Losses were substantial for the army too, especially in the final campaigns of the war. The combined naval and land assault during

---

[133] Nunn, *Yesterday's Soldiers*, 190.

the Arica battle was a costly victory for both arms. The war experience also had revealed many defects in military organization. The prosecution of the war was marked by improvisation, administrative disorganization, breakdown in the chain of command, and incompetent leadership on the battlefield.[134] Even while Chile was still at war, political and military leaders began to voice the need for modernization and professionalization of the military.[135]

The main purpose of the remainder of this chapter is to detail Chile's changing threat levels, corresponding to the timing, pace, and scale of its military emulation. The discussion begins with an examination of Chile's geopolitical situation, assesses the repercussions of the Second War of the Pacific, and analyzes its external balancing options.

CHILE'S PERSISTENT VULNERABILITY

Chile's decision to invest in large-scale military emulation was a response to external threats to its national security. The timing of its emulation, and each of its distinct phases, corresponded to steep, adverse changes in its external security environment. Chile's military emulation process was intense as it was extensive – far more so than any of its neighbors. For the theory of emulation, this rapid pace and vast scale is to be expected given the proximity, persistence, and scale of the military threats arrayed against it.

Nineteenth-century Chile was a case study in how the pressures of an anarchic international system condition the internal evolution and external behavior of states. Chile was the closest thing South America had to Prussia in terms of grand strategy and geopolitics. It was first among its neighbors to establish durable central authority under a unitarian constitutional order.[136] Chile was also an activist state from early on, one that directly and indirectly fostered the husbanding of the productive bases of national power. It was first to organize a standing national army, in contrast to the irregular forces and warlord militias of neighbors like Argentina.[137] It was small, exposed,

---

[134] On the military's own assessment of its performance and condition during and after the Pacific war, see Ministério de Guerra, Estado Maior General del Ejército, *Historia del Ejército*, vol. 6, *El Ejército en la Guerra del Pacífico: campañas de Monquegua, Tacna y Arica, Lima, la Sierra, Arequipa, y término de la guerra* (Santiago: Estado Maior General del Ejército, 1980); and *Historia del Ejército*, vol. 5, *El Ejército en la Guerra del Pacífico: ocupación de Antofagasta y campaña de Tarapacá, 1879* (Santiago: Estado Maior General del Ejército, 1980).

[135] Vial, *La sociedad chilena*, 785–88.

[136] Arthur A. Stein, "Conflict and Cohesion: A Review of the Literature," *Journal of Conflict Resolution* 20, no. 1 (March 1976): 143–72.

[137] For a discussion of nineteenth-century civil-military relations in Chile, see Nunn, *The Military in Chilean History*; North, *Civil-Military Relations*. See also Blakemore, "Chile," in Bethell, ed., *The Cambridge History of Latin America*, 33–86; Simon Collier, "Chile: From Independence to the War of the Pacific," in Bethell, ed., *Cambridge History of Latin*

and surrounded on all sides by enemies. Disputes over ill-defined borders and conflicting territorial claims poisoned relations with all three principal rivals, Peru, Bolivia, and Argentina. From the start it faced a multifront war problem.

Chile, in other words, was perennially insecure. Its compact size, lack of resource self-sufficiency, absence of allies, and geographic exposure generated predictable patterns – from the standpoint of neorealism – in its national security behavior and military policy.[138] Two themes dominated Chile's external relations and grand strategy: fear of encirclement and vulnerability to attack, primarily from the seas.[139] The singular objective of its diplomacy was preventing an encircling alliance. States that are similarly situated as Chile will devote close and sustained attention to the relative size and effectiveness of their military systems. Their military doctrines emphasize preemption, offensive action, and mobile forces. This, in turn, means that national safety and physical security can only be guaranteed by the strength of arms. In both Pacific wars, Chile struck first, taking the fight to its enemies.

Chile, thin and compact, was vulnerable and easily conquered. Its geography was its biggest strategic liability. Nineteenth-century Chile was geographically an altogether different country than Chile today.[140] It really was small and compact, in both territory and population, prior to 1883. Its population of two and a half million in 1885 was dwarfed by that of its neighbors. It resembled a city-state, long and narrow. The country was confined to the central third of its claimed national territory up to 1883, stretching from just south of the present-day Antofagasta to Concepción in the south. Its main population and production centers were concentrated in the central valley region, the heartland between the port city of Valparaíso and Concepción and comprising a radius of about two hundred miles. The central valley itself was no more than forty-five miles across. Thus, Chile's vital centers were exposed by land and sea. Its concentration and confinement between ocean and mountains made it practically indefensible. Domínguez

---

America, 1–32. See also *Chile Since Independence,* ed. Leslie Bethell (Cambridge: Cambridge University Press, 1993); Simon Collier and William F. Sater, *History of Chile, 1808–1994* (New York: Cambridge University Press, 1996); Alain Rouquié, *The Military and the State in Latin America* (Berkeley: University of California Press, 1981).

[138] On the relationship between a state's strategic setting and its national security behavior, see Barry Posen, *The Sources of Military Doctrine: Britain, France, and Germany Between the World Wars* (Ithaca: Cornell University Press, 1984).

[139] On Chile's diplomatic history and national security concerns, see Robert N. Burr, *By Reason or Force: Chile and the Balancing of Power in South America, 1830–1905* (Berkeley: University of California, 1965). See also Emilio Meneses Ciuffardi, "Coping with Decline: Chilean Foreign Policy during the Twentieth Century, 1902–1972," Ph.D. diss., Oxford University Press (1988); Mário Barros, *Historia diplomática de Chile, 1541–1938* (Santiago: Ediciónes Ariel, 1970).

[140] On Chile's geography, see Gilbert J. Butland, *Chile: An Outline of its Geography, Economics, and Politics* (Westport: Greenwood Press, 1981).

suggests that one way to think about threat levels is the number of frontiers along which war is possible.[141] War was possible on all sides, maritime and terrestrial. As the war with Spain illustrated, it was vulnerable to seaborne attack; both wars against the Peruvian–Bolivian federation were primarily maritime affairs. Thus, a well maintained and powerful navy had been the pivotal component of its grand strategy. Command of the seas was as critical to successful prosecution of war as it was to national survival.

To be sure, Chile's geographic exposure was not absolute.[142] It benefited from some advantages of geography – as long as its enemies did not possess power projection capabilities to overcome them. The Andes mountain chain, which stretched unbroken the length of Chile's territory, was a formidable natural barrier. The chain increased in altitude from the central to the northern third of the territory. In the northern portion bordering Argentina (near the Puna de Atacama) and the Atacama desert, the Andean peaks soar above fifteen thousand feet. The Andes suddenly taper off at the northern portion of the Atacama desert, where Chile shares borders with Bolivia and Argentina. Unlike the southern third of its territory, the northern border is open desert.

The Andes provided a defensive barrier, but the independence wars had proven that the *cordilleras* were not impassable. More still, the Andes themselves became the object of bitter dispute between Chile and Argentina, old rivals who shared the range as natural border. The open desert bordering historic enemies Peru and Bolivia was more liability than advantage. Even more worrisome was the country's maritime exposure. For a country so heavily dependent on commerce, its main port city of Valparaíso and entrance into the central valley had few natural defenses. The port city was razed by the Spanish fleet's bombardment during the 1865–66 war with Spain. Bolivia and Peru possessed substantial naval capabilities prior to 1883 (with Peru, in fact, considered the dominant naval power in the region). Such defensive liabilities explain why Chile was so sensitive to the regional naval balance and favored a well-organized and equipped navy. The war ministry put it succinctly in 1885: "Chile, because of its geographic location and conditions, needs, more so than other countries, a powerful navy that will serve not only to guarantee its autonomy, but also to give life and stability to its commerce."[143]

THE ABSENCE OF ALLIES

The vigor and alacrity with which Chile moved to modernize its military forces can be explained by the dire circumstances it faced during and immediately after the Pacific War: encirclement and threats of war by

[141] Professor Jorge I. Domínguez, Harvard University, comments to author on an earlier draft.
[142] Butland, *Chile*, 2.
[143] Ministério de Guerra, *Memória, 1885*, 7.

declared enemies, on one hand, and the absence of effective external alliance options on the other. Chile was surrounded by powerful enemies, Argentina, Peru, and Bolivia. Its external balancing options were as limited as they were unreliable. Consequently, the absence of credible allies, in an environment where encirclement was a continual possibility, had a profound effect on security thinking and military planning.[144]

Chile anchored two major, interlaced balance-of-power subsystems on the continent – the Andean and Pacific subsystems, whose core members also included Peru, Bolivia, Colombia, Ecuador, and Argentina. It derived partial, but undependable, relief from the fact that it was part of two interlocking subregional power balances, or security subcomplexes.[145] The Pacific system, comprising primarily Chile, Bolivia and Peru, was marked by constant instability (fueled in large measure by internal instability in Chile's neighbors) and crosscutting antagonisms. The geopolitical consequences of the collapse of Iberian rule and the independence wars affected Chile and everyone else in the region.[146] Chile repeatedly clashed with Colombia and Peru over the territorial integrity of Ecuador.[147] Conflicting territorial claims poisoned relations between Chile and Peru, while the latter pursued political union with Bolivia. Thus encircled by enemies with pretentions to confederacy, Chile developed an early interest in the territorial integrity of its neighbors, even though the relationships were frequently tumultuous. It vigorously opposed any efforts at territorial union between Peru and Bolivia.[148] Chile's strongman, Diego Portales, warned that "united, these two states will always be more powerful than Chile in all ways and circumstances."[149] By the 1870s the Pacific and Andean subsystems had merged into one.

---

[144] Meneses Ciufardi, "Los limites." See also his important study, Meneses Ciuffardi, "Coping With Decline," chap. 1.

[145] Barry Buzan, "Security Complexes in Structural and Historical Perspective," in Brian L. Job, *The Insecurity Dilemma: National Security of Third World States* (Boulder: Lynne Rienner, 1992): 167–90.

[146] See the collection of essays in *The Cambridge History of Latin America*, vol. 3, ed. Leslie Bethell (Cambridge: Cambridge University Press, 1986).

[147] Paradoxically, the very weakness of these neighbors constituted a security problem for Chile. Peru's post-independence years were marked by a high degree of political and geographic fragmentation and *caudillo* warfare. The same story was repeated in Bolivia. For Chile, another source of concern with the domestic affairs of its neighbors was that Bolivia and Peru openly supported and harbored exile forces that wanted to overthrow the central government in Santiago.

[148] The two classic works by Burr on Chilean and regional diplomatic history provide an excellent account of this point. See Robert N. Burr, *The Stillborn Panama Congress: Power Politics and Chilean-Colombian Relations During the War of the Pacific* (Berkeley: University of California Press, 1962), and *By Reason or Force*.

[149] Quote cited in Heraclio Bonilla, "Peru and Bolivia From Independence to the War of the Pacific," *The Cambridge History of Latin America: From Independence to 1870*, vol. 3 Leslie Bethell, ed., (Cambridge: Cambridge University Press, 1985): 569.

In the span of forty years Chile fought three major international wars, two against a coalition of its Pacific neighbors. The First War of the Pacific (1836–39) was precipitated by commercial rivalry and trade wars with its northern neighbors.[150] The underlying cause of the war was Chile's fear of the newly created, albeit artificial, confederation between Peru and Bolivia declared in 1835–36. Despite early battlefield setbacks and inferior numbers, Chile defeated the confederate forces (who were also opposed by northern Peruvian rebels) and occupied Lima, Peru's capital.[151]

Chile was again at war by the time the United States was embroiled in its own civil war. In 1865–66 Spain sought to take advantage of the United States's distraction with a blundering attempt at imperial restoration. The Spanish threat temporarily overrode the mutual hostility that simmered among the Andean countries. Chile was joined by its otherwise historic rivals Ecuador, Bolivia, and Peru, though the bulk of the fighting was done by Chile and Peru. Spain was rebuffed, but Chile suffered heavy costs. The Spanish fleet nearly destroyed Valparaíso.

The war with Spain had two major consequences for Chile. The war spurred Chile to launch a military buildup, particularly in the areas of coastal defense, naval modernization, and fortification. More important, it spurred the creation of a large, blue water navy.[152] Second, the war with Spain soured Chile's relations with the River Plate powers as well as with the United States. Chile had repeatedly asked Brazil, Argentina, and Uruguay – who at the time were warring against Paraguay – to close their ports to the Spanish fleet which, Chile believed, Spain was using as a base of operations and resupply. The war's main impact on Chile's foreign affairs was in its relations with the United States.[153] During the war Chile asked the United States to invoke the Monroe Doctrine. Ironically, Chile had never supported the Monroe Doctrine, which it viewed as a pretext for U.S. intervention and hemispheric hegemony.[154] Relations between the two countries were never good since the days of independence. The nonintervention of the United States raised Chile's distrust.

Chile's traditional fear of encirclement was compounded by the fact that it lacked any effective external balancing options. Its commercial and military ties with Britain, and later Germany, did not translate into actual or promised

---

[150] On the First War of the Pacific see Collier, "Chile."

[151] For a brief synopsis of the war, see Nunn, *The Military in Chilean History*, 46–50.

[152] On the history of the Chilean navy, and naval modernization and emulation, see Emilio Meneses Ciuffardi, *El factor naval en las relaciones entre Chile y los Estados Unidos, 1881–1951* (Santiago: Ediciónes Pedagógicas Chilenas, 1989), and "Los limites"; Robert Scheina, *Latin America: A Naval History, 1810–1987* (Annapolis: Naval Institute Press, 1987); Philip D. Somervell, "Naval Affairs in Chilean Politics," *Journal of Latin American Studies* 16, no. 2 (November 1984): 381–402.

[153] On this point, see Pike, *Chile and the United States.*

[154] Pike, *Chile and the United States,* 24–25.

military backing – though there are grounds to view such ties as Chile's effort to secure diplomatic backing and neutralize the United States or other hostile great powers.[155] This fact was made painfully clear during its clash with the United States during the *Baltimore* incident and again during the 1898–1902 war scare with Argentina, when both Germany and Britain backed away from declaring any support for Chile.

Chile was not entirely without external balancing options. The problem was the reliability and military value of these options. Brazil, Ecuador, and Colombia were the only realistic options. Long-running antagonism and territorial clashes between Peru, on one hand, and Ecuador and Colombia on the other, made the latter pair natural options for Chile. Indeed, it cultivated close ties with Ecuador. (It would later even send military training missions to both.) Yet Ecuador and Colombia combined were *quantité négligeable*. Chile's only hope for external relief – Brazil – was largely fictional, given the military disrepair of the South American giant during the last two decades of the century. As with Ecuador and Colombia, the Brazil option was a byproduct of the "enemy of my enemy is my friend" dynamic, since they shared Argentina as an historic enemy. Their relations since the early post-independence years are often described as a sort of unwritten alliance, what Valdão referred to as "an alliance without treaty."[156] Relations were close and cordial.[157] Though commercial and other links between them were nonexistent, more brought them together than separated them. Both were isolated on the continent. Both had ongoing border disputes with Peru and Bolivia, which forced their adversaries to consider the reactions of the other when confronting one of them. Chile could and often did play the "Brazil card" when dealing with its Andean neighbors. The Brazil alliance option was effective as long as Argentina remained disunited and militarily weak.

The high point of the Chilean–Brazilian relationship came right before and during the Second War of the Pacific. Brazil alerted Chile to the 1873 secret treaty being negotiated among Bolivia, Peru, and Argentina.[158] Chile turned

---

[155] Meneses Ciuffardi, "Los limites." See also Warren Schiff, "German–Latin American Relations: The First Half of the Twentieth Century," *Journal of Inter-American Studies and World Affairs* 22, no. 1 (February 1980): 109–17.

[156] Alfredo Valdão, *Brasíl e Chile na época do Império: amizade sem exemplo* (Rio de Janeiro: Livraria J. Olympio Editôra, 1959): 85.

[157] On Chilean–Brazilian relations see: Juan José Fernandes, *La República de Chile e el Imperio del Brasil: historia de sus relaciones diplomáticas* (Santiago: Editorial Andres Bello, 1959); Valdão, *Brasíl e Chile*; Burr, *By Reason or Force*, and *The Stillborn Panama Congress*; Ron L. Seckinger, "South American Power Politics During the 1820s," *Hispanic American Historical Review* 56, no. 2 (May 1976): 241–67.

[158] Juan José Fernandez Valdés, "El tratado secreto peruano-boliviano de 1873 y la diplomacia brasileña," *Boletin de la Academia Chilena de la Historia* 23, no. 55 (1956); Barros, *Historia diplomática de Chile*, chap. 10.

to Brazil to secure a "true and sincere alliance," as the Chilean representative in Rio de Janeiro put it.[159] Brazil declined a formal alliance, but it pressured Peru and sent warnings to Buenos Aires. Nonetheless, Brazil's lukewarm response to Chile's initiative in 1874 demonstrated to *La Moneda* the limits of Brazilian support.[160]

The tacit alliance with Brazil proved ineffectual in the years Chile most needed it – the late 1880s and 1890s period when security threats mounted. Brazil's military power languished after the Paraguayan war, and by the mid-1880s it was engulfed in internal political turmoil. Cordial relations alone could not make up for Brazil's severe military weakness. After the 1889 military coup in Brazil, Chile effectively lost Brazil as a potential military ally. First, the ouster of the Brazilian emperor, whom the Chileans considered a personal friend, effectively sealed any hopes Chile may have had. Second, the new republican government in Rio de Janeiro inaugurated a radically different foreign policy, one of detente with Argentina. Third, Argentina's unification and military modernization changed the strategic balance. Relations between the two Platine neighbors improved so much that by early 1890s there were rumors in the region of an impending triple alliance among Brazil, Argentina, and Peru directed against Chile.[161] The British minister in Santiago observed that "Chile now fears lest the common interests which have united her with Brazil should disappear under the new influences at Rio de Janeiro and lest also the late Empire should be divided into three or four independent states none of which for years to come could be a useful ally to Chile. It is this feeling of isolation and anxiety as regards the future which predominates in Chile."[162]

THE SECOND WAR OF THE PACIFIC AND ITS AFTERMATH

A few short years after the war with Spain, Chile was again at war. The Second War of the Pacific (1879–83) was precipitated by the same old disputes and confederation between archrivals Bolivia and Peru. Its consequences reverberated throughout the continent, and prompted Chile's military modernization.

The immediate cause of the war were efforts by Bolivia and Peru to hamper Chilean commerce, including the seizure of its profitable mining enterprises across the border in the Bolivian and Peruvian provinces of Antofagasta

---

[159] Quote cited in Fernandes Valdés, "El tratado secreto," 12.

[160] Fernandes Valdés, "El tratado secreto," 13.

[161] Michael G. Varley, "The Aftermath of the War of the Pacific: A Study in the Foreign Policy of Chile, 1891–1896," Ph.D. thesis, Cambridge University (1969): 38.

[162] British Minister Kennedy to Foreign Office, in Varley, "The Aftermath of the War," 33.

FIGURE 4.1. The Pacific Subsystem and Chilean Expansion, 1879.

and Tarapacá.[163] War had been in the making since 1873, when Peru and Bolivia signed a secret treaty directed against Chile. Argentina was a reputed signator to the pact, adding a new and more ominous element. For Chile, fear of complete encirclement had finally materialized. Its immediate response to the secret treaty was a naval armaments buildup to bring it into parity with Peru's navy. To neutralize Argentina, Chile approached Brazil in 1874 for a formal treaty.[164] Though no formal alliance treaty with Brazil resulted, the uncertainty over how Brazil would react appeared sufficient reason to prevent Argentina's participation. Another factor keeping Argentina on the sidelines was Peru's fear of the ramifications of a Chilean–Brazilian alliance for its interests in the Amazon basin bordering Brazil.[165]

Chile's military strategy emphasized preemption, offensive action, and combined arms. It was first to mobilize and deploy its forces, taking the war immediately to Bolivian and Peruvian territories. It adopted combined arms strategies, employing naval and ground forces to rout its allied foes and capture enemy territory despite some early battlefield setbacks. By mid-1880 the war was militarily decided, though it was not until 1883–84 that Peru and Bolivia finally succumbed. The Chilean army once again occupied Lima. A formal peace treaty (the Treaty of Ancón) was signed with Peru in 1883, and an uneasy truce signed with Bolivia in 1884. Chile thus remained in a technical state of war with Bolivia until 1904, when the latter finally relented to Chilean terms.

Chile dictated the terms of surrender and the postwar settlement. In addition to financial reparations exacted on both, it annexed Peru's Tarapacá and the Bolivian littoral province of Antofagasta, which ever since deprived Bolivia of access to the sea. Both territories were home to large U.S. and British mining operations. Under the terms of the Treaty of Ancón, Peru ceded Tarapacá in perpetuity. In addition, it ceded the provinces of Tacna and Arica, immediately north of Tarapacá, for ten years, after which a plebiscite was to be held to determine sovereignty. Arica was eventually annexed, and Tacna restored to Peru only in 1929. Chile suddenly grew by a almost one-third, and so did its national defense needs. Antofagasta province alone added over 60,000 square miles of territory and some 200 miles of coastline. The Second War of the Pacific brought substantial booty to Chile. It was a very profitable war for Chile.[166] The new threats engendered by the war spurred military emulation, while the war booty financed it.

---

[163] On the causes of the War of the Pacific, and its diplomatic and military aspects, see: Barros, *Historia diplomática de Chile*; William F. Sater, *Chile and the War of the Pacific* (Lincoln: University of Nebraska Press, 1986); Luís Ortega, "Nitrates, Chilean Entrepreneurs, and the Origins of the War of the Pacific," *Journal of Latin American Studies* 16, no. 2 (1984): 381–402. On Bolivia and Peru, see Bonilla, "Peru and Bolivia."

[164] Fernandez, "El tratado secreto." See also Burr, *By Reason or Force*, 129, and *The Stillborn Panama Congress*, 30.

[165] Burr, *By Reason or Force*; Fernandez, "El tratado secreto."

[166] Bowman and Wallerstein, "The Fall of Balmaceda," 446.

The genesis of Chile's large-scale military emulation thus lies in the Second War of the Pacific. The war and its aftermath spurred modernization in four interrelated ways. First, the war revealed serious flaws in military organization. While its military may have been better organized relative to its neighbors, in absolute terms the military suffered from defects and was incapable of meeting its new missions. Second, the war's aftermath increased its insecurity and defensive needs, both from the standpoint of military defense of the newly acquired territories as well as the political isolation that resulted from conquest. Individually, Chile's neighbors did not present an immediate military threat right after the war. But its defeated foes continued openly to contemplate revanchism. A decade after losing the war and recovering from internal turmoil, both countries began to rebuild and modernize their military forces. Indeed, starting in the mid-1890s, both countries sought to obtain German military missions.[167] In addition, soon after the war they began to canvass regional and international support to build an anti-Chilean coalition.[168] Third, new threats emerged right after the war, as Chile found itself in near-war crises with Argentina and the United States. The immediate military threat came, not from neighbors, but from the United States and some of the European great powers. Chile's conquest and annexation upset the commercial interests of the United States, Britain, and France.

The conduct of the war revealed many defects in military organization, prompting scattered efforts at reform and improvisation in the midst of battle. Chile fought and won the Second Pacific War with a broken army. The severity of the problems led to initial battlefield setbacks. Only the greater incompetence and disorganization of its numerically superior foes saved Chile from disgrace. It fought the war with an army characterized by improvisation, administrative chaos, breakdown in the chain of command, and poor operational leadership.[169] General Francisco Javier Diaz noted that "despite the triumph of 1879, the Chilean army suffered from grave deficiencies, which were evident in the absence of an optimal state [of readiness] to confront the contingencies that arose from the war."[170]

---

[167] Peru and Bolivia hired foreign military missions to direct modernization. Both first attempted unsuccessfully to hire a German mission. Bolivia's first known attempt was an 1894 unsuccessful request for a French mission. It hired a handful of individual German instructors on private contracts in 1901. A formal German mission arrived in 1910. Peru turned to the French in 1896.

[168] Meneses Ciuffardi, "Coping with Decline," chap. 1.

[169] On the military's own assessment of the military during and after the Pacific war, see Ministério de Guerra, Estado Maior General del Ejército, *Historia del Ejército*, vol. 6, *El Ejército en la Guerra del Pacífico: campañas de Monquegua, Tacna y Arica, Lima, la Sierra, Arequipa, y término de la guerra* (Santiago: Estado Maior General del Ejército, 1980), and *Historia del Ejército*, vol. 5, *El Ejército en la Guerra del Pacíifico: ocupación de Antofagasta y campaña de Tarapacá, 1879* (Santiago: Estado Maior General del Ejército, 1980).

[170] Quote cited in Quiroga and Maldonado, *El prusianismo*, 38.

Sater, in his unflattering study of the military during the Pacific War, counters the widespread myth that Chile had a well-prepared military going into the war.[171] Chile's army suffered from extensive defects: incompetent leadership, nonexistent supply and medical services, severe recruitment problems. A major problem during the war was the poorly delineated chain of command, which many commanding officers wanted to reform.[172] Chile's military and political leaders may not have fully agreed with Sater's scathing assessment, but they acknowledged that flaws existed. Right after the war, they moved to correct them by commissioning an internal study to analyze the military's battlefield and organizational performance. The goal was to suggest reforms in light of the changed external security situation.[173] The study concluded that Chile needed a peacetime military that was well organized and combat ready, with a trained reserve, a general staff for planning and study, modern instruction, new regulations, and modern armaments.[174]

The second major factor prompting large-scale modernization was the need to hold and defend the spoils of war. The acquisition of Antofagasta, Tarapacá, and Tacna–Arica enlarged Chile's national territory by a third. Chile also occupied other stretches of territory, the most significant being the Puna de Atacama bordering along Antofagasta on the Argentine side. The strategic result was that Chile's military needs increased with territorial expansion. Territorial conquest thus imposed additional demands on a military already overstretched and poorly organized. The conquered territories, rich in nitrates and other minerals, represented an enormous economic boon and financial windfall to Chile. Overnight, Chile monopolized world production of nitrates and copper. In 1890, revenues from nitrates exports accounted for 52 percent of the government's total.[175] Financing for modernization would come from the very same territories the military had to defend. The real problem for Chile was that defense of the territories did not entail a simple task of fending off its dismembered neighbors, but warding off the United States and European great powers intent on rolling back Chile's gains.

Third, the conquered territories became a double-edged sword for Chile. Their legal status was undefined, and neither foe accepted dismemberment. The annexation of the territories created the same military and diplomatic problems for Chile that the acquisition of Alsace–Lorraine created for

---

[171] Sater, *Chile and the War of the Pacific.*
[172] Sater, *Chile and the War of the Pacific,* 35–36.
[173] Ministério de Guerra, *Reorganizacíon del Ejército,* 17.
[174] Ministério de Guerra, *Reorganizacíon del Ejército,* 17–18.
[175] Blakemore, "From the War of the Pacific to 1930," 41. See also Bowman and Wallerstein, "The Fall of Balmaceda." The war ministry's own calculation on the percentage of nitrates in national revenues was in 1880: 5%; 1883: 23%; 1886: 24%; 1889: 39%; 1890: 49%. See Ministério de Guerra, Estado Maior del Ejército, *Historia del Ejército,* vol. 6, *El Ejército en la Guerra del Pacifico, companias de Moquegua, Tacna y Arica, Lima, la Sierra, Arequipa y Término de la guerra* (Santiago: Ministerio de Guerra, 1980): 381.

Germany after 1870, as one Brazilian war minister put it in 1918.[176] Chile's conquests alarmed her neighbors as well as gave them common cause against her.[177] Anti-Chileanism was continent wide, and the fear of a coalition to contain Chile and restore the prewar territorial status quo preoccupied Chilean policy from 1883 to 1930.[178] Though it feared the real possibility of revanchism by Peru and Bolivia, the conquered territories caused serious problems for Chile's diplomatic relations. Their dispute heightened Chile's continental isolation and vulnerability.[179] In the meantime, one of the many complications that would arise over this territory was Bolivia's decision in 1889 to cede to Argentina part of its territory, Puna de Atacama, then occupied by Chilean troops, as incentive to win Argentine backing against Chile.

From the close of the war up until the mid-1920s Bolivia and Peru launched a dogged international campaign to win support for their cause and orchestrate international pressure against Chile. Argentina was a natural and receptive audience for Bolivia and Peru. It capitalized on Bolivia's hopes by pulling it under its political and economic sway. In the decades after the war, Argentina was an unrelenting interloper in their dispute, and it took up the cause of Bolivia and Peru. Thanks to Bolivia's desperate generosity, it had real land to fight over. This was a major flashpoint during the two decades after the war. At every opportunity Argentina demanded Chile relinquish the occupied territories. More problematic from Chile's standpoint, Argentina led the regional call to make compulsory arbitration part of the convention in the hemisphere. At various points in its own bilateral disputes with Chile, including the crucial Pactos de Mayo negotiations, Argentina introduced the status of the territories as a prerequisite for agreement. For their part, and with Argentine backing, Peru and Bolivia sought to put the status of the territories on the agenda of international forums in the hope that they could get a favorable resolution and have Chile forced into compulsory arbitration. Prior to 1879 Chile had been wary of international congresses and loath to compulsory arbitration; after the war it became even more

---

[176] João Pandia Calogeras, *Problemas de administração*, 2nd ed. (São Paulo: Cia. Editôra Nacional, 1938/1918).

[177] Varley, "The Aftermath of the War of the Pacific," 25.

[178] Burr, *By Reason or Force*, 169.

[179] From 1883 to the early 1930s these territories constituted the bulk of Chile's international affairs, consuming nearly all of its diplomatic attention. There are several good studies of Chile's foreign relations during this time period. The often-cited work by Barros, *Historia diplomática de Chile*, is impressive in scale and reach but not very well documented. It is unabashedly pro-Chile, conservative, and has frequent racist overtones. The study by Jaime Eyzaguirre, *Chile durante el gobierno de Errázuriz Echaurren, 1896–1901* (Santiago: Empresa Editora Zig-Zag, S.A., 1957) is rich and well documented, albeit with a pro-Chile bias. Burr's, *By Reason or Force*, remains the best work in English on Chile's foreign relations. Pike's *Chile and the United States* is also nicely written and well researched.

defensive and wary.[180] Most states in the hemisphere, particularly the United States, sympathized with Chile's foes. Reluctantly Chile participated in the Pan American conferences only on the condition that compulsory arbitration would not be discussed nor the status of Tacna and Arica. Chile preferred to deal with Peru and Bolivia bilaterally. An essential component of its postwar foreign policy was the pursuit of a divide-and-rule strategy when dealing with Peru, Bolivia, and Argentina.[181]

In addition to the hostility of its neighbors, Chile feared the real possibility of a diplomatic or military intervention by the European great powers and the United States seeking to deprive Chile of the spoils of victory.[182] This fear arose while the Second War of the Pacific was in progress, as the United States, Britain, France, and Italy sought at various times to intervene militarily and diplomatically in the war and arrange a settlement. Meddling by the United States was especially extensive and biased. The actions and attitudes of these powers, some with considerable economic and strategic interests in Peru and Bolivia, were decidedly anti-Chilean. All of these powers, in concert and individually, involved themselves in the conflict – ostensibly to mediate an end to the war – and devised plans to intervene militarily.[183] This is particularly true once it became clear that Chile would emerge victorious. In July 1880, for example, Italy initiated a proposal for a joint Italian, French, and British armed intervention under the pretext of Chile's actions against their expatriates and violations of international law and codes of armed warfare.[184] Chile resented and was suspicious of the United States.[185] The United States openly declared its goal of preventing a Chilean victory.[186] Of the great powers, only Germany abstained from intervening in the war.[187]

After the war, Chile moved quickly to ease tensions with the Europeans by settling their financial claims over alleged losses suffered during the war.

[180] On this point, see Barros, *Historia diplomática de Chile*; Meneses Ciuffardi, "Los limites"; Burr, *By Reason or Force.*

[181] On this point, see Varley, "The Aftermath of the War of the Pacific"; Burr, *By Reason or Force*; Barros, *Historia diplomática de Chile.*

[182] Barros, *Historia diplomática de Chile*, chaps. 11 and 12; Varley, "The Aftermath of the War of the Pacific."

[183] Miguel Cruchaga Tocornal, "Actitud de Alemania durante la Guerra de la Pacífico," *Boletin de la Academia Chilena de la Historia* 16, no. 40 (1949). See also Ministério de Relaciones Exteriores, *Memória*, (Santiago: Imprenta Nacional, 1883). Burr, on the other hand, maintains that the danger of great-power intervention was minimal. See Burr, *By Reason or Force*, 167–68.

[184] Cruchaga Tocornal, "Actitud de Alemania," 33.

[185] Pike, *Chile and the United States*; Sater, *Chile and the United States.*

[186] Pike, *Chile and the United States*, 59. See also Stephen D. Brown, "The Power of Influence in Chilean–United States Relations," Ph.D. thesis, University of Wisconsin–Madison (1983): chap. 3.

[187] Cruchaga Tocornal, "Actitud de Alemania."

In sharp contrast, relations with the United States deteriorated after the war. Simultaneously, its relations with historic rival Argentina also worsened. Chile's grand strategy was a continental (and certainly Andean) balance of power that was favorable to its position, and which could thereby protect its war gains. The United States and the other great powers, individually or in concert with Chile's regional enemies, were capable of upsetting this balance. At war's end in 1883 Chile found itself more encircled than ever before; the scale of military threats were greater than ever, including a revamped Argentina. Alone and without any effective external balancing options, Chile had to rely on the strength and efficiency of its own arms. President Balmaceda summed up the view succinctly in 1885, noting that "Chile should be able to resist on its own territory any possible coalition.... It should at least prove that there is no possible profit in starting a war against Chile."[188]

POSTWAR CHILE AND THE NEW THREATS

From the immediate postwar years to 1902, Chile faced an even more hostile international environment than it had before or during the Second Pacific War.[189] The timing and scale of Chile's military emulation cannot be understood apart from its adverse security situation during and immediately following the war. The logic of anarchic systems is such that blowback is inevitable. Chile's wartime and immediate postwar actions, intended to bring greater security, resulted in postwar insecurity spirals that eventually eroded its position. Conquest resulted in booty and extended frontier. But Chile's territorial aggrandizement also sparked fear among all its neighbors, especially Argentina, spurring them to build up their arms and collude against Chile. Its expansion also threatened the commercial and strategic interests of great powers like the United States. The outcomes of the War of the Pacific were universally interpreted as Chile's bid for continental hegemony. The Buenos Aires daily, *El Tiempo*, echoed the fear when it warned that Chile's "political and economic hegemony" resembled that of Prussia, and that soon it will turn Peru, Bolivia, and other neighboring countries into satellites. "The extraordinary significance of Chile's actions for the balance in South America," the paper declared, "cannot be ignored by anyone."[190]

The most critical strategic development in the postwar years was the simultaneous emergence of both Argentina and the United States as military threats. The United States and Argentina were intent on rolling back Chile's

---

[188] Quote cited in Sater, *Chile and the United States*, 52.
[189] Gonzalo Vial Correa, "La vida internacional," in *Historia de Chile, 1891–1973*, vol. 2, tome 1, *Triumfo y decadencia de la oligarquía, 1891–1920* (Santiago: Santilla del Pacífico, S.A., 1982).
[190] *El Tiempo*, 14 Mai 1895. Quote cited in Barros, *Historia diplomática de Chile*, 505.

regional position. Their actions during the Pacific War served as important motivation in Chile's decision to modernize its armed forces. Chile's military emulation, especially during its second phase, thus had dual-balancing objectives. Its rivalry with Argentina is discussed in the next section.

Between the War of the Pacific and World War I, the United States played a major role in Chile's national security policy.[191] Each side came to consider the other as a threat to its physical security and hemispheric interests. Chile's fear of a U.S. attack, and opposition to a U.S. presence in the region, did not subside until the 1930s.[192] Obscured in the historiography is Chile's role in triggering the development of modern U.S. naval power in the last two decades of the nineteenth century.[193] A series of incidents, together with the incessant diplomatic maneuvering of third-party states to capitalize on their mutual animosity, brought Chile and the United States to the brink of war. These incidents reflected a larger dynamic: a brief but intense power struggle between a Chile intent on preserving a South American continental balance in its favor and an expansionist United States intent on stamping its dominance southward from Central America.[194] Foreign-relations documents indicate that the United States was hostile toward Chile in the postwar years.[195]

Long before the Second War of the Pacific, relations between Chile and the United States already had an undertone of mutual suspicion and dislike. It started with the tardy recognition by the United States of Chile's independence. As noted previously, Chile's distrust of the United States resurfaced during the Spanish attacks in 1865–66.[196] The War of the Pacific stoked this suspicion into open hostility.[197] The behavior of the United States during the Pacific War was one of open hostility to Chilean aims.[198] In fact, Chilean military and political leaders came to see the United States as a supporter for the cause of Peru and Bolivia, both during and after the war, even

---

[191] Meneses Ciuffardi, *El factor naval,* and "Los limites"; Pike, *Chile and the United States*; Sater, *Chile and the United States*; Seward W. Livermore, "American Strategy Diplomacy in the South Pacific, 1890–1914," *Pacific Historical Review* 12, no. 1 (March 1943): 33–52. See also George T. Davis, *A Navy Second to None: The Development of Modern American Naval Policy* (New York: Harcourt, Brace & Co., 1940); Harold Sprout and Margaret Sprout, *The Rise of American Naval Power, 1776–1918* (Princeton: Princeton University Press, 1946).

[192] Meneses Ciuffardi, *El factor naval,* 17.

[193] Brown, "The Power of Influence"; Davis, *A Navy Second to None*; Livermore, "American Strategy"; Kenneth J. Hagan, *American Gunboat Diplomacy and the Old Navy, 1877–1889* (Westport: Greenwood Press, 1973).

[194] Meneses Ciuffardi, *El factor naval,* and "Los limites." See also Barros, *Historia diplomática de Chile*; Livermore, "American Strategy."

[195] See *Foreign Relations of the United States* (FRUS), 1883 to 1914.

[196] On Chile's attitude toward the Monroe Doctrine, see Pike, *Chile and the United States,* 24–25; Sater, *Chile and the United States,* 3–4.

[197] Sater, *Chile and the United States,* chap. 2, passim.

[198] Livermore, "American Strategy"; Meneses Ciuffardi, *El factor naval*; Sater, *Chile and the United States*; Brown, "The Power of Influence," especially chap. 3.

though much of U.S. policy was the work of inept representatives in the region.[199]

First, in the midst of the war, the United States attempted to act as a not-so-neutral mediator. The U.S. minister in Santiago recalled in 1911 that "Chile has always feared our attitude in their troubles with Peru – almost to the point of considering us an ally of that country."[200] During the fighting, the United States entered negotiations with Peru for commercial privileges and rights to a naval base. The two governments, in fact, were discussing the lease of the port of Chimbote in return for a U.S. guarantee against the looming territorial dismemberment of Peru.[201] The United States, moreover, sought to mediate at the point where the contest had been decided militarily in Chile's favor. Representatives of the United States in the region did not conceal their interests in Peru nor their opposition to Chilean victory. They acted in "utter disregard of every rule of prudence and propriety," as Secretary of State James G. Blaine admitted.[202] In mid–1881 the United States announced it opposed territorial dismemberment of any belligerent, and sought to pressure Chile from including territorial concessions in the terms of peace.[203] By this time Chile already had settled the contest of arms. Efforts by external powers to shape the terms could only be viewed as damaging to its war aims.

Maneuvering of the United States in the region was part of its wider imperial ambitions in the hemisphere. On one hand was its long-standing anxiety over the presence of the European great powers in the hemisphere. On the other was a concern that a militarily powerful Chile was an obstacle to its regional ambitions, including ambitions in Central America.[204] The United States wanted to get rid of the European presence. Sater notes that the United States regarded the war essentially as a British plot.[205] Chile's postwar ties to Germany added more fuel to already poor relations with the United States. By the 1890s, Germany surpassed Britain and France as the main rival for the United States both in the new world and elsewhere, particularly in the Far East and the Asian South Pacific. Germany became a permanent feature in U.S. strategic thinking.[206] The U.S. strategy was to roll back Chile, and was simultaneously one of strategic denial aimed at Germany.

---

[199] Brown, "The Power of Influence."

[200] Cable from the U.S. minister to the State Department, 31 October 1911. Quote cited in Livermore, "American Strategy Diplomacy," 49.

[201] Meneses Ciuffardi, *El factor naval*, 33.

[202] Quote cited in Brown, "The Power of Influence," 214.

[203] Brown, "The Power of Influence," 219–20.

[204] In early 1895 the Chilean minister in Washington cabled the foreign ministry in Santiago that the United States may yet succeed in establishing a "protectorate over all of Latin America." Cable from Chilean minister to ministry of foreign relations, 24 April 1895, cited in Pike, *Chile and the United States*, 137.

[205] Sater, *Chile and the United States*, 39.

[206] Davis, *A Navy Second to None*, 123.

For the United States, the strategic problem posed by a militarily powerful, victorious Chile was not just the imaginings of overzealous diplomats. Chile's superior naval power had effectively prevented the United States from achieving its objectives during the war and after. Chile emerged from the war as the principal naval power in the South Pacific. For a brief window, Chile's naval capabilities outmatched that of the United States, whose navy may have been larger in size but was composed of aging, poorly constructed, wooden-hulled vessels, compared to Chile's modern, iron-plated battleships.[207] In the years immediately following the war some U.S. political and military leaders regarded Chile as a physical threat.[208] A powerful Chile blocked U.S. pretensions in the Caribbean basin. In 1885, when Colombia and the United States clashed over Panama, the dispatch of Chile's powerful battleship, the *Esmeralda*, to the Isthmus proved sufficient to thwart an early U.S. effort to acquire the Isthmus.

For Chile, the threat posed by the United States did not abate with the close of the war. It increased. By the late 1880s the United States was engaged in its own large-scale naval modernization program.[209] It remained an active player in the region's affairs after the war.[210] The strategy of Peru and Bolivia was simple: to secure the diplomatic (and, if possible, military) backing of the United States and Argentina to press Chile to return the conquered territories. Peru's major bargaining chip and inducement for U.S. backing was the port of Chimbote.[211] In light of U.S. actions during and after the war, Chile could only assume that any confrontation with Peru and Bolivia would draw U.S. intervention.

Relations between Chile and the United States progressively worsened after the war. Tensions mounted anew during Chile's 1891 civil war from a combination of U.S. meddling and great-power rivalry. Britain, France, and Germany were sympathetic to the rebel congressional cause – mainly out of commercial reasons (since the rebels controlled the mineral-rich northern provinces) and the military and naval ties that the rebel forces had already established with Germany and Britain.[212] The United States, on the other hand, favored presidential forces, and considered Britain and the other European powers supporters of the rebels.[213] The U.S. detained the rebel transport ship *Itata*, which was carrying rebel arms from San Francisco. Also

---

[207] Davis, *A Navy Second to None*.

[208] Meneses Ciuffardi, *El factor naval*, chap. 2, passim; Davis, *A Navy Second to None*.

[209] Davis, *A Navy Second to None*.

[210] Livermore, "American Strategy."

[211] Livermore, "American Strategy," 34.

[212] Barros, *Historia diplomática de Chile*, chap. 12; Cruchaga Tocornal, "Actitud de Alemania"; Pike, *Chile and the United States*, chap. 3.

[213] See various cables between the U.S. minister in Santiago, Patrick Eagan, and the State Department in *Foreign Relations of the United States (FRUS)*, 1891. See especially cables from Eagan to the State Department 14 April 1891 and 17 September 1891.

asylum was provided to presidential supporters at the U.S. Embassy. These were two of many instances that led the victorious parliamentary forces to suspect U.S. motives. The dispatches of Ambassador Robert Eagan displays an unambiguous bias toward the presidential forces and hostility toward the rebel forces.[214]

Barely had the civil war ended when a near-war crisis erupted as a result of the infamous *Baltimore* incident, when a barroom brawl in Valparaíso ended in the deaths of U.S. sailors.[215] The United States, observed British diplomats, turned the barroom brawl into an international incident and casus belli. The United States interpreted the events in Valparaíso, and the Chilean government's initial handling of the incident, as "cruel work," "injurious to the United States," "offensive," and a sign of hostility toward the United States.[216] By January 1892, as the U.S. fleet assembled off the south Pacific coast in preparation for war, President Harrison was laying the groundwork for a declaration of war.[217] An imposing U.S. Pacific fleet, composed of eight major warships and augmented by elements of the Atlantic fleet, assembled off the coasts of Peru and Chile.[218] Chile was surrounded by three hostile neighbors spoiling to join a United States in war against Chile. Argentina communicated to the United States its desire to join in a war against Chile. As the crisis unfolded, Argentina provided the United States with military intelligence on recent Chilean arms acquisitions.[219] This period corresponds to the second major phase of military emulation.

Chile responded to the threat of war by speeding up its military emulation as well as seeking protection from the European great powers. Chile's ministers in Paris, London, and Berlin were told not to expect any European support, and counseled to accede to U.S. demands.[220] Germany regarded the incident as a U.S. effort to find a pretext for war to displace European commercial interests in the region, and warned Chile not to provoke the United States.[221] The confrontation with the United States spurred Chile to engage in an arms buildup program that essentially did not end until 1902. Invariably,

---

[214] United States, Department of State, *Foreign Relations of the United States* (FRUS), 1891. See various cables between Eagan and the State Department from January to August 1891.

[215] Joyce S. Goldberg, *The "Baltimore" Affair* (Lincoln: University of Nebraska Press, 1986).

[216] *Foreign Relations of the United States (FRUS)*, 1891, State Department cable to Eagan, 23 October 1891; Goldberg, *The "Baltimore" Affair*.

[217] On the preparations for war by the U.S. Pacific fleet, see Meneses Ciuffardi, *El factor naval*, chap. 3.

[218] Meneses Ciuffardi provides a good discussion of the war preparations on both sides. See Meneses Ciuffardi, *El factor naval*, chap. 3, especially 63–79; Goldberg, *The "Baltimore" Affair*, 119–23.

[219] Meneses Ciuffardi, *El factor naval*, 79–81. See also Goldberg, *The "Baltimore" Affair*, 120–21.

[220] Pike, *Chile and the United States*, 78; Meneses Ciuffardi, *El factor naval*, 83; Goldberg, *The "Baltimore" Affair*, 124–28.

[221] Goldberg, *The "Baltimore" Affair*, 126.

Chile's arms buildup to prepare for war with the United States provoked alarm in Buenos Aires, which continued to view Chile's war machine as the country's biggest threat. It came as no surprise that relations with Argentina would grow tense just as the crisis and arms racing with the United States unfolded. This spiral of fear and insecurity had a rachet effect on Chile's military modernization. Chile averted war with the United States, but its war preparations intensified old security problems. As war with the United States appeared to pass, war with Argentina loomed. Argentina now replaced the United States and the other traditional rival, Peru, as Chile's number one military threat. General Saez Morales, a key participant in the reform process, recounted that "the danger of a war with Argentina had made the government understand the necessity of reconstituting, rapidly, an army whose efficiency would be the guarantee of international security, a task which was entrusted to General Körner."[222]

CHILE AND ARGENTINA

By the mid-1880s Chile and Argentina were locked in the biggest and most expensive competitive military emulation in Latin American history. Chile and Argentina share a history of bitter rivalry, which even today still casts a long shadow. The frequency of a diplomatic tiff between them today betrays sensitivy to a long history scarred by mutual hatred. Their enmity dates to the independence wars. The usual territorial disputes clouded relations, and each treated the other with suspicion and racist overtones. Yet as long as Argentina continued to be a loose confederation of unruly and warring provinces, as it was before 1880, Chile could approach their disputes with equanimity. The military threat presented by Argentina, by itself, was neither immediate nor serious.[223]

Prior to the Second War of the Pacific their rivalry remained largely in the background, given Argentina's internal disunion and military weakness. Argentina's national unification in 1880 elevated the rivalry to a qualitatively different level. It now represented a real threat. The Pacific war made it a direct participant in Chile's immediate arena of competition. Even a militarily weak Argentina worried Chile because of the real likelihood of an encircling alliance led by Argentina. The strategic problem for Chile worsened in 1880. Unification was coupled with military buildup in Argentina which launched its own vast military modernization. Chile's attempt to gain more security by building up its arms led to its unraveling. No other single factor would do more to undermine Chile's relative position than the rise of a unified, large, and wealthy Argentina.

Three sets of issues intensified the historic rivalry by the Second War of the Pacific. The first was Argentina's behavior during the war. Argentina openly

---

[222] Saez Morales, *Recuerdos de un soldado*, 24.
[223] Burr, *By Reason or Force*, 167.

supported Chile's enemies during both Pacific wars. Its alleged participation in the 1873 secret treaty between Bolivia and Peru earned it Chile's enduring wrath. Argentina, of course, was key to complete encirclement. Chile was able to neutralize Argentina's formal participation in the war, but its Andean rival nevertheless supplied material support to Bolivia.[224] Argentina joined the United States in pushing forward the principle of territorial integrity of all the belligerents. From Argentina's perspective, anything that could obstruct augmentation of Chilean power was a net benefit to its security. All that Chile saw was encirclement and collusion.

The second set of issues involved the many territorial disputes between the two rivals dating back to independence. During the war, Chile assuaged Argentina through a series of protocols meant to keep it from entering the war. For its part, Argentina sought ways to capitalize on Chile's distraction with the war. In 1880, while Chile was battling Peru and Bolivia, Argentina seized the opportunity to occupy disputed territories in the Patagonia and force Chile to agree to a disadvantageous settlement. In the 1881 agreement Chile surrendered nearly all of the Patagonia region. Although it retained much of Tierra del Fuego territory and the Straits of Magellan, its claim over the vast Patagonia since 1810 had extended its eastern borders to the Atlantic coast. The 1881 agreement, however, did not fully settle their disputes in the region, nor ease Argentina fears over Chilean expansionism.

Chile's conquest of Bolivian and Peruvian territories heightened Argentina's fear of Chilean power and territorial ambitions. Their many disputes, which had begun to flare up in the early 1870s, were aggravated by Argentina's acquisition of Chilean-occupied Bolivian territory. In 1889 and 1893 Bolivia ceded to Argentina its territories of Puna de Atacama and the Chaco Central, none of which had any agreed upon demarcation. The Puna de Atacama, comprising over 150,000 square miles and most of it lying in present day Argentina, was occupied by Chile during the war. Argentina became a direct participant in the affairs of the Pacific system, as Bolivia effectively turned its territorial dispute with Chile to a Chilean-Argentine dispute. Chile had always feared that its disputes with Argentina would become enmeshed with its Peru-Bolivia quagmire. For its part, Argentina did not abstain from using this possibility as a bargaining chip to force Chile to be more conciliatory in their own border demarcation settlements in the 1890s. The arid Puna plateau stretched north–south for nearly 400 miles and consisted of high mountain ranges and desert. The Puna became the source of a war crisis by 1898, though the real fight was over more than just desert. The two rivals did not resolve the Puna de Atacama dispute until 1902, after first peering into the chasm of war.

It was the fallout of the Second War of the Pacific that embittered relations most. Chile's victory and territorial expansion was looked upon as

---

[224] Barros, *Historia diplomática de Chile*, 354–56.

nothing less than menacing by Argentina.[225] Indeed, Chilean expansionism and postwar military buildup were the chief causes for the gaucho republic's own military emulation. Argentina openly denounced Chile's "violent conquests," as Foreign Minister Bernardo de Irigoyen noted in 1880, adding that "the areas taken by force of arms [constitute] senseless aggression."[226] For their part, military and civilian leaders in Argentina believed that Argentine territory, especially the undefended bordering provinces, would be attacked by Chile. For the next two decades Argentina did all it could to obstruct Chilean efforts to settle the disputes with Bolivia and Peru. Chile's foreign minister cabled the ambassador in La Paz to "remain there until the treaties are finalized. Argentina will make every effort to obstruct."[227]

In the course of the postwar decades Argentina became a nominal protector of Chile's foes, especially Bolivia, which increasingly fell under its sway. To undercut Argentina's role and neutralize the joint action of its foes, Chile mounted a series of bilateral negotiations to settle outstanding border disputes. In particular, it approached Argentina to resolve their Andean frontier and settle the status of the Puna de Atacama. Negotiations stalled. Chile was well aware that its position rested on a delicate (if not fleeting) balance. Two motivations lay behind its push to resolve quickly all disputes with Argentina. The first was to remove the grounds of common action among its neighbors. The second was to take advantage of its relative power over the still militarily weak but rich Argentina. Chilean leaders viewed the rise of Argentine power as inevitable. The British minister in Santiago succinctly described Chile's strategic dilemma in 1896 when he observed that "the government of Chile is very attentive to the growing importance and wealth of the Argentine republic and feels that if it cannot *increase its military resources by means of secure alliances*, Chile will one day be annexed by Argentina."[228]

By 1892 the two countries were locked in a naval arms race, a situation made worse by talks of an alliance between Argentina and the United States. The *Baltimore* affair had the effect of bringing Argentina and the United States closer, and provided motive for joint action against their common enemy. Even after the threat of war between Chile and the United States subsided, unofficial talks were taking place between Argentina and the United States regarding a possible treaty – talks that were known in both

---

[225] Burr, *By Reason or Force*, 154–55.
[226] Argentine Foreign Minister, Bernardo Irigoyen, 1880. Quote cited in Thomas F. McGann, *Argentina, the United States, and the Inter-American System, 1900–1914* (Cambridge: Harvard University Press, 1957): 83.
[227] Quote cited in Meneses Ciuffardi, "Los limites," 105.
[228] Quote cited in Meneses Ciuffardi, "Los limites," 100, and "Coping with Decline," 27. Emphasis added.

Chile and Britain.[229] Chile's reaction was to approach Britain as a possible source of support, and seek an alliance with Brazil (whose short-lived detente with Argentina had come to an abrupt end by this time).[230] Argentina, emboldened by its approximation with the United States, responded with what Chile considered stalling tactics.[231] Border negotiations with Argentina were abruptly broken off in 1895 when Argentina asked for the dismissal of the Chilean representative on the joint border demarcation commission. Chile, frustrated over what it considered Argentina's obstructionist and delaying tactics, responded with a brisk military and naval arms buildup, including a new warship and several thousand more Mauser rifles.[232] The impasse worsened when Argentina and Bolivia ratified their treaty on the Puna de Atacama. Argentina rejected Chilean protest, and asserted that it would not give up the territory under any circumstance.[233]

Relations reached a nadir during 1895–1902.[234] The unintended consequence of Chile's military modernization was to spur arms racing throughout the region. More detrimental to its own position was that it unwittingly spurred a countermodernization by the larger, richer Argentina. Relations escalated into an "armed peace," as the U.S. ambassador in Buenos Aires described it in 1898.[235] Both sides prepared for war, and mobilized their forces on several occasions during 1898–1902. The U.S. minister in Santiago cabled Washington to warn that "the [Chilean] government is undoubtedly making war preparations on an extensive scale. The navy is being put in the best possible condition and the army is being subjected to a severe and continuous drill."[236] Chile and Argentina found themselves locked in an escalating naval arms race throughout the 1890s and 1900–02. By the first half of the 1890s Argentina was amassing modern armaments. This arms buildup intensified in the naval area beginning in 1890, though Chile's naval modernization program of 1887 may have acted to spark the naval arms race.

The problem for Chile was that it became painfully clear that it could not afford an arms race with the wealthier, larger, economically more productive Argentina. The British minister in Santiago forecasted Chile's difficulty in 1896, noting that "Chile, with the assistance of German officers, has perfected its military organization and awaits the fleet of warships from England. *But it feels that it is now less capable of realizing its plans than six*

229 Varley, "The Aftermath of the War of the Pacific," 79–81.
230 Varley, "The Aftermath of the War of the Pacific," 80–81, 155–57.
231 On this point, see Eyzaguirre, *Chile durante el gobierno de Errázuriz.*
232 Meneses Ciuffardi, "Los límites," 105.
233 Quote by Argentine President Júlio Roca, cited in Meneses, "Los límites," 105–06.
234 For a nicely documented study on this period (though from a Chilean perspective), see Eyzaguirre, *Chile durante el gobierno de Errázuriz.*
235 United States, Department of State, National Archives, *Dispatches from U.S. Minister to Argentina, 1817–1906,* Film S-1040, M69, Roll 31. Cable from Buchanan to State Department, 5 August 1898. (Note: original document spelled as "Despatches.")
236 Quote cited in Meneses Ciuffardi, "Coping With Decline," 43.

months ago, and that while it is no longer capable [of sustaining] a greater increase in its military power there is no limit to the wealth that Argentina possesses."[237]

The militarily weaker but wealthier Argentina was well aware of this. In 1895 Argentina's economy was already twice the size of Chile's. An influential journalist noted that Chile's hurry to settle its disputes with Argentina was motivated by a desire to "exploit [its] fleeting advantage, which it will soon lose." He added perceptively that "Chile today has reached its maximum military preparation possible; never will it be able to surpass it. Neither its present population, nor its impoverished finances ever will allow it the illusion of achieving it. Moreover, it cannot maintain for much longer the current war footing; its resources are depleted. Argentina, on the other hand, can easily double its present preparation. It has the sufficient population and resources. *If war does not erupt now, each day that passes is a loss for Chile and a gain for Argentina."*[238]

Earlier in the decade, October 1893, Argentina's foreign minister cabled his legation in Lima to outline the course of Argentine foreign policy in the region. He reminded the legation that "Chilean preponderance deserves to be taken into account, but it is also true that it should be no danger for Argentina if we are able to maintain peace and good government for some years. The adversary will be left well behind and we will impose ourselves without sacrifice."[239] By forcing Chile, which still had superior land and naval forces, into an expensive arms race Argentina hoped to trigger financial-economic collapse on the other side of the Andes. Chile's president Errázuriz Echaurren succinctly noted Chile's predicament in early 1898, noting that "[a] situation like the one that is rapidly transpiring will ruin Chile and produce an economic disaster from which it cannot come out of as long as its fiscal resources are sunk in armaments. The government estimates that a day will come when a supreme resolution will have to be taken which avoids the disastrous war that threatens us, or we [give it] the security of victory."[240] Argentine leaders were no more sanguine. José Uriburu was pessimistic about the prospect for peaceful resolution, noting that "we will not be able to live in peace with such a powerful neighbor."[241]

Waiting for War and the Pactos de Mayo

The first half of 1898 was a time of war preparation on both sides of the Andes. The situation for Chile worsened rapidly on all fronts. Peru and

[237] British Minister Kennedy, quote cited in Meneses Ciuffardi, "Los limites," 100. Emphasis added.
[238] Ernesto Quesada, *La política argentina respecto de Chile, 1895–1898* (Buenos Aires: Editor Arnoldo Moen, 1898): 77, 109.
[239] Quote cited in Meneses Ciuffardi, "Coping With Decline," 27.
[240] Quote cited in Eyzaguirre, *Chile durante el gobierno de Errázuriz*, 190.
[241] Quote cited in Barros, *Historia diplomática de Chile*, 525.

Bolivia, sensing an inevitable confrontation between the two dominant Andean powers, stepped up their diplomatic alliance with Argentina and began to press Chile for an immediate settlement of their disputes.[242] Chile made an effort to deflect Peru and Bolivia, and quickly signed a protocol with Peru in 1898. By the middle of the year, news emerged that Argentina was to acquire a second modern capital ship, putting Chile in a position of naval inferiority. By this time, however, Chile could no longer finance the arms race. Argentina's strategy of driving Chile into economic ruin was working. The armed peace with Argentina came at precisely the point when world market prices for nitrates plummeted (1897–99). To make matters worse, as war loomed closer Chile was unable to secure foreign loans. The economic situation, already in serious recession in 1897, reached a critical point in the wake of a banking crisis in late 1898.

Cabinet meetings on national security were continuous during the first half of the year.[243] A key participant in these meetings was the chief of the general staff of the army, Emil Körner.[244] Körner, though he favored war, told the cabinet that the army was not fully prepared for war.[245] Körner proposed the immediate acquisition of armaments to equip an army of 150,000. Chile, it should be noted, viewed war with Argentina as primarily a land affair, with the army delivering the decision and doing so on the enemy's territory. The general staff, though concerned with the naval balance, noted that "the decision must be obtained on land by the army, which will cross the *cordilleras* and drive to the enemy's capital."[246]

As war approached, in 1898, Chile was forced to choose among unpleasant alternatives: war or capitulation to Argentina's terms. Waiting was simply not an option, for within a few months Argentina would eclipse Chile's naval capabilities and wreck its economy. Chile seriously contemplated war (as did Argentina) as a means to close the rapidly growing window of vulnerability.[247] Prominent among the advocates for a preventive strike against Argentina was Chile's minister in Buenos Aires, Joaquin Walker. Exasperated at Argentina's delaying tactics, in August 1898 he cabled to his foreign minister an argument for preventive war against Argentina. "These people are fooling us in order to gain the time necessary to finish placing themselves in an invincible position," he argued. Argentina, he added, "will delay as much as possible until the arrival of the warships. You know what the warships will mean in the balance of our small navies. Our [leaders] will reason that it is not worth fighting for desolate territories from a position of inequality.

[242] See Vial, *Triunfo y decadencia de la oligarquía.*
[243] Eyzaguirre, *Chile durante el gobierno de Errázuriz*, 189.
[244] Ibid.
[245] Vial, *Triunfo y decadencia de la oligarquía*, 251, 273.
[246] Ministério de Guerra, Estado Maior General del Ejército, *Memorial del Estado Maior General del Ejército*, no. 1 (15 June 1906): 13.
[247] Eyzaguirre, *Chile durante el gobierno de Errázuriz.*

And then we will just capitulate and appear [weak] before the whole world."
Walker's words have been echoed throughout the ages by leaders optimistic
about their ability to control human affairs and predetermine the outcomes
of war. He boasted: "Today Chile's triumph is guaranteed. A naval campaign
would settle the contest. In another three months our chances at sea will be
the opposite and we will have to attend simultaneously to the defense of the
[Andean] territories."[248]

Walker was right. Argentine leaders were in no rush. Carlos Pellegrini,
former Argentine president and close ally and adviser to President Júlio Roca,
confided to one of Roca's ministers that "to me, Roca's present policy is
perfectly calculated. Our race with Chile is an arms race. The longer it is,
the more advantageous it is for us, since the rate of our growth is immensely
superior to that of Chile. If the definitive resolution of our dispute drags on
for another ten years, it will be prejudicial to Chile and not to us."[249]

By June, Chile was already opting for a peaceful settlement of its disputes with Argentina, and sought the mediation of outside powers. Chile
approached Britain both to act as an arbiter and to put pressure on Argentina
to agree to an arbitration settlement. Walker, on the other hand, continued to
advocate preventive war while the balance of capabilities was still in Chile's
favor. In particular, he keenly observed that Chile had the advantage on land
as well, since Argentina, which had not yet launched full military emulation, possessed a disorganized, untrained military. In a September cable to
the ministry he picked up where he had left off in his previous cable: "On
what basis does this faith in a peaceful solution rest? I declare to you that I
do not find any foundation for this faith and I cannot understand this loss
of time which can only translate into obvious disadvantages for our arms."
Walker noted that now was the time to strike. Argentina's military was disorganized, he said, "and a rapid action on our part will ensure a superiority
which may disappear later on. Chile, I repeat, is at the mercy of the goodwill
of a country which hates us with a hatred of which there is only one example
in South American history. Today our military power is undoubtedly sufficient to provide a solution to a state of affairs which has [turned into] a crisis
that no diplomacy can exorcise."[250]

Walker's faith in preventive war was never put to the test. The British-
mediated peace settlement between Chile and Argentina, accords which
collectively came to be known as the "Pactos de Mayo," was a major water-
shed in their bilateral relations.[251] In one stroke, Chile resolved its most

[248] Quote cited in Eyzaguirre, *Chile durante el gobierno de Errázuriz*, 208–09.

[249] Carlos Pellegrini, 29 January 1901, quote cited in Rosendo María Fraga, *Roca y Chile* (Buenos Aires: Editorial CEUNM, 1996): 56.

[250] Quote cited in Eyzaguirre, *Chile durante el gobierno de Errázuriz*, 215–16.

[251] On the Pactos de Mayo, see Oscar Espinoza Moraga, "Los Pactos de Mayo," *Boletín de la Academia Chilena de la Historia* 19, no. 46 (1952).

urgent security problem. In addition to mending (but not resolving) the territorial disputes, the settlement was also one of the world's first naval arms control agreements. The armed peace itself had greatly increased the pace and scope of Chile's military emulation between 1897 and 1906, dates which corresponded to the two major reorganizations since the civil war as well as the deepening of the German model.

The overall effect of the 1902 agreements on the military competition and emulation of both sides of the Andes was somewhat ambiguous. On the one hand, by putting an end to the naval arms race, resolving outstanding territorial disputes, and outlining each power's sphere of influence, the agreements dampened the sharpness and intensity of security competition between the two that had marked their relations between 1895 and 1902. But each continued to view the other as a likely battlefield enemy, and both continued to modernize their armed forces. In many ways, the peaceful settlement in 1902 reflected the decline of Chilean power more than anything else.[252] Chile entered the twentieth century bankrupt, with a large and expensive military apparatus whose supporting pillar was a feeble economic-financial base. It could no longer keep up with its larger neighbor. By 1910 Argentina had eclipsed Chile in every category of national power.

THE REEXPORT OF THE GERMAN MODEL

Chile, just as Prussia had done after 1870, began to generate widespread appeal throughout Latin America. The real appeal was the German army, but that a sister republic in the hemisphere had successfully embraced it and now generated respect and admiration amongst its neighbors provided reinforcement for would-be emulators. Though Chile had not fought any wars with its new military system, its successful adoption of the German system lessened the uncertainty and reservations would-be emulators in the region may have had. Chile itself became a model for the second wave of emulators of the German system.

Since the 1890s military officers from Paraguay, Ecuador, and elsewhere had been studying in Chilean military schools.[253] In 1900 Ecuador contracted a Chilean military mission to supervise its military reorganization. The mission remained in Ecuador from 1900 to 1916. In 1903, a Chilean military mission arrived in El Salvador, where it remained until 1964. Another mission was in Colombia between 1907 and 1915; individual Chilean officers were contracted again between 1933–35 and 1958–61. A Chilean mission also guided Venezuela's modernization during 1907–14. Honduras contracted the Chileans in 1911. The military missions Chile sent abroad spread the

---

[252] Meneses Ciuffardi, "Coping With Decline."
[253] Vial, *Triumfo y decadencia de la oligarquía*, 273.

German system throughout much of the hemisphere, and served as a useful tool through which Chile could spread its influence. These missions were also an integral part of, and reflected the change in, Chile's grand strategy. With the rapid and inexhaustible rise of Argentine power by 1910, and its own bankruptcy, Chile's relative position was declining precipitously. Chile's grand strategy turned to deterrence and external accommodation. The military missions abroad were meant to supplement its rapid decline through strategic diplomacy.[254]

In the years prior to World War I, Chile sought to cope with decline by favoring an entente among the three big powers. Chile's motivation was to soften its precipitous decline, to find new ways to shore up its diplomatic position regarding the conquered territories, and to neutralize the United States. The origins of the so-called ABC treaty are not fully clear. Meneses dates the start of negotiations among Argentina, Brazil, and Chile to 1907.[255] Barros dates it to early 1914 when Brazil proposed a nonaggression pact with Argentina.[256] That same year British diplomats were reporting on the ABC treaty, which the British ambassador interpreted as an instrument to counterbalance the United States.[257] In mid-1915 representatives from Argentina, Brazil, and Chile signed the ABC pact, though it was never ratified. It remained a gentlemen's agreement up to 1917.[258] For Chile, the ABC was a desperate attempt to arrest its relative decline, and to buy security through external accommodation. It favored a stronger alliance than what materialized.[259] Its leaders saw the pact as an instrument to soften the country's declining position. "The unequal growth of the American states," observed Foreign Minister Alejandro Lira in 1915, "requires a diligent diplomatic action [on our part] to maintain the dignity of our situation."[260]

The Decline of Chilean Power

Germany's defeat in 1918 was a terrible blow for Chile and its army.[261] This was not so much because the Chileans were ardent admirers of German

[254] Meneses Ciuffardi, "Coping With Decline," and "Los limites."
[255] Meneses Ciuffardi, *El factor naval*," 132.
[256] Barros, *Historia diplomática de Chile*, 615.
[257] Cable from British ambassador in Santiago to foreign office, 30 May 1914. Cited in Meneses Ciuffardi, *El factor naval*, 132.
[258] Barros, *Historia diplomática de Chile*, 615.
[259] Meneses Ciuffardi, "Los limites," 96.
[260] Meneses Ciuffardi, *El factor naval*, 135.
[261] On the impact of World War I on the Chilean military and postwar reforms, see Chile, Ministério de Guerra, Estado Maior General del Ejército, *Historia del Ejército*, vol. 8, *La primera guerra mundial y su influencia en el Ejército, 1914–1940* (Santiago: Ministério de Guerra, 1980).

military prowess, but more so because of their heavy dependence on Germany for commerce and armaments. The war severed the official military exchange between the two countries. The Treaty of Versailles not only disarmed Germany but it also prohibited the export of German armaments and military personnel. Chile no longer needed foreign missions. Indeed, it was sending its own military trainers abroad to train the armed forces of others. Nevertheless, during the interwar years individual German military officers continued to serve in Chile and the rest of South America despite the Versailles ban.[262] A small number of individual German officers remained in Chile during the 1920s and 1930s.[263] They were usually "retired" officers on private contracts, and their activities were categorized as unofficial. Some simply emigrated and became citizens of the host country. The United States representative in Berlin cabled the State Department in 1930 that at least ten German officers "have been carrying out their duties in Chile with much dedication and have confined themselves entirely to the technical advice for which they have been employed."[264] The German officers served either as advisers to the general staff or as instructors at the War academy.

Despite the evisceration of Germany, Chile's adherence to the German military system did not wane after World War I. Why? The theory expects states to maintain their existing model in the absence of a critical juncture that compels them to switch to a new model. The 1902 détente with Argentina did not fully remove all of its external security threats, nor did it put an end to the historic rivalry. It did reduce them to manageable levels. The challenges posed by Peru and Bolivia, while real, were also manageable, given their own internal disorganization. Aside from a brief war scare with Peru in the early 1920s, Chile's external security environment remained fairly stable, albeit in the context of continuing relative decline of its power.

Chilean admiration for the German military system never disappeared. It was too deeply rooted. The French victory did spark some appeal in Chile. The influence of the French system was mainly at the doctrinal level.[265] But the appeal of the French was neither deep nor lasting. The United States was also generating much appeal in South America, particularly in naval organization and technology. Chile, in fact, had already begun to look to the United States on the eve of the war as it prepared naval reorganization. In 1913 Chile contracted individual U.S. naval officers for instruction in coastal artillery and to organize a coastal artillery school.[266] But this is as

---

[262] Nunn, *Yesterday's Soldiers*, 183.
[263] Nunn, *Yesterday's Soldiers*, 182–92, 211–12.
[264] Quote cited in Nunn *Yesterday's Soldiers*, 212.
[265] Nunn, *Yesterday's Soldiers*, 186, 190.
[266] Meneses Ciuffardi, *El factor naval*, 128.

close as Chile would approach U.S. military organization and technology in the period before the Second World War. Chile would continue to regard the United States with some coolness.

Chile clung to the past. The Chilean military remained essentially unchanged in the interwar period. Vial, in fact, argues that the Chilean military had been stagnating since the incomplete success of the 1906 reforms.[267] There were no major reorganization or reforms that altered significantly the interwar military from the one organized by Körner. It was not until a decade after the war that the strategic and tactical lessons of the war were being implemented.[268] During this period the only reform spurt of substance was 1924–31.[269] The power of the inspector general was reduced, and the new post of commander-in-chief of the army was created as the highest rank in the hierarchy. The general staff was reorganized in 1925, but it remained a subordinate advisory organ, dedicated solely to war planning.

The interwar years were mainly years of stagnation for the Chilean military.[270] The stagnation in military organization, doctrine, and technology in the 1920s was reflective of the overall precipitous decline in Chile's relative position as a power on the continent.[271] Chile's occupation of the top rank among the major powers was brief. Small in territory and population, with limited natural resources and a negligible industrial base, Chile could not keep up with its larger, economically more vigorous neighbors. By the turn of the century, Argentina was outdistancing Chile in national wealth and population. The development of a large and complex mass army taxed Chile's financial resources, and the armed peace bankrupted it.

The Second War of the Pacific catapulted Chile to the dominant position in the Pacific system of balancing. Chile's stay at the top was brief, and the benefits of victory illusory. Continental mastery was fleeting since it lacked the capacity to sustain its relative position in the long run. Chile's continental primacy was based largely on a combination of temporary and fortuitous factors.[272] Primacy was also temporary because its major rival, Argentina, possessed greater size and productive capacity. Chile's newly found source of revenue was Faustian. It was able to undertake massive public expenditures in social areas as well as finance military modernization. Yet the international market for nitrates was highly unstable. Predictably, Chile succumbed to the "Dutch disease" syndrome, as the economy turned to monoculture export

---

[267] Vial, *La sociedad chilena*.
[268] Estado Maior General del Ejército, *La Primera Guerra Mundial*, 48.
[269] On military reforms in the 1920s, see Estado Maior General del Ejército, *La primera guerra mundial*.
[270] Estado Maior General del Ejército, *La Primera Guerra Mundial*.
[271] On Chile's decline, see Meneses Ciuffardi, "Coping With Decline."
[272] Varley, "The Aftermath of the War of the Pacific," 19; Meneses, "Los limites."

production and the state came to rely on these export duties as its chief source of revenues.[273]

Chile's relative decline from the ranks of the major continental powers began almost immediately upon arrival at the top. Chile's eclipse was evident early on. The U.S. ambassador noted in 1899 that, unlike its neighbor to the east, Chile's structural weaknesses meant that the "improvident maintenance of an army, the size of which was far beyond its capacity to sustain, has greatly weakened the country commercially. [Chile's] ascendancy soon waned, and has now passed from it to [Argentina], where, from natural geographic and economic conditions, it is liable to remain for a long time."[274] Argentina was developing the economic-industrial base to sustain a large, well-equipped military. Chile, on the other hand, lacked the economic-industrial base to keep up with the minimum requirements of national competitive effectiveness, let alone sustain the large and impressive military power it already possessed.

---

[273] On this point, see Bowman and Wallerstein, "The Fall of Balmaceda."

[274] United States, Department of State, *Dispatches from U.S. Minister to Argentina, 1817–1906*, Film S-1040, M69, Roll 32, 3 August 1899.

5

Military Emulation in Argentina, 1895–1930

"It is no longer possible to improvise armies as in the past," warned Argentina's War Minister, Guillermo Villanueva, in 1896, as the country prepared to match the military developments under way in the region.[1] Argentine journalist Ernesto Quesada was more insistent and denigrating, decrying in 1898 Argentina's military "negligence" in the face of "military imbalance" favoring the "Chilean hordes."[2] In the decade after the start of Chile's military emulation Argentina relied on its old army to face the growing power of its rival across the Andes. Yet it did so for other than financial reasons.

Argentina in the 1890s was entering the new century as the most developed and prosperous of the Latin American republics and one of the richest nations in the world. Between the time of effective national union in 1880 and the First World War, Argentina experienced one of the world's most rapid economic growth rates. Its average annual growth rate between 1870 and 1914 was an estimated 5 percent, fueled by a tremendous expansion in agricultural and livestock production, and a large influx of foreign capital and immigrant labor.[3] Argentina's was an export-led economy, with its

---

[1] Minister of War Guillermo Villanueva, in Argentina, Ministério de Guerra y Marina, *Memoria del Ministério de Guerra y Marina, 1896* (Buenos Aires: Ministério de Guerra, 1896): 7. The *Memoria del Ministério de Guerra y Marina* is the official annual report of the ministry of war and navy. Collection consulted in the army historical archives, Servicio Histórico del Ejército, Buenos Aires. Hereafter cited as Ministério de Guerra, *Memoria*.

[2] Ernesto Quesada, *La política argentina respeto de Chile, 1895–1898* (Buenos Aires: Editor Arnaldo Moen, 1898): 103.

[3] On the growth of the Argentina economy, see Carlos F. Díaz Alejandro, *Essays on the Economic History of the Argentine Republic* (New Haven: Yale University Press, 1970); Roberto Cortés Conde, "The Growth of the Argentine Economy, 1870–1914," in *Argentina Since Independence*, ed. Leslie Bethell (Cambridge: Cambridge University Press, 1993): 327–53; *Relevamiento estadístico de la economia argentina, 1900–1980*, ed. Banco de Análisis y Computación (Buenos Aires: Banco de Análisis y Computación, 1982).

major strategic sectors controlled by foreign (mainly British) capital.[4] During this same time period, Argentina also experienced enormous social and demographic changes, essentially turning from a Latin to a European country in the makeup of its population, society, and cultural habits. Its average annual population growth rate was over 3 percent, going from a population of 1.7 million in 1869 to 8 million in 1914. This population growth was driven by the enormous influx of immigration from Europe (mainly Italy and Spain); an estimated 6 million, half which settled permanently.[5] Immigration and export-led growth spurred an unprecedented expansion in national wealth which fueled both conspicuous consumption as well as social modernization.

This wealth and social modernization did not extend in any serious way to the modernization of the armed forces prior to the mid-1890s. Having overcome over half a century of bloody internecine warfare and political fragmentation, Argentina first turned its seemingly unlimited wealth and resources toward the modernization of its social, economic, and administrative institutions. Yet, five years after unification in 1880 and the start of Chile's military emulation, the country's military lagged far behind the modernization taking place in other areas.[6] Chile's military buildup changed everything. As the threat of war with the militarily stronger Chile loomed large in the latter part of the 1890s, Argentina quickly turned to the buildup and modernization of its armed forces with alacrity and boundless energy. Like its archrival Chile, it too launched large-scale military emulation based on the German mass army. By the First World War, Argentina had eclipsed both of its historical rivals on its flanks to become the most potent military power on the continent.

The start of Argentina's military emulation can be dated to 1895, when its first request for a German military training mission was rebuffed. Its initial response to the rise of Chilean power was an arms buildup beginning in the early 1890s. A German mission was formally contracted in 1899, but the

---

[4] H. S. Ferns, *Britain and Argentina in the Nineteenth Century* (Oxford: Oxford University Press, 1960); *Historia argentina: la república conservadora*, vol. 5, ed. Túlio Halperin Donghi (Buenos Aires: Editorial Paidos, 1984); Roger Gravil, *The Anglo–Argentine Connection, 1900–1939* (Boulder: Westview Press, 1985); Andrew Thompson, "Informal Empire? An Exploration in the History of Anglo–Argentine Relations, 1810–1914," *Journal of Latin American Studies* 24, no. 2 (May 1992): 419–36.

[5] On population and immigration, see Diaz Alejandro, *Essays on the Economic History of the Argentine Republic*. Note that only 2% of the immigrants during 1857–1930 were of German origin, and about 46% were Italian.

[6] For overviews on early Argentine military history, see Argentina, Ministério de Guerra, Estado Maior General del Ejército, Comando en Jefe del Ejército, *Reseña histórica y organica del Ejército argentino*, 3 vols., vol. 2, *1862–1917* (Buenos Aires: Círculo Militar, 1971). Hereafter cited as Ministério de Guerra, *Reseña histórica*. See also Colonel Augusto G. Rodriguez, *Reseña histórica del Ejército argentino, 1862–1930* (Buenos Aires: Secretaria de Guerra, 1964).

initial request indicated an earlier decision had been made to adopt military emulation as the primary balancing strategy. When the German mission arrived in 1899, Argentina became the second of the three big regional powers to embark on a massive project of military modernization. That states like Argentina, in particular, assiduously attended to the relative capability of their military system is neither surprising nor unexpected. The *gaucho* republic was haunted by its perennial security predicament – sandwiched by historical enemies, Chile and Brazil. The tacit alliance of its two principal rivals was pure balance-of-power politics, since they shared Argentina as enemy. Throughout the period between 1885 and 1914 the Pacific, Andean, and La Plata subsystems experienced a continually rising level of hostility, arms racing, and war preparation. Argentina was at the epicenter of these trends, the bridge linking power competition in the two subsystems.

Argentina's military modernization was explicitly undertaken in response to the growth in the military power, territorial expansion, and competitive arms racing of its two main rivals, primarily Chile. It launched large-scale modernization precisely when its external security environment turned for the worse. It had been building up and modernizing its military and naval capabilities since the latter 1880s and early 1890s, purchasing enormous quantities of advanced weapons technology in Europe. By the mid-1890s its ability to free ride on the anti-Chilean coalition vanished, as detailed in the previous chapter. Now much more was required. It could not chance the risks of being militarily unprepared while flanked by powerful enemies. Come 1895, immediate war with Chile appeared inevitable, just as relations with Brazil worsened over border disputes. War was likely now on both flanks in 1895. No one inside Argentina could ignore the vast military power neighboring Chile was amassing, or dismiss the Brazilian factor.

MILITARY MODERNIZATION IN ARGENTINA, 1895–1930

There were three main phases to military modernization in Argentina, 1880–98, 1899–1914, and 1914–30, each corresponding to peaks in the country's worsening external security environment.[7] Large-scale military emulation comprised the first two phases, when the entirety of the German model was implanted. The first phase, 1880–98, was characterized by steady and extensive buildup of the latest European armaments, though little in terms of deep organizational reforms despite Chile's frantic and massive

---

[7] For a survey on Argentina's military modernization during the 1880–1914 period, see Ministério de Guerra, *Reseña histórica*; Gilberto Ramírez, Jr., "The Reform of the Argentine Army, 1890–1904," Ph.D. thesis (University of Texas–Austin, 1987); Frederick M. Nunn, *Yesterday's Soldiers: European Military Professionalism in South America, 1890–1940* (Lincoln: University of Nebraska Press, 1983); Alain Rouquié, *Poder militar y sociedad política en la Argentina, hasta 1943*, vol. 1 (Buenos Aires: EMECE Editores, 1981).

undertaking. However, by 1894 reformers had decided on a strategy of large-scale modernization, as its request in 1895 for a German training mission indicated. The second phase, roughly spanning 1899–1914, was the defining period. The armed peace and near-war crisis with Chile during the period 1898–1902 provided the backdrop for the hiring of a German training mission. In the third phase, 1914–30, minor reforms continued, but it was primarily a time of consolidating its position as the wealthiest and most powerful of the South American republics. As in Chile, military emulation in Argentina covered every area of the military system. What separated Argentina from the other regional states was that it alone had the industrial and productive base (as well as political stability) to build and sustain a large and expensive military system.

The Early Phase of Reforms

Argentina's emulation of the German military system followed the same pattern as elsewhere. It began to emulate the German system only after the 1870s, and initially confined its borrowing to armaments. As in the other republics, prior to 1870 the predominant organizational, technological, and doctrinal influence on the Argentine military was French.[8] French influence was partly superficial. First, it was confined to armaments. Argentina adopted French infantry light arms since the Paraguayan war. The Minié rifle was the standard infantry equipment since the Paraguayan war, as was French-made cast-iron and bronze artillery. After 1881 Argentina began to acquire the first series of Krupp field artillery.[9]

The other reason why foreign influence remained superficial prior to the 1880s relates to Argentina's own internal disunion. The Argentine army was established as a permanent national force only in 1880. Until this point the Argentine confederation had been basing its national defense largely on independent provincial militias (composed in part by the nominal national guard) and private *caudillo* (warlord) armies. There was a token federal army in existence since the Paraguayan war. Yet in the context of interprovincial warfare and shifting coalitions, the "federal" army acted more like a private or provincial force depending on the fortunes of whichever province or coalition claimed national power.[10] The core of what became the national army consisted of the force involved in the decades-long extermination campaigns against the Indian nations in the Patagonia and southern regions. The

---

[8] Ministério de Guerra, *Reseña histórica*; Miguel Angel Scenna, *Los militares* (Buenos Aires: Editora Belgrano, 1980); Lieutenant Colonel Augusto A. Maligne, *Historia militar de la República argentina durante el siglo de 1810 a 1910* (Buenos Aires: La Nación, 1910).

[9] Ministério de Guerra, *Reseña histórica*, 118.

[10] On the effects of the Paraguayan war on national unification and military organization, see Juan Bautista Alberdi, *La Guerra del Paraguay* (Buenos Aires: Hyspamérica Ediciones, SA, 1988).

leader and military hero of these campaigns was Júlio Argentino Roca, who effectively unified the country with his election in 1880.

Once Chile initiated military modernization in 1885, Argentina quickly found itself in a position of military inferiority. As expected by the theory, its initial response to the growth of Chilean power with its own armaments buildup, is detailed below. Military expenditures increased by 150 percent between 1891 and 1898.[11] Soon both sides found themselves embroiled in one of the most expensive and dangerous arms races in the region's history. Chile was dominant on land and at sea, and because naval capabilities would be so crucial in any war, Argentina turned first to modernizing and building up its navy.[12] Historically, Argentina feared the possibility of Chile having bioceanic capabilities, giving Chile the ability to cut off its economic lifeline and effectively quarantine the country. As both powers plunged into an escalating, costly arms race during the second half of the 1890s, Argentina kept a nervous eye on Chilean military capacity and improvements.[13] Indeed, all three, Argentina, Brazil, and Chile, expanded their powers and the scope and intensity of their information gathering and military intelligence on each other's military system.

REFORMERS AND THE GERMAN SYSTEM

A March 1894 correspondence between the two main figures in Argentine military modernization, two-time president Júlio Argentino Roca and Berlin-based military attaché Lieutenant Colonel Pablo Riccheri, is revealing for several reasons. In the letter, the former president and sitting Senator Roca expressed his worries about "this perspective of war with Chile, at a time when we have so much to anticipate and prepare in all areas, from soldiers' shoes to higher organization and strategic concepts, and for this reason I believe that the [war ministry] should have at its side an officer like you, the author of all our recent reforms and progress in everything concerning the art of war."[14] First, the specter of war with Chile was already looming large. Second, reformers saw thorough modernization as the only real solution. Finally, it may or may not be reasonable to read into Roca's conclusions validation of the German model, but the recent reforms he alluded to were the German-inspired ideas and reform measures of Riccheri.

Argentina's military modernization, as in Chile and Brazil, was largely the work of a cadre of young officers and their backers in the high command.

[11] Ministério de Guerra, *Reseña histórica*, 511. Expenditures for the army alone rose from 8 million pesos in 1891 to 20 million in 1898.

[12] Robert Scheina, *Latin America: A Naval History, 1810–1987* (Annapolis: Naval Institute Press, 1987).

[13] On this point see Ramirez, "The Reform of the Argentine Army," chap. 7.

[14] Correspondence Roca to Riccheri, 3 March 1894, in Rosendo Fraga, *La amistad Roca–Riccheri: a Través de su Correspondencia* (Buenos Aires: Círculo Militar, 1996), 68.

Argentina, in contrast to Chile but similar to Brazil, began to adopt the German military system mainly through the work and direction of its own European-trained officers. A conscious decision was made in the first half of the 1890s to develop a cadre of officers, all of whom would be sent to the elite academies of Europe for instruction, and who would return to direct the military modernization program upon their return home. Germany's initial refusal in 1895 to send an official mission, as discussed below, proved the wisdom of the decision. The goal was to "form a good nucleus of those who have seen European armies and know what good officers are worth," as one officer put it in 1888.[15] A similar philosophy would mark Brazil's initial approach to large-scale emulation.

The most important figure in Argentina's military reform movement was Pablo Riccheri.[16] Riccheri and the other reformers had as their institutional home the Comisión Técnica de Armamentos (Technical Commission on Armaments, also named Arms Purchasing Commission), established in 1890 to test and purchase European armaments. Records are imprecise as to the composition of the commission over time. The commission, and later the general staff, became incubators for reformers. Both experienced a good deal of promotions into their numbers during 1889 and 1890.[17] The commission was based in Berlin, and headed by Riccheri, who spent nearly all of the 1890s in Europe. The commission, especially Riccheri, established close personal and professional relations with members of the German army as well as German war industry. It was highly regarded within the German military and the rest of Europe for its technical and professional competence, particularly its strict scientific testing and control procedures in the purchasing of armaments.[18] Thus, the same officers who came to head large-scale emulation had the most extensive, direct, firsthand knowledge of European military systems and Germany's in particular.

Riccheri is widely credited by historians as the founder of the modern Argentine military. He was also the individual most responsible for the contracting of a German military mission.[19] He became the protégé of General

15 Quote cited in Ramirez, "The Reform of the Argentine Army," 165.
16 On Riccheri, see General Rodolfo Martínez Pita, *Riccheri* (Buenos Aires: Círculo Militar, 1952).
17 Argentina, Archivo General de la Nación, Archivo Roca, Caja 1379. The National Archives in Buenos Aires maintains several document collections, among them the personal letters and documents of President Júlio Roca, organized in separate folders (Caja). The individual archives are also referred to as "Fondo." Hereafter cited as Archivo Roca.
18 On the armaments commission, see Ramirez, "The Reform of the Argentine Army," chap. 4.
19 Studies on Riccheri include: Martínez Pita, *Riccheri*; Plácido Grela, *Fuerzas Armadas y soberania nacional: vida y obra del Ten. General Pablo Riccheri, forjador del moderno Ejército argentino* (Rosarios: Littoral Ediciones, 1973).

Júlio Roca, the war hero turned first president of unified Argentina during 1880–86.[20] Both had intimate knowledge of the military. After his successful desert campaigns against indigenous nations, Roca was nominated war minister in 1878, while Riccheri completed his studies in the Colégio Militar. Riccheri would later (1897) direct the war arsenal, head the general staff (1898), and serve as war minister during the pivotal 1900–04 years. The young Riccheri, an artillery officer, rose quickly through the ranks. Already in 1890 he was a major in the 1st Division of the main general staff and based in Europe. Riccheri himself was a graduate of Belgium's Superior War Academy, where he enrolled in 1883 and conducted research on the Belgian military system and European systems of command.[21] He later served as Argentina's military attaché in Paris, then in Berlin where he observed the annual Imperial war maneuvers in 1889.

From the start, Riccheri had no doubts as to what he believed to be his mission in Europe, where he met Roca for the first time. One year after the start of Chile's large-scale military emulation, he noted in a December 1886 cable to the foreign ministry that his "most fervent desire is to employ my time here [in Europe] to undertake studies for the purpose of improving our military institutions." Advances in technology and the "art of war have been tremendous in the *past sixteen years*," he noted, providing Argentina the template to modernize its armed forces. He concluded pointedly that "if our country wishes to preserve the hegemony granted to it by its geographic situation and its intellectual and material progress, it must vigorously acquire a new base for the establishment of its military institutions – a base that naturally conforms to the necessities of the nation and which takes into account the situation of the neighboring powers."[22] Riccheri's primary motivation in calling for emulation was Chile's military modernization. His cables frequently cited the Chilean threat. His overarching goal was not simply to counter Chile's buildup, but to provide Argentina with the capabilities to surpass Chile's power; to preserve a hegemonic position in the region which the Argentines believed was their natural right and destiny. Germany was to be the model for his project of national greatness.

Argentina had been studying the German military organization since the early 1880s. Germany's general staff drew particular attention.[23] By 1891 military contacts and arms trading between Argentina and Germany had deepened greatly. Yet, as is clear from Riccheri's 1886 cable, Argentina

[20] On Roca and Riccheri, see Fraga, *La amistad Roca–Riccheri*.

[21] Grela, *Fuerzas Armadas*.

[22] Pablo Riccheri, 25 December 1886 cable to Argentine legation in London. Quote cited in Grela, *Fuerzas Armadas*, 76. Emphasis added.

[23] See series of studies by J. A. Mendoza in *Revista Militar y Naval*, vols. 6 and 7 (November/December 1884).

wanted more than arms transfer. It wanted direct transfer of technical expertise and professional training. For quite some time, Argentina, like the other
South American powers, had been hiring individual European officers as
instructors in the military schools and field units. European military advisers
were present in Argentina since the late 1860s. There were many transplanted
European officers (mainly German, French, and Italian) in the Argentine
army.[24] By the late 1880s they became exclusively German in origin.

Why Germany's Imperial army? General Rafael Aguirre put it succinctly:
"The German Army represents the mightiest military organism that exists.
As a result of its integrity, its level of training, its *practical experience*, and
its historical tradition, the German Army is *the best example we could have
chosen to imitate.*"[25] Beginning in the early 1890s, Argentine officers were
engaged in the direct study and observation of the German military system – through the armaments commission – and indirectly through the
military literature. Why did the Argentines choose to import the German
military system as opposed to that of France, Britain, or Italy with whom
it already had extensive commercial and cultural ties and to whom it
looked as models for its growing, modernizing navy?[26] Why might it adopt
the same military system of its rival and most likely battlefield opponent,
Chile?

Despite past French intellectual and doctrinal influence, and the political
and ideological orientation of the Anglophile civilian leadership, there was
growing admiration for the German military system in the country. As in
Chile, this admiration turned into religious fanaticism on the part of some
officers. Individual enthusiasts were plenty, and by the mid-1880s a discernible Germanophile faction had emerged within the army. In a series of
studies in the widely read *Revista Militar y Naval* (later renamed *Revista
del Club Naval y Militar*), the journal's director, J. A. Mendoza, proposed
that the newly established Argentine general staff be modeled after that of
Germany. Mendoza, a colleague of Riccheri in the pivotal 1st Division of
the general staff, anticipated many of the arguments that future reformers
and defenders of the German model would turn to in their justification for

---

[24] Ramirez, "The Reform of the Argentine Army," 325.
[25] General Rafael M. Aguirre, war minister, 1912. Quote cited in Elizabeth B White, *The German Influence in the Argentine Army, 1900–1945* (New York: Garland, 1991): 16. Emphasis
added.
[26] Even after the start of emulation, Germany still lagged behind Britain in terms of its economic
position in Argentina. Britain remained the overwhelming economic actor in Argentina even
after 1914. As of 1904, Germany had surpassed France to become Argentina's second largest
trading partner. In 1913 Argentina accounted for 35% of Germany's exports to Latin America, and 41% of its imports from Latin America. See Ramirez, "The Reform of the Argentine
Army," chap. 2; Bill Albert, *South America and the First World War: The Impact of the War
on Brazil, Argentina, Peru, and Chile* (Cambridge: Cambridge University Press, 1988).

military emulation. He advocated the organization of a true general staff, adding that the "best organized of all is the German one."[27] He cautioned that Argentina should not imitate the Germans indiscriminately. He noted, "there is something [in the German model] that can be adopted, other things would require modifications, and even then we should not believe that we can approximate the perfection of the organization of the German army."[28]

The appeal of the German model was strongest among the younger officers. As in the case of Brazil, the reformers within and outside the military equated military modernization with national progress, and equated both with Germanization. One young officer remarked in 1889 that Germany was a "warrior nation par excellence," which "marched at the vanguard of progressive nations."[29] Admiration for the German system was evident as well in the upper ranks. The minister of war noted in his annual report of 1880 that "the general staff is the key, it is the great engine of the army, it is the depository of war, as is said of the Prussian [general staff]."[30] General Alberto Capedevilla, later an opponent of extensive reforms, argued in an article that the German infantry manual could serve as an excellent guide for officer instruction.[31] During the last phase consolidating the full emulation of the German system, War Minister Aguirre noted that "the German army has been chosen as the exclusive source for the formation of [our] officers, not just as a result of the ample support the Imperial government and the Prussian war minister has offered us, but also because, as has been said, we aspire persistently to [that level] of instruction, qualities which that army possesses in eminent degree."[32]

Details about Argentina's decision to hire a full German military training mission are missing from the archival records examined. German military advisers on independent contracts were in Argentina in the early 1890s.[33] Schiff reports that there were German and other European military advisers in Argentina even earlier during Roca's first presidency (1880–86).[34] German advisers, few in number and largely inactive officers, were serving in various

---

[27] J. A. Mendoza, *Revista Militar y Naval* 6, no. 1 (November 1884), 436. The *Revista*, an official publication, renamed *Revista del Club Naval y Militar*.

[28] J. A. Mendoza, articles on general staff organization, *Revista Militar y Naval*, vols. 6 and 7 (November/December 1884).

[29] Quote cited in Ramirez, "The Reform of the Argentine Army," 164.

[30] Ministério de Guerra, *Memória, 1880*, 21.

[31] Article by General Alberto Capdevilla, *Revista del Club Naval y Militar* 24, no. 6 (December 1895).

[32] Ministério de Guerra, *Memória, 1907–1908*, 108.

[33] White, *The German Influence*, 3.

[34] Warren Schiff, "The Influence of the German Armed Forces and War Industry on Argentina, 1880–1914," *Hispanic American Historical Review* 52, no. 3 (August 1972): 436–55, 438.

capacities throughout the army. German war ministry records show that by the mid-1890s there were numerous German officers applying for advisory service in Argentina.[35]

As noted above, Argentina made an early appeal to the German government for a military mission – conveying a formal request in 1895.[36] Its request was unsuccessful. The German emperor, Wilhelm II, feared that granting Argentina a mission would damage the close and lucrative military and commercial ties with Chile.[37] Delicate diplomatic relations were not the only factors stymieing Argentina's attempt to get a training mission. Argentines were also unsure about the wisdom of having a foreign mission. Argentine military and civil leaders had a jaundiced, skeptical view of Chile's experience and the role of the German military mission in the Chilean army and politics. They believed that Chile had turned itself into a satellite of Germany and were apprehensive about what they perceived to be meddling in Chile's internal affairs by German corporations and government. For reformers and Germanophiles like Riccheri, the question of a German training mission was even more awkward and complicated. Anti-German sentiment was widespread among ordinary and elite Argentines. Germany was seen as a protector and ally of their country's greatest enemy. Roca confided to Riccheri his own preoccupation in 1894. He wrote that the German government was viewed with suspicion and antipathy because of its military assistance to Chile and, as a result, feared the Chileans might be tempted to try "new adventures."[38] It is impossible to know the impact of each of these considerations. But as war with Chile seemed imminent, and the problem of reform became more urgent, Argentina saw a military mission as a necessary component of its modernization plans.

The German Military Mission

The 1898–1902 near-war crisis with Chile prompted Argentina to undertake a much more rapid, immediate, and extensive overhaul of its military system. A lengthy, uncertain go-it-alone strategy would no longer suffice in view of the intensified military competition with its neighbors. In 1899 the Argentine minister in Berlin, General Lúcio Mansilla, was instructed by Buenos Aires to contract a German military mission for the purpose of organizing and staffing a new superior war academy, the Escuela Superior de Guerra (ESG). This time Argentina's request received the approval of the German government, a decision which drew immediate criticism from Chile. The reasoning

[35] Schiff, "The Influence of the German Armed Forces," 438.
[36] White, *The German Influence*, 3.
[37] Ibid.
[38] Correspondence Roca to Riccheri, 3 March 1894, in Fraga, *La amistad Roca–Riccheri*, 67–68.

behind Germany's reversal on a military mission to Argentina is a matter of conjecture – all the more so coming at a time of war crisis between the Andean rivals. For its part, Chile's only recourse was to express its displeasure.

For head of mission, Argentina first approached General Colmar von der Goltz, who had successfully directed the reorganization of the Turkish army.[39] Goltz declined but recommended in his stead Lieutenant Colonel Alfred Arent, a cavalry officer and former member of the Great General Staff. Argentina's war minister, General Luis Campos, proudly reported that, "the moment has come when the government is concerned with facilitating the scientific formation of our future military leaders, taking as a model those European systems. [I have been] authorized to hire Colonel Alfred Arent to found and direct our Escuela Superior de Guerra."[40] Arent headed a small, five-man mission to help found and teach at the war academy. Arent himself was to direct the academy, formally established in 1900 to train general staff officers. While unable to get von der Goltz, the Argentines did get a competent, respected military planner and tactician in Arent. Like his Chilean counterpart Körner, Arent was a decorated veteran of the Franco–Prussian War (1870) and staff officer.

The Argentine mission, in contrast to Chile's, remained relatively small. Its small size, and its more circumscribed role, partly reflected the complicated triangular political relations among Germany, Chile, and Argentina rather than Argentina's desire to rebuild and expand its military power. Other factors were in play as well. Though technically proficient, Arent's personal and diplomatic blunders, including an antagonistic relationship with Riccheri, hampered the work of the German mission. Arent's troubles, the negative publicity the mission attracted to itself, and the prejudiced view that Argentines already had about the German mission in Chile nearly ruined Argentina's attempt at full-scale emulation of the German army. Consequently, the mission remained small and confined in its work. In 1912, for instance, the British reported only eight German military advisers in Argentina, six of whom were at the war academy (ESG) and one attached to the general staff.[41]

Large-scale modernization, based on the German model, had strong backing in the highest reaches of authority, including that of President Roca. During the first decade of the twentieth century there were many Germanophile officers in strategic posts within the military. Among other early supporters of the German model were the influential General Francisco Seeber, Lieutenant

[39] Ramirez, "The Reform of the Argentine Army," 368; White, *The German Influence*, 3–5.

[40] Ministério de Guerra, *Memória, 1898–99*, 10.

[41] Britain, Foreign Office, British Documents on Foreign Affairs: Reports and Papers From the Foreign Office Confidential Print, pt. 1, series D, Latin America, *1845–1914*, vol. 9, *The Latin American Republics, 1910–1914*, ed. George Philip (Bethesda: University Press of America, 1991): 262.

Colonel José Rojas, a future director of the ESG, and José Felix Uriburu. Uriburu had trained and served in the German army, and was one of the most ardent Germanophiles in the Argentine army.[42] Aside from the backing reformers and Germanophiles received from Roca, most of the war ministers between 1900 and 1914 were strong advocates of the German model, especially General Rafael M. Aguirre. Moreover, leading figures of the "old army" and veterans from the Paraguayan and Indian wars supported military reforms, including generals Bartólomeu Mitre, Nícolas Levalle, Luis Maria Campos, and Donato Alvarez.[43] Outside of the military, where reformers and Germanophiles were the dominant faction, extensive reforms and the German model received the backing of Argentina's powerful and assertive foreign minister, Estanislao Zeballos. Much like his equally influential counterpart and personal rival in Brazil, the Baron of Rio Branco, Zeballos was ardent in his admiration and advocacy for the German military system.

ARMAMENTS

The army reforms undertaken after 1880, when a national military under centralized command and political control was firmly established, looked to Germany's Imperial army as a model. Many of these founding reforms were initiated under Roca's first presidency (1880–86). Roca, the hero of the desert wars against the Indian nations of the Patagonia, had served as war minister in 1878. The bulk of military reforms in this first phase involved the acquisition of modern armaments. Argentina began to invest in a vast rearming of its land and naval forces by purchasing the latest military technologies in Europe. Argentine military expenditures during the second half of the 1890s were astronomical, and remained high to 1914 (see Figure 5.1).[44] It should be mentioned briefly, however, that some modest organizational reforms were also implemented during this first phase. In 1884 a permanent general staff was created, and later restructured in 1896, though it remained largely administrative in function. A new conscription law acted as a prelude to full obligatory military service, requiring all eligible males to serve in the line army for two months of training.

Armaments buildup defined the first phase. We expect states confronted by a serious and growing threat, as Argentina was, to turn to the quickest and easiest balancing strategy, such as beefing up its armaments. While here we focus only on the army, it should be noted that an equally intense

---

[42] For a study on Uriburu see Pedro Fernandez Lalanne, *Los Uriburu* (Buenos Aires: EMECE Editores, 1989).

[43] Rouquié, *Poder militar*, 83.

[44] See Robert Potash, *The Army and Politics in Argentina, 1928–1945: Yrigoyen to Peron*, vol. 1 (Stanford: Stanford University Press, 1969): chap. 1; Ministerio de Guerra, *Reseña histórica*, vol. 2, *1862–1917*, 512–15.

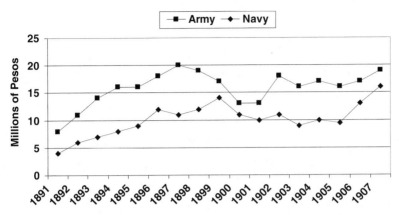

FIGURE 5.1. Trend Line of Argentine Army and Navy Expenditure, 1891–1907. (*Source:* Ministério de Guerra y Marina, *Reseña histórica*, 511. Figures represent totals from regular budget, and do not include extraordinary, or emergency, expenditures.)

naval modernization competition was consuming the energies of the three South American rivals in the last quarter of the century. Like Chile, the navy constituted the main pillar of Argentina's national defense. The ocean was its lifeline, all the more as its export-led economy accelerated its pace of growth. Its extensive coastline, together with its national well-being, could only be defended by a fast and powerful navy. Argentina's naval modernization had been underway since 1895, experiencing another major (and revolutionary) spurt in 1908–14 with the acquisition of dreadnought warships during the naval arms race with Brazil. Like its rival Chile, Argentina turned to the British Royal Navy as its source of inspiration and hardware. Italy as well became a major source.[45] A new naval expansion program was launched in 1926 in response to Brazil's 1924 push to modernize its fleet.

In a lengthy cable from Berlin to Roca in the fall of 1895, Riccheri focused at length on the "grave situation" with Chile and its modernization led by the "imminent General Körner," arguing that "the better armed we are the more chance we have to maintain peace."[46] The major push in arms buildup corresponded with the peak periods of armed confrontation with Chile (see Table 5.1). The armed forces' share of the national budget between 1890 and 1897 averaged 30 percent, nearly approaching one half in 1896

[45] For an excellent discussion of this issue see, Varun Sahni, "Not Quite British: A Study of External Influence on the Argentine Navy," *Journal of Latin American Studies* 25, no. 3 (October 1993): 489–513; Scheina, *Latin America*.

[46] Correspondence, Riccheri to Roca, 10 October 1895, in Fraga, *La amistad Roca–Riccheri*, 230–31.

TABLE 5.1. *Military Expenditure as Percent of Total Expenditure. Average for Selected Year Ranges, 1884 – 1917*

Year	Army	Navy
1884–1891	15	6
1892–1902	20	13
1895–1899	22	12
1907–1917	9	8

Source: Data compiled from, Ministério de Guerra, *Memoria*, during selected years, and from Ministério de Guerra, Reseña histórica, 509 – 15.

alone.[47] In 1906 and 1907 additional emergency war expenditures were approved, averaging 17 percent of the public budget. Expenditures for the army alone averaged 15 percent of total expenditures during 1902–07, while the navy's share hovered at 10 percent.[48] The acquisition of German arms accelerated as the country found itself in an arms race with Chile by the mid-1890s. As is common with military emulators, armaments buildup is the first and easiest stage of borrowing. Not surprisingly, the switch to the German model occurred more quickly in the area of armaments. As early as 1873 Argentina was acquiring its first pieces of Krupp artillery.[49] After 1881 Argentine artillery was exclusively of German origin, and by the early 1890s Germany was the exclusive supplier of all weapons and equipment for Argentina's land forces.[50] In 1889 Argentina purchased 60,000 Mauser rifles from Germany.[51] In 1894 an emergency national defense budget was approved in preparation for war with Chile.[52] A huge order of arms, munitions, and equipment in 1896 was described by Riccheri as giving Argentina the capacity to "burn half of Chile and Körner with all his helmeted Germans."[53] After 1898 more weapons were acquired, including field canons, coastal fortifications, Maxim guns, and shells.

Far from random, Argentina's arms buildup was studied and coordinated by the aforementioned armaments purchasing commission. Indeed, the process of armaments acquisition became pivotal to the wider modernization process. The commission acted as the principal organ to test and purchase European armaments. The commission was based in Berlin, Germany from 1890 to 1914. War ministry records, however, show that as early as 1881

---

[47] Ramirez, "The Reform of the Argentine Army," 191.
[48] Ministério de Guerra, *Reseña histórica*, 512.
[49] Schiff, "The Influence of the German Armed Forces," 47.
[50] Ministério de Guerra, *Reseña histórica*.
[51] Ramirez, "The Reform of the Argentine Army," 169–70.
[52] Schiff, "The Influence of the German Armed Forces," 438.
[53] Ramirez, "The Reform of the Argentine Army," 183.

Argentina was attempting to establish a permanent armaments commission in Europe.[54]

Argentina imported both military hardware as well as know-how from Germany. One of the more significant episodes in its modernization process was the decision in 1891 to equip its army with the Mauser rifle, which Argentina redesigned and modified (through the work of its arms purchasing commission in Europe).[55] Argentina received German licensing authority to begin manufacturing an Argentine model of the Mauser rifle. The Model 91 Argentine Mauser became standard equipment in the region. According to Riccheri, it was subsequently adopted by Germany, Britain, United States, Spain, Brazil, Sweden, Bolivia, and even rival Chile. It remained standard issue for the Argentine army up to the eve of World War I.

By 1900 Argentina had amassed enough armaments and equipment to outfit a standing force of 150,000.[56] The year 1908 saw a major acquisition of new artillery, all from Krupp, including twelve 13 cm siege canons, twenty-six 10.5 cm canons, and thirty-six 10.5 cm campaign artillery pieces.[57] In 1910 the army was equipped with 1891 and 1909 models of the Mauser rifles, and Krupp pieces of 75 mm, 105 mm, and 130 mm, mostly 1898 models.[58] The other major prewar instance of large-scale arms acquisition and buildup occurred during the 1906–14 arms race with Brazil. By the early 1890s Germany had already become Argentina's exclusive supplier of arms and equipment for its land forces.[59] Its reliance on German arms was one of almost total dependence.[60] This high dependence on German arms meant that for Argentina and Chile, in contrast to Brazil, the First World War and the restrictions of the Versailles treaty amounted to an even greater disruption for their militaries.

Aside from the armaments commission in Europe, the rest of the army's technical and storage infrastructure was weak. This reflected the overall administrative disorganization and functional disarticulation of the army's supply system, statistical services, and lack of storage facilities. These too were to be restructured. The army's supply and arsenal system was reorganized with the establishment of the Intendencia de Guerra (War Intendancy). Aside from the formal German mission attached to the military academies and upper military administration, Argentina also contracted individual

---

54 Ministério de Guerra, *Memória, 1880*, annex.
55 Ramirez, "The Reform of the Argentine Army," 170.
56 Ramirez, "The Reform of the Argentine Army," 334.
57 Rodriguez, *Reseña historica*, 123–24.
58 Maligne, *Historia militar*, 183.
59 See G. Pope Atkins and Larry V. Thompson, "German Military Influence in Argentina, 1921–1940" *Journal of Latin American Studies* 4, no. 2 (November 1972): 257–74. By the eve of World War I, Argentina began to acquire some of its smaller warships and torpedo boats from Germany. Britain, France, Italy, and the United States were its main suppliers of its capital warships.
60 Atkins and Thompson, "German Military Influence in Argentina," 258.

German and other European military technicians to direct and provide technical support in the arsenals and the small arms and munitions factories. In 1912 the British reported that there were eight such foreign technicians.[61]

While the South Americans were driven by security needs to modernize their armed forces and to look to European armies as models, the European great powers were driven by their own commercial and geostrategic considerations. Wealthy and fast-growing Argentina, very much like the other South American republics, was a lucrative market for European manufactured goods and, more important, their emerging global war industry. Argentina and the other republics were, naturally, targets of fierce competition among the European arms manufacturers, a competition that was politically corrupting and that spilled into divisive domestic politics.[62] Similarly, secondary states like Argentina were always vulnerable to the whims and bullying of the global great powers, on whom they were highly vulnerable given their dependence on European (mainly British) markets, capital, and credit. Grela argues that Argentina was coming under heavy pressure from Britain – whose dominant position in the River Plate economy led many to describe Argentina as an informal colony – not to purchase German weapons.[63]

CONSCRIPTION

A year after Chile instituted obligatory military service, Argentina implemented its own, weeks before the military was put on war footing and following nearly a year of debate and redrafting. The adoption of obligatory military service in 1901 (amended in 1905) was a major reform measure. The law was adopted at the peak of the near-war crisis with Chile. Universal military obligation was a crucial component of military modernization. The previous 1895 reforms introduced limited obligatory service. The 1895 law still left Argentina with a woefully inadequate and disorganized reserve system. The 1901 law was intended to correct these flaws. It stipulated obligatory, universal, and personal service (though, once again, the new law included exemptions that tended to benefit the wealthy). Argentina's adoption of obligatory service, though repeatedly couched by its defenders in democratic, nation-building language to placate congressional opponents, was explicitly a response to Chile's efforts. Riccheri noted during a congressional hearing that "obligatory military service [based on] a regional system is the most rational system in which all the powers of Europe base their military organization; and *it is the principle upon which is found the military*

---

[61] Philip, ed., British Documents on Foreign Affairs, The Latin American Republics, 262.
[62] On this point, see White, *German Influence*; Schiff, "The Influence of the German Armed Forces"; Atkins and Thompson, "German Military Influence in Argentina."
[63] Grela, *Fuerzas Armadas*, 75.

organization system of one neighboring power, which has an organization already far advanced, and which our country cannot neglect.[64]

Most scholars agree that the basic legislation was drafted by the Arent mission, though it appears that versions of the legislation were in debate since 1899.[65] Like Chile, Argentina patterned its conscription system on Germany's. The 1901 law, revised in 1905, provided for obligatory and personal service by lottery, fixing the length of service at one year (originally two years) in the regular army and two years in the navy. The second contingent of lottery-eligible males and all other liable males were required to serve three months in the army.[66] The impact of the law was immediate. During the first year alone some 68,000 men were incorporated.[67] Since Argentina was in the grips of the war scare with Chile, the quality of training for the new recruits is unclear. Riccheri reports that in 1902 over 90,000 men served or trained in the regular army.[68] He assured Roca, as both stood on the precipice of war, that the "army finds itself in condition to respond successfully to any eventuality" as a result of the new obligatory service law.

Riccheri and the reformers followed closely the Prussian example of creating a small but solid military apparatus capable of rapid expansion and mobilization. Unable to contain his pride and enthusiasm, he reported that as a result of recently adopted reform measures the present organization of the army easily permitted its expansion with trained reserves, "sufficient to create an army of 60,000 men, with all elements of armaments and equipment necessary, to enter immediately into combat."[69] The national army was organized, as in Germany, into the first line army and its reserves, the national guard, and the territorial guard. With respect to reserve service, after a tour in the active army there awaited nine years in the reserves for both those who served the full year as well as those incorporated for only three months. Reservists underwent two-month-long periods of maneuvers and exercises annually. The law required a further ten years of service in the national guard and five in the territorial guard, each also requiring multiple periods of annual exercises. The territorial guard was based on German principle, a reserve force independent of the first line army and charged exclusively with the mission of frontier guard.

---

[64] Pablo Riccheri, quote cited in Grela, *Fuerzas Armadas*, 196. Emphasis added.

[65] See, for example, White, *German Influence*; Nunn, *Yesterday's Soldiers*; Rouquié, *Poder militar*; Atkins and Thompson, "German Military Influence in Argentina"; Schiff, "The Influence of the German Armed Forces." The correspondence examined here between Roca and Riccheri does not make any mention of German participation.

[66] Brazilian officer Duval estimated that annually only about 25% of all eligible males were called up for duty. See Armando Duval, *Argentina, potencia militar*, 2 vols., vol. 2 (Rio de Janeiro: Imprensa Nacional, 1922): 21.

[67] Ministério de Guerra, *Memória, 1901–1902*, 6.

[68] Ministério de Guerra, *Memória, 1901–1902*, 14.

[69] Ministério de Guerra, *Memória, 1901–1902*, 6.

By 1910 Argentina could field a standing force of 250,000 (regular army plus reserve forces), of which at least half had some minimal level of instruction.[70] In 1922 Argentina's mobilizational capacity was estimated at 140,000–155,000 of first line army and reserves, with 660 canons. Its overall combat force was estimated to be a grand total of 695,000, which included the first line army and reserves, the national guard, the territorial guard, and untrained reserves.[71] No other South American country could match Argentina's mobilizational potential. One influential general staff officer noted that, in the event of any war against its neighbors, Argentina was capable of rapid, violent, and deep offensive operations.[72] Aside from this numerical superiority and organizational efficiency, Argentina's extensive rail network also assured rapid mobilization and concentration of forces.[73] From 9,400 km in 1890, Argentina's rail network had exploded to 33,900 km, making it one of the top ten largest rail networks in the world.

Conscription into the Argentine army, like its German and Chilean counterparts, was regional and decentralized. Argentina developed one of the most well-organized conscription systems in the region. The conscription system was run by the military itself, even at the local district level, and not by civilian politicians. This method of organization inoculated the system from politics and political interference, though the system was never fully immune nor without loopholes that benefited the elite. Conscription fell under the jurisdiction of the general staff and was administered regionally by the field staffs. The national territory was divided into five military regions, each composed of a division and its general staff. Each region or zone, which corresponded with population distribution and strategic importance, was further subdivided into two smaller zones, and each in turn subdivided into six military districts. Conscription and the instruction of new draftees were run by each military district. As in Germany, the system was organized as the smallest level of the country's military division, whereby the local military district would be responsible for the maintenance of a list, running the lottery, and incorporating new draftees. With the 1911 modified law, every eighteen-year-old male was required to register with the services and receive a *"cardenetta de alistamiento,"* a registration card that doubled as a voter registration card.[74] Argentina also adopted Germany's practice of a one-year reserve officer training program. This was intended largely as a way to address the shortage of reserve officers. The system was organized around a three-month training program, utilizing civilian schools, in addition to other special courses.

---

[70] Maligne, *Historia militar*, 180. See also Duval, *Argentina, potencia militar.*

[71] Duval, *Argentina, potencia militar*, vol. 2, 583, 597, 600–03.

[72] Maligne, *Historia militar*, 180.

[73] Duval, *Argentina, potencia militar*, vol. 2, 589.

[74] Duval, *Argentina, potencia militar*, vol. 1.

OFFICER FORMATION AND TRAINING

The greater part of Argentina's military modernization took place between 1900 and 1914. This second reform phase was a period of deepening of the German model. The army's intellectual formation occupied most of the work of this second phase. The German imprint was deep, penetrating all three vital springs of intellectual development: officer formation, general staff organization, and military doctrine. The German mission's principal task was to establish and direct a war academy to train officers for general staff service and senior command. Like its Chilean counterpart, the Escuela Superior de Guerra (ESG) was modeled after the Kriegsakademie. The ESG became the main locus of German efforts and influence within the Argentine army. The creators of the ESG planned to use it as the main platform and instrument through which uniformity in the corps could be achieved, not only through formal instruction but also by providing special courses, directing field combat training, and large-scale joint maneuvers.[75]

Arent became the director of the academy, and five of the initial faculty were German officers.[76] The ESG had a three-year curriculum (originally two), and was opened to first lieutenants and captains from the three combat arms. In 1904, the ESG curriculum was expanded to train officers for superior command. Like its German counterpart, the ESG's curriculum and philosophy stressed practice and contact with the troops. It required of each prospective candidate for admission at least three years (later extended to five) of active service in the field. Regular contact with line forces was part of the coursework. War gaming and field exercises modeled on the Franco-Prussian War were also key components of its three-year curriculum. Entrance and graduation examinations were drawn up by the German instructors. Admissions requirements were stringent, but even more stringent were the qualifications for general staff service. As with the procedure in the Kriegsakademie, the top graduates of the ESG became *oficiales alumnos*, probation candidates for staff service, after a period of which a select few would be incorporated in the general staff. Others received adjunct status. The graduates of the ESG rose quickly through the ranks, and even the army itself noted that the top graduates of the academy would receive priority in promotions.[77]

---

[75] On the Escuela Superior de Guerra, see Escuela Superior de Guerra (ESG), *Cincuentenario de la Escuela Superior de Guerra: homenage tributado a su fundador, Tenente General Luís Maria Campos* (Buenos Aires: ESG, 1951), in Ministério de Guerra, Arquivo Servicio Historico del Ejército, Buenos Aires.

[76] Duval, *Argentina, potencia militar*, vol. 2, 369. See also Escuela Superior de Guerra, *Cincuentenario*. The ESG staff included Colonel Alfred Arent, director; Lieutenant Colonel José A. Rojas, subdirector; José Armand, secretary. Other staff and professors: Rolo Kornstzki, Jorge Felgenhauer, Beltran Schunk, Alfonse Diserens, Gunter Bronsard von Schellendorff, Carlos Sarmiento, Gerardo Aranzadi, Luis Dellepiane, Carlos Corazzi, Marcial Quiroga.

[77] Ministério de Guerra, *Reseña histórica*, 308.

Germans also established and staffed the various specialized schools for each combat service as well as schools for junior officers. The Colégio Militar (Military School), which had gone through various cycles of reform and disruption, was reorganized as the Escuela Militar y de Aplicación in 1904. It offered a three-year course of study for officers in artillery and engineering. A special eight-month course of study was started for all officers and previous graduates of the military schools. It provided revision courses to ensure uniformity in instruction and doctrine in the officer corps. In 1908 the Escuela de Clases (renamed Escuela de Suboficiales in 1916) was established with the purpose of creating the noncommissioned cadre for all the combat arms. Argentina also emulated Germany's longstanding and successful practice of a one-year voluntary officer training program. It also consolidated a reserve officer formation system in 1905, utilizing civilian schools and requiring training for three months.

New promotions and service qualifications were devised to achieve the same goal: to raise the technical and professional level of the officer corps as well as create a homogenous, Prussianized officer corps.[78] As part of the 1905 reforms, the new service requirements stipulated that only graduates of the Colégio Militar could be commissioned. The new regulations also required that to qualify for promotions officers must first graduate from the advanced military schools, to undergo examination at the ESG before promotion to the ranks of major or higher. By 1908 the influence and activities of the German military mission had gradually expanded into other areas of the Argentine military system, including promotions. German officers came to have a controlling voice in senior rank officer promotions (an issue that would later cause a good deal of opposition and resentment within the military).[79]

The influence of the German model was deepened by the reforms of 1905–06, and reinforced by the 1907–08 wholesale adoption of German regulations and field manuals. The war department celebrated the adoption of German regulations, which "give us an indispensable foundation" and provide a uniform method of training and deployment of troops.[80] This was followed up in 1909 with required examination in field service and troop command to ensure knowledge of the new regulations.[81] Suitable or not, wise or foolish, Argentina had effectively adopted German war doctrine with these reforms.

The key piece of reform in this deepening of the German model at the intellectual and doctrinal level was a new agreement with Germany to allow

---

[78] Rouquié, *Poder militar*, 93–97. See also Potash, *The Army and Politics*, 2–3.

[79] Schiff, "The Influence of the German Armed Forces," 444.

[80] Ministério de Guerra, *Memoria, 1907–1908*, 106. It is worth noting that Riccheri's immediate successor as war minister was General Godoy, who had opposed Riccheri's reform plans and emulation while serving in the congress. Nevertheless, in his brief tenure he continued and, in some instances, broadened those reforms.

[81] White, *The German Influence*, 13.

Argentine officers to serve in the Imperial army as well as, more importantly, to gain admissions into the Kriegsakademie. As evident in the large number of Argentine officers who would eventually go to Germany, the sending of officers for formal direct training in the Imperial army was Argentina's principal strategy for large-scale emulation. The idea was to create a cadre of German-trained officers who would then return to lead the army and direct the modernization process. Two categories of officers were sent. One group was sent annually to serve directly in German regiments; the other went to Germany for advanced instructions to prepare a body of faculty for the nation's military schools. A new regulation required that all officers being sent abroad for instruction and training were to go exclusively to Germany. Those already serving elsewhere in Europe were reassigned to German units for eighteen months.[82]

From 1905 onwards Argentine officers served in Germany in various capacities. Some were sent to German military schools. Some were incorporated into German regiments, while others attended the annual maneuvers of the Imperial army as special observers. In 1906 the Argentine government received approval from Germany to send thirty officers for training, five of whom were to study at the Kriegsakademie to become professors at ESG. In 1908 over sixty Argentine officers were serving in Germany. Up until World War I, upward of 173 officers had been sent to Germany.[83] Between 1909 and 1914 additional officers were sent to observe the annual German imperial maneuvers.[84] The exact number of Argentine officers who served in Germany between 1906 and 1914 is unknown, and war ministry records are unsystematic. Potash estimates that about 140 in number are known, but that the real figure may well be somewhere between 150 and 175 to the eve of World War II.[85] When war was declared in the summer of 1914 there were an estimated forty Argentine officers in Germany.[86] Duval, the astute Brazilian military attaché, estimates that over half of the Argentine officer corps had passed through the German army and German military schools, nearly all of which occupied the highest positions in military administration, schools, and troop command.[87]

German-trained officers came to play important roles in Argentine national life in the postwar period.[88] The most outstanding and influential of the German-trained officers was José Felix Uriburu, who became

---

[82] Estado Mayor General del Ejército, *Boletín Militar*, 18 October 1905.

[83] Atkins and Thompson, "German Military Influence in Argentina," 259. See also Potash, *The Army and Politics in Argentina*, 4, fn. 6.

[84] Duval, *Argentina, potencia militar*, vol. 2, 379.

[85] Rouquié, *Poder militar*, 90.

[86] Potash, *The Army and Politics*, 4, fn. 6; Rouquié, *Poder militar*, 92.

[87] Duval, *Argentina, potencia militar*, vol. 2, 371.

[88] See Schiff, "The Influence of the German Armed Forces"; Potash, *The Army and Politics*, chap. 1.

director of the ESG (1907–13), inspector general and army chief (1923–26), and acted as interim president (1930–32) of Argentina after the 1930 coup. Uriburu was one of the top graduates of the ESG, and subsequently served as artillery officer in Germany's First Regiment of the Artillery Guard and the Second Uhlans. He was the leading and most respected supporter of the German mission and emulation of the German system. Uriburu favored the expansion of the German mission's activities and authority throughout the army.[89] Other influential German-trained officers were the war ministers between 1932–38, General Manuel Rodriguez and Basílio Pertiné. Another important officer was General Juan Bautista Molina, a political maverick and later head of the arms-purchasing commission in Europe (1926–32).

The ESG remained the bastion of German influence and the dissemination of the German model. Its graduates, together with those officers who had served in Germany were the main carriers of the German model. German professors at the ESG inculcated their students in the virtues of offensive action, encirclement, preparation, and rapid mobilization. Hans von Below, professor at the ESG in 1907 and director of the army's war games and maneuvers, in the *Revista Militar*, explained the virtues of German war theory: "success lies in the offensive, for the defense by itself can never win and nor is it necessary always to have numerical superiority for offensive action." Mouthing the teachings of the Kriegsakademie since the time of Moltke, Below went on to explicate key pillars in German operational doctrine: "the envelopment of the enemy," and "the freedom of action [for subordinate commanders] is indispensable such that it is unnecessary to wait for orders" once contact with the enemy has been made.[90] The interruption caused by the First World War was a serious blow to further development of the German organizational and technological influence, but at the doctrinal-intellectual level this influence persisted strongly into the interwar years.

GENERAL STAFF ORGANIZATION

"The general staff is the key," declared the war ministry's annual report in 1880. "It is the great motor of the army, it is the repository of war, as they say of the Prussian."[91] As in Chile, substantial reform measures were taken to organize a modern general staff to serve as the brain of the army. Both Chile and Argentina adopted Germany's open and decentralized staff system, though neither matched the level of authority and control over military affairs of the Grosser Generalstab.

[89] On Uriburu see, Schiff, "The Influence of the German Armed Forces." See also Nunn, *Yesterday's Soldiers*, chap. 4; Potash, *The Army and Politics*, 4–5.
[90] Professer Hans von Below, "Las maniobras Imperiales alemanes en 1906," *Revista Militar* 6, no. 168 (January 1907): 19–20.
[91] Ministério de Guerra, *Memória, 1880*, 21.

The genesis of a modern Argentine staff system began with the reforms of 1895, which gave the general staff wider powers and technical orientation.[92] Development of a modern general staff, institutionalized and permanent, broke with the tradition of *caudillos* and warlord armies. The new staff's chief became the immediate commander-in-chief of the army. This exalted position and authority of the general staff and its chief, however, existed more on paper than in practice. The 1895 reforms gave the general staff three main departments – a technical division, inspection, and instruction – as well as a small administrative section. A solid organization would emerge only during Roca's second presidency and under the tenure of Riccheri as chief of staff. Soon after his election, Roca summoned Riccheri from Europe to resume his duties, writing that "here we are awaiting for you to organize the general staff, which today remains of provisional character, and I wish to give it a more definitive organization, in accordance with the latest progress in military science."[93] Even before Riccheri could return from Berlin, where he was making new armaments purchases, Roca cabled him again to nominate him as war minister.

A new decree was issued in late 1900 reorganizing the general staff and streamlining military hierarchy. It proposed a clearer division of labor in the war department among the military cabinet, central administration, and the general staff. Command was reserved exclusively for the war minister, and exercised through the military cabinet. The 1900 reorganization reduced the general staff's role in command, and endowed it with purely war-planning and preparation functions. The 1900 reforms and subsequent reorganizations also gave it greater organizational and departmental differentiation.[94] The staff was subdivided into six departments (mobilization, military operations, geography, transportation, information and statistics, and military history), but field staffs were not created. Some essential functions, such as conscription and military schools, were placed under the jurisdiction of the military cabinet. In a vague provision, the chief of staff was responsible for the "technical inspection" of ESG.[95] Argentina moved closer to the German model only with the 1904 reorganization. The length and detail of the 1904 decree was an indication of both the scope of the reorganization as well as the extent to which reformers sought to correct the many flaws of the past.

The 1904 reorganization further streamlined the general staff and aimed to replicate more closely the German standard. The new measures sought to

---

[92] On the early history of the general staff, see Ministério de Guerra, *Reseña histórica*.

[93] Correspondence Roca to Riccheri, 9 June 1899, in Fraga, *La amistad Roca–Riccheri*, 97.

[94] On the 1900, 1904, and 1916 reforms of the general staff, see Ministério de Guerra, *Reseña histórica*; Argentina, Congresso Nacional, *Leyes y decretos militares de la República Argentina*, vol. 6, *1899–1905* (Buenos Aires: Congresso de la Nación, 1905).

[95] Ministério de Guerra, *Monografia histórica de Estado Maior del Ejército Argentino* (Buenos Aires: Círculo Militar, 1929): 84.

give the organ, as explained in the 1904 decree, "an essentially technical role, having in its responsibility the direction of the tasks of war preparation."[96] The general staff was divided into the Gran Estado Mayor (the main general staff) and the Estado Mayor de los Comandos de Tropas (field staffs), and given a more elaborate organization. The fields staffs were directly under the command of the main staff, though the field staff's relation to the regional commanders remained unclear. The great general staff was subdivided into two main departments: operations and services. Each was further subdivided into functional sections. The services department was given four major divisions, each further subdivided and encompassing standard general staff functions like mobilization, transportation, and geography. New sections and functions included full jurisdiction over the ESG and study of foreign militaries. The general staff was responsible for war plans, mobilization plans, fortification plans, and overall national defense planning, but its plans were to be submitted to the war minister for approval. Only graduates of ESG could serve in the general staff. The spirit of the new organization called for an open staff system, though the language of the decree was imprecise. Upon graduation from ESG, prospective candidates could be required first to spend an indeterminate time in a combat regiment. Alternatively, candidates could enter directly to the main general staff or the field staffs. The 1904 reform called for rotation of all personnel, and embraced the principle of having general staff officers knowledgeable about all aspects of the general staff's work.

Unlike the situation in Chile, the Argentine general staff was not subject to the direct influence and functions of the German mission. As the threat of war with Brazil intensified during the 1906–10 period, the role of German military advisers in the general staff's war-planning functions grew.[97] The German mission's influence in war-planning and general staff operations remained indirect. The mission trained the candidate members of the general staff, and it had a hand in the selection of candidates for admissions to the ESG as well as the selection of graduates to serve in the general staff.[98]

Argentina emulated every aspect of Germany's Generalstab, including its more ambiguous and potentially crippling aspects. Specifically, peacetime and wartime delineation of command functions and prerogatives between the general staff (its chief) and unit commanders were vague. Germany had sought to turn this ambiguity into an advantage by stressing partnership and collegial decision making. Argentina appears to have attempted the same. The field staffs, Duval reports, were at once subordinate to the field

---

[96] Congresso Nacional, *Leyes e decretos militares*, decree of 17 January 1904. See also Ministério de Guerra, *Monografia histórica*.
[97] Schiff, "The Influence of the German Armed Forces," 444.
[98] White, *The German Influence*, 19.

commanders but also directly responsible to the great general staff.[99] The 1904 decree reorganizing the general staff stated that the higher function of the general staff's chief was "to facilitate the command and direction of the army during wartime." It went on to offer that the chief, "in wartime will be the chief of the great general staff of the army and will accompany in this function the commander in chief of army in operations, for whom he will be a legitimate and constant counselor."[100]

An integral piece of the general staff's war planning was to ensure uniformity in doctrine. The general staff organized and directed all large-scale maneuvers and training exercises, including annual staff rides. In 1913 the first divisional staff ride, lasting ten days, took place in the first military region. Further to ensure uniformity in doctrine, the general staff was given sole responsibility for military regulations. Argentina attempted to adopt Chile's decentralized system in 1905 when the country was divided into five military regions. It fell short of Chile's extreme form. The 1904 measure proposed that the general staff become an organization whose "arteries" penetrate throughout the army, to diffuse practical knowledge as well as produce a "common body of principles and doctrine."[101]

Whereas in the past the chief of the field staff was the regional commander as well, now each military region had its own commander, with the field staff playing only an advisory and collaborative role. The powers of the general staff were reduced by the 1916 reforms. It no longer played a role in the immediate chain of command, functions that passed on to the new post of inspector general. This powerful new body duplicated many of the functions of the subordinate general staff, including preparation, mobilization, and instruction. The new general staff was put in charge of war planning, mobilization, transportation, among other functions. By 1920 the post of inspector general became the top rank in the military, the virtual commander in chief of the army.

EXPLAINING MILITARY EMULATION IN ARGENTINA

Argentina, the most Europeanized of all Latin American countries, is an ideal candidate for cultural explanations. Neither the cultural affinity nor the sociological institutionalism explanations, however, can account for Argentina's choices and decisions. It had much more in common with France and Italy than with Germany. The argument that countries emulate the most prestigious and widely accepted symbols of statehood for the purpose of

---

[99] Duval, *Argentina, potencia militar*, vol. 1, 42–44.
[100] Congresso Nacional, *Leyes e decretos militares*, decree of 23 December 1904; Ministério de Guerra, *Monografía histórica*, 96.
[101] Ministério de Guerra, *Monografía histórica*, 97.

social fitness is appealing even if ultimately difficult to falsify. Yet it too cannot account for the timing and the frantic pace, especially in the second phase. Given its proclivity to mimic all things European, including its famed tango, a cultural tolerance argument appears to fit well. As with all other cultural explanations, it cannot account for all the main aspects of emulation.

Given its tumultuous political history, Argentina is also an ideal candidate for a regime insecurity explanation. Its history of incessant interprovincial warfare and centrifugal *caudillo* strife presents a ready-made case for domestic political explanations of military modernization. This is a common, but erroneous, explanation in the literature.[102] The argument is that the ruling elite, or at least those with unification ambitions, needed a modern military to suppress the *gaucho* militias and centrifugal claims of provincial warlords. There is no doubt that the process of national consolidation was violent and protracted. No one province or warlord was able to impose its will or monopolize force. Each attempt at unification involved bloodshed, but resulted only in partial and unstable arrangements. The war ministry's annual reports prior to 1880 occasionally make reference to rebellions, domestic "order," "bandits," and the "black flag of *caudillism*."

The year 1880 was for Argentina a significant historical marker politically as well as strategically. First, it marked the beginning of a qualitatively different external situation from the standpoint of its national security. By 1880 the outcome of the Second War of the Pacific among its northern neighbors was already decided. The other significant historical marker in 1880 was that, for the first time since independence, Argentina could be treated as a unified nation-state. Though historians disagree on the matter, I maintain that we cannot really speak of an "Argentina" or Argentine state until 1880. Argentina finally achieved effective national consolidation and internal order in 1880 with the presidential election of military hero, Júlio Argentino Roca. The election of Roca inaugurated a thirty-six-year stretch of one-party rule under a thinly democratic constitutional system. Argentina's unification appears to have had its own internal logic, though we cannot fully discount the influence of external forces such as the rise of Chile.

Effective unification in 1880 was a combination of imposed will as well as tenuous and informal coalition bargaining among warlords and oligarchs. Roca's triumph in 1880 was made possible by a solid coalition of ruling oligarchs from interior provinces. But the country was polarized between his supporters and the opposition, based in Buenos Aires and Corrientes provinces, which took up arms in a failed attempt to block his ascendancy. The decades of military modernization that followed unfolded under the political monopoly of a single party, the Partido Autonomista Nacional

[102] Marvin Goldwert, *Democracy, Militarism, and Nationalism in Argentina, 1930–1966: An Interpretation* (Austin: University of Texas Press, 1972).

(National Autonomist Party, PAN), which was widely accused of using the army to impose its rule. PAN rule did not go unchallenged and was confronted with feeble armed uprisings in 1890 and 1893. One of Roca's first acts was to abolish the provincial militias. Argentina's strong presidential system gave the president constitutional authority to intervene in the provinces, an authority Roca (and his successors) used deftly to eliminate or neutralize opposition. The federal army was occasionally used as a tool to achieve political ends in the provinces. Moreover, the opposition, led by the Radical Party, actively conspired inside the military and sought to draw it into the political fray. The matter was of sufficient concern to prompt Riccheri in 1903, on the eve of presidential elections, to issue an internal confidential memorandum to all military chiefs reminding them of the "necessity to keep the army away from political fights."[103]

Yet there is nothing in the timing and scale of military modernization to support a regime insecurity account. First, there is no reason why insecure rulers should opt for such an expensive and revolutionary form of military power to deal with domestic opponents. Why bother to emulate the German, or any other, system? Second, the post-1880s period was actually one of relative and unprecedented domestic peace and tranquility. There were no major provincial uprisings during Roca's first presidency (1880–86). The 1890 and 1893 uprisings were exceptions. In fact, what is remarkable is the sudden drop in uprisings and *caudillo* challenges after 1880. This is not to suggest that the country had suddenly transformed itself into a genteel democracy. PAN's rule was autocratic – at best a restricted constitutional system with limited democratic practice and ample fraud. PAN established a powerful and highly centralized rule based on an imperial presidency and robust informal accord among oligarchs. Third, domestic disturbances, in the form of labor strikes, anarchism, and partisan power struggles, emerged as a serious problem long after modernization was well under way. The heavy use of armed force to put down opposition and provincial unrest occured much later, especially during the post–World War I Yrigoyen years. This political tumult was normal politics, as it was universal; the natural pressures for liberalization inherent in all restricted systems. The United States experienced the same tumult at the time. For the most part, PAN had to contend only with its own internal factions. Modernization could have been initiated at any time the PAN government wished and at any scale it pleased. Finally, creating a powerful modern mass army, with its own bureaucratized procedures and institutional autonomy, threatened strongman rule.

Unsurprising but also inconsequential, was the presence of domestic political opposition to military emulation. If the defensive tone of the war ministry's annual reports and the proceedings of congressional debates are any

[103] Riccheri, "Circular Reservada," 25 September 1903, in Fraga, *La amistad Roca–Riccheri*, 162.

indication, both large-scale military modernization and the emulation of the German system encountered strong domestic political opposition. According to some scholars, stiff opposition forced Roca and the government to scale back their original intention to contract a large German mission.[104] The opposition came mainly from congress, and more often than not appeared motivated by interparty rivalry and backbenching politics than opposition to military reforms per se.[105] Schiff notes that the decision to contract a German mission was highly controversial.[106] Opposition to a German mission, especially in congress, persisted over the next decade as interparty competition increased as a result of greater political liberalization. For instance, the new reform measures introduced in 1905 (the so-called "Godoy" reforms) originally provided for the hiring of a sixty-man German military mission, but congressional opposition forced the government to halve the mission to thirty-five officers who arrived in 1906.[107] As noted previously, domestic political and intramilitary opposition are natural and expected parts of the emulation landscape. Domestic politics do not simply come to a halt just because structural pressures prevail in the decision making of national leaders. The fact that opposition was strong and yet large-scale emulation occurred strengthens the role of structural pressures driving Argentine behavior.

Though the political elite in the country had come to recognize the need for military reforms as a result of the confrontation with Chile, there was ample disagreement over the character and scale of these reforms. As with debates over military spending all over the world, much of the debate in Argentina turned on a guns-and-butter issue. Opponents of large-scale military modernization pointed to the tremendous cost of such an undertaking, especially at a time of financial crunch. The reform measure that drew most fire from opponents inside and outside congress was the obligatory military service law introduced by the government in 1900.[108] Deputies called it the "most expensive recruiting system imaginable."[109] Many were also concerned about the negative economic impact a conscript army would have for a rapidly growing country with a tight labor market. War Minister Nicolas Lavalle retorted that full obligatory service is the "only practical and economical means to have a solidly founded army."[110] Congressional opponents of the government's measure, ironically, were led by two former generals turned deputies, Alberto Capedevilla and Enrique Godoy. Their opposition was partisan, being opponents of Roca rather than of the reforms per se. (Although

[104] Schiff, "The Influence of the German Armed Forces," 439.
[105] Ramirez, "The Reform of the Argentine Army," traces this debate.
[106] Schiff, "The Influence of the German Armed Forces," 439.
[107] White, *The German Influence*, 9.
[108] On congressional and political debates surrounding the obligatory military service law see Grela, *Fuerzas Armadas*, 191–96.
[109] Quote cited in Ramirez, "The Reform of the Argentine Army," 351.
[110] Quote cited in Ramirez, "The Reform of the Argentine Army," 279.

Capedevilla's sentiments in floor debates suggest he opposed emulation of foreign systems.) They had previously introduced a more restricted version of obligatory service. Riccheri was unsparing in his counterattack. He told the parliamentary armed services committee that Argentina faced a similar situation to that of France and Prussia in 1870. He admitted that his reform proposals may not achieve the "perfect military organization" of Prussia, but the legislation favored by the opponents were no better than what France had on the eve of the war.[111] Riccheri and defenders of military obligation, though successful in the end, were forced to do some backtracking. The new law allowed for ample loopholes, in the form of exemptions, substitutions, and fees, which benefited the elite classes.

Some opponents of military reforms based their position on more than technical differences with the government. Some, particularly members of opposition parties in congress, questioned the government's true motivations in creating a large, powerful military establishment. Fears of central government power characterized all the partially democratic federal republics of the region. The venerable former president, Carlos Pellegrini, criticized Riccheri's extensive reform program, not just because of its high costs, but because it would result in militarizing the country.[112] This fear was fueled in large part by the popular perception many had about the Prussian/German model that reformers wanted to emulate. Prussian military organization had come to acquire a popular image all over the world as antidemocratic and antirepublican, and Germany as a militarized, aggressive state. The argument was a powerful one – an argument which, ironically, many scholars later on would embrace to account for the military's intervention in politics.[113] One deputy accused the reformers of being people "who in the America of free institutions system want to implant the iron system of the Germanic empire."[114]

The argument was strengthened by the widespread view and ridicule in Argentina of Chile as a case of runaway Prussianism. One influential commentator in 1898 described Chile as "Körner's military autocracy."[115] Whether accurate or not, this view of Chile's experience was widespread. Riccheri himself often derided the Chileans for blindly imitating the Germans and handing over control of their army to German advisers. This wariness on the part of Argentine reformers to avoid the Chilean experience, and their sensitivity to the popular perception of German influence prevailing in the media and society, explains much of the cautionary, circumscribed approach taken by the reformers with respect to the size, functions, authority, and visibility of the German mission.

[111] Riccheri testimony before the war commission, chamber of deputies, 4 September 1901, cited in Fraga, *La amistad Roca–Riccheri*, 130.
[112] Ramirez, "The Reform of the Argentine Army," 339.
[113] The two leading exponents of this argument are Nunn, *Yesterday's Soldiers*, and Goldwert, *Democracy, Militarism, and Nationalism.*
[114] Quote cited in Ramirez, "The Reform of the Argentine Army," 273.
[115] Quesada, *La política argentina*, 105.

Reformers also had to contend with nationalist opposition, even though Argentina had a sizable German population by this time. Though favorable to military modernization, many opponents objected to the hiring of foreign missions as opposed to a nationalist solution. The influential and widely circulated daily, *La Nación*, while an early supporter of German military training, later questioned whether a mission was necessary as opposed to a more energetic home-grown strategy of modernization.[116] Philip argues that, in contrast to Chile and Brazil, there was a much greater level of nationalist opposition in Argentina to military emulation.[117] One influential officer who opposed the German system argued that military institutions "are like plants, neither can be transplanted very well under a strange sky." He added that "the integral adoption of the German or the French or the Italian military system is useless, although the latter are less exotic for us; it cannot transform [our] mentality."[118] Pellegrini, a one-time Roca ally and supporter of Riccheri, now ridiculed Riccheri's attempt to "transplant this seed" as a "military error."[119]

Reformers became even more defensive, since such prickly criticisms could trigger a nationalist backlash that could unravel all reforms. In 1899, Minister of War General Campos, had already warned of the political and social difficulty involved in adopting the German model. He warned that, "diverse causes have obstructed such legitimate aspirations [for reforms], and among them [is] the resistance of customs and practices consecrated by [tradition]."[120] Riccheri was forced to defend his project in congress. In one of several marathon sessions in congress, he assured the deputies that "the system that will be established is not the German system, nor it is French, nor Italian, etc., because not everything that is effective and judicious in one country will produce the same results [when] literally transplanted to another [country], whose environment and social norms, politics, economy and even geography are distinct."[121] He continued to sound defensive in response to congressional criticism. He declared in another hearing that military emulation would not involve the wholesale importation of a foreign model, but would involve selective adoption modified to Argentina's needs and circumstances. "We are mindful," he observed, "of the peculiar modality of the country, and borrow from those [European] systems – without a doubt the most perfect – as well as from the existing military legislation in Argentina, whenever capable of responding to [our] ideas and goals, and are susceptible

[116] *La Nación*, 12 February 1899, 5, cited in Schiff, "The Influence of German Armed Forces," 439.

[117] George Philip, *The Military in South American Politics* (London: Croom Helm, 1985): 102. See also, Schiff, "The Influence of German Armed Forces," 445.

[118] Augusto Maligne, cited in Schiff, "The Influence of the German Armed Forces," 444–45.

[119] Carlos Pellegrini, quote cited in Fraga, *La amistad Roca–Riccheri*, 141.

[120] Ministério de Guerra, *Memória*, 1898–1899, 3.

[121] Ministério de Guerra, *Memória, 1900–1901*, 7–8.

to being adapted to our means and necessities, they are incorporated into [our] reform program, in this way resulting in a solid foundation."[122]

Finally, even though opposition to the German model within the military was manageable, the German training mission encountered serious difficulties in its work. As noted earlier, much of the difficulty appeared to stem from poor personal relations. By 1913 serious strains had developed between the German-trained directors of the Escuela Superior de Guerra and the mission.[123] Opposition to the influence, authority, and even presence of the German military mission grew throughout the army, and nationalist officers (many German trained) made a push to bring an end to the German mission's participation in areas such as promotions.[124]

Opposition to large-scale military modernization, while a natural part of the process, affected the details of individual reform measures. Yet every aspect of Argentina's military emulation occurred as expected by the theory of emulation. As in the other cases, there was an impressive array of domestic political reasons, intraorganizational obstacles, and even cultural reasons for Argentina *not* to emulate. Variance in security threats, not domestic politics or notions of cultural fitness, explains Argentina's military modernization. As we delve into the archival materials and trace in detail the deliberations and decisions, we encounter Argentine leaders preoccupied with technical specifications of alternative armaments, the quality of the armaments rivals possessed, or the country's level of military preparedness. Indeed, we find in the archives hundreds of reports and memos on tedious and boring matters such as artillery specifications or expenditure accounting, not lofty cultural analysis. Above all, we encounter Argentine leaders moving quickly to match each major improvement in Chile's military power. When Chile drastically altered its capacity to mobilize and quickly deploy a trained mass army by adopting universal military service in 1900, Argentina responded immediately with own mass conscription measure, difficult and contentious as the legislation was.

FIRST PHASE OF REFORMS AND RISING THREAT LEVELS

"It is no longer possible," explained a senior Argentine military leader defending the military modernization under way, "for the Republic to continue basing its defense on such precarious elements [as the old army]. Its security, even its freedom of action, requires the transformations that are now being realized."[125] Argentina did not have the option or the luxury to

---

[122] Ministério de Guerra, *Memória, 1900–1901*, 8.
[123] Schiff, "The Influence of the German Armed Forces," 446.
[124] Ibid.
[125] General Rafael M. Aguirre, minister of war, Ministério de Guerra, *Memória, 1907–1908*, 117.

indulge in old military practices and traditions. The old army was obsolete. It was made obsolete, not because of Argentina's desire or intention, but by the unavoidable reality on the other side of the Andes. Rival Chile had amassed military capabilities of a qualitatively higher grade. Argentina had to keep up, for the consequences of falling behind were too great. National survival, and not simply a victorious outcome in war, was at stake. "To achieve this indispensable victory," Aguirre insisted, "there is only one road: that of thorough and extensive military preparation. No improvisation is permitted in this matter."[126]

The explanation for Argentina's military emulation is to be found in its external security situation between the 1880s and World War I. Argentina was the least ambiguous of the three historical cases in tracing the weight of structural forces. As expected, its military emulation was reactive and defensive. The threat of Chilean military power was the driving force behind its military modernization. Equally expected given its strategic predicament – sandwiched between its two main enemies – its response to one threat triggered military competition on its other flank. A competitive security logic drove its military modernization. Indeed, as noted in earlier chapters, only a competitive security logic can explain the chain-reaction dynamics of military emulation in South America. The timing of Argentina's buildup, its pace and scale, all corresponded with adverse turns in its security environment. Minister of War Riccheri was emphatic in his reasons for military modernization. In his usual succinct and blunt style, he told a congressional committee that, while his government worked to maintain external peace in the region, "we cannot look with indifference at the progress in military arts or the organization of the armed forces of the countries that surround us. As soon as any of them organizes its army in a solid manner, we must do the same, such that we can never be caught by surprise by any eventuality."[127] Just as Argentina celebrated the arrival of internal peace in 1880, its external security environment began to shift adversely. On the other side of the Andes, Chile was amassing the machinery for war and conquest.

The most important issue to address during the first phase of Argentina's military emulation, 1895–98, is that of timing. Why does Argentina launch military emulation a full decade after the start of Chile's, rather than immediately? Another intriguing question is why Argentina emulated the same foreign model as its historic adversary. We would expect that, given their historic rivalry, Argentina would respond immediately to the rise of Chilean power. A careful examination of Argentina's changing external security situation during the last two decades of the century reinforces our confidence in the neorealist theory of emulation. To anticipate, first, it began immediately

---

[126] General Rafael M. Aguirre, minister of war, Ministério de Guerra, *Memória, 1907–1908*, 60.

[127] Riccheri testimony before congress, 4 September 1901, in Fraga, *La amistad Roca–Riccheri*, 132.

to build up and modernize armaments for its army and navy. Military spending averaged over a 20 percent share of total government expenditures during the latter half of the 1880s, and continued upward in the 1890s. Expenditures jumped 150 percent between 1891 and 1898.[128] Second, in the years immediately after the Second Pacific War, Argentina was a security-free rider on the postwar anti–Chilean coalition led by the United States. Brazil, another historic enemy, was a stagnant military power at the time. By the mid-1890s, its security situation worsened precipitously. In sum, Argentina initially responds to the Chilean threat with a combination of internal and external balancing.

To explain the timing, pace, and scale of Argentina's military emulation, the balance of this chapter will examine closely its changing levels of external threat during the period. Four critical components of its strategic situation merit close inspection. The first is the matter of external balancing options. We begin here largely because this factor alone plays a determining role in explaining the seemingly delayed start of its military emulation in response to the Chilean challenge. The second component is the rise of Chilean power. The third part of the chapter examines the security competition with Brazil. Finally, Argentina's own military preparedness, or lack thereof, contributed to its level of insecurity, and thus a big part of its decision to adopt large-scale modernization.

EXTERNAL BALANCING OPTIONS

The Second War of the Pacific (1879–83) between Chile and the Peruvian–Bolivian coalition changed Argentina's strategic environment. A good portion of the strategic dynamic put in play by the War of the Pacific has been discussed above. The first phase of Argentina's military emulation has its genesis in the war and its aftermath. The war's immediate strategic ramification for Argentina was that it did not have to face its historic enemy alone. Indeed, it benefited from a fortunate, if temporary, set of favorable strategic circumstances. By the mid-1890s these advantages eroded, but in the meantime they gave the *gaucho* republic some breathing room.

In the immediate years after the Second War of the Pacific, Argentina enjoyed a measure of security advantages from: geography, the weakness of its La Plata River Basin rival (Brazil), and the containment of Chilean power. Argentina's great size, the dispersion of its main population-economic centers, the barrier provided by the Andes *cordilleras*, and the buffer provided by defeated Paraguay comprised the key pillars of its defensive advantages and relatively lower vulnerability into the early 1890s.[129] The Andes, though passable, constituted an impressive natural land barrier as long as an external

---

[128] Data calculated from Ministério de Guerra, *Reseña histórica*, 510–11.
[129] Gilbert J. Butland, *Latin America: A Regional Geography*, 3rd ed. (London: Longman Group Ltd, 1972), chaps. 17–22.

power did not have the delivery and projection capabilities to threaten Argentina's heartland.[130] The flat and rich Pampas powered Argentina's rapid growth and national wealth in the fifty years after national consolidation. The insatiable demand for food and raw materials in Europe's sprawling industrial cities drove Argentina's primary export-dependent economy, and the Pampas laid the golden eggs. The Pampas became the source of both vast wealth and, thus, insecurity.

Argentina's principal strategic good fortune was its ability to free ride on the anti-Chilean coalition that emerged during and after the war. Argentina was able to free ride a fortuitous but transitory set of strategic conditions that kept its primary threat contained in the west, while security of its eastern flank was assured by the military weakness of its other rival. Its ability to free ride was far from a passive set of conditions. Rather it was also the work of its own astute, Machiavellian diplomacy. Argentina deliberately stoked the anti-Chile hatred to keep Chile bogged down. That is to say, Argentina's first response to the emerging Chilean threat was to adopt a strategy of forward containment – capitalizing on Chile's many troubles to keep it bogged down. It maneuvered quickly while the war was still going on to put in place the pieces of Chile's containment.

First, it capitalized on its natural alignment affinity with Chile's battlefield foes. Chile's enemies, Peru and Bolivia, were Argentina's natural friends. Argentina effectively joined the Pacific balance-of-power subsystem and aligned with Chile's wartime opponents. Second, it deliberately sought to draw in the United States into the anti-Chilean bloc, going as far as proposing alliance with the United Staes.

Argentina worked during and after the war to contain and roll back Chilean power. It intervened in the Second War of the Pacific to support Peru and Bolivia. Argentina's blundering attempt to join a Peru–Bolivian secret military alliance made it the target of renewed Chilean (and Brazilian) hostility.[131] It cowed under pressure from its rivals, but relations between Chile and Argentina soured further during the war. Argentina continued to extend diplomatic and material support to Peru and Bolivia during the war, including the transfer of arms and war material to Bolivia and allowing the transport of Bolivian arms acquisition through its territory.[132] Finally, in

---

[130] English describes the Andes as "largely impenetrable." See Adrian J. English, *Armed Forces of Latin America: Their Histories, Development, Present Strength, and Military Potential* (London: Jane's, 1985): 17.

[131] On the 1873 secret treaty between Peru and Bolivia and Argentina's involvement see, Juan José Fernandez Valdéz, "El tratado secreto peruano-boliviano de 1873 y la diplomacia brasileña," *Boletín de la Academia Chilena de la Historia* 23, no. 55 (1956). See also Robert N. Burr, *By Reason or Force: Chile and the Balancing of Power in South America, 1830–1905* (Berkeley: University of California Press, 1965).

[132] Mário Barros, *Historia diplomática de Chile, 1541–1938* (Barcelona: Ediciones Ariel, 1970): 354.

1881, it capitalized on Chile's wartime preoccupation by militarily occupying a disputed territory in the Patagonia region and forcing an (ill-defined) agreement with Chile.

The 1881 agreement, while ambitious in its inclusion of most of the territories and border demarcations under dispute, was too ambiguous.[133] It created more problems than it solved. Essentially, Chile interpreted the treaty in a way in which the demarcation would give it possession of lands east of the Andes in the Patagonia region. Argentina, on the other hand, saw the treaty as stipulating a more westerly demarcation along the highest peaks of the Andes. Repeated diplomatic initiatives and binational commissions met with failure. Bilateral negotiations often became entangled in larger territorial disputes and postwar fallout in the Andean subsystem.

In the postwar years, Argentina continued its backing of the anti-Chilean coalition formed by Peru and Bolivia, both of whom continued to harbor desires for a war of revanchism. All three sought to internationalize their dispute with Chile. This anti-Chilean coalition nominally included the United States, which acted as an informal protector of Peru during the immediate postwar period and which actively sought basing rights in that country. Argentina deliberately fostered greater animosity between Chile and its erstwhile foes, exploiting the rift, and openly backed Peru and Bolivia in their efforts to recoup lost territories.[134] On the diplomatic front, it championed the Peru–Bolivia cause, particularly by pushing the principle of retroactive obligatory arbitration in several Pan American congresses. Both Peru and Bolivia came to believe that Argentina would come to their defense in the event of another war with Chile. The possibility of a military alliance among the three was small. Both Peru and Bolivia were too severely weakened militarily and domestically. Though both were engaged in military modernization by the late 1890s, they were likely to be more of a liability than an asset in a major confrontation with Chile, which was arming for a multifront war. Yet the net effect was to keep Chile diverted and embroiled in intractable disputes with its defeated neighbors.

The second external balancing option Argentina was able to free ride on was the poisoned relationship between the United States and Chile. Here, too, Argentina deftly exploited U.S.–Chile rancor in the postwar years in order to contain Chilean power. The irony is that Argentina's relations with the United States were anything but cordial.[135] Yet the threat of Chilean power

---

[133] The 1881 treaty covered the regions of Patagonia, the Straits of Magellan, and Tierra del Fuego. The treaty put off the actual demarcation of borders to a later date.

[134] Michael G. Varley, "The Aftermath of the War of the Pacific: A Study in the Foreign Policy of Chile, 1891–1896," Ph.D. thesis, Cambridge University (1969).

[135] On Argentine–U.S. relations see: Thomas F. McGann, *Argentina, the United States, and the Inter-American System, 1880–1914* (Cambridge: Harvard University Press, 1957); Joseph S. Tulchin, "The Origins of Misunderstanding: United States–Argentine Relations, 1900–1940," in *Argentina Between the Great Powers, 1939–1946*, ed. Guido di Tella and

overrode any qualms Argentina may have had about the United Sates. Chile was the greater threat. From the Pacific War to the first half of the 1890s Argentina and the United States mounted a tacit alliance against Chile. Like Argentina, the United Sates supported Peru and Bolivia and opposed Chile's territorial annexations. In the postwar period, both smaller powers drew protection from the United States and Argentina. The height of Argentina's rapprochement and free riding with the United States came during the 1892 face-off between Chile and the United States, a crisis in which both sides prepared for and nearly declared war. Argentina offered assistance, in the way of bases and transit, to the United States in the event of a war with Chile.[136] In early 1892 a U.S. navy squadron paid an extended visit to Buenos Aires, and unofficial discussions took place regarding a possible treaty between the two countries.[137] The coincidence of interests between Argentina and the United States did not solidify into anything durable, nor did it wash away Argentina's historic wariness of the United States. Yet the practical effect was to purchase, temporarily, more security through external balancing. Argentina returned to its traditional anti–American stance soon after 1892, coinciding with the first major push to reequip and modernize its land and naval forces.[138]

SECURITY AND INSECURITY ON THE EASTERN FLANK

From the mid-1800s to the 1980s, Argentina's national security rested on its ability to manage an unfavorable and unforgiving geographic reality: being hemmed in on both sides by its historic rivals. Its national safety rested on, above all else, its ability either to prevent a Brazilian–Chilean alliance and combined assault or, alternatively, to amass sufficient military capabilities to fight a multifront war against both enemies. It sought to do both. Its foreign policy behavior during each major crisis during the century spanning the 1890s to the 1980s involved making concessions and easing tensions with one rival while confronting the other. Its military emulation, and subsequent buildup of its military power in the interwar period, was its insurance policy should its diplomatic gamble fail.

Of Argentina's two historical rivals, Chile and Brazil, the former represented the bigger military threat up to World War I. The Chilean threat is

D. Cameron Watt (London: Macmillan Press, 1989): 34–55; David Healy, "Admiral William B. Caperton and United States Naval Diplomacy in South America, 1917–1919," *Journal of Latin American Studies* 8, no. 2 (November 1976): 297–323.

[136] Varley, "Aftermath of the War of the Pacific," 73–74; Emilio Meneses Ciuffardi, *El factor naval en las relaciones entre Chile y los Estados Unidos, 1881–1951* (Santiago: Ediciones Pedagógicas Chilenas, 1989): 79–82.

[137] Varley, "Aftermath of the War of the Pacific," 80–81.

[138] Arthur P. Whitaker, *The United States and the Southern Cone: Argentina, Chile, and Uruguay* (Cambridge: Harvard University Press, 1976): chaps. 2 and 16, passim.

discussed later. As for Brazil, it was militarily negligible into the early years of the new century. Yet given its gargantuan size, their history of armed clashes, and its territorial expansionism, Argentine leaders never lost sight of the fact that Brazil would eventually supplant Chile as their biggest military threat. Declared Riccheri: "I repeat it again and again, the international policy of the Republic should be today and always – we turn our backs to Chile and look in front to Brazil."[139] Though weak and internally disorganized, Brazil still constituted a strategic problem for Argentina because it always had to take into account Brazil's reaction in dealing with Chile.

The rivalry across the Paraná River dated back to Iberian colonial rule. The Spanish colonies early on developed suspicions over Lusophone Brazil's expansionist tendencies. It was a rivalry for continental primacy, and one marked by racist overtones and mutual dislike between the two peoples. Power competition in the La Plata Basin was primarily for continental dominance, but relations were also strained by border disputes which erupted anew in 1895. An international arbitration of the Misiones territory left both sides embittered, but Argentina lacked the military wherewithal to confront Brazil while at the same time confronting Chile over their own territorial disputes. The Misiones confrontation with Brazil, which Argentina practically lost, acted to provide further motive for large-scale military emulation.

Brazil's domestic turmoil and military disrepair effectively removed it as a major player in the continental system of balancing. Brazil's weakness during the last two decades of the nineteenth century allowed Argentina to focus all its attention westward to its primary military threat, Chile, worrying only about a potential encircling alliance between its historic foes. More opportune for Argentina was their short-lived détente. The 1889 military coup in Brazil, followed by a drawn-out period of internal political turmoil, temporarily weakened its close relationship with Chile. In fact, republican Brazil entered a brief rapprochement with Argentina, which eagerly courted the new regime in Rio de Janeiro.

Still Brazil could not be discounted entirely. It outsized Argentina in every category, and its close relations with Chile were long-standing. Argentina could never risk the ever-present prospect of an encircling alliance of its rivals. Pablo Riccheri complained about Argentina's complacency and inattention toward its eastern rival. While in Europe he urged that "the moment for military and naval reforms has arrived for our country," but the leadership places faith in Argentine valor. They naively believe, he continued, that there is no necessity "to prepare to defeat our powerful enemies." He warned that the country risked "disaster and irreparable harm if we were to rely solely on the Argentine valor in an armed contest against Chile, or against both of them which is not impossible."[140] Though Brazil's military

---

[139] Riccheri, quote cited in Grela, *Fuerzas Armadas*, 88.
[140] Riccheri, quote cited in Grela, *Fuerzas Armadas*, 77.

preparation was negligible prior to 1906, the very prospect of encirclement was sufficient to make Argentina pause or moderate its actions. In the heat of the near-war crisis with Chile, President Roca traveled to Brazil in the autumn of 1899 to smooth relations and solicit Brazilian assurances to remain neutral in any trans-Andean conflagration.

Another important factor contributing to Argentina's security concerns on its eastern flank was Brazil's close relationship with the United States. Argentina, as noted above, staunchly opposed US presence in the region, despite their brief hiatus of common cause against Chile in 1892. Brazil and the United States, on the other hand, had warm ties historically, ties that became even closer after 1900. Relations between its historic rival and the United States, as leaders in Buenos Aires saw it, resembled a kind of an alliance.[141] The U.S. factor in Argentine strategic thinking should not be underestimated. The South American power was historically opposed to the expansion of a U.S. presence and influence in the region, and it remained wary of the pretensions of the United States to hemispheric leadership well into the Second World War. With visions of its own great-power status, Argentina historically saw itself in competition with the United States for hemispheric leadership. It saw itself as the self-anointed defender of the hemisphere against U.S. imperial ambitions.[142] Argentina never ceased denouncing the Monroe Doctrine. It feared that someday it too would become target of continual military interventions by the United States in the hemisphere. In response to U.S. and European great power military intervention in Venezuela to collect debts, Argentina announced its own counterpoise to the Monroe Doctrine. The 1902 Drago Doctrine, which Roca and Ricchieri helped draft with Foreign Minister Luíz Drago, opposed all forms of European territorial occupation in the Americas and declared that military force cannot be used to collect debt. More worrisome for Argentina was the U.S.-Brazil nexus, and the possibility that the United States would use Brazil as a proxy or back it in a military confrontation with Argentina. Argentine leaders, the U.S. Embassy reported in 1922, regarded U.S.–Brazil ties as an alliance, and worried about the role of the United States in a possible war with Brazil.

By the early years of the new century, Argentina could no longer write off Brazil as a negligible military threat. By this time the rivalry in the Basin intensified, re-ignited by the 1895 misiones dispute. Brazil began to lay the groundwork for its own military modernization on land and sea, beginning with an ambitious naval modernization project launched in 1904. Argentina's second phase of modernization was well under way. That same year Brazil annexed by force Acre territory from Bolivia, a client of Argentina. Argentina bitterly protested Brazil's actions to no avail. In 1906 Brazil made its first real

---

[141] Healy, "Admiral William B. Caperton."
[142] On this point, see Tulchin, "The Origins of Misunderstanding."

attempt to undertake large-scale military emulation. Between 1906 and 1914 Argentina and Brazil found themselves engaged in an expensive, and tense arms race. The bulk of this arms race was at sea, as both scrambled to acquire the largest and most modern warships from Europe and the United States. Brazil became one of the first countries in the world to acquire the revolutionary, British-built dreadnought. The naval arms race between Argentina and Brazil quickly dragged in Chile, as both Andean rivals agreed in 1910 to scrap the 1902 naval limitations treaty. Relations between Argentina and Brazil suddenly escalated to a near-war crisis during 1907–08. Brazilian leaders warned of an impending war against Argentina in 1907, while Argentina announced plans for large naval maneuvers off the Brazilian coast.[143]

Argentina continued its military modernization after World War I, long past the mellowing of Chilean power. It had good security reasons to do so. With the waning and eventual eclipse of Chilean power after World War I, relative to its own growth in power, Argentina's main security concern turned to Brazil. The rivalry intensified. Its pro-Axis neutrality during World War I caused further deterioration in relations with Brazil and the United States, leaving it isolated on the continent. After efforts to persuade it to join the Allied cause failed, both the United States and Brazil sought to contain Argentina during the war. Relations again escalated into near-war crises in the late 1920s and again in the late 1930s. In 1919, Brazil launched its large-scale military emulation and buildup. Argentina responded with its own arms buildup on land and at sea, the bulk of which occurred during 1926–29 and 1936–38.[144] Relations tumbled in the wake of Brazil's decision to contract a U.S. naval mission, which Argentina opposed and perceived as threatening. In 1925 a United States minister in Buenos Aires cabled Washington that "the general feeling in Argentina is that the next war which Argentina engages in will be against Brazil, and each country has their army located with this in view."[145] U.S. presence in Brazil did not help matters. U.S. diplomats correctly predicted that the naval mission would trigger a new round of naval arms competition among the three regional powers. As late as 1936 U.S. diplomats were reporting the "considerable apprehension" with which Argentine leaders regarded U.S.-Brazil ties.[146]

---

[143] On these points, see E. Bradford Burns, *The Unwritten Alliance: Rio Branco and Brazilian–American Relations* (New York: Columbia University Press, 1966): 185; Luís A. Moniz Bandeira, *Presença dos Estados Unidos no Brasíl: dois séculos de história* (Editôra Civilização Brasileira, 1973): 179.

[144] Potash, *The Army and Politics.*

[145] United States, War Department, *Military Intelligence Reports: Argentina, 1918–1941* (UPA, 1984), Cable #3550, 10 September 1925, 1.

[146] Foreign Relations of the United States (FRUS). See, for example, 26 June 1924 cable from State Department to Embassy in Brazil, and 18 March 1936 cable from U.S. Embassy in Buenos Aires to State Department.

THE CHILEAN MILITARY THREAT

The rivalry between Argentina and Chile dated to the wars of independence. Its essence was a struggle for regional hegemony, and territorial disputes provided the fuel.[147] Both emerged with ambitions for regional leadership of the newly independent Spanish republics. Conflicting territorial claims and ill-defined borders ruined relations from the start. Chile's postwar conquest and massive military buildup elevated the competition and mutual suspicions. Argentine animosity toward Chile bordered on racist. Argentines did not hesitate to portray Chileans as warlike, aggressive, hateful, and racially contaminated. An Argentine consular official in Chile reported to his superiors in Buenos Aires that "if peace holds it is because of the *cordilleras*, not the Chilean people. They hate us. Many [Chileans] believe the only solution is war."[148] "It is a matter of the idiosyncrasy of a people, their way of life, their addictive adventurism, and their easy past conquests," argued Argentina's ambassador in La Paz, Bolivia.[149] Interim president José Uriburu, and father of German-trained José Felix Uriburu, assailed the "stubborn malevolence of our Chilean brothers."[150]

Chile's military power was the most serious and immediate threat to Argentine security, and the trigger for its own large-scale modernization. Yet in the ten years after the start of Chile's modernization, Argentina found itself militarily inferior. Its immediate response to the Chilean threat consisted of two major balancing strategies. First, it built up its own forces through countermeasures such as arms armaments acquisition. Second, it pursued external balancing options to contain Chilean power. Both strategies were stop-gap measures while the country prepared for full-scale modernization.

Bilateral relations between Chile and Argentina deteriorated rapidly after the Pacific war. By 1894 tensions escalated. In a letter to Riccheri in Europe, Roca made note of the fact that there was widespread "national sentiment here against the Chileans," and everyone in the country was asking the government to arm.[151] The aftermath of the Second War of the Pacific engulfed most of the continent and divided it into hostile camps, with the larger, anti-Chilean camp led by Argentina.[152] Argentina had aided Chile's battlefield

---

[147] Emilio Meneses Ciuffardi, "Los limites del equilíbrio de poder: la política exterior chilena a fines del siglo pasado, 1891–1902," *Opciones* 9 (May–September 1986); Ramirez, "The Reform of the Argentine Army." For general reference, though biased, see Miguel A. Scenna, *Argentina–Chile: una frontera cáliente* (Editorial de Belgrano, 1981).

[148] Archivo Roca, Sala 7, Caja 1384. Report by Luis [surname unintelligible], 24 May 1898.

[149] Archivo Roca, Caja 1384. Report from the Argentine Legation in Bolivia to President Júlio Roca, 8 August 1900, 17.

[150] Quote cited in Lalanne, *Los Uriburu*, 161.

[151] Correspondence Roca to Riccheri, 3 March 1894, in Fraga, *La amistad Roca–Riccheri*, 67.

[152] On the diplomatic and strategic aftermath of the war of the Pacific, see Varley, "The Aftermath of the War of the Pacific"; Seward W. Livermore, "American Strategic Diplomacy in the South Pacific," *Pacific Historical Journal* 12, no. 1 (March 1943): 33–51.

enemies and backed their postwar diplomatic offense to block Chilean annexation of their territory. An editorial in *La Tribuna*, a Buenos Aires press favoring Roca's presidential bid, complained that Chile's "program of conquest" harmed regional commerce.[153] The editors of *La República* asserted that Argentina "founded" the independence of Peru and Bolivia, and therefore reserved the right to invoke international law against Santiago's aggression "so that no other power in this part of the Americas would suffer immediately and directly the conquests of Chile and the heavy burdens that it has imposed on Peru and Bolivia."[154] The March 12, 1879, edition of *El Parlamento* accused Chile's "ambitious government" and "fierce soldiers" of committing "crimes" in Peru and Bolivia.

Long-standing border disputes of the Andean rivals resurfaced with much more intensity and mutual recriminations after the war. The fear of Chilean territorial expansionism was more real and immediate. Argentina not only feared that Chile would settle their pending territorial disputes by force of arms, but also that it might easily expand its conquest into thinly populated and poorly defended bordering provinces. Argentine leaders regarded such expansionism as the only way resource-poor, land-starved Chile could expand its power. One prominent Argentine legislator, Roman Pacheco, insisted that "Chile cannot develop, squeezed between the *cordillera* and sea. To the north the Atacama Desert unavoidably limits expansion; to the South, the strip becomes narrower and narrower. By reason or force, it needs territory for its overflowing population and to meet this need the meadows of the Andes are perfect and Chile will not cease dreaming of them until it falls vanquished."[155] Chile's "conquests are necessary to its existence," asserted an Argentine ambassador.[156] "Chile lives for military conquest, with which it grows and with which they believe they can become even bigger."

In view of Chile's dismemberment of Peru and Bolivia, Argentine fears of Chilean expansionism and preemptive attack were well-founded. Official records show that Chilean leaders were, indeed, contemplating such options against their still militarily inferior neighbor. Chile combined ambition with military might. Chile's territorial conquests augmented its power. This thesis was clear and simple, and echoed frequently by Argentine diplomats. Writing in the midst of the clamor surrounding a final peace treaty between Chile and Bolivia (which was to determine the status of Chilean-occupied Antofagasta), Argentine diplomats in Santiago advised that Chile should not be allowed to keep the conquered territories and most likely would end up annexing

---

[153] *La Tribuna*, "Nuevos Horizontes," 26 October 1879, 1.
[154] *La República*, 29 November 1879, 1.
[155] Roman Pacheco, quote cited in Ramírez, "The Reform of the Argentine Army," 13–14. For similar sentiments regarding Chilean territorial ambitions see, Quesada, *La política argentina*.
[156] Archivo Roca, Caja 1384. Report from the Argentine Legation in Bolivia to President Júlio Roca, 8 August 1900, 17–18.

all of them. As long as possibility of further Chilean expansion existed, they warned, the result would be "greater increase in its power" and a continuation of "distrust, fear and, in consequence, this armed peace."[157] Argentina particularly feared its neighbor's covetous eyes on its productive pampas and Patagonia provinces.[158] Congressional debates in 1881 focused on the precarious defenses of outlying provinces and territories like Rio Negro. One deputy in the chamber of deputies, pleased with Argentina's occupation of new territories down to the Rio Negro (acquired by Roca at the expense of native populations), exclaimed that "we no longer have this door opened for a Chilean invasion."[159] Deputy Castro added that "in the event of a war" the economic and population centers of Argentina would be in "imminent danger" by the "completely open" outlying provinces bordering "that well-known perfidy of a certain ambitious neighbor."[160] Chile's expansion, by augmenting its power, represented "always a danger to Argentina."[161]

Historically the Argentine public and their leaders were suspicious of what they believed to be Chile's aggressive and expansionist ambitions. Roca spoke of Chile's bellicose impulses.[162] By the early 1890s it became apparent, from Argentina's point of view, that Chile had more appetite for territory and had the requisite military might to realize it. Additionally, Chile was a bioceanic power, putting Argentina's economic lifeline – international trade – at risk. Argentina, while gradually building up its forces but nervous about its vulnerability, grew alarmed at the likelihood of a preemptive, knock-out strike by the militarily more vigorous Chile. As Chilean power grew on land and sea, Argentine leaders became increasingly concerned about their vulnerability to such an attack. An array of strategic surveys by the general staff and reports commissioned from foreign experts all pointed to this vulnerability and military inferiority.

Argentina also worried that a stronger Chile would dictate the terms of their border settlement. It is this rationale that military and civilian leaders cited most frequently in defense of large-scale military modernization. The head of a congressional military reorganization commission, General Francisco Bosch, put it succinctly: "On the other side of the Andes the sounds of armaments can be heard. It is possible to witness the efforts that leaders

---

[157] Report, Argentine Embassy in Santiago, Chile, in Ministerio de Relaciones Exteriores y Culto, *Memórias, 1903–1904*, 250.

[158] For a more alarmist view on Chile's aims and capabilities see collected articles by a key legislator and journalist, Quesada, *La política argentina respeto de Chile.*

[159] Deputy Tamini during congressional session of 23 February 1881; transcribed in *El Parlamento*, 12 March 1881, 2.

[160] Deputy Castro during congressional session of 23 February 1881; transcribed in *El Parlamento*, 12 March 1881, 2.

[161] Report, Argentine Embassy in Santiago, Chile, in Ministerio de Relaciones Exteriores y Culto, *Memórias, 1903–1904*, 252.

[162] Felix Luna, *Soy Roca*, 6th ed. (Buenos Aires: Editorial Sudamericana, 1990), 325.

are making to bring their army to a level of preparation capable of putting it in a position to undertake by force solutions that calm reason dictate ought to be resolved by diplomacy and by treaty." He concluded that "it behooves us to follow this development, to put ourselves in turn in a position to prevent such things from happening."[163]

There was no doubt in the minds of the military and civilian leadership that Chile was building up its arms for one sole purpose: to prepare for a war with Argentina. In the judgment of Argentina's ambassador to Bolivia, "I fear a war [with Chile] more or less in the long term but it is irreversible and inevitable."[164] Indeed, Chilean records show that the decision to launch full-scale military emulation was based on the fear and estimation of a likely future war with Argentina.[165] Ernesto Quesada, an influential commentator, warned about the "military disequilibrium," citing Chile's "complete preparation" and Argentina's military "negligence."[166] He argued that, with the latest reforms of 1897 and given its excellent rail network, Chile could mobilize 50,000 trained men within twenty-four hours, and place 80,000 troops on Argentina's borders within two days. Of grave concern to Argentina was not just Chile's overall military preparedness but the offensive strike and mobilizational capacity it amassed. Chile had constructed an impressive rail network, much of which concentrated on the Argentine border, permitting rapid mobilization and concentration of forces. An influential, if alarmist, semiofficial Argentine study put out in 1898 warned that Chile's "railroads permit it rapidly to concentrate its forces and mass at all threatened points."[167]

Argentine leaders, cognizant of their own military weakness, feared a Chilean invasion of the poorly defended border provinces and coastline. An undated general staff report, noting the strategic importance of the Rio de la Plata as the "key to our international trade," observed that it is "relatively undefended."[168] The report focused mainly on the strategic significance of the naval imbalance facing Argentina. In light of Chile's well-defended and fortified ports and coastline, the Chilean navy was thus released from defensive duties and could "with total confidence abandon its perfectly defended coastline and dedicate all its forces to carrying out purely offensive

---

[163] Argentina, Congresso Nacional, *Diario de Sessiones de la Camara de Diputado* (Buenos Aires: Congresso de la Nación, 1900): 966.

[164] Archivo Roca, Caja 1384. Report from the Argentine Legation in Bolivia to President Júlio Roca, 8 August 1900, 16.

[165] On this point, see Vial, *La sociedad chilena*.

[166] Quesada, *La política argentino*, 103–05.

[167] *El Ejército de Chile y la guerra de mañana* (Buenos Aires: Compañia. Sud-America, BD, 1898). The booklet does not list an author. Collection in Servicio Histórico del Ejército.

[168] Archivo Roca, Caja 1384, army general staff report, unsigned, undated, untitled, 2. The report was probably completed after 1902, since it makes reference to the naval arms control negotiations which emerged after the 1898–1902 war crisis.

operations."[169] This was not so for Argentina. Its naval forces, according to the report, may have the margin in terms of total tonnage, but Chile had "an effective superiority in the number of torpedo boats and transport." Krupp naval experts, hired by the Argentine general staff, made similar conclusions with regard to defending Buenos Aires from enemy attack. The Krupp report noted that "Brazil and Chile would be the only powers Argentina should fear in terms of a possible international conflict."[170] Another report commissioned from Italian naval experts noted that Argentina's extensive coastline could not be defended by fortifications and other defensive measures alone. Argentina had to rely on the "power and velocity of its navy."[171]

Foreign observers had the same assessment of the military balance and Argentina's vulnerability. "Recent events have proved Chile to possess an excellent and serviceable fleet," observed the British ambassador in Buenos Aires, "and an army in effective trim, well commanded and well armed, besides enjoying unlimited credit in a pecuniary sense, [whereas Argentina is] in a very different situation."[172] Chileans were even more optimistic, perhaps boastful, of their relative military position, leading many senior Chilean leaders to agitate for preventive war. Senior Chilean leaders noted as early as 1896 that "Argentina will not start [a war] because it fears Chile and respects it. It knows that on the battlefield it cannot win."[173]

ARGENTINA'S MILITARY INFERIORITY

Chile's qualitative jump in military capabilities changed Argentina's strategic landscape. Argentina's old army was inadequate – indeed a dangerous basis on which to rest its national safety given the impending territorial disputes with both historic rivals as well as the demonstrated willingness of both to use armed force for expansionist aims. Its postwar reliance on the anti-Chilean coalition partly offset, and perhaps hid, its military weakness. Its countermeasures were insufficient, given the qualitative jump in Chile's capabilities. It was acquiring vast quantities of new weapons, but still had a feeble organization. The result was that its military inferiority grew worse each passing day. Fear of the rapid growth in Chilean power, combined with their own disorganization, prompted both civilian and military leaders to call for a much more fundamental and extensive military modernization than hitherto undertaken.

---

[169] Archivo Roca, Caja 1384, army general staff report, unsigned, undated, untitled, 2.
[170] Archivo Roca, Caja 1384, Lieutenant Colonel Dienner, corps of engineers, Prussian army, "Proyecto de fortificación del Banco Chico en el Rio de la Plata," undated 10.
[171] Archivo Roca, Caja 1384, army general staff, Guillermo Villanueva, "Defense de las costas Atlánticas de la República Argentina," 21 June 1898.
[172] Quote cited in Varley, "Aftermath of the War of the Pacific," 68.
[173] Quote cited in Eyzaguirre, *Chile durante el gobierno de Errázuriz*, 111.

Argentina had a lot of catching up to do to close the gap in military capabilities. Military spending, especially on armaments, took place at a feverish pace, but its military was deficient in every other category. Though Rouquié argues that the officers and commanders of the *gaucho* armies and desert campaigns were professional and competent in their own way, the level of technical-professional training (as defined by Huntington) of the officer corps remained dismal into the turn of the century.[174] In 1893 the war ministry estimated that out of 1,400 total officers in the army only about thirty had technical training in the higher military academies.[175]

The country's lack of military preparedness was a major issue in public discourse and official attention.[176] Military leaders complained of the total lack of military preparation and organization in the face of a likely war. General Bosch complained that the "permanent army is falling apart."[177] General staff officer and head of the army's 2nd division, General Lorenzo Vintter, criticized the dilapidated state of Argentina's armed forces, and became a major advocate of complete overhaul. In an 1894 memorandum to the minister of war, Vintter, then army chief of staff, argued for the "absolute necessity" of reforms, and called for "a vast and thorough plan to reorganize the army."[178] In his many reports to the general staff he complained about a broad range of deficiencies in the Argentine military system, from the lack of adequate training, the "extremely deficient enlistment," to the absence of modern communications. Another memorandum to Roca's minister of war noted that, in contrast to Argentina, "today all the more advanced nations in the art of war have rushed to utilize the latest advancements that science has placed at their disposal."[179] His sense of urgency notwithstanding, Vintter also counseled against a "radical" reform that could produce "negative results."[180] Vintter's caution seems to have been based on his view that the reforms already under way were facing many difficulties, largely because "the basic foundation to support them are lacking."[181]

Argentina, it should be noted, had been closely monitoring the progress of Chile's military modernization.[182] By the turn of the century, all the major powers in the region had their own civilian and military observers stationed

---

[174] Rouquié, *Poder militar*, chap. 2.

[175] Ramirez, "The Reform of the Argentine Army," 144.

[176] Ramirez, "The Reform of the Argentine Army."

[177] Argentina, Congresso Nacional, *Diario de Sessiones*, 1900, 967–68.

[178] Archivo General Lorenzo Vintter, Archivo Nacional, Sala 7, Caja 1161. Untitled memorandum, army general staff, 8 December 1894, 2, 4. Hereafter cited as Archivo Vintter. Collection in Servicio Histórico del Ejército.

[179] Archivo Vintter, "Memorandum," 24 October 1894, 1.

[180] Archivo Vintter, "Memorandum," army general staff, 8 December 1894.

[181] Archivo Vintter, "Memorandum," army general staff, memorandum to minister of war, undated.

[182] On this point, see also Ramirez, "The Reform of the Argentine Army," chap. 7.

in one another's capitals. Argentina was no exception to this military information and intelligence gathering. Since the mid-1890s a stream of military reports had been arriving, carefully assessing the strengths and weaknesses of Chilean military power and reforms. Some warned of Chile's open confidence in its superiority and victory in war with Argentina.[183] Riccheri warned that without serious reforms Argentina would be confronted with a "French 1870" situation in a possible conflict with Chile.[184]

The "Armed Peace"

The latter half of the 1890s constituted the pivotal moment in Argentina's military modernization. The festering border dispute with Chile quickly escalated into what a U.S. diplomat called an "armed peace."[185] Tensions escalated. War appeared imminent, so much so that Argentines turned once again to Roca as the uncontested presidential candidate in 1898. The near-war crisis dragged on for four years, 1898–1902. Relations between the Andean rivals had been deteriorating precipitously after 1895 as a result of conflicting interpretations over the Patagonia territory. Border negotiations stalled. The cold war between the two Andean powers would eventually draw the attention and mediation efforts of the great powers. The first major attempt at international arbitration was made by the United States in 1898. It was unsuccessful. Argentina and Chile stood on the brink of war. To Roca, the source of the problem was Chile's "bad faith." Chile possessed a powerful navy and army, said Roca, and it wanted to "take advantage of this exceptional moment to accomplish its long-standing dream to hold on to Patagonia and acquire an outlet to the Atlantic."[186] The war crisis was set off by all the classic ingredients found in the anarchic structure of the international system: territorial disputes, arms racing, and power competition.

Arms racing accelerated. Both sides braced for war and mobilized their armed forces. The start of an arms race is never clear cut, making it difficult to point to an exact date or event that sets it in motion. The arms race between Argentina and Chile was no different. Chile had been building up its military since the mid-1880s, and continued to keep a brisk pace throughout the 1890s. For its part, Argentina had begun to acquire massive amounts of modern weapons from Europe beginning in the late 1880s. Despite severe fiscal and budgetary problems, Argentina's buildup accelerated in 1892, leading one United States diplomat to observe that its military

[183] Ramirez, "The Reform of the Argentine Army," 311–18.
[184] Quote cited in Ramirez, "The Reform of the Argentine Army," 280.
[185] United States, Department of State, National Archives, *Dispatches from U.S. Minister to Argentina, 1817–1906*, Film S-1040, M69, Roll 31.
[186] Luna, *Soy Roca*, 306.

TABLE 5.2. *Chile–Argentina Naval Balance of Power, 1902*

Main Battle Ships		Reserve Forces		Torpedoes		Transports and Aux. Ships	
Tons	Canons	Tons	Canons	Number	Tubes	Number	Tons
Argentina	44673	76	12500	5	15	37	8	30,080
Chile	43392	72	7218	2	21	49	20	63,060
Difference	+1281	+4	+5282	+3	−6	−12	−12	−32,980

Source: Argentina, Archivo General de la Nación, Archivo Roca, Caja 1384, Special Memorandum on Naval Agreements, Undated, Unsigned, 9. Memorandum likely prepared in late 1902 by the general staff.

expenditures "in no way point to the economies one would expect in the time of financial difficulty."[187]

The arms race turned predominantly into a naval affair during 1898–1902. Both rushed to acquire some of the largest and most advanced warships built in Europe. Argentina was able to close the naval gap rapidly, and the balance of naval capabilities became so delicate as to generate further instability and brinksmanship. Argentina sought to improve its naval power with the purchase in May 1898 of the Italian cruiser *Garibaldi*, the second cruiser it acquired during the first half of the year. Chile considered the acquisition of the *Garibaldi* as a move that would place it in a position of naval inferiority, making an ultimatum to Argentina to agree to arbitration before the arrival of the ship.[188] The naval arms race was capped in 1902 when Argentina ordered two more ironclads. Chile responded by ordering two large ironclads, to which Argentina responded by ordering two additional, much larger ironclads. The two powers were deadlocked at rough parity by the end of the naval arms race, though Argentina enjoyed a slight advantage in aggregate tonnage while training and discipline favored Chile.[189]

For all practical purposes, Chile and Argentina were in a de facto state of war. Throughout much of 1898–1902, on several occasions both powers mobilized their forces in preparation for war.[190] As the crisis peaked, the Argentine congress finalized the universal conscription legislation introduced by Riccheri. By 1901 President Roca and his war minister, Riccheri, were in near-continuous emergency sessions to review war plans.[191] Roca ordered Riccheri to mobilize the armed forces in December 1901. On Christmas Eve 1901 the Argentine government notified its representatives in Santiago,

---

[187] Quote cited in Varley, "Aftermath of the War of the Pacific," 88.
[188] Eyzaguirre, *Chile durante el gobierno de Errazuriz*, 194.
[189] "Chili and Argentina," *Army and Navy Journal*, 39, no. 18 (4 January 1902): 446.
[190] On Argentine war preparations, see Grela, *Fuerzas Armadas*, 128–29.
[191] Grela, *Fuerzas Armadas*, 100; Roca, *Soy Roca*, 328–32.

Chile, of its decision to break diplomatic relations with Chile. In Riccheri's sobering estimate of the situation, he noted "we were practically in a state of war, all that was missing was the firing of a shot in the *cordilleras.*"[192] Argentina expected a multifront, combined land and sea attack. Adding to the war scare in Buenos Aires, alarming reports were coming in from military attachés and embassies in the region. Throughout 1900 Argentine military attachés in Bolivia were reporting continuous Chilean military exercises along the Bolivian border.[193] The Argentine mission warned that Chile might attack Bolivia as well. Chile's military preparations and the activities of its military attachés in Bolivia, warned the Argentine ambassador, "point to one end, a plan of military invasion into one or another side of this country or even Peru." Such an invasion would only be a prelude to a "war against Argentina." Chile "is emboldened by its prior and easy conquests, and Chileans believe they can field two armies in a war against Argentina." The report concluded with a sobering tone that "for these reasons, [I] fear a war is likely.[194]

The near-war crisis of 1898–1902 was finally resolved in 1902 through British mediation and the signing of a series of multifaceted agreements that became known as the Pactos de Mayo.[195] An important component of the settlement was one of the world's first naval arms limitations agreements. The naval agreement, signed in July 1902, called for "discrete equivalence" and recognized the natural sphere of influence each country claimed in the Pacific and Atlantic respectively.[196] The spheres of influence stipulation was standard balance of power practice, by states big and small, but novel to the South American system in the form of an explicit agreement. The effect of this provision was profound. In essence, what broke the deadlock was Argentina's agreement to end its meddling in Pacific affairs and terminate its support to Peru and Bolivia. To avoid war with Chile, still at the peak of its power, Argentina had to abandon the Peruvians and Bolivians to their own fate. As Roca himself later acknowledged, this aspect of their relations had always been a major source of Chilean antipathy and distrust.

[192] Grela, *Fuerzas Armadas*, 100.
[193] See for example Archivo Roca, Caja 1384. Report from the Argentine Legation in Bolivia to President Júlio Roca, 8 August 1900, 5, 7–8.
[194] Archivo Roca, Caja 1384. Report from the Argentine Legation in Bolivia to President Júlio Roca, 8 August 1900.
[195] On the 1902 accords between Chile and Argentina, see Burr, *By Reason or Force*; Meneses Ciuffardi, "Los límites"; Oscar Espinoza Moraga, "Los Pactos de Mayo," *Boletín de la Academia Chilena de la Historia* 19, no. 46 (1952).
[196] Archivo Roca, Caja 1384, Special Memorandum on Naval Agreements, undated, unsigned. Memorandum likely prepared in late 1902 by the general staff. The full translated phrase is: "Para establecer una discreta equivalencia entre las escuadras chilena y argentina. . . ."

The Pactos de Mayo ended the near-war crisis. In a lengthy report to Roca on military expenditures in early 1902, Riccheri observed that "we traversed critical moments."[197] The arms limitation agreements and nonaggression pacts with Chile in 1902 did not significantly dampen Argentina's military modernization. The arms limitations articles dealt exclusively with naval forces, and naval expenditures remained fairly stable up to 1908. The question is why Argentina continued extensive military modernization when the wide-ranging Pactos de Mayo accords appeared to remove the sources of conflict between the two Andean powers? The 1902 accords provided for the settlement of most, not all, the outstanding territorial disputes between Chile and Argentina. More important, the settlement brought an end to the naval arms race, which was creating preemptive-war incentives on both sides of the *cordilleras*. But it was a temporary truce.

The clash between the two regional powers was about much more than the immediate issues of dispute (territorial demarcation), as the arms race showed. They were symptomatic of the larger struggle for regional mastery and military advantage. The U.S. ambassador in Argentina was prescient in his observation: "I am convinced that both countries will maintain their present war footing up to the time that this [border] limits questions is settled, and I am inclined to believe they will [continue to] to do so thereafter. There is considerable truth to what many believe here, viz: that the limits question between the two countries is but an incident; that behind all else lies the question of supremacy in South America and therefore there is little likelihood of any material diminution in the military status of either."[198] Argentina's ambassador in La Paz added that "we are dealing neither with boundaries nor borders; but rather with political and military preponderance aspired to by a country that is essentially adventurous and poor, which seeks to enrich itself by the fortune of its arms which up to the present has been favorable and easy."[199]

Notwithstanding the accords, Argentina still found itself in a militarily inferior position relative to Chilean power – although it had closed the gap (and perhaps even achieved a marginal advantage) in naval capabilities. Argentina's army, on the other hand, still paled in comparison in terms of training, organization, and planning. President Roca, who opposed the accords' stipulation regarding Argentine neutrality in Chile's Pacific sphere of influence, noted in 1902 that, "Chile should not augment its power in the process of settling the pending questions with Bolivia and Peru, because this

---

[197] Ministério de Guerra, *Memoria*, 1902, 9.
[198] United States, Department of State, *Dispatches from the U.S. Minister to Argentina, 1817–1906*, Film S1040, M69, Roll 32, 22 September 1898.
[199] Archivo Roca, Caja 1384. Report from the Argentine Legation in Bolivia to President Júlio Roca, 8 August 1900, 14.

would be a serious danger for us. This perspective, this danger, requires us to arms ourselves."[200]

Uncertainty lingered as to Chile's short-term intentions. As did fears of a Chilean preemptive invasion or move to occupy by force disputed lands. Late into 1900 the expectation of a Chilean attack still prevailed. The Argentine minister in Bolivia reported that from "conversations with the Bolivian president, Chilean plans, in the opinion of the [president] envisage war, which he believes inevitable for the reasons he lays out in this report."[201] Riccheri confided in 1893 that Argentine military modernization had one single objective: to make Argentina "speak with the authority of the first power in South America."[202]

The 1902 peace accords, therefore, did not solve fully Argentina's military inferiority. Nor did the accords settle their border disputes with any finality. (Eight decades later both countries would stand again on the precipice of war, as the entire world braced for a South Atlantic war in 1978.) Argentina continued to fear a Chilean preventive war. The underlying problem, as Roca himself recognized, was the inevitable power transition, rather than a few square kilometers of barren territory. The real problem, said Roca, was the "hegemonic position that many Chileans wished to give their country over South America."[203] Roca told congress in 1903 that the country cannot put an end to modernization simply because of the 1902 accords, for "the eventualities that led us to initiate the work of perfecting our military institutions have not disappeared."[204]

Argentina was still vulnerable to, and feared, Chile's military power. The U.S. minister in Buenos Aires, commenting on Argentina's lack of military preparedness and the "smallness of the Argentine army and navy," went on to note that "as a matter of fact, it is extremely doubtful whether the Argentine government would have been able at the time, considering the unorganized condition of its military force, to have successfully resisted the trained battalions of Chile and prevented an invasion of her territory. [The near-war crisis] taught Argentina a lesson which has not passed unheeded."[205] Argentine leaders were as aware of the country's military situation, notwithstanding the peace accords and naval limitations treaty. Argentina's legation in Santiago cabled a lengthy study to Buenos Aires in June 1903, noting that, "the [accords] cannot offer guarantees. Chile must not augment its [military] power in the wake of the territorial dispute settlement, for it will present a

[200] President Júlio Roca, quote cited in Grela, *Fuerzas Armadas*, 229.
[201] Archivo Roca, Caja 1384, Argentine Mission to Bolivia, Memorandum, 8 August 1900.
[202] Quote cited in Ramirez, "The Reform of the Argentine Army," 182.
[203] Luna, *Soy Roca*, 306.
[204] Roca, speech before congress, 1 May 1903, cited in Fraga, *La amistad Roca–Riccheri*, 158.
[205] United States, Department of State, *Dispatches from the U.S. Minister to Argentina, 1817–1906*, Film S1040, M69, Roll 32, 3 October 1900.

grave danger for us. This perspective, this danger obliges us to undertake our armament."[206]

Despite the political turbulence and the financial crisis, made worse by the escalating arms race, Argentines had two major answers. First, they once again turned to the old veteran and military hero, Júlio Roca, to lead the country, believing only he could lead the country out of crisis and bring success in the event of a war with Chile. Carlos Pellegrini, the leading candidate who bowed out of the race in favor of Roca explained, "only Roca will be able to prevent a war with Chile, and this question is more important than any other national interest."[207] Second, both opponents and proponents of military modernization agreed on the necessity of immediate military reforms, even if they continued to disagree on the details.

THE INTERWAR PERIOD

On the eve of the First World War, Argentine leaders were confident in the progress they had made modernizing the armed forces. Of equal significance was the confidence they exuded in the German model they adopted, even though initially they had reservations about the strategy. "The German methods that we have adopted have been assimilated with ease and enthusiasm by our officers, who are now awakened to the scientific foundation of these methods, its irrefutable logic and its indisputable efficiency."[208]

The interwar years were a period of unrest and disorder inside and outside the military. It was also a period of consolidation for the army reforms, as the military experienced simultaneously greater professionalization and politicization. The First World War caused serious disruptions in economic and military spheres.[209] The war was a serious blow to military emulation in terms of the formal contacts and relationship between the Argentine and German armies. The most visible disruption occurred at the level of armaments, the formal military mission, and the training of Argentine officers in Germany. These were the three main channels and carriers of the German model. The post-WWI. period was essentially a period marked by consolidation of the prewar reforms and adjustments. The primary trend in the Argentine military in the interwar years was steady growth in size and armaments as military competition with Brazil stiffened. The military grew in both strength and resources, increasing in size by 26 percent between 1920 and 1930.

---

[206] Argentina, Ministerio de Relaciones Exteriores y Culto, *Memorias, 1903–1904*, 248–49.

[207] Quote cited in Ambrosio Romero Carranza, Alberto Rodríguez Varela, and Eduardo Ventura, *Historia política y constitucional de la Argentina*, 3 vols., vol. 3, *Desde 1868 hasta 1989* (Buenos Aires: A–Z Editora, 1993): 272.

[208] Ministério de Guerra, *Memoria, 1912–1913*, 8.

[209] Percy Alvin Martin, *Latin America and the War* (Baltimore: Johns Hopkins University Press, 1925) remains a classic study on this question.

The other dominant trend in the interwar years was internal factionalism and politicization of the officer corps. Though elements in the army had been politically involved in the past – especially those linked to the Radical Party – the army's politicization during this period came largely in response to the policies and interventions of the Radical government into military affairs. Argentina was a one-party dominant political system under PAN, but pressure has been building since 1890 to open the system to greater contestation and inclusion. These pressures did not abate despite electoral reforms in 1911, and labor strikes swept the country in the immediate post-WWI years. The military became infected. The military coup d'état in 1930 became the first in a long and tragic series of interventions.

Long before the tumult of the interwar years, Argentina had already imported much of the German model. Thus, the postwar years found its army and navy well equipped and organized. Moreover, it had formed a large cadre of German-trained officers who carried out the final steps in emulating the German system and consolidating the reforms. Argentina, unlike Chile and Brazil, was always less dependent on direct and formal links with the model being emulated. Unlike both neighbors, Argentina's military strength did not erode. Several reform initiatives were launched in the 1920–30 period – corresponding closely to Brazil's own efforts – and raised tensions between the two historic rivals.

The 1920s witnessed a dramatic expansion in the numerical size of the army, with a 40 percent increase in annual conscription during 1920–30.[210] In 1920, active army strength stood at 26,000, but by 1930 it had expanded to 33,000. Military expenditures increased sharply, doubling during 1916–22, a period corresponding to the launching of military emulation in Brazil. As a percentage of the national budget, military expenditure (for both the army and navy) averaged around 20 percent during the 1920s.[211] This period also witnessed an extensive program aimed at improving the military's physical plant, installations, and equipment. The other major reform spurt occurred in 1926–27, again corresponding to renewed tensions with Brazil. This spurt consisted mostly in the huge acquisition of new armaments from various parts of Europe. The trend in military expenditures during 1931–37 was one of steady growth.

Despite Germany's defeat, the pull of the German system remained strong within and outside the Argentine army, as it did in neighboring Chile.[212] Indeed, Argentine governments in the 1930s and the Peronist period modeled themselves after fascist Germany and Italy. For both Nazi hunters and Hollywood films, Argentina became a notorious haven for Nazi officials escaping

---

[210] Potash, *The Army and Politics*, 6–7.
[211] Potash, *The Army and Politics*, 6–8.
[212] On postwar military emulation in South America and changes in foreign influence, see Nunn, *Yesterday's Soldiers*, chap. 6.

prosecution. To the frustration, of the United States Argentina adopted a distinctly pro Axis policy. Argentina's-pro-Axis neutrality in the First World War was widely attributed to the strength of the German influence in the armed forces. This influence remained strong even during the Second World War, in which Argentina again assumed a pro-German neutrality, though eventually it was pressured to join the Allied cause in the last few days of the war. Within the army the intellectual influence remained despite Germany's emasculation. Rouquié notes that Argentine military academies in the 1920s continued to study the Franco-Prussian war and World War I from Germany's perspective.[213] Of the 126 military texts published between 1918 and 1928, 60 were German translations (many direct translations of German works on World War I), and only 20 were French.[214]

More important, despite the restrictions of the Treaty of Versailles, German military advisers and informal missions continued to be active in Argentina during the interwar period. The evidence is spotty as to their exact number and activities. On account of the Versailles treaty, German officers hired in South America ostensibly did not receive sanction from the German government but worked as private contractors; though many of these officers in South America were being promoted on the active list in the German army at the same time.[215] Secondary sources disagree on the extent of the presence. Duval reports that in 1920–21 there were no foreign military personnel in Argentina's military schools.[216] Potash, on the other hand, argues that after 1921 there were a few individual German military advisers in Argentina, and there remained a small, unofficial German mission into the 1930s.[217]

The first group of officers are said to have arrived in Argentina in 1921.[218] The officers of this unofficial mission were former members of the prewar mission to Argentina, led by the controversial and well-traveled Wilhelm Faupel. Though he would work in Argentina without an official contract, Faupel became the personal adviser to Uriburu. Many of the German officers became instructors at the war academy (ESG), the infantry and cavalry schools, in addition to directing the training of cadets and noncommissioned officers, air tactics and armor combat, and also directing maneuvers.[219] The German presence in Argentina once again caused great controversy within the military and political establishment during the latter part of the 1920s.

[213] Rouquié, *Poder militar*, 94.
[214] Rouquié, *Poder militar*, 97.
[215] Atkins and Thompson, "German Military Influence in Argentina," 261–62. Moreover, to bypass Versailles restrictions German officers became naturalized citizens in the host country, without losing their German citizenship.
[216] Duval, *Argentina, potencia militar*, vol. 2, 369
[217] Potash, *The Army and Politics*, 5.
[218] Atkins and Thompson, "The German Military Influence in Argentina," 261.
[219] Atkins and Thompson, "The German Military Influence in Argentina."

Nonetheless, the size and functions of German military advisers grew rapidly in the 1930s, especially after the rise of Adolph Hitler and the beginning of Germany's rearmament. During the early 1930s the size of the unofficial German mission in Argentina was six, rising to eighteen in 1939.[220] Moreover, during the 1930s it is estimated that over fifty Argentine officers were sent to Germany for military instruction.[221]

Why did Argentina not "switch" to the model of the Allied victors? Argentina did flirt with the French model immediately after the First World War. Potash reports that there was a major push within the military to emulate the French army after the war.[222] Between 1916 and 1928 almost one third of the Argentine officer corps went to Europe for training and instruction, most going to France and Italy.[223] Potash also argues that it is in the 1920s that factionalism rose within the army, partly due to the split between Francophiles and Germanophiles. The factional split between Francophil and Germanophil officers was perhaps more pronounced in Argentina than in Chile and Brazil. The depth of the bitterness and public controversy surrounding the 1909–10 contract negotiations over the purchase of new artillery, and subsequent competition between France and Germany to secure support inside the military, is only one nascent indication of the seriousness of the split.[224] The prominent Colonel General Colmar von der Goltz, attending Argentina's centennial celebration in 1910, noted that while the German military system had many admirers within the Argentine army, the German mission was a means by which such admirers could strengthen "their position with respect to the old *gaucho* generals and the friends of the French, who still exercise a certain influence and today once again are in the leadership."[225]

During the interwar years, Argentina was the dominant military power on the continent. It had already begun to eclipse Chilean power by 1910, and would cast a long shadow over Brazil well into the 1930s. Argentina had what its two rivals lacked: the dynamic economic-industrial base on which to create and sustain a large, well-equipped military system. It outmatched Chile in every category of national capabilities. It had all the raw resources of national power, the necessary base to sustain its pre-WWI rank as one of the world's ten richest nations. What it lacked, but which Chile had up into the early 1970s, was political stability, and an inability to break its economy away from its dependency on a primary products monoculture.

---

[220] Atkins and Thompson, "The German Military Influence in Argentina," 269. See also Nunn, *Yesterday's Soldiers*, 213; Grela, *Fuerzas Armadas*, 204.

[221] Atkins and Thompson, "The German Military Influence in Argentina," 270. Nunn, *Yesterday's Soldiers*, 215, estimates that twenty Argentine officers went to Germany.

[222] Potash, *The Army and Politics*.

[223] Rouquié, *Poder militar*, 96.

[224] White, *The German Influence*; Schiff, "The Influence of the German Armed Forces."

[225] Quote cited in Ramirez, "The Reform of the Argentine Army," 98.

Brazil had the size and power potential, which Argentines constantly feared would materialize one day. But it too lacked political stability, despite possessing in ample supply all the material ingredients of national power. Similar to Argentina, the weight of Brazil's economic mismanagement and chronic political turmoil undercut the Luso giant's aspiration.

6

Military Emulation in Brazil, 1870–1930

Brazil's war minister in 1894 protested that the country's military disrepair was becoming "more and more urgent with each passing day." Nearly all departments, he said, "have antiquated organization, which are not in step with the exigencies of the advancements in military science."[1] His successor recommended that "we need to adopt to our conditions the principles and the perfections sanctioned by [the] experience of the more advanced nations."[2] Brazil's military languished, while on the other side of the Paraná River historic rival Argentina was amassing an impressive military machinery. Military weakness was not the only problem besetting the Old Republic. From the overthrow of the monarchy in 1889 to its demise in 1930, the troubled Old Republic was mired in a long cycle of political and social turmoil. Brazil was last among the three regional powers to adopt military emulation, and it emulated the least. The process of modernizing its armed forces was tortuous, replete with fits and starts. Reform plans came and went, few were implemented or allowed to root.

Brazil's military emulation is theoretically fascinating as well as challenging. The wider spectrum of its balancing behavior, including spurts of arms racing, responded to external pressures, primarily the menace of Argentine military power. Of the three cases, it represents the clearest case of switching from one model (Germany up to 1914) to another (France in 1919) midstream. It confirms our theoretical expectations that countries emulate proven success, and switch models accordingly. As expected, given its strategic situation, the pace and scale of its emulation were modest compared to the other two cases. The late start, modest scope, and fitful nature of Brazil's

---

[1] Brasíl, Ministério de Guerra (ministry of war), *Relatório do Ministério de Guerra, 1894* (Rio de Janeiro: Imprensa Nacional, 1895): 4. The full title of the annual reports is *Relatório do Ministério de Guerra Apresentado ao Presidente da República dos Estados Unidos do Brasíl pelo Ministro*. Hereafter cited as *Relatório*.

[2] Ministério de Guerra, *Relatório, 1899*, 9.

military emulation was very much a product of its external security situation. First, its principal military threat and geopolitical adversary, Argentina, did not initiate full-scale military emulation until 1899. Thus, as expected Brazil's own efforts came *after* that of its principal rival. Second, unlike its neighbors to the west, the South American giant was endowed with ample defensive advantages afforded by geography and the good fortune of free riding on the power of Chile and the United States. The result was an unsteady and uncertain process of military modernization.

Brazil's military emulation is an ideal case for domestic political explanations. In sharp contrast to the other two cases, domestic forces seemingly overpowered external ones to thwart competitive emulation. We cannot ultimately discount the weight of domestic factors. The havoc surrounding the post-1889 political breakdown and the rebellious impulse in the heart of the military, necessarily impeded military modernization. This implosion did not just interrupt military modernization; it tore apart the institution. More often than not, national upheavals had their origins inside the military. The military as an institution was a microcosm of all the disarray and paralysis of the enfeebled Old Republic. The country's military modernization could not escape the consequences of the deeply afflicted, ultimately unworkable, Old Republic.[3] From an empirical standpoint, Brazil is challenging to study because so much of the implementation stages of emulation were either disrupted or stillborn as a result of the many crises inside and outside the military.

In this chapter I examine Brazil's efforts to modernize its military system between the Paraguayan war (1865–70) and the years of the Old Republic (1889–1930).[4] I first detail the process of military emulation, focusing primarily on the period from 1898 to the early 1930s. There were three defining reform spurts, notable for their shortcomings as much as their ability to set the modernization agenda in national discourse: the 1898–1901 years, the ambitious efforts of the *jovem turcos* (Brazil's own Young Turks) to import

---

[3] A good general reference in English is *Brazil: Empire and Republic, 1822–1930*, ed. Leslie Bethell (Cambridge: Cambridge University Press, 1989).

[4] I rely primarily on archival records from the Brazilian army's Arquivo Histórico do Exército (AHEX, army historical archive), in Rio de Janeiro. I also acknowledge the insights and contributions of Professor José Faria, resident scholar in AHEX and grandson of the famous Brazilian general by the same name. On secondary literature on Brazilian military history during 1870–1930, see Nelson Werneck Sodré, *História militar do Brasil* (Rio de Janeiro: Editôra Civilização Brasileira, 1965); João Batista Magalhães, *A evolução militar do Brasil: anotações para a história* (Rio de Janeiro: Editôra Nacional, 1950); Edmundo C. Coelho, *Em busca de identidade: o Exército e a política na sociedade brasileira* (Rio de Janeiro: Forense–Universitaria, 1976); Robert A. Hayes, *The Armed Nation: The Brazilian Corporate Mystique* (Tempe: Arizona State University Press, 1989); *Perspectives on Armed Forces in Brazil*, ed. Henry H. Keith and Robert A. Hayes (Tempe: Arizona State University Press, 1976); General Francisco de Paula Cidade, *Síntese de três séculos de literatura militar brasileira* (Rio de Janeiro: Gustavo Cordeiro de Faria, 1959).

the German system during 1906–14 and the period of the French military mission beginning in 1919.[5] The modern Brazilian military was in the throes of creation during these years. I will trace first the emulation of the German system, followed by a discussion of the emulation of the French system. The second section of the chapter presents the theoretical explanation for Brazil's emulation. I will highlight only those aspects and developments that bear on emulation efforts.

MILITARY MODERNIZATION IN BRAZIL, 1898–1930

Prior to the coming of the French military mission to Brazil in 1919, there were three noteworthy reform pushes: the latter half of the 1890s, corresponding with the eruption of the Misiones border dispute with Argentina; the ambitious naval modernization program begun in 1904, which coincides with the brief war with Bolivia over Acre territory; finally, the 1906–14 push to emulate the German army. These pre-WWI reforms halted decades of decline, but failed to solve Brazil's military problem. The reform spurt begun in the late 1890s, as with the other two, was notable less for its results than for its ability to put military modernization on the national agenda. A general consensus appeared to be emerging that the military needed to be reorganized. The problem in Brazil continued to be implementation. As a result, its armed forces continued their postwar decline. The Paraguayan war itself had revealed the military's gaping flaws. It had fought the war with a slave army, led by officers with little or no formal training. Many officers came to blame the total lack of prewar preparation and the exclusive reliance on wartime improvisation for the tremendous losses and repeated battlefield setbacks suffered by the army in the course of the war.[6] The Brazilian military of the late nineteenth century was an archaic and stagnant institution.

Beginning in 1898 there came to power war ministers who used their positions to advocate and implement modernizing reforms as well as encourage reformers in the ranks. Prominent among them were General João de Medeiros Mallet (1898–1902), Brigadier General Francisco de Paula Argollo (1902–05), Marshall Hermes da Fonseca (1906–10), and Marshal José Caetano de Faria (1914–18). Their annual reports to the legislature and the executive, the *Relatório do Ministério de Guerra* (*Annual Report of the Ministry of War*), were frank and detailed. Their reports called for a complete reconstitution.[7] The most critical aspect of their tenure, however, was the

---

[5] For an informative survey of foreign military influence in Brazil see Frank D. McCann, "A influência estrangeira e o Exército brasileiro, 1905–1945," in *A Revolução de 30: seminário internacional*, ed. CPDOC (Brasília: Ed. Universidade Brasília, 1982): 211–247.

[6] See reports of field commanders in Ministério de Guerra, *Relatório, 1871*, annex B. See also, Davis Ribeiro Sena, "O desenvolvimento do Exército e o oficial de Estado Maior," *Revista do Exército Brasileiro* 126, no. 3 (July–September 1989): 54–63.

[7] See annual reports by Mallet, Ministério de Guerra, *Relatório, 1898–1901*.

stability and continuity in leadership and planning that the armed forces had been lacking. (Brazil averaged one war minister annually during 1889–98.) The first phase of reforms can be traced a few years earlier to a series of coherent reform proposals outlined in the 1894 *Relatório*.[8] These criticisms and recommendations were repeated the following year. War Minister Bernado Vasques observed that the military needed a "complete reconstitution, in its very organization, personnel, and materiel."[9] More significant, he went on to observe that Brazil needed a "complete reform so that we do not appear in a condition of inferiority relative to the other American republics, who have boldly undertaken and go on to realize a complete transformation of their military power."[10]

Mallet's tenure at the war ministry was a turning point. His annual reports called for complete overhaul.[11] In every *Relatório* Mallet stressed the importance of peacetime preparation as the basis for victory in wartime. Improvisation was no longer possible. Mallet's first three reports highlighted conscription and officer instruction, though all of them were wide ranging in their discussion and recommendations. He was the first minister to advocate the adoption of the military systems of the leading great powers, though he felt Brazil should adopt only general aspects of these systems. He argued that "we need to adopt to our conditions the principles and the perfections sanctioned by *experience* of the more advanced nations."[12] Military modernization also received vocal backing from Brazil's powerful foreign minister, José Maria da Silva Paranhos, better known as Baron Rio Branco, who served during 1902–12.[13]

Mallet established a commission in 1899 to prepare a reorganization plan.[14] Among the members of the commission was Tasso Fragoso, a major proponent of reforms and later chief of the general staff (1923–29).[15] The goal of the reorganization commission was to "adopt, in accord with our capacity and circumstances, all that is indispensable, without deforming the essence of general principles."[16] The reform recommendations were not explicitly modeled after foreign practices. The commission concluded that Brazil's lack of an industrial base and technically skilled officers "prevents

[8] Ministério de Guerra, *Relatório, 1894.*
[9] Ministério de Guerra, *Relatório, 1895,* 5.
[10] Ibid.
[11] See especially *Relatório, 1901.*
[12] Ministério de Guerra, *Relatório, 1899,* 9. Emphasis added.
[13] José Maria da Silva Paranhos, Barão do Rio Branco, *Obras do Barão do Rio Branco,* vol. I (Rio de Janeiro: Ministério de Relações Exteriores, 1948): 104. A nicely documented biography of Rio Branco is Luís Viana Filho, *A vida do Barão do Rio Branco* (Brasília: Senado Federal/Fundação Alexandre de Gusmão, 1996).
[14] Ministério de Guerra, *Relatório, 1899,* 9.
[15] On Fragoso, see General Tristão de Alencar Araripe, *Tasso Fragoso: um pouco de história do nosso Exército* (Rio de Janeiro: Biblioteca do Exército, 1960).
[16] Ministério de Guerra, *Relatório, 1900,* 72.

us from modeling completely our army on those of the European powers."[17] Herein was the genesis of the idea to send officers abroad for training. Mallet's reorganization plan met the same fate as so many other reform measures before and after it. His 1901 report complained bitterly that the reorganization had not yet received any legislative attention.[18] He noted that the army was in "urgent necessity of reorganization," and that "this issue is made more urgent with each passing day."[19]

Mallet's successor, General Argollo, likewise highlighted the need for deep reforms. He blamed congress, "political speculators," and "anarchist politicians" for the military's disorganization and internal divisions.[20] Argollo noted that Brazil could not rely solely on diplomacy and international law to guarantee its sovereignty and freedom of action. Reminiscent of Thucydides' *Melian Dialogue*, and cognizant of the imperialist scramble then taking place to carve out parts of the world, Argollo argued that the international system is a realm in which "the weak countries are condemned to the degrading tutelage of the powerful, who deem themselves to have the right to command them, to lead them, and even reprimand them, making a fiction of their independence and autonomy."[21] Echoing Argollo's sentiments, Foreign Minister Rio Branco told a cavalry regiment in 1909 that "peace does not depend solely on our wishes, but also and principally on the wishes of numerous neighbors who encircle us. In order that none of our neighbors contemplate injury against us, it is necessary that we are prepared for an immediate and effective repulsion [of an attack]."[22]

Prior to 1906, explicit calls to emulate foreign practices or hire foreign training missions were muted. There was a notable reluctance to hire a foreign military mission and embrace foreign models. These doubts quickly abated. The examples of Chile and Argentina acted both to stimulate Brazil to reorganize its own military system and, indirectly, to reduce Brazil's own uncertainty about the viability of emulating foreign ways and practices. The more intriguing emulation example Brazilians pointed to was Japan. Japanese military modernization and adoption of foreign military practices were singled out by Brazilian reformers as confirmation of the validity of an emulation strategy. The appeal of the German model in Brazil, as elsewhere in South America, was considerably boosted by Japanese military successes and Japan's meteoric rise from the periphery to world power. Brazil was particularly impressed by the fact that Japan was victorious in a major war (the

[17] Ministério de Guerra, *Relatório, 1900*, 72.
[18] Ministério de Guerra, *Relatório, 1901*, 6.
[19] Ministério de Guerra, *Relatório, 1901*, 3.
[20] Ministério de Guerra, *Relatório, 1904*, 9.
[21] Ministério de Guerra, *Relatório, 1903*, 4.
[22] Rio Branco, *Obras do Barão*, vol. 1, 222.

Russo–Japanese war, 1905) against a European great power. The Japanese army had been reorganized and modernized under German supervision since the late 1880s. Brazil's war minister said admiringly that "Japan has stopped being a backward country, of inferior rank, has stopped being considered a simple prize coveted by all and is now treated with respect and even admiration by the civilized nations after it became evident that it possesses a military power significantly strong to defend itself against them and even fight against anyone of them."[23] Brazilian reformers repeatedly pointed to "the formidable military power of Japan" as the goal Brazil should aspire to, and as late as 1917 military leaders were urging Brazil to follow the "Japanese example."[24] The Russo–Japanese war was widely studied all over the region. In Brazilian military journals around this time the Russo–Japanese war received more mention than the Franco–Prussian war or any other conflict. Brazilian officers were particularly interested in the tactical and organizational aspects of the war. War Minister Faria, lamenting that Brazil lacked a peacetime military organization that could quickly convert to war footing, noted that "this is a classic formula whose disregard was one of the principal reasons for Russia's failure in the war against Japan."[25]

Before elaborating the army modernization measures of the 1906–18 reform phase, a brief mention of the 1904 and 1906 naval modernization is necessary. Brazil, as I have emphasized, was both last and slow moving in launching military emulation. Moreover, military modernization was marked by advances and reversals, progress and setback. This pattern of apparent failure to respond, and respond effectively, to adverse changes in its external security environment, stands in contradiction to our theoretical expectations. Yet such an assessment is premature for two reasons. One reason is that Brazil was a security free rider. The other reason is intimately bound up with the naval modernization program. Brazil initially adopted a countermeasuring strategy to respond to the rise of Argentine power. The naval program approved in late 1904 was a direct response to Argentina's buildup – a result of the intense Argentine–Chilean naval arms race during 1898–1902. In the wake of the Argentine–Chilean truce in 1902, Argentina's naval and land power now became Brazil's problem. It was unsurprising Brazil would fear Argentine naval power. It was too big for land conquest and the terrain difficult for offensive military operations, but an enemy with naval supremacy could effectively choke off the country's commerce and well-being. In late 1904, a plan was approved to purchase advanced warships from Britain, including ordering the construction of three modern dreadnoughts and three cruisers (two of the main battleships were delivered

---

[23] Ministério de Guerra, *Relatório, 1903*, 4.
[24] Ministério de Guerra, *Relatório, 1904*, 4, and *1917*, 5.
[25] Ministério de Guerra, *Relatório, 1914*, 4.

in 1910). Brazil's naval modernization, in response to Argentina's earlier buildup, triggered a new round of arms racing with Argentina that reached near-war crisis by 1908.

BRAZIL'S "YOUNG TURKS" AND THE GERMAN ARMY, 1906–1918

Aside from the naval buildup, the first real attempt at military modernization came in 1906–18 under the leadership of War Minister Marshall Hermes da Fonseca.[26] Fonseca, later president and the most respected military figure of the day, was a strong supporter of modernization and a Germanophile.[27] The 1906–18 reforms were explicitly modeled after the German army, especially in the area of armaments, officer formation, doctrine, and general staff organization. There were three significant components to the Fonseca reforms of 1906–18: an extensive armaments program, the 1908 obligatory military service, the sending of junior officers to Germany for training. Most of the important reform measures were adopted during the period 1906–10, and the rest during the wartime years.

Aside from Fonseca, another key proponent of modernization based on the German model was Baron Rio Branco.[28] The durable foreign minister was an admirer of the German military system. Prior to heading Itamaratí, the foreign ministry, Rio Branco served as Brazil's chief diplomatic representative in Europe and ambassador to Germany. Unlike his counterparts in Chile and Argentina, he was a big supporter of the Monroe Doctrine, and would engineer a close relationship with the United States as a key pillar of Brazil's grand strategy. Rio Branco, who may have viewed himself as a Latin Bismarck, saw a strong and well-equipped military as the keystone to an effective foreign policy. He often noted that "the diplomat and the soldier are partners, they are collaborators who mutually assist each other greatly."[29] He distrusted Spanish America, with nearly all of whom he had quarrels. He feared an Argentina sneak attack to capitalize on its vast military superiority. Brazil's military disrepair, he warned, would result in national disgrace. As changes in military organization began sweeping across the region, and power differentials quickened, he seized upon their significance for Brazil. As early as 1882, while serving in Britain, he protested that "we have no navy, we have no torpedoes, we do not have an army, and the Argentines have all of this. For the first time, we find ourselves at the mercy of our neighbors, at

---

[26] Hermes da Fonseca Filho, *Marechal Hermes: dados para uma biografia* (Rio de Janeiro: Instituto Brasileiro de Geografia e Estatistica, 1961). See also Roberto Piragibe da Fonseca, *A ressurreição do Exército nacional através da reforma de 1908: fatos e inferências* (Rio de Janeiro: Instituto Histórico e Geográfico Brasileiro, 1974).

[27] Fonseca Filho, *Marechal Hermes*. See also Fonseca, *A ressurreição*.

[28] Fonseca, *A ressurreição*, 83–88.

[29] Rio Branco, *Obras do Barão*, vol. 1, 104.

a time when the means of war cannot be improvised in months or weeks."[30] Brazil's great difficulty dispatching a small force to Acre territory during the war with Bolivia in 1904 may have been the breaking point for Rio Branco. Whereas the success of the 1906 reforms was uneven, the proposal to send Brazilian officers to Germany was an unambiguous success. Rio Branco obtained German agreement for Brazilian officers to receive training and advanced instruction in the Imperial army.[31] Three contingents of officers were sent to Germany in 1906, 1908, and 1910, the most notable of the three. Among the 1910 mission's twenty-one members were the two leading members of the German-trained junior officers who collectively became known as the *jovem turcos*, Young Turks (a deliberate appellation after their Ottoman namesake). Among the prominent members of the Young Turks were: Estevão Leitão de Carvalho, who served with the fourth infantry regiment of Turingin, and Bertoldo Klinger, who served with the 24th Holstein field artillery regiment, during their years in Germany.[32] Carvalho, Klinger, Souza Reis, Pargas Rodrígues, and Furtado do Nascimento were the core organizers, intellectual leaders, and political strategists.

The Young Turks came to comprise a much larger group of junior officers (nearly all of whom were captains and lieutenants) than just those who served in Germany.[33] The label also came to apply to other junior officers closely allied with the original contingents, and who actively adhered to their emulation reform program and Germanophilia. Prominent among the associated Young Turks were Pedro Aurélio de Góes Monteiro, Francisco de Paula Cidade, and José dos Mares Maciel da Costa.[34] Although they came to

---

[30] Baron Rio Branco, personal correspondence, 5 September 1882, in Viana Filho, *A Vida do Barão*, 106.

[31] José Murilo de Carvalho, "As forças armadas na Primeira República: o poder desestabilizador," in Boris Fausto, ed., *História Geral da Civilização Brasileira*, vol. 3, tome 2, O *Brasil Republicano , 1889–1930* (Rio de Janeiro: Difel, 1977): 183–234, 198.

[32] Bertoldo Klinger, *Narrativas aotobiográficas*, 2 vols. (Rio de Janeiro: O Cruzeiro, 1944). Klinger reports twenty-one Brazilian officers in the 1910 group sent to Germany. The war department reports nine officers sent in 1908. Other prominent, original members of the group included Joaquím de Souza Reis Neto, Cesar Augusto Parga Rodrígues, Eduardo Calvacante de Albuquerque Sá, Euclides de Oliveira Figueiredo, Furtado do Nascimento, Mario Clementino, Epaminodas de Lima e Silva, Manuel de Castro e Silva, and Evaristo Marques da Silva.

[33] On the ideas and role of the *jovem turcos*, aside from the Klinger and Carvalho memoirs, see Frank D. McCann, "The Formative Period of Twentieth Century Brazilian Military Thought, 1900–1922," *Hispanic American Historical Review* 64, no. 4 (November 1984): 737–65. The exact number of Brazilian officers who trained in Germany is unclear. McCann, "A influência estrangeira," 215, puts the number at thirty-four.

[34] Góes Monteiro became the most controversial of the associated members. His association with the Young Turks and subsequent joining with the *tenentes* in the military-civilian rebellion of 1930 lent credence to the argument that the Young Turks were political. Góes was, above all, an opportunist. Opportunism notwithstanding, he was a diehard Germanophile

have innumerable sympathizers throughout the corps, and were the army's best trained soldiers, the *jovem turcos* comprised a relatively small group of officers. Most of them were based in the capital city, Rio de Janeiro, where nearly half of the officer corps and military detachments were also located. This gave them a huge audience to disseminate knowledge of the German system and to garner support in the senior ranks.[35]

Whilst still in Germany the *jovem turcos* began to organize as a group to plan the army's transformation once they returned to Brazil.[36] They returned to Brazil to find no infrastructure or plan in place to make use of them, to disseminate and capitalize on their experience and knowledge. Klinger and Carvalho bemoaned how they were received and reassigned.[37] Some of their fellow German-trained officers were randomly dispersed in the military bureaucracy. Most were scattered in regimental duty in and around the capital, where they began to implement reforms on their own, such as regular field training, formal instruction (including basic literacy classes and courses for sergeants), marches, weapons handling, and regular physical exercises.[38]

Emulation of the German model would be aborted soon after it started, cut short by the great war in Europe. Yet the Young Turks were able to achieve partial success emulating German practice. Despite their small numbers, their partial success stemmed from three factors. They were organized, they were able to garner powerful backing in the hierarchy, and as a result, they were able to colonize key parts of the military bureaucracy. Fonseca and Marshall José Caetano de Faria, chief of general staff (1910–14) and later war minister (1914–18), were the most important senior-level supporters of the Young Turks.[39] With Faria's backing, many of the *jovem turcos* began to populate the war ministry, general staff, and the principal military academy, the Escola Militar at Realengo in Rio de Janeiro. Faria relied on their knowledge and expertise. With his support, the Young Turks, like Góes Monteiro

---

and convert to the reform of the Young Turks. See Lourival Coutinho, *O General Góes Depõe* (Rio de Janeiro: Ed. Coelho Branco, 1956).

[35] See Estevão Leitão de Carvalho, *Memórias de um soldado legalista*, 3 vols. (Rio de Janeiro: Imprensa do Exército, 1961): vol. 1, 176–79, on this point.

[36] Leitão de Carvalho, *Memórias*, vol. 1, 115, 154.

[37] Klinger, *Narrativas*; Leitão de Carvalho, *Memórias*. See also Leitão de Carvalho, Estevão Leitão de Carvalho, *Dever militar e política partidária*, 2 vols. (São Paulo: Editôra Nacional, 1959): vol. 1, 34–37.

[38] Leitão de Carvalho, *Memórias*, vol. 1.

[39] On Faria and the Young Turks see: Ministério do Exército, *Coleção Marechal José Caetano Faria*, Arquivo Histórico do Exército (AHEX); Estevão Leitão de Carvalho, *Centenário de nacimento do Marechal José Caetano Faria* (Rio de Janeiro: Instituto de Geografia e História Militar do Brasíl, 1955). See also Cláudio Moreira Bento, "Marechal José Caetano de Faria: projecção de sua obra como chefe do Estado Maior do Exército e Ministro da Guerra na reforma militar," undated manuscript, in Faria Collection, Arquivo Histórico do Exército, Brazil; Leitão de Carvalho, *Memórias*, vol. 1, 176, 183–87.

and Klinger, began to populate the general staff, whose authority and influence over military affairs grew steadily after 1914. Moreover, Young Turks were frequently used by the general staff in unofficial capacity or as outside aides and consultants commissioned for special studies and projects.[40] The chiefs of the general staff from 1914 to the late 1920s were all supporters or sympathizers of the Young Turks and their reform project, among them Faria, Bento Ribeiro, Setembrinho de Carvalho, and Tasso Fragoso. Coelho describes the general staff in the late 1920s and 1930s as "controlled" by the *jovem turcos*, though this may be an exaggeration.[41] General Justino Alves Bastos, an opponent of the Young Turks and son of an interim chief of staff at the time, noted that by the early 1920s the "Young Turks had established their headquarters [in the general staff]," and opposed the work of the French mission.[42] In addition, Young Turks were in the decision-making military cabinet of Faria's war ministry, where they played a key role designing major reorganization measures during the war.[43] Prominent among them was Souza Reis (who later played an instrumental role in contracting the French). They served as a kind of "kitchen cabinet" for the minister. Though more complete biographic information is needed, it appears that during his tenure in the war ministry Faria assembled around him a "brain trust," a loose grouping of officers from the war ministry and general staff responsible for reform planning and study. The Young Turks were key participants in this group.[44]

The biggest impact of the Young Turks was intellectual. They took it upon themselves to found a modern Brazilian army beginning with its intellectual regeneration. Few in numbers, the key was to find an effective channel to disseminate their knowledge and promote their reform agenda.[45] In 1913 they founded the semiofficial military journal, *A Defeza Nacional* (*The National Defense*), which quickly became the most widely read publication in the military. The journal was to be the principal "organ in the [army's] renovation campaign."[46] Carvalho, Klinger, Francisco de Paula Cidade,

---

[40] Leitão de Carvalho, *Memórias*, vol. 1.

[41] Coelho, *Em busca de identidade*, 82.

[42] General Justino Alves Bastos, *Encontro com o tempo* (Porto Alegre: Editôra Globo, 1965), 24.

[43] Jehovah Motta, *Formação do oficial do Exército: currículos e regimes na Academia Militar, 1810–1944* (Rio de Janeiro: Editôra Compania Brasileira de Artes Grandes, 1976); Leitão de Carvalho, *Memórias*, vol. 1.

[44] See documents in Ministério do Exército, *Coleção Marechal José Caetano Faria*, Arquivo Histórico do Exército (AHEX). See also Leitão de Carvalho, *Dever militar*, 47, and *Memórias*, vol. 1, 183–87. See also Ministério de Guerra, *Relatório, 1918*, 18–26.

[45] Soon after they returned home, Carvalho and others began to publish regular columns on military affairs in Rio de Janeiro's leading daily, *O Jornal do Cómercio*.

[46] Leitão de Carvalho, *Memórias*, 175. The analysis of the reform and doctrinal ideas of the Young Turks relies heavily on content analysis of *A Defeza Nacional* – deliberately misspelled with a "z" – conducted at the official military history archive, the Biblioteca do Exército, in

Pargas Rodrígues, Mario Clementino, and other young officers trained in Germany were founding members and editors.[47] Klinger, Carvalho, and Pargas Rodrígues served as the journal's first editors.

A Defeza Nacional – the same name used by the Ottoman Turk reformers for their journal – quickly became the leading forum for debate and discussion of technical and organizational matters.[48] *A Defeza Nacional* was not the first or only proreform journal, but it was by far the most outspoken. It was severe in its criticism of military readiness, and its combative approach resulted in censure from the high command on more than one occasion. Its principal founders, Bertoldo Klinger and Estevão Leitão de Carvalho, deliberately patterned it after the influential German military weekly, *Militarwochenblatt*.[49] *A Defeza Nacional* became one of the main platforms for the dissemination of knowledge about the German military system. The journal was not an official military publication; it was not funded, printed, or published by the high command.[50] It was, on the other hand, semiofficial to the extent that it received de facto blessing (more accurately, tolerance) from the hierarchy. In addition, contributors to its pages often included senior officers and commanders. Technical orientation, combative editorials, and Germanophilia were the journal's hallmarks. Naturally, the journal became the main vehicle outlining the Young Turks' reform program – religiously modeled on the German system.

The apex of the German model's appeal and influence in Brazilian military thinking was between 1900 and 1914.[51] Brazil began to adopt several aspects of the German military system as the result of the work of the Young Turks. The appeal of the German system, however, predated them as far back as the Paraguayan war in 1870.[52] As illustrated in the pages of the *Revista Militar* and the *Boletim Mensual do Estado Maior General do Exército*, Brazilian officers devoted extensive study to the German military system, both through direct observation as well as Portuguese translations of German military literature.[53] German-trained Estevão Leitão de Carvalho, for example, was

---

Rio de Janeiro. It should be noted that the archive's collection of the journal is incomplete and uneven by volume and number.

[47] The original "Grupo Mantenedor," or editorial board, included eight original turks: Carvalho, Klinger, Souza Reis, E. de Lima e Silva, Parga Rodrígues, Figueiredo, Amaro de Azambuja Vilanova, Francisco Jorge Pinheiro and four adherents: Paula Cidade, Brasílio Taborda, José Pompeu Calvacanti de Albuquerque, and Mário Clementino.

[48] On the role of the *A Defeza Nacional*, see Paula Cidade, *Síntese*; McCann, "The Formative Period."

[49] Leitão de Carvalho, *Memórias, 174.*

[50] Leitão de Carvalho, *Memórias*, vol. 1, 174–75.

[51] On intellectual influences and military literature, see Paula Cidade, *Síntese*.

[52] Motta, *Formação*, 184.

[53] See, for example, Major Dias de Oliveira, "O Exército alemão," *Revista Militar* 3, (1901); Tasso Fragoso, "Serviço do Estado Maior," *Revista Militar* 2, no. 1 (1900).

the author of a detailed, four-part study on the German infantry for the general staff in early 1913.[54] The German system was by far the most studied and cited of any other military in the world.[55] Between 1900 and 1906, for instance, a series of elaborate studies on the German military and the general staff system appeared in the *Revista Militar*.[56] A high ranking officer in the war ministry in 1920 summed up the German influence in the Brazilian military during 1900–14. He observe that "despite the influence of French books adopted by our professors in all the courses, Germany, as a result of its innovations, practical achievements, and its brilliant specialized books, was the country most admired and respected in our country during the time of our youth."[57] One general staff officer later recounted that "Germany, in the field of military [organization] and war, was in those days a nation highly esteemed and followed in our country."[58]

The Young Turks pushed for emulation of the German system. "Germany demonstrated to the world in the most brilliant manner," they argued, "the value of a nation being completely prepared and equipped for war and that the money invested in this yields excellent results in peacetime and incalculable results in war." The value of modernization, they stressed repeatedly, was not confined to just military power. The German model also "showed that complete preparation and [equipment] is not incompatible with the maximum development of the nation."[59] The Young Turks wanted to transplant onto Brazilian soil the main principles of the German military system. Yet they did not see military modernization in narrow technical or even strictly military terms. Their modernization project was far bigger, far more ambitious. Theirs was a nation-building project. Indeed, for good or ill, the reform program and ideas of the Young Turks, so passionately expressed in the pages of *A Defeza Nacional*, became the intellectual wellspring of the National Security and Development Doctrine embraced by the Brazilian and other Latin American militaries during their brutal rule of the 1950s to 1980s.[60] Their nation-in-arms philosophy saw the military as the motor of

---

[54] Ministério de Guerra, Estado Maior General do Exército, *Boletim Mensual do Estado Maior do Exército* 5, nos. 1–4 (January–April 1913).

[55] Number of articles on foreign systems in *Revista Militar, 1899–1908*: Germany (106); France (47); Argentina (40); United States (38); Japan (38); Britain (37); Chile (30); Portugal (19); Russo–Japanese War (16).

[56] See, for example the study on the German army by Major Dias de Oliveira, "O Exército alemão," *Revista Militar*, 3 (1901).

[57] Egydio Moreira de Castro e Silva, *À margen do Ministério Calógeras*, vol. 1 (Rio de Janeiro: Editôra Melso, S.A., 1960): 29.

[58] Castro e Silva, *À margen do Ministério Calógeras*, 38.

[59] *A Defeza Nacional* 3, no. 25 10 October 1915, 4.

[60] The classic study remains Alfred Stepan, "The New Professionalism of Internal Warfare and Military Role Expansion," in *Authoritarian Brazil: Origins, Policies and Future*, ed. Alfred Stepan (New Haven: Yale University Press, 1973): 47–68 and *The Military in Politics:*

national economic and social development, including citizenship formation. The Young Turks, never advocated an explicit political role for the military and, with one important exception, remained neutral and uninvolved in the many political upheavals of the Old Republic.

The Young Turks concentrated primarily on conscription, officer formation, and general staff organization. They were least successful in conscription and general staff reform. The biggest impact of the Young Turks, and the area of the most visible changes, was in the military's intellectual formation.

Armaments

The Fonseca–Young Turks reform measures of 1906–14 concentrated in five areas: military regulations, armaments, officer instruction, conscription, and general staff organization.[61] The bulk of these efforts were devoted to armaments, the area of deepest reform, and German emulation. Germany became the dominant, but not exclusive, supplier of armaments to Brazil up to 1914.[62] An extensive project was launched to reequip the army with modern (mainly German) armaments and equipment.[63] Up to this point, Brazil's army remained equipped with outdated armaments, mainly French.[64] But as early as 1870 there were calls to equip the army with Krupp field artillery and Dreyse needle rifles.[65] Brazil began to equip its land forces with German weapons in the early 1890s, albeit on a small scale. The 1881 *Relatório do Ministério de Guerra* notes that Brazil was purchasing Krupp artillery pieces at this time. An arms purchasing commission was established and sent to France and Germany in 1893. Yet Brazil opted for Krupp artillery exclusively.

During this period, when relations with Argentina deteriorated, Brazil undertook an extensive arms buildup. The arms purchasing commission, based in Europe, acquired enough armaments to equip an army of half a million men.[66] Brazil purchased several hundred thousand Mauser rifles, Luger pistols, and new Krupp cannons after Fonseca's 1908 visit to Berlin.[67]

Changing Patterns in Brazil (Princeton: Princeton University Press, 1971); Eliézer Rizzo de Oliveira, *As Forças Armadas: política e ideologia no Brasil, 1964–1969* (Petrópolis: Vozes, 1976).

[61] On the 1908 reforms, see Fonseca, *A ressurreição*.

[62] On Brazil's arms imports and supply dependence, see Stanley E. Hilton, "The Armed Forces and Industrialists in Modern Brazil: The Drive for Military Autonomy (1889–1954)," *Hispanic American Historical Review* 62, no. 4 (November 1982): 629–73.

[63] For an elaborate discussion on the armaments buildup and renovation at this time see, Fonseca, *A ressurreição*.

[64] Fonseca, *A ressurreição*.

[65] Ministério de Guerra, *Relatório, 1870*.

[66] Fonseca, *A ressurreição*, 79.

[67] Hilton, "The Armed Forces," 634.

Between 1911 and 1913, for example, it acquired an estimated 300,000 Mauser rifles.[68] It also turned to Germany (Krupp) for machinery and equipment in the manufacture of munitions, though production in its poorly run arsenals was negligible.[69] Privately contracted German technicians were present in some of the arsenals and factories.[70]

The naval modernization program, approved in late 1904 and begun in earnest in 1906, also became part of the armaments buildup. The warships were exclusively of British design and construction. During the Fonseca armaments buildup, the United States also became a major source of technology and expertise, especially in light infantry arms and munitions. Indeed, this period marked the beginning of Brazil's long relationship with the DuPont corporation of the United States. Brazil also turned to the United States for machinery and technical assistance.[71] It had been relying on the United States in the area of small arms, factory construction, and powder-chemical manufacturing as early as 1905. During the buildup, transport equipment was singled out, to permit "a rapid movement across the frontiers of the country."[72] Brazil's arms buildup remained static between 1914 and 1918 as a result of the war in Europe.[73] In 1917 an arms purchasing commission was sent to the United States.[74] It began to purchase its armaments, especially naval and coastal artillery weapons, from the United States. After the Great War, France became the predominant supplier for Brazil's army's equipment, while it turned to the United States to equip its naval forces. Interestingly and unexpectedly, Brazil would return to purchasing German arms again in the late 1930s, placing a contract with Krupp in 1937 for field artillery. A six-year contract was signed in 1938 for a total of 900 pieces, but the outbreak of war in Europe (and British blockade) prevented their delivery.[75]

Conscription

The Young Turks' centerpiece reform was universal obligatory military service. German influence, however, was negligible in this area, inasmuch as anything approaching a conscription system can be said to exist in Brazil up until the coming of the French mission in 1919. Despite the fact that

---

[68] General Alfredo Souto Malan, *Missão militar francesa de instrução junto ao Exército brasileiro* (Rio de Janeiro: Biblioteca do Exército, 1988), 36.

[69] Hilton, "The Armed Forces," 639.

[70] Castro e Silva, *À margem do Ministério Calógeras*, 32.

[71] McCann, "A influência estrangeira"; Hilton, "The Armed Forces."

[72] Ministério de Guerra, *Relatório, 1910*, 5.

[73] On this point, see Joseph S. Tulchin, *The Aftermath of War: World War I and U.S. Policy Toward Latin America* (New York: New York University Press, 1971).

[74] McCann, "A Influência estrangeira," 216.

[75] Hilton, "The Armed Forces," 649.

archrival Argentina had adopted universal military service, which gave it tremendous mobilizational capacity, Brazil in 1906 was still relying on the outdated old army of long-serving, mostly illiterate conscripts. The Young Turks and other reformers understood that obligatory service was key to organizing a mass army. It was the leading topic in almost every issue of *A Defeza Nacional* during its first several years. They believed a transformation had taken place in the nature of warfare and the relationship between the state, society, and military power. Brazil, they argued, lagged woefully behind these changes. They called for the creation of the mass conscript army as the primary method to bring about the country's material and social development, and not just modernize its military capabilities. "The nation is the army, and the army is the nation," declared Lieutenant Alves Tavora in one of the first editions of their journal.[76]

The Young Turks advocated mass conscription for two reasons. The first was military power and the second was nation-building. For them, obligatory military service was the primary vehicle for military and national renewal, the country's "salvation," as one editorial put it.[77] The mass conscript army was to be "the school for the nation," a place where patriotic, soldier-citizens were formed. "Secure nations," they argued, "are able to turn their energies to progress and credit, engendering their wealth and the development of sources of production."[78] Military power depended not so much on the country's armaments but on the quality of its people; on its overall ability to cultivate the nation's human and material resources in wartime.[79] Military power and development depended on many factors, but of primary importance was the "moral and intellectual capacity" of its people, their "social discipline," "education," "citizenship," their "subordination and respect for the institutional order."[80] Although their language often betrayed a preoccupation with social control, their doctrine remained true to the German idea that linked mass conscription, nationalism, and combat power.[81] In addition to obligatory military service, the Young Turks called for the establishment of obligatory national primary education, one with "a patriotic orientation."[82]

Given its political and social ramifications, obligatory service was a hotly contested political question everywhere on the continent. Brazil was no exception. Conscription had long been a vexing topic inside and outside the military. As exemplified by the 1910 elections, barely won by Hermes

---

[76] *A Defeza Nacional*, 10 December 1915.
[77] *A Defeza Nacional*, 10 January 1915.
[78] *A Defeza Nacional*, 10 January 1917.
[79] *A Defeza Nacional*, 10 January 1915.
[80] These themes appear in nearly every issue of *A Defeza Nacional*. See, for example, Captain Luiz G. Borges Fortes, "Preparo do homen para a patria," *A Defeza Nacional*, 10 October 1919.
[81] *A Defeza Nacional*, 10 January 1915.
[82] Ibid.

da Fonseca, obligatory military service became a divisive issue in the politics of the Old Republic. The state governments, who controlled the national guard, opposed it. A similar situation was replayed in the United States. The question of the national guard was itself a major obstacle, since creating a true reserve army would require converting the provincially controlled guard into a federal force. The needs of the enlistment system were great. It was described by one war minister as "a corrupt, vexatious, unequal, and insufficient system." The war minister proposed that Brazil should strive for the "rigorous features of the Prussian system."[83] By 1910, universal service and rapid modernization had given Argentina the ability to mobilize and field a trained fighting force of 250,000 within weeks.[84] The legal size of the Brazilian army in 1910 was a paltry 20,000, and without a trained reserve.

The first major push to change the status quo came in the form of the 1907 military service law, amended in 1908, which called for personal, obligatory service based on lottery and volunteers.[85] German influence appeared to be minimal. Reformers hoped to create a first line army that would have a trained and ready reserve at its disposal. Individuals called to duty were to serve two years, after which they were to pass to the reserves for seven years with annual training exercises. All lottery eligible recruits not incorporated into active duty were to pass directly to the reserves. The law allowed that the military would first try to fill the ranks with volunteers, leaving ample opportunity to avoid the full application of the law. The military was reorganized into regional corps groups, reminiscent of German decentralized distribution. As in Germany, recruitment and training were to take place at the regional level. However, the 1906/1908 reorganization adopted political criteria, not military efficiency, in its regional organization, creating twenty-one military regions corresponding to each state and the federal district. Thus, enlistment was to occur by state, giving regional power brokers and governors substantial power to influence the process. The obligatory military service law remained unimplemented.

In 1916 the Young Turks assisted Faria in amending and implementing the 1908 obligatory service law, based on a lottery draft and one-year length of service. The national guard was finally abolished in 1918, and reconstituted as the federally controlled second line reserve army. The Young Turks had hoped to emulate Germany's three-tier reserve system, the third of which would be a federally controlled territorial guard similar to the Landwehr. Under this system, conscription, training, and incorporation were to be regionally administered and regimentally based. Despite severe administrative and enforcement problems in the conscription system, some 50,000

---

[83] Ministério de Guerra, *Relatório*, 1871, 3.
[84] Lieutenant Colonel Augusto A. Maligne, *Historia militar de la República Argentina durante el siglo de 1810 a 1910* (Buenos Aires: La Nación, 1910): 180.
[85] Ministério de Guerra, *Relatório*, 1907.

draftees were called through the lottery in 1918, with only 16,000 incorporated in some capacity.[86] The results of the 1916–18 changes were minimal. Political opposition, rampant draft dodging, physical disqualifications, and budgetary constraints precluded the full realization of the system and incorporation of draftees, but so too did organizational weaknesses and constraints of the military. Faria and the *jovem turcos* recognized the army was far too small and disorganized to be able to incorporate effectively the large numbers of annual recruits obligatory service would generate.[87]

Military Regulations

The area of perhaps the most substantial, albeit short-lived, German emulation was the military's internal regulations and doctrine. The Young Turks wanted to introduce modern ideas and strategic concepts. As noted earlier, a good deal of emulation efforts during this time period did not follow any systematic plan or reorganization design. Initially many reforms modeled on the German system were carried out in isolation, in individual units to which Young Turks were assigned. Other German-modeled reforms were army wide. Beginning in 1908, for example, the army's engineering combat arm was reorganized according to that of Germany's, "whose military organization had served as the norm to realize, in the words of Lieutenant Colonel Alexandre Vieira Leal who was assigned to make a study of the German engineering arm.[88]

Largely through the efforts of the Young Turks, Brazil began to adopt German infantry and artillery combat regulations in 1910.[89] While in Germany, they translated German military regulations and combat manuals, which they forwarded to the war ministry and general staff back home. Soon after they returned, Carvalho and Klinger began systematically to translate other German regulations and manuals, focusing on small unit training exercises and physical education.[90] They also translated German regulations for large unit operations and deployment. During 1912–13 Klinger and Carvalho translated the German regulation and manual on gymnastics and infantry training, the *Regulamento de Ginástica para Infantaria e Tropas a Pé*. War Minister Faria ordered that it be adopted in the Brazilian army.

With the collaboration of other Young Turks, Klinger and Carvalho turned their efforts to what became the two principal internal regulations of

---

[86] Ministério de Guerra, *Relatório, 1918*, 60.

[87] Leitão de Carvalho, *Centenário*, 211.

[88] Ministério de Guerra, Estado Maior General do Exército, *Boletim Mensual do Estado Maior General do Exército* 7, no. 6 (June 1914): 382. Hereafter *Boletim*.

[89] Ministério de Guerra, Estado Maior General do Exército, *Boletim* 7, no. 3 (March 1914): 173.

[90] Klinger translated German regulations prior to his service in Germany; he published them in a semiofficial journal, *O Combate*. See Klinger, *Narrativas*, 154.

the military, the Regulations for Instruction and General Services (RISG) and the Regulations for Administrative Services (RSA), both patterned closely after German regulations. Klinger and Paula Cidade collaborated on another critical military regulation, the *Manual for the Command of Troops*, which they modeled on Germany's *Handbuch für den Trunpenführer.*[91]

Officer Formation

One of the biggest deficiencies in the Brazilian military was the intellectual and technical formation of its officer corps. Mallet had described the officer corps in 1900 as being in a state of ignorance.[92] The recruitment and instruction of the officer corps remained haphazard and unsystematic well into the 1920s, despite the heroic but unsystematic efforts of the Young Turks. Officer instruction and technical training between 1870 and 1918 were poor in quality, irregular, and lacked uniformity.[93] In fact, it was only after 1910 that minimum educational qualifications were enforced in the recruitment and advancement of officers. Promotions had always been based on favoritism and political connections. Up until the Young Turks' reforms, military instruction in Brazil was encyclopedic, with the curriculum at the military schools based primarily on the natural sciences and mathematics.[94] "What is worse," complained one officer in 1890, "is that these military schools are before all else civilian schools because the military content is secondary and almost of no value."[95]

The *joven turcos*, along with reformist but more nationalist officers at home, formed the so-called Missão Indígena (Indigenous Mission) which operated out of the Escola Militar, the main academy for officer instruction and general staff service. They revamped the curriculum and introduced more technical and practical instruction. The Missão Indígena, with their institutional base at the school and with powerful backers in the war ministry and general staff, lasted as an important reform constituency between 1916 and 1924. By 1919 the Escola Militar resembled a true military school in its curriculum and internal regulation, particularly its rigid disciplinary code. Motta notes that it had a "touch of Prussianism."[96]

New reforms in military instruction were introduced in 1913, and modified in 1918. The objectives were to eliminate traces of theoretic instruction, reduce the number of schools to the Escola Militar and the Escola Práctica (School of Applications), and introduce more stringent qualifications for

[91] Paula Cidade, *Síntese*, 278.
[92] Ministério de Guerra, *Relatório, 1900*, 27.
[93] Motta, *Formação do oficial.*
[94] Magalhães, *A evolução militar do Brasíl*, 328.
[95] Quote cited in Motta, *Formação do oficial*, 220.
[96] Motta, *Formação do oficial*, 313.

the teaching staffs.[97] The curriculum at the Escola Militar was reduced to two years, with an additional year for cavalry and infantry officers and two years for artillery and engineering officers. In 1913 the curriculum was revamped at the Escola do Estado Maior do Exército (Army General Staff School, ECEME) which was located at Praia Vermelha in Rio and reopened in 1905. It started functioning in 1907. The course of study was reduced to two years, and an attempt made to inject more practical, technical studies into the curriculum. Instructional texts, field manuals, training, and campaign regulations were translations from the German. The military school remained under the Indigenous Mission after 1919 despite the fact that the French military mission had been given authority to revamp the entire military education system. The military school, paradoxically, would become a hotbed of radical activism and rebellion that burst on the scene in 1922. Though no Young Turks participated in the 1922 revolt at the school, their students did.

An important component of officer formation begun under the 1906 reforms was the initiative to send Brazilian officers to Germany for training. There were three main contingents between 1908 and 1914. At least thirty Brazilians officers benefited from advanced instruction in Germany. The war department stated in its 1912 annual report that the practice of sending officers abroad was producing good results. It noted that many more officers ought to be sent, but that budgetary constraints limited the program.

General Staff Organization

Military modernization in Brazil was frustratingly slow and haphazard. The Young Turks' success in Germanizing the Brazilian army was spotty. The dream of a powerful directing brain of the army, modeled after Germany's, would never be realized. Brazil lacked a true general staff service in the period preceding the French mission. The Young Turks were not alone in advocating a powerful general staff, based on the German model. Fragoso, later chief of staff, wrote admiringly of the German staff model, which offered "in peacetime and wartime a novel way to command great masses of combatants."[98] Yet the Young Turks did succeed in establishing the main components of such an organ.

A general staff service was finally created in 1896, but it existed only on paper. It remained an administrative, powerless body, its functions poorly specified, and with little jurisdiction over matters that normally fell under the purview of its counterparts elsewhere. In 1902 the general staff had two main sections. The first prepared regulations and published the *Revista Militar*. The second department was responsible for the study of theaters

---

[97] Motta, *Formação do oficial*, 297, 304.
[98] Tasso Fragoso, "Serviço do Estado Maior," *Revista Militar*, 2, no. 1 (1900): 381–82.

of operation, mobilization plans, topography, and foreign military systems. There was yet no uniform, institutionalized system of officer formation for general staff service. Fonseca and the Young Turks set out to create a modern general staff system. "The general staff," he complained, "has bureaucratic features, which is not consistent with its elevated role in peacetime as well as wartime."[99] Fonseca noted that when it was first created the general staff was intended to perform the same functions as "the general staffs of the European powers."[100] He said "the open [staff] system of Germany is the ideal to attain."[101] The general staff was reorganized in 1906 and again in 1908, and based on a transitional formula that combined elements of both the open and closed staff systems. Most of its administrative functions were eliminated. It was put in charge of studying organization and command questions and developing a unified doctrine for the armed forces. Fonseca hoped the "Brazilian general staff will be like the German, like the Japanese, the true brain of the army, the organizer of victory."

His optimism was premature. The general staff remained in the backwaters of the organization, its functions and jurisdiction poorly delineated. It was subordinate to the war ministry and military command. Some of its formal functions and jurisdiction were familiar to its German counterparts – military instruction, mobilization plans, foreign military intelligence, geography. On the other hand, its role in war planning was limited to helping choose plans. Despite ambiguities in some areas of its function, the new regulations made it explicit that the general staff was not to interfere in command functions. The 1906 and 1908 reforms also created a new department of war, with more direct command participation and functions that overlapped or infringed on those of the general staff.

Nonetheless, in part due to its colonization by the Young Turks, the general staff became more vocal and active, especially in terms of disseminating information and providing outlets for debate and intellectual renewal. It acquired a more expanded role in promotions and its control over military instruction put it in position to shape the army's intellectual and doctrinal formation. As war in Europe approached, reports warned that mobilization was crucial to victory, as demonstrated by the armies of Germany and Japan, and that Brazil might end up like France in 1870.[102] The general staff was unsparing in its assessment. "Here in Brazil nothing can be done in this regard to advance [a mobilization plan]. First, because we still do not have obligatory military service. Second, because, even if we had such a service, we are lacking in the indispensable means of communications and the rapid

---

[99] Ministério de Guerra, *Relatório, 1906*, 7.
[100] Ministério de Guerra, *Relatório, 1907*, 26.
[101] Ministério de Guerra, *Relatório, 1907*, 27.
[102] Ministério de Guerra, Estado Maior General do Exército, *Boletim* 7, no. 3 (March 1914): 190.

means of transportation," it argued. It cited a cultural explanation for the country's military ills, arguing that "we do not want to enter into a reckoning with the frankly antimilitaristic tendency of the Brazilian."[103]

In 1912 the general staff underwent another amendment. The new reorganization plan decreed that the general staff was "an essential organ of the high command," and named as its mission the preparation of the army for war and the study of national defense.[104] Its functions were listed as organizing troop formation and distribution for deployment, military education, preparing the general outlines of a mobilization plan, transportation, and studying probable theaters of operations. The new regulation assigned the general staff a coordinating role in all operations and services during wartime to assist the command. More important, the general staff was formally divided between the main staff and field staffs assigned to each of the military divisions and inspectorates. Consistent with German practice, Brazil adopted an open staff system, requiring some regimental duty of all staff officers as well as allowing for alteration between the main and the field staffs. The main staff was subdivided into four sections. On paper, the new regulation appeared to give the chief of staff wide powers over military affairs, giving the chief complete authority over all functions that fell under the general staff. It also gave the chief responsibility (in conjunction with the high command) over the professional preparation of troops, the means of defense, mobilization, armaments, and war planning.

A major reorganization was initiated in 1915, the most important measure being the restructuring of the general staff. War Minister Faria built on the proposals of the Young Turks for an autonomous, powerful organ for military planning. Just as the Young Turks had been recommending, the general staff began to assume more and more control over matters relating to preparation, mobilization, defense planning, and military instruction. It was also becoming the principal locus of institutionalized study in the military. Under the 1915 reorganization, the general staff formally became part of the high command, though the proper delineation of authority and jurisdiction remained vague.[105] On paper it seemed to approximate the German ideal. It was nominally second in the chain of command under the war ministry, followed by the inspector general of the army and the command of the large units and military districts.[106] The minister of war was to exercise command over all other organs and officials. But confusion still prevailed. The general staff was to be purely auxiliary, its proposals and measures were

---

[103] Ministério de Guerra, Estado Maior General do Exército, *Boletim* 7, no. 3 (March 1914): 192–93.

[104] See decree No. 9.338, 17 January 1912, in *Boletim Mensual do Estado Maior do Exército* 2, no. 6 (March 1912).

[105] Ministério de Guerra, *Boletim do Exército*, no. 410 (6 March 1915).

[106] Ibid.

to be submitted to the war minister for approval. "The chief of the general staff is not to partake in the authority of high command from the point of view of the effective command of the forces."[107] The same paragraph adds that the general staff may "act independently of orders and instructions" in carrying out its projects. Even further from the German ideal was that the general staff lacked both technical expertise and intellectual formation.

A GERMAN MILITARY MISSION?

From the start Brazil showed considerable reluctance – and nationalist opposition – to a foreign military mission. Instead, Brazil's preference was to create a cadre of European-trained officers who would lead the modernization effort. There were, nonetheless, attempts to hire a German mission. Under Fonseca, as war minister and later president, attempts made to hire a German mission were unsuccessful. Fonseca was invited by the German emperor in 1908 to visit Germany to observe the annual military maneuvers of the Imperial army. His first-hand observation of German maneuvers convinced him of the need for modernization, and one directed by German officers.[108] It is not clear whether an official request was made in 1908 to contract a mission. According to Bertholdo Klinger, Fonseca promised to hire a mission if he won the upcoming presidential elections.[109] Official talks were initiated in 1910 and a group of German officers were designated for the mission.[110] The German mission was reportedly to be headed by General Colmar von der Goltz, the famed reformer of the Turkish army.[111] But the mission never materialized, mainly because congressional and intramilitary opposition was severe. Presumably, part of the difficulty in hiring a German mission had to do with Imperial Germany's concerns about upsetting relations with Brazil's rival, Argentina.

Opposition to modernization had been stiff, confined largely to the old guard within the military and their civilian backers. By 1906 reformers were ascendant, but they themselves were split. On the one hand, the Young Turks and their allies were unabashedly proemulation and vocal in their calls for a German training mission. The other group of reformers, the nationalist faction, opposed foreign missions. The nationalists did not, in principle, oppose selective emulation. They favored the sending of Brazilian officers abroad for training, with the objective of having a foreign-trained cadre. A major figure

[107] Ministério de Guerra, *Boletim do Exército*, no. 410 (6 March 1915): 297.
[108] Frederick M. Nunn, *Yesterday's Soldiers: European Military Professionalism in South America, 1890–1940* (Lincoln: University of Nebraska Press, 1983): 132.
[109] Klinger, *Narrativas*, vol. 1, 165.
[110] Malan, *Missão militar*, 56.
[111] Fonseca Filho, *Marechal Hermes*, 122.

among the nationalists was Faria.[112] During the 1908 and 1910 attempts to hire a German mission, Faria headed the general staff and contributed to the successful torpedoing of the idea. From 1914 to 1918 he served as war minister, and used his institutional position to block efforts to hire a foreign mission. Faria was one of the biggest supporters of modernization and an important defender and protector of reformist junior officers like the Young Turks. Yet he preferred indigenous solutions. In 1918, in the midst of debates about contracting a French military mission, he argued that "I am opposed to [a French mission]. I [also] contributed to the failure of [the] contract [of a German mission]. The army can only be national in its doctrines, its theories, in its spirit as well as tactics. Moreover, I know our officers are very jealous of their rights and I don't believe that they will subject themselves to the command of foreign officers."[113]

EMULATING THE FRENCH MILITARY SYSTEM, 1919–1930

The reforms of 1906–16 were of limited success and spotty in emulation. The defects of the Brazilian military were great. The army was severely tested in its campaign to put down ragtag paramilitary forces in the southern provinces during the Contestado rebellion. The country could barely muster a token show of force after it declared war on Germany in late 1917. Despite the limited reforms of 1906–16, the military was still being described as "an ancient military machine" by its own leaders.[114] Commander of the federal forces during the Contestado, Brigadier General Fernando Setembrinho de Carvalho, noted that the army found itself in a "situation which originated in the distant past and which unfortunately still persists to this day."[115] The war ministry pronounced in 1919 that "nobody can ignore the fact that Brazil is almost entirely defenseless."[116]

The war in Europe, and Germany's eventual subjugation, undercut the limited modernization under way by depriving Brazil of its principal supplier of armaments and undermining the legitimacy of the army's leading reformers. The threat posed by German submarines to Brazilian shipping sealed the fate of the German model. In late 1917, Brazil declared war on Germany, definitively closing the chapter on its brief experiment with German practice. During the years between the start of the Fonseca reforms and

---

[112] On Faria and his views toward reforms and foreign missions, see Carvalho, *Centenário*.

[113] Quote cited in Malan, *Missão militar*, annex 2, 218.

[114] Ministério de Guerra, *Relatório, 1918*, 5. The 1918 *Relatório* is one of the most detailed and extensive of all the annual reports. It discusses at length the French training mission and elaborates the reform program.

[115] Brigadier General Fernando Setembrinho de Carvalho, summary of report, in *A Defeza Nacional* 4, no. 47 (10 August 1917): 357.

[116] Ministério de Guerra, *Relatório, 1919*, 43.

the declaration of war, Brazil's security situation went from bad to worse. The war years were years of panic, as discussed in the next section. Fear of invasion, from Germany and from Argentina, gripped the country. It comes as no surprise that Brazil would persist in its efforts to modernize the armed forces.

A new chapter started. Brazil turned immediately to the French system as the war ended. Renewed calls emerged among senior officers to contract a foreign military mission to direct a complete overhaul of Brazilian military capabilities. By 1918 no one believed Brazil could reorganize its forces at such a late hour without the help of a foreign mission.[117] Even Faria was publicly committed to a foreign mission, arguing at one point that a mission in Brazil would be better than sending officers to France for training.[118] In favoring a French training mission, Faria stressed the value of proven effectiveness, arguing "it is best to look outside for masters who are already formed by a long and cruel campaign [WWI]: elite officers, who are in a position to greatly facilitate our tasks, making our transition rapid, and in short order giving rise to a new generation of officers, who are practical and disposed to carrying out their mission."[119] Other prominent officers and civilians who favored a foreign mission were Major Alfredo Malan d'Angrogne, Brazil's military attaché in Paris, and João Pandia Calógeras, future war minister and civilian member of Brazil's delegation to the Versailles Peace Conference. Malan unambiguously favored a French mission. He cited the fact that the United States itself had been contracting individual French officers to train its army. In a letter to Faria, Malan argued forcefully that, "more so than in the case of the United States, I believe we need a mission: not a small one, but a large one." The objective of hiring the mission, he continued, "should be to create anew. I believe we need a mission not just for the schools, but also for the entire military – for the general staff, for military administration. And this [we need] more today than yesterday. Tomorrow may be too late. I think that [our] forces should be reorganized as if we had to repel an immediate attack."[120]

The new war minister, Calógeras, argued that "a great [military] mission will save the army, as it will save the navy and, along with them, Brazil."[121] Calógeras summarized his scorching indictment thus: "The grave crisis of the armed forces is evident in the most irresponsible way, a crisis of command and the labor of the young [officers] to overcome the intellectual and

[117] Carvalho, *Memórias*, vol. 2, 22.
[118] See correspondence between Faria and Malan in *Coleção Faria*.
[119] Ministério de Guerra, *Relatório, 1918*, 25.
[120] Correspondence from Major Malan to War Minister Faria, 1 November 1917, in *Coleção Faria*.
[121] João Pandia Calógeras, *Problemas de adminístração*, 2nd ed. (São Paulo: Compania Editôra Nacional, 1938; originally published 1918): 36.

professional ankylosis that emanate from the incompetence of the high command." Calógeras insisted that the "only solution is to contract a great
mission which can only be French, not so much because of our affinity of
racial temperament, but also because of the experience drawn from the excellent results achieved in São Paulo with the collaboration of officers from the
[French] army and the state militia."[122]

In his well-documented study of the French mission in Brazil, General
Pedro Malan, son of Alfredo Malan, credits his father as the first to call for a
French military mission in an October 1917 cable to the war ministry.[123] The
first concrete proposal from inside the military to contract a foreign mission
came in 1918, when the war ministry issued an extensive study on the state
of the military.[124] The report was wide-ranging in its critique and recommendations. It recommended the creation of a permanent body that could
organize and carry out extensive study, reform measures, and overlook their
implementation. It proposed the creation of a council of national defense,
to be composed of the president, the military chiefs of all the services, and
the heads of the major civilian departments. The council, an idea Brazil borrowed from the French, was to be responsible for all matters military. (The
1918 war department annual report noted the council was first proposed by
the general staff in 1916.) Finally, the report concluded by recommending the
contracting of a foreign, namely French, military mission. Brazil lacked the
technical skills and expertise to carry out modernization, argued the report,
"hence the idea of contracting a French mission, composed of officers of
valor, to help us in this *large scale* task of reforms."[125]

The French initially rebuffed Brazil's first overture for a training mission.[126] Discussions took place during the Versailles conference.[127] Calógeras,
who became war minister in 1920 and a key backer of reforms, was one of the
participants in these discussions.[128] He participated in negotiating the contract in Paris as well as choosing the head of the eventual mission, General
Maurice Gamelin, a veteran divisional commander and general staff officer. The obscure Gamelin was the recommendation of War Minister Joseph
Joffre, though the Brazilians at first were considering the names of Man-
gin, Guillaumant, Sauret, Nerel, and Foch.[129] Gamelin would later have the
ignoble distinction, as chief of the French general staff (1931–40), of heading
the army that collapsed in the face of German blitzkrieg.

---

[122] Calógeras, *Problemas de administração*, 115.

[123] Malan, *A Missão militar*, 49.

[124] Ministério de Guerra, *Relatório, 1918.*

[125] Ministério de Guerra, *Relatório, 1918*, 25.

[126] Report no. 1119 from French attaché to war ministry in Paris, 26 September 1917, cited in
Malan, *Missão militar*, 44–45.

[127] Castro e Silva, *À margem do Ministério Calógeras*, 39–40, 52–53.

[128] Castro e Silva, *À margem do Ministério Calógeras.*

[129] Malan, *Missão militar*, 59–63.

The French military mission to Brazil was formally contracted in September 1919.[130] In August of the same year Brazil also contracted from France an aviation mission. In order to preempt the Argentines, Brazil attached certain stipulations. The Brazilian minister in Paris, Raul Regis de Oliveira, cabled Rio de Janeiro that the delegation wanted a stipulation in the contract that "the French government promises not to send a military instruction mission to any other country in South America without our prior approval."[131] Gamelin made a preliminary visit to Brazil in early 1919. The full mission arrived in Brazil in March 1920, consisting of twenty-three middle and senior ranking officers plus a few aides. The various individual missions to Brazil were generally composed of higher ranking officers, in contrast to Chile and Argentina. The French military mission remained in Brazil from 1920 to 1940, and each two-year mission averaged about thirty, usually higher ranking, officers and aides.[132] (In 1922 Brazil contracted a U.S. naval mission and launched a major naval arms buildup in 1924. U.S. naval officers had been in Brazil since 1917 training Brazilian officers; in 1932 a small U.S. army mission was hired to organize the coastal artillery. The U.S. naval mission remained until 1978.)[133]

The decision to contract a French mission did not generate much controversy within the army, nor did it spark resistance from Germanophiles. The Young Turks had declared in early summer of 1914 that a "Military Mission to Brazil has to be German."[134] But Germany's attack on Brazilian shipping, the ambiguous status of the German émigré population and, of course, Germany's defeat, undercut the position and prestige of the Young Turks.[135] Klinger and Carvalho note in their memoirs that they supported the French mission and wanted to assist its efforts in whatever

---

[130] On these points, see Malan, *Missão militar*, 65–95. Months prior to the federal government's contract with the French mission, the state of São Paulo, the same year, renewed its contract with its French military mission. It should be noted that Brazil also contracted individual Austrian specialists in 1920 to provide technical knows how to the military's geographical services. During the 1920 and 1930s Brazil hired a number of professionals on individual contracts from various nationalities.

[131] Malan, *Missão militar*, 87, 88.

[132] Frederick M. Nunn, *The Military in Chilean History: Essays in Civil-Military Relations, 1810–1973* (Albuquerque: University of New Mexico Press, 1976): 7.

[133] On the United States as a model for Brazil's naval and aviation forces, see McCann, "A influência estrangeira"; Joseph Smith, *Unequal Giants: Diplomatic Relations Between the United States and Brazil, 1889–1930* (Pittsburgh: University of Pittsburgh Press, 1991). On the overall influence of the United States on Brazil's military system, see Frank D. McCann, Jr., *The Brazilian–American Alliance, 1937–1945* (Princeton: Princeton University Press, 1973); David Healy, "Admiral William B. Caperton and United States Naval Diplomacy in South America, 1917–1919," *Journal of Latin American Studies* 8, no. 2 (November 1976): 297–323. Brazil also contracted U.S. advisers to organize coastal artillery, military arsenals and munitions factories.

[134] *A Defeza Nacional*, 5 May 1914.

[135] General Justino Alves Bastos, *Encontro com o tempo* (Porto Alegre: Editôra Globo, 1965).

capacity.[136] Magalhães notes that the Germanophiles did not hesitate to lend their support to the French mission.[137] The headline of *A Defeza Nacional* declared "Foreign military mission, welcome!" on the eve of the French arrival, though the journal would keep a critical eye on the work of the French.[138] In general, the French mission would encounter numerous obstacles and opposition to its work from a variety of sources.[139] Right before assuming office as war minister, Calógeras noted that in "the generalty and in the superior posts [the French mission] encounters its most fierce opponents."[140]

Notwithstanding opposition inside the military, the French also had their defenders, especially War Minister Calógeras. He was one of the first civilians to occupy the post, and came into office with a wide-ranging reform program focusing on conscription, technical organs, war materiel and armaments, and military instruction.[141] He was regarded as an expert in military affairs. Before coming to office he had written an important study on government administration that provided a detailed (and somber) analysis of the organizational and materiel situation of the military.[142] An area of urgent concern was armaments and equipment. Calógeras warned that Brazil had been losing valuable time "in the face of Argentina, much more prudent and provident than us and disposing reserves of almost half a million men." Brazil therefore had "to follow the example of Prussia after the disaster at Jena," and quickly modernize its military system.[143]

The French quickly began their work. Their first act was to conduct a survey of the military defense situation in the southern states of Brazil. Gamelin presented the general staff and the government with an elaborate report that discussed existing military problems, outlining what the future military system should look like.[144] He proposed a ground force of three army groups, consisting of eight infantry divisions, three cavalry divisions, and three mixed formations, all with their accompanying reserves and armaments, as well as a heavy artillery detachment.[145] A war ministry staff officer recounted that Gamelin's report "was a sweeping summary of the [military] situation of our country in the face of that of neighboring countries; it established, in

---

[136] Klinger, *Narrativas*; Leitão de Carvalho, *Memórias*.

[137] Magalhães, *A evolução militar do Brasíl*, 349.

[138] *A Defeza Nacional* 6, no. 67 (10 April 1919).

[139] McCann, "A influência estrangeira"; Magalhaes, *A evolução militar do Brasíl*, 350–53; Leitão de Carvalho, *Memórias*, vol. 2; Nunn, *Yesterday's Soldiers*, 192–97.

[140] Calógeras, *Problemas de administração*, 35.

[141] Castro e Silva, *À margen do Ministério Calógeras*, 80. See also Ministério de Guerra, *Relatório*, 1920, 1921, and 1922.

[142] Calógeras, *Problemas de administração*.

[143] Calógeras, *Problemas de administração*, 89.

[144] Castro e Silva, *À margen do Ministério Calógeras*, 70–71.

[145] Castro e Silva, *À margen do Ministério Calógeras*, 71.

general terms, how our ground forces should be organized. General Gamelin discussed all that which we needed, having in view a [successful] encounter in the first battles of an international war."[146]

The activities of the French military mission were extensive, spanning across organization, armaments, and doctrine – though initially its functions were limited to military instruction and its authority defined as strictly "advisory." French influence was largely confined to the army, though the army's aviation service also came under French influence initially. The original 1918 war ministry report outlined the various areas in which the French mission would be active, concentrating mainly on all levels of officer formation and general staff organization.[147]

ARMAMENTS AND REGULATIONS

In relatively short time Brazil had acquired advanced weapons from Germany to outfit its army during the 1906–14 reform period. Yet the Brazilian army in 1920 was still outfitted with obsolete equipment. Calógeras's assessment was that "the most important and urgent [are] expenditures for military arms and equipment."[148] During the last few years of the war in Europe the United States provided Brazil with armaments, partly as a way to entice it to declare war on Germany. With the hiring of the French mission, France became Brazil's supplier – though not entirely by choice. The French government initially made approval for a military mission conditional on Brazil agreeing to purchase French armaments exclusively.[149] This was one of the several conditions that stalled negotiations on various occasions.[150] Another was the French demand that only French military advisers be used to direct or provide technical assistance in areas such as military arsenals and factories and coastal artillery. The two governments finally agreed on a language that stipulated in the contract that Brazil would give preference to France as a source of arms and all other technical advisers.[151]

In 1920 an arms purchasing commission was dispatched to France to acquire armaments. France became the source of mortars, machine guns,

---

[146] Castro e Silva, *À margen do Ministério Calógeras*, 71, 72.
[147] See Brazil, Ministério de Guerra, *Relatório*, 1918.
[148] Calógeras, *Problemas de adminístração*, 38.
[149] It was evident from the start that the French were very interested in the commercial returns of a possible military mission to Brazil. In his first communiqué suggesting the idea of a mission to Brazil, the French attaché in September 1917 noted that while a mission may be too premature at the moment, "it would be prudent to study the economic side of the question, such that the Brazilians do not purchase their materiel from others (particularly the United States which offered them favorable terms in this area)." Report no. 1119, from De la Horie to war ministry, 26 September 1917. Cited in Malan, *Missão militar*, 44–45.
[150] On these issues see, Malan, *Missão militar*, chap. 4.
[151] Malan, *Missão militar*, 89–95.

artillery, and armored vehicles. In all, Brazil's arms purchases from France during the 1920s were modest, primarily as a result of the country's financial difficulties.[152] Military spending during 1918–22 hovered around 20 percent of the total budget.[153] Budgetary constraints forced both the army and the navy to scrap several ambitious programs. Light and heavy weapons received from France soon became a point of dissatisfaction and controversy. Brazilians often accused France of providing them with *ferro velho* (junk), outdated surplus weapons from the war.[154] Brazilians were particularly not satisfied with the quality of the Schneider and Saint-Chamonte artillery, which many deemed inferior to the Krupp counterparts.[155] Brazilian dissatisfaction was also directed at the quality of French war planes as well as the instruction Brazilian aviators were receiving from the French mission.[156] Brazilian officers, some with first hand knowledge, considered the equipment and training of the U.S. army's air forces superior to those of the French. By 1928 Brazil was openly seeking an aviation mission from the United States.[157] Financial constraints and dissatisfaction with French arms meant that the army was equipped with a mixture of armaments and equipment during the 1920s.[158] Individual units were often equipped with arms from the United States, Germany, or France, causing severe training and logistical problems. As for the navy, an ambitious program was launched in 1924 to acquire twelve new warships to replace Brazil's aging fleet which the U.S. state department described as "obsolete." The new ships were to come from the United States, and "will place her in a very superior position" in the state department's estimate.[159]

Military regulations became one of the first areas of work for the French mission. In general, French imprint was deep and lasting in military doctrine. First, by the 1930s and 1940s nearly all of the military hierarchy had been graduates of the French-run military schools and had taken special courses at home. A few were sent to France to further their training. Second, the French immediately set out to rewrite all combat and internal regulations, including command regulations for the large combat units, combat and exercise regulations for the infantry, artillery, and cavalry, troop instructions, military regions, inspection services, communications, supply and support

[152] Hilton, "The Armed Forces," 634.
[153] Estevão Leitão de Carvalho, *Estudo comparative das despezas militares do Brasíl, Chile, e Argentina*, paper presented at V Conferência Pan-Americana de Santiago, Chile, 1924. Report in AHEX collection.
[154] Quote cited in McCann, "A influência estrangeira," 219.
[155] McCann, "A influência estrangeira," 219.
[156] On this point, see McCann's detailed study, "A influência estrangeira."
[157] McCann, "A influência estrangeira," 223.
[158] Hilton, "The Armed Forces," 637.
[159] Foreign Relations of the United States, 1924. Cable, 26 June 1924, from State Department to U.S. Embassy in Brazil.

services, as well as the major regulations for the army in campaign, general staff service, and the general staff school. The work of the Young Turks was pushed aside. The French wrote most of the combat and organizational regulations adopted by the army. These included the *Regulamento para a Direção e Emprego das Grandes Unidades* (Regulation for the Direction and Employment of Large Units), Brazil's war doctrine adopted in 1921. The Regulamento was based on France's *Provisional Instructions on the Tactical Employment of Large Units*, also adopted in 1921 and revised in 1936.[160]

Brazil, in essence, adopted a war doctrine which had traditionally been defense oriented, especially in the latter interwar years. Gamelin himself was an influential figure in the development and formulation of French war doctrine during the interwar period. General Humberto Castelo Branco, the first head of the military government in 1964, noted in 1957 that the French mission emphasized tactical defensive maneuvering, defensive positioning, and created a "national psychosis of the defensive."[161] Like France, Brazil would enter the Second World War with its own intellectual Maginot Line. The weight of the army's defensive mentality, and the total absence of initiative and offensive action, proved costly to its expeditionary force on the bloody Italian front in World War II.[162]

CONSCRIPTION

As for conscription, the 1908 obligatory military service law had been modified and implemented in 1916 by War Minister Faria.[163] As noted previously, its impact was negligible due to financial and administrative limitations.[164] In 1918, over 50,000 conscripts were called, but only 17,000 incorporated. The war ministry in 1918 proposed a length of service of eighteen months, instead of two years. Despite some innovative measures by Calógeras to augment the military budget, financial constraints continued to hamper the full implementation of obligatory service. Calógeras initiated a new round of efforts to rationalize the conscription system. He favored regional conscription, and in 1922 recommended that the country be divided into military recruitment regions. Each region was to correspond to a division, each of

[160] Paula Cidade, *Síntese*, 366. On France's military doctrine and the provisional regulations, see Robert Allan Doughty, *The Seeds of Disaster: The Development of French Army Doctrine, 1919–1939* (Hamden, CT: Archon Books, 1985).

[161] Quote cited in Malan, *Missão militar*, 186–87. Malan himself notes that the French reinforced Brazil's own "defensive mentality."

[162] On these points, see McCann, "A influência estrangeira," and *The Brazilian-American Alliance*.

[163] On the revised law itself see, *Boletim do Exército* 142 (15 January 1918): 72–80.

[164] Frank D. McCann, "The Nation in Arms," in *Essays Concerning the Socioeconomic History of Brazil and Portuguese India*, ed. Dauril Alden and Warren Dean (Gainsville: University of Florida Press, 1977): 211–43.

which would be subsequently subdivided into brigade districts, and then regiments of inscription.[165] This system corresponded closely to Argentina's German-inspired system, though well within the French practice of regional conscription and incorporation.

Another administrative innovation Brazil borrowed from Argentina was the *carteira de reservista*, an official registration card for all those who qualify for the draft. Incorporation continued to be based on the lottery. Up until the 1930s the length of service for draftees was one year. The goal was to generate as rapidly as possible, a large trained reserve. Calógeras's view was that, the country had lost too much time, and had to play catch up to its rival, Argentina. A short length of service was crucial to avoid disaster. "We must, therefore, follow the example of Prussia after the disaster at Jena," he argued, "and intensify the training of recruits whose time of service has to be short, with the objective of augmenting as rapidly as possible the number of trained classes."[166] A functioning system of obligatory service was finally put in place only in the 1939 draft law, which amended the defects of previous laws. The size of the army nearly doubled between 1930 and 1940 from roughly 47,000 to 80,000.

OFFICER FORMATION AND TRAINING

The area in which the French military mission made a big impact was officer formation, though the army's dispersion meant some units were left untouched. Here too the results were uneven. Commenting on French military instruction in Brazil, a United States military attaché observed in 1926 that, "I think little of this knowledge has penetrated to the individual soldier. The officers of the general staff, however, have benefited greatly from it."[167] The British ambassador in Rio de Janeiro reported to the foreign office in 1923 that "the French officers have the worst opinion of the efficiency of the army. The French Military Mission, as I have been told by members of it, look upon it as an almost hopeless task to produce anything even commencing to resemble an army out of the material they have to handle."[168]

The French mission reorganized the entire system of officer recruitment and instruction.[169] French officers established and staffed most of the military academies and specialized schools (with the notable exception of

---

[165] Calógeras, *Problemas de administração*, 86.
[166] Calógeras, *Problemas de administração*, 89.
[167] Quote cited in Nunn, *Yesterday's Soldiers*, 192.
[168] British ambassador to the foreign office, cable, 2 May 1923. Cited in Stanley E. Hilton, "Brazil and the Post-Versailles World: Elite Images and Foreign Policy Strategy, 1919–1929," *Journal of Latin American Studies* 12, no. 2 (November 1980): 341–64, 348. Emphasis added.
[169] On officer formation during this time, see Motta, *Formação*; Sena, "O desenvolvimento do Exército."

the Escola Militar at Realengo). The mission established several new schools and revision courses: aviation, general staff, supply services, veterinary, and the special revision course for general staff officers and large unit commanders. The revision courses were intended primarily for those officers who had already gone through the Escola Militar or who had received instruction in Germany. The aim was to create a uniform officer instruction system as well as ensure doctrinal uniformity. Most of these schools and courses were added when Calógeras came into office. Some of the schools had previously existed but either operated intermittently or never functioned. The general staff school never really functioned on a regular basis. A new ECEME was established in 1920, offering a two-year course of study, but also a parallel one-year special course and a revision course.[170] French officers acted as the directors of curriculum at the newly revived Escola Superior de Guerra (Superior War School) and the Escola de Aperfeiçoamento (School of Revision), which offered refresher courses. In 1925 a cavalry school, and specialized schools for the other combat arms, were opened. The only school that initially escaped French influence was the Escola Militar, where the Missão Indígena was still based. The 1922 lieutenants' revolt at the school led to its temporary closure. When it was reopened in 1924 the military school was placed under French direction. Its internal regulations and plan of study were overhauled. The school offered an additional year for officers in each of the combat arms. French instructors coordinated all of the school's tactics courses, in addition to teaching military history.[171]

An integral part of the training and instruction of officers, especially for general staff service, was the use of large-scale field maneuvers and military exercises. The first such maneuvers were held in 1920 and again in 1922. The maneuvers and exercises, which attempted to simulate battlefield conditions and combat operations, were carefully studied by the French in the formulation of a reform program.[172] These exercises had the effect of displaying the full extent of the military's needs and defects. A report by the French mission summed up the performance of the army in the 1922 maneuvers as one of complete disorganization, with units far off from achieving their objectives, unable to practice combined arms tactics, or just completely lost as a result of lack of adequate maps, cartography skills, and disorientation.[173]

Unlike Argentina and Chile, large numbers of whose officers went to Germany for advanced training, there were surprisingly few Brazilian officers attending French schools. Malan reports only seven Brazilian officers between 1919 and 1940.[174] Finally, the French were instrumental in drafting

---

[170] Malan, *Missão militar*, 100.
[171] Motta, *Formação*, 322.
[172] Malan, *Missão militar*.
[173] Leitão de Carvalho, *Memórias*, 58.
[174] Malan, *Missão militar*, 18.

the new 1934 law on promotions, which established strict merit-based guide-lines, qualifications, and timetables, and created a separate promotions com-mission to oversee the process. Unlike Argentina and Chile, military emula-tion in the area of officer formation did not involve sending Brazilian officers for formal instruction and service to France, at least in large numbers. There is no satisfactory explanation for this.

REORGANIZING GENERAL STAFF SERVICE

In sharp contrast to the wide powers and influence the French mission had over military instruction, it had limited control over the general staff.[175] The general staff was, in theory, to act as the codirector of Brazil's military modernization in conjunction with the French mission. Both McCann and Magalhães argue that the army's central organs of command, especially the general staff, were hostile to the French mission and jealously guarded their authority and turf against French intrusion.[176] Alves Bastos claims that the general staff was dominated by the *jovem turcos* which explains its resis-tance to the French mission.[177] The relationship between the French mission and the general staff would remain strained throughout the long stretch of the mission's work in Brazil. More than one general staff chief or senior commander pushed to have the mission terminated.[178] In 1931 the French mission was reduced from seventy officers to a six-man mission.[179]

Nonetheless, the French influenced the general staff's formation indirectly through officer training. Even Tasso Fragoso, who would later break with the mission, credits the French with introducing the first true, modern general staff service in Brazil.[180] The French arrived to find largely an administra-tive service, though on paper individual reform measures since 1915 had widened its authority and jurisdiction. Moreover, unlike the case in Chile and Argentina, no procedure of recruitment and training for general staff service existed. It was only after the arrival of the French military mission that the technical functions and authority of the general staff were aug-mented, formally and in practice.

The general staff was divided into two principal sections in 1920. The first was in charge of operational planning and instruction. The section brought together mobilization, military organization, and services. Much

---

[175] This is the assessment of the great majority of military historians. See, for example, Magêlhaes, *A evolução militar do Brasíl*; McCann, "A influência estrangeira."

[176] McCann, "A influencia estrangeira"; Magalhaes, *A evolução militar do Brasíl*, 350.

[177] Alves Bastos, *Encontro com o tempo*, 24.

[178] McCann, "A influência estrangeira," 221. On the friction between the French mission and the Brazilian military hierarchy, see Bastos, *Encontro com o tempo*; Paula Cidade, *Síntese*, 364–65.

[179] McCann, "A influência estrangeira," 225.

[180] Sena, "O desenvolvimento do Exército," 60.

of its activities focused on war preparation and study of theater operations. At this time also the French mission and the directory of the general staff collaborated to produce the Regulation for the Command and Employment of the Large Units, which served as Brazil's war doctrine. The high command was reorganized in 1921, with the chief of the general staff, the Germanophile Setembrinho de Carvalho, becoming the immediate chief of the army, followed by the regional military inspectors, and regional and divisional commanders.

The general staff would reach the peak of its authority and command over military affairs only with the 1934–35 reforms. The 1934–35 reforms centered the army's high command in the general staff, which shared wartime command with the superior war council. The general staff was designated as the "highest technical organ of national defense."[181] All traces of administrative functions were eliminated or transferred to the war ministry. The chief of the general staff, in effect, became the commander in chief of the army in both peacetime and wartime. He was no longer subordinate to the war minister, but became a collaborator with the war minister in command and control over all aspects of the military and national security policy. Though command and control was concentrated in it, the general staff itself was decentralized, with its individual sections enjoying ample autonomy and jurisdiction over the matters that fell within their individual functional areas. The section heads could deal directly with the troops or regional commands without the mediation of the chief or the war ministry. This ascendancy was short lived. The general staff would subsequently lose its authority under the 1937–39 reorganization. Peacetime and wartime command and control were transferred back to the war minister, and the chief of staff became once again a subordinate to the war minister.

EXPLAINING MILITARY EMULATION IN BRAZIL, 1870–1930

Military emulation in Brazil was slow and uneven. Unlike Chile, Brazil responded to victory in the Paraguayan war with complacency and stagnation. Like Chile and Argentina, it too employed a foreign military training mission to direct its modernization. Yet even under French guidance, emulation was not the same wholesale remaking that it was in the other two cases. Brazil did engage in other internal balancing efforts, such as its arms buildup and naval arms race during 1906–14, but the scale and pace of modernization were modest. The rise of Argentine power notwithstanding, Brazil emulated its rivals the least, and seemined not to have their sense of urgency and peril. In the remainder of this chapter, I elaborate my argument that the timing, pace, and scale of Brazil's military emulation were products of its structural position. Ample defensive advantages and opportunities for

---

[181] Magalhaes, *A evolução militar do Brasíl*, 368.

external balancing, in sharp contrast to its two neighbors, allowed it the luxury to move more slowly and modestly in remaking its military power.

Brazil appears to be a strong case for alternative explanations. Social theories, however, do not find confirming evidence in its behavior or in its archives. Aside from all the other reasons already cited, social theory makes a presumption of full-scale emulation. That is, if states pursue social fitness through emulation in order to enhance their security, presumably they will strive for fidelity and completeness in their efforts. If social fitness is crucial even to national security, why might Brazil put off its emulation for so many years after that of its neighbors? To the extent that Brazil's emulation was spotty and halting, and perhaps the result of internal developments, unit-level explanations are more likely to account for these outcomes. Military reformers consistently pointed to the Argentine military threat, not internal concerns, as the reason for modernization.[182] While these domestic factors are not the ones cited by the regime's insecurity or military organizational explanations, their impact on timing and scale of emulation cannot be discounted entirely.

In contrast to its neighbors, Brazil had no shortage of internal impediments to modernization. These internal impediments existed inside as well as outside the military. Brazil during the Old Republic (1889–1930) was a politically and institutionally dysfunctional state, one in the throes of breaking down across four decades. For the majority of this period, the country underwent a procession of constitutional crises, military revolts, popular uprisings, and provincial rebellions. Brazil did not have a full-on civil war, as in Chile, but rather a series of mini internal wars and rebellions that likely proved both more disruptive and more destructive institutionally given their chronic, protracted nature. More often than not, the military was at center stage, as it was in the 1920s. The military revolts and provincial uprisings of the 1922–34 years were the most debilitating for the military as an institution and damaging to the work of the French mission. Under these circumstances, modernization resembled the plight of Sisyphus. Each military revolt or provincial uprising was a major setback for military reform.

The Old Republic finally collapsed under its own weight in 1930.[183] The causes and details of Brazil's political implosion during 1889–1934 need not detain us here. The root cause was that the Old Republic had been infirm from the beginning, built on rotten foundations. The country, like its military, was fractured, governed by an internally divided governing elite. Each

---

[182] References to internal order appeared several times in the annual war ministry reports during the Contesdo rebellion, as they did during the 1893 naval revolt, but there is nothing unusual about this.

[183] Thomas E. Skidmore, *Politics in Brazil, 1930–1964: An Experiment in Democracy* (New York: Oxford University Press, 1967): chap. 1, passim. For a discussion in English of the military's participation in the political breakdown, see Keith and Hayes, eds., *Perspectives on the Armed Forces in Brazil*.

presidential succession was a traumatic moment. Aside from the many armed uprisings within the military, there were other popular armed uprisings, countryside rebellions, and armed federal interventions in the states. The two most serious and protracted of these popular rebellions were the bloody Canudos rebellion in the northeast (1893–95) and the Contestado rebellion in the south (1912–16).[184] These two rebellions by ragtag rural forces would further expose the weaknesses and defects of the army. The provincial uprisings and military revolts were equally indicative of the underlying structural weaknesses of the Old Republic, and more destructive for the military. The most significant of these provincial uprisings occurred in near-rapid succession in the two big states of São Paulo and Rio Grande do Sul in 1924, 1930, 1932, and 1934.

As in pre-1880 Argentina, national politics boiled down to interprovincial power struggles to control the national government or struggles over the balance of power between federal and state prerogatives. Nearly all the military revolts, and all the provincial rebellions, had their origins in the country's hyperfederalism. Brazil's states were practically sovereign fiefdoms. A major source of opposition to modernizing the federal military was the state governments and provincial elite. In this regard, Brazil closely resembled the domestic politics of military reform in the United States. The theory of emulation easily accounts for why Brazil emulated, why it emulated Germany and then France, it easily accounts for the overall variance in Brazil's military emulation, and none of these provincial or military rebellions were explicitly directed against modernization. Nevertheless, the theory cannot rule out the significance of this hyperfederalism as a practical obstacle to the process. It would be disingenuous to deny it mattered in blocking the implementation of universal military service, for example. The fact was that a weak federal government with a small and weak military was crucial to many actors in the brittle political bargain of the Old Republic. Reformers like the Young Turks challenged more than the status quo inside the military.

The Old Republic – that is, every presidential administration and congress – rested on a delicate and usually combustible politics of coalition among the elite and governors of the big states. Each state had its own national guard militia. From the standpoint of the states, the dual threats to their interests posed by military modernization were that the elimination of the state militias would be required, and the often-interventionist federal government's coercive powers would be strengthened. Indeed, the period

[184] On these rebellions, see Todd Diacon, "Bringing the Countryside Back In: A Case Study of Military Intervention as State Building in the Brazilian Old Republic," *Journal of Latin American Studies* 27, no. 3 (October 1995): 569–92; Tristão de Alencar Araripe, *Expedições militares contrá Canudos: seu aspecto marcial* (Rio de Janeiro: Biblioteca do Exército, 1985). The classic work on the infamous Canudos rebellion is Euclides da Cunha, *Rebellion in the Backlands* (Chicago: University of Chicago Press, 1944).

witnessed repeated federal armed interventions in the states to prop allied local elites. The states opposed any buildup of federal military power, especially the land forces. (Aside from the budget, all military legislation had to receive approval in the provincially controlled federal legislature.) In fact, the powerful states of São Paulo and Minas Gerais, the economic centers of the country, made sure their state militias were better organized and equipped than federal forces. In 1906 the powerful, semi-independent state of São Paulo contracted a French military mission to direct the modernization of the state militia.[185] The French mission, small and headed by veteran officers who had served in Indochina, remained in the state until 1914. São Paulo's military emulation, its desire to establish a powerful and well organized military force, was symptomatic of the strength of centrifugal forces in Brazil and the provincial opposition to a strong, modernized federal military.

As a result of the violent upheavals and political chaos of the Old Republic, the military was divided. It fought against itself, pitting legalists against dissidents. Political upheaval, a polarized civilian elite, and federal power struggles undermined military reforms. More important this political instability aggravated the already brittle military organization, one in which factionalism ran deep and discipline fragile. The military as a whole was heavily politicized, and civil-military relations constantly strained.[186] The politically appointed brass owed primary allegiance to the political leadership and partisan cliques.[187] The military was split vertically and horizontally.[188] It experienced continuous internal turmoil; conspiracies were as many as were their motives. Hierarchic control was brittle and intermittent. The junior officer movement itself was a heterogeneous jumble of interests and agendas. Paradoxically, none of this radicalism and open revolt had anything to do with reforms or emulation. In other words, the combination of the political system's dysfunction and subjective control of the military, to use Huntington's phrase, resulted in frequent ruptures in civil-military relations. There were

[185] On the French mission in São Paulo, see Dalmo de Abreu Dallari, *O pequeno exército paulista* (São Paulo: Editôra Perspectiva, 1977). The decision to contract a French mission appears to have been made largely on the basis of personal contacts the state governor had with the French. The state government had first contacted Foreign Minister Rio Branco, who suggested a German mission be hired.

[186] On civilian hostility, see Coelho, *Em busca de identidade*; June E. Hahner, *Civilian-Military Relations in Brazil, 1889–1898* (Columbia: University of South Carolina Press, 1969).

[187] Brazil's pattern of civil-military relations resembled Huntington's "subjective control" pattern. Samuel P. Huntington, *The Soldier and the State: The Theory and Politics of Civil-Military Relations* (New York: Random House, 1957).

[188] José Murilo de Carvalho, "As forças armadas na Primeira República: o poder desestabilizador," *História geral da civilização brasileira*, Boris Fausto, ed., vol. 3, tome 2, *O brasil republicano, 1889–1930* (Rio de Janeiro: DIFEL, 1977): 183–234, provides the best analysis on military factionalism during the Old Republic. See also William S. Dudley, "Institutional Sources of Officer Discontent in the Brazilian Army, 1870–1889," *Hispanic American Historical Review* 55, no. 1 (February 1975): 44–65.

plenty of debates about, and opposition to, military reforms. But none of the more serious intramural ruptures had anything to do with reforms or emulation.

Junior officer radicalism and discontent ran deep, animated by positivist ideas and anticivilianism dating back to the monarchy. Unlike Chile and Argentina, Brazil experienced a more violent, frequent, and temperamental junior officer movement. The notable exceptions were the apolitical *jovem turcos*. Junior officers were consistently inclined to push their claims outside the institution and resort to armed protests. Military revolts came with dizzying frequency. Some were serious, some minor.[189] At the military school in Praia Vermelha alone there were revolts in 1895, 1897, and 1904, forcing the government each time to close the school. Discontent and radicalism also infested the lower and noncommissioned ranks, as illustrated in the violent 1915 Sergeants' Revolt. Though the navy was on the whole better organized and more cohesive than the army, it too suffered several revolts. The most serious military uprising was the 1893 naval revolt in the federal capital, followed by another in 1910. The first lasted a few months and triggered the involvement of foreign powers. Warships from the United States, Britain, Portugal, Italy, and France forced the Brazilian government to cease operations against rebel forces under the pretext of protecting foreign nationals.[190]

The single most devastating of these junior officer rebellions, of course, was the *tenentes* (lieutenants) movement (1922–35), which touched off state uprisings in the process. It plunged the country into a drawn-out, low-intensity civil war that led to the Old Republic's eventual collapse in 1930, when dissident high command officers deposed the sitting president.[191] The *tenentes* were contemporaries of the Young Turks; indeed many were their students at the military school. Political concerns, and a virulent anticivilianism directed at a political leadership they considered corrupt, drove the *tenentes* and their rebellion. The point merits repeating that their revolt was animated by political, not military, goals, and was not directed against modernization. Their ideology was a jumble of military honor, anticorruption, and national salvation. With one important exception, the Young Turks did

[189] Carvalho, "As Forças Armadas," 185, table 1, lists eighteen separate revolts by the army and navy between 1889 and 1930.

[190] See, for example, Ministério de Relações Exteriores, *Relatório, 1893*.

[191] One of the best studies on the *tenentismo* movement is José Augusto Drummond, *O movimento tenentista: intervenção militar e conflito hierárquico, 1922–1935* (Rio de Janeiro: Edições Graal, Ltda., 1986). See also Hélio Silva, *1922: sangre na areia de Copacabana*, 2 vols., 2nd ed. (Rio de Janeiro: Civilização Brasileira, 1971); Carvalho, "As Forças Armadas"; John D. Wirth, "Tenentismo in the Brazilian Revolution of 1930," *Hispanic American Historical Review* 44, no. 2 (May 1964): 161–79; Robert J. Alexander, "Brazilian 'Tenentismo,'" *Hispanic American Historical Review* 36, no. 2 (May 1956): 229–42; João Quartim de Moraes, *A esquerda militar no Brasíl: da coluna à comuna*, vol. 2 (São Paulo: Ed. Siciliano, 1994).

not join the uprising. The *tenentes* rebellion became a low-intensity insurgency, led by the famous Coluna Prestes, the more radical faction. It traversed several states for a decade, often intermingling with provincial uprisings. The work of military modernization did not halt, implementation did. By the mid-1930s the French mission was still trying to implement basic reforms.

How much did these domestic level forces impair the timing, pace, and scale of military emulation? Impossible to say with any precision, or to determine how much of the residual variance is explained by them. I argue that it is largely an empirical, not theoretical matter. First, domestic level factors clearly did not affect whether Brazil emulated or which models Brazil emulated, adopting the only criterion we expect in anarchic competition. Second, Brazil did not face the same acute geostrategic exposure, as Chile did, nor the scale and immediacy of threat as had Argentina. Third, Brazil did balance, and did so on-the-cheap. It built up its armaments in response to Argentina's buildup. More important, it was adept at passing the buck and seeking external means to shore up its weaknesses. It watched the Chilean–Argentine spiral with satisfaction, since it meant the attention of its primary military threat was otherwise occupied. Just when it was abandoned by Chilean power, it turned to the United States as a counterweight.

BRAZIL'S DEFENSIVE ADVANTAGES

An explanation that focuses on Brazil's external security situation provides sufficient account for the overall variance in its military emulation. Such an account explains the timing and modest scale of emulation. Two external security factors are especially important. The first is Brazil's defensive advantages, and the second is its utilization of external balancing options.

Brazil was difficult for anyone to conquer because of the immense expanse of its land mass and extensive natural barriers. Its enormous size was a double-edged sword in view of the poor state of its military.

Given the technology of the time, its size and natural barriers presented serious obstacles to any power intent on conquest and occupation. Though it borders every state in South America except Chile and Ecuador, the impenetrable and expansive Amazon jungle carpeted most of this frontier. With neighbors to the south and west, Brazil shared river borders and marshlands. These provided less of an absolute barrier to an invading army, but acted as a defensive advantage over an invading army given the nature of the military capabilities its neighbors possessed up to the turn of the century. Though it has an extensive maritime frontier – and by the 1880s its economy had come to depend heavily on foreign trade – it faced no immediate maritime threat until 1900. Argentina did not have a true navy until the late 1890s, and the Atlantic expanse kept the European great powers far off (though Brazilians were wary of the dangers). Defeated Paraguay and politically dominated Uruguay were natural buffers against its principal adversary, Argentina.

These defensive advantages were not fixed. They were advantages only insofar as its main enemy – Argentina – lacked the land and naval power to put Brazilian national security at risk. For its part, Brazil stood still for much of the period between the Paraguayan war and the implosion of the Old Republic. Its huge size was prohibitive to any would-be conquerer, but this also meant that it had numerous borders and vast territory to defend. It lacked the military capabilities to defend this vast frontier, as well as the internal policing and central state capacity to govern its interior reaches. In addition, expansive territory and endless borders also meant it had a long list of border disputes and unsettled boundaries. Tensions marred Brazil's relations with all bordering countries, from Argentina, to Peru, to Colombia, to British Guayana and French Guiana. A number of these disputes were the direct result of its own migrating population of entrepreneurs, adventurers, bandits, traders, and fortune seekers. Brazil spent the four decades of 1870– 1910 preoccupied with and demarcating its borders with a combination of armed force and negotiations.[192]

BALANCING THROUGH EXTERNAL MEANS

Of the three major powers, only Brazil was able to derive substantial, prolonged value from the availability of external balancing and free riding. Unlike Chile and Argentina, Brazil was able to benefit indirectly from two sources of external balancing: Chile and the United States. In other words, Brazil was able to offset, partially and without formal alliance treaties, its military weakness and put off military emulation by free riding on Chilean and U.S. power.

Brazil's primary military rival, Argentina, was already a full decade into its military buildup by the start of the 1906 Fonseca reforms. It was Argentina's misfortune, and Brazil's good fortune, to be hemmed in by its two historical enemies. More important, up until the 1902 Andean settlements Argentina's attention was turned westward to its primary military threat, Chile. Naturally Brazil and Chile balanced against Argentina. Relations between Brazil and Chile, sharing a common enemy and no borders, were historically friendly and close diplomatically.[193] Their relations have been described by Valdão as a "friendship without treaty."[194] The relationship was far more

---

[192] See foreign ministry reports during the time period, in Ministério de Relações Exteriores, *Relatório.*

[193] On relations between Brazil and Chile, see Juan José Fernandes, *La República de Chile e el Imperio del Brasil: historia de sus relaciones diplomáticas* (Santiago: Editorial Andres Belo, 1959), and "El tratado secreto peruano-boliviano de 1873 y la diplomacia brasileña," *Boletín de la Academia Chilena de la Historia* 23, no. 55 (1956); Robert N. Burr, *By Reason or Force: Chile and the Balancing of Power in South America, 1830–1905* (Berkeley: University of California Press, 1965); Alfredo Valdão, *Brasíl e Chile na época do Império* (Rio de Janeiro: Livraria Olympio Editôra, 1959).

[194] Valdão, *Brasíl e Chile,* 85.

valuable to the militarily weaker Brazil. For Brazil, the diplomatic and military value of its close relations with Chile was indirect and subtle, acting as a check on Argentina. A formal treaty was never signed (though discussed on more than one occasion), yet Argentina could not contemplate action against one without fearing the reaction of the other.[195]

Tripolar balancing in the Andean–La Plata system contained Argentine power on several occasions. Its attempt in the early 1870s to join an anti-Chile treaty with Peru and Bolivia was aborted when Chile approached Brazil for a counteralliance.[196] Chilean representatives in Buenos Aires cabled back home that Argentina would not sign the secret treaty because it feared Brazil.[197] Brazil's ability to use the "Chile card" was particularly valuable as Argentina modernized and its own military decayed. In the absence of armed conflict, it is impossible to measure how much weight Argentine decision makers placed on the Brazil–Chile connection. Argentine diplomacy during the 1890s suggest that they placed a lot of weight on it. Argentina was far more concerned with Chilean power, the effect of which was to divert attention away from Brazil. The specter of Chilean power on its western flank, combined with its own military unpreparedness, was a pivotal factor in dissuading Argentina from pressing its position on the Misiones dispute with Brazil in 1895. It grudgingly acquiesced to the U.S.-arbitrated settlement award to Brazil because its relations with Chile had worsened badly.

Brazil's free riding on Chilean power came to an abrupt end at the turn of the century. From a longer term standpoint, Chile's power had waned considerably relative to Argentina's. Costly arms racing with the wealthier, economically thriving Argentina crippled the foundations upon which its military power rested. By 1914 Argentina was amassing the capabilities to fight on two fronts simultaneously. The 1902 Argentine–Chilean accords and détente effectively removed Chile as a player in the La Plata balancing subsystem. In fact, one of the stipulations of the treaty was a pledge by both Argentina and Chile to abstain from meddling in the affairs of their respective spheres of influence, the Andean and Platine subsystems.[198] Put bluntly, Chile abandoned Brazil. Astute Argentine diplomacy minimized the prospects of Chilean–Brazilian entente, thereby decoupling the two subsystems of competition.

Brazil lost its Chilean card exactly at a time when relations with its western Amazonian neighbors and Argentina were turning for the worse. In 1903–04 Brazil engaged in a brief armed skirmish with Bolivia for control of

---

[195] On this point, see Burr, *By Reason or Force*.

[196] Communiqué from the Chilean mission in Rio de Janeiro to the Brazilian government, 21 January 1874. Cited in Fernandes, "El tratado secreto," 12.

[197] Cable from Chilean mission in Argentina to foreign ministry, 16 February 1874. Cited in Fernandes, *La República de Chile*, 76–77.

[198] On the 1902 treaties, see Oscar Espinoza Moraga, "Los Pactos de Mayo," *Boletín de la Academia Chilena de la Historia* 14, no. 46 (1952); Burr, *By Reason or Force*.

Brazilian-occupied but disputed Acre territory. Acre, claimed by Brazil, Bolivia, and Peru but largely occupied by Brazilian settlers and traders, was South America's equivalent of the Texas territory in United States–Mexican relations in the 1830s and 1940s.[199] Brazil's occupation and subsequent annexation of Acre stirred protest from both Peru and Argentina. Argentina, like its other Spanish American neighbors, interpreted Brazil's actions as nothing less than a revival of Luso–Brazilian aggressive expansionism.

Brazilian diplomacy, not its arms, had been the strength of its external relations throughout its modern history. Brazil developed one of the hemisphere's best skilled diplomatic corps – one that became the spearhead of its national security strategy.[200] Just as it lost the ability to free ride on Chilean power, its adroit diplomacy secured another source of free riding. This time from the United States, historically antagonistic to Argentina save for the brief years of the *Baltimore* crisis. To compensate for its military inferiority, and shore up its bargaining position in relation to Argentina and Peru, Brazil turned to a policy of closer relations with the United States.

Relations between Brazil and the United States had been cordial since the days of the empire.[201] From the days of the monarchy, Brazil was one of the few Latin American countries that welcomed U.S. expansion (even if by force) into Latin America. In particular, Brazil supported the Monroe Doctrine early on, and gave its diplomatic support to U.S. police actions in the hemisphere.[202] During the Rio Branco years as foreign minister, 1902–12, Brazil adopted a more concerted diplomatic strategy to win U.S. backing. This strategy of alignment with the United States, which Rio Branco referred to as "our great sister of the North," was unabashedly one intended to shore up Brazil's weakness in the face of Argentine power, and generally secure diplomatic backing necessary in its many dispute with all bordering countries.[203]

Brazilian–U.S. relations during this period is often described as an "unwritten alliance."[204] Brazil's ambassador in Washington, Joaquim Nabuco,

[199] Smith, *Unequal Giants*, 39.
[200] On Brazilian foreign relations, see *Sessenta anos de polítca externa brasileira, 1930–1990*, ed. José Augusto Guilhon Albuquerque (São Paulo: Cultura Editores, 1996).
[201] On Brazilian-United States relations, see E. Bradford Burns, *The Unwritten Alliance: Rio Branco and Brazilian-American Relations* (New York: Columbia University Press, 1966); Luis A. Moniz, *Bandeira, Presença dos Estados Unidos no Brasíl: Dois Séculos de História* (Rio de Janeiro: Civilização Brasileira, 1973) Smith, *Unequal Giants*; McCann, *The Brazilian-American Alliance*.
[202] Calógeras, *Problemas de administração*. See also Smith, *Unequal Giants*; Burns, *The Unwritten Alliance*.
[203] Barão do Rio Branco, speech to the foreign ministry, 10 November 1906, in *Obras do Barão do Rio Branco*, vol. 1, *Questões de limites entre o Brasíl e a República Argentina* (Rio de Janeiro: Ministério de Relações Exteriores, 1948): 103.
[204] Burns, *The Unwritten Alliance*; McCann, *The Brazilian-American Alliance*; Smith, *Unequal Giants*.

in a January 1908 cable to Rio Branco, explicitly identified the approximation with the United States as a means to strengthen Brazil's national security.[205] Closer ties with the United States, according to Nabuco, "would be better than the largest army or navy."[206] The benefits to Brazil were the doubts created in Argentina's calculations about war and peace. Indeed, one finds these considerations salient in Argentine diplomatic correspondence even as late as the 1970s. Brazil allied with the United States during World Wars I and II, serving as a base of operations in both. In addition to having the United States as a major source of armaments, it also received a large U.S. naval training mission in 1922 to direct its naval modernization program.

Strategically, what mattered was not whether the U.S.–Brazilian relationship was a formal alliance, but the possibility of U.S. support or intervention on Brazil's behalf. Uncertainty had deterrent value.[207] Argentina's behavior is again illustrative. During the crisis of 1907–08 Argentina approached the United States for reassurances that it would not back Brazil militarily in the event of an Argentine–Brazilian war.[208] Argentine misgivings never dissipated, nor were they lost on the United States. In late 1992, the U.S. embassy in Argentina reported that political and militay leaders regarded U.S. ties with Brazil as an alliance.[209] Approximation allowed Brazil to deprive other Latin American countries of U.S. support in the event of a crisis or dispute settlement. It allowed Brazil to checkmate U.S. involvement and backing of others in issues (especially border demarcations) where Brazilian interests might be engaged – thus allowing Brazil to deal with smaller, less diplomatically adept neighbors bilaterally. Approximation with the United States was as much about free riding as it was about strategic denial of its Spanish neighbors.

There were limits to this free riding. For its part, the United States had interests in the region that went beyond Brazil – and often conflicted with those of Brazil. During World War I it worried that its close relations with Brazil would upset the rest of South America – at a time when the United States was attempting to recruit them to join the Allied cause. In 1917 the United States sent its South Atlantic fleet to Brazil, ostensibly to join the British navy in patrolling the South Atlantic and to guard the northeastern bulge of Brazil. The fleet was instrumental in reassuring Brazil of U.S. support. But the United States was aiming for a regional policy, and soon after the fleet arrived in Brazilian ports it was dispatched to Uruguay and Argentina for formal visits.[210] Concerns of the United States, with how its

[205] Quote cited in Burns, *The Unwritten Alliance*, 171.

[206] Ibid.

[207] McCann, *The Brazilian-American Alliance*, 6, makes a similar point.

[208] Smith, *Unequal Giants*, 65.

[209] Foreign Relations of the United States (FRUS), 20 December 1922, cable from U.S. Embassy to the State Department.

[210] Healy, "Admiral William B. Caperton."

Brazilian policy could upset relations elsewhere were again displayed with the decision to provide Brazil with a naval mission.[211] Argentina adamantly opposed the U.S. naval mission, which remained in Brazil until 1978. The United States stressed that the mission was purely technical, and that it did not signify a commitment of military backing. It initially opposed Brazil's extensive naval buildup, and threatened to withdraw the mission. It feared that such a program would alter the balance of power in the region. "The Department feels so strongly about the matter," wrote Secretary of State Robert Lansing, "that it would recall the Naval Mission rather than assume the responsibility for the naval program."[212]

Thus, for Brazil, there were limits to its relationship with the United States, even though its relations with the United States were closer than were those of any other Latin American Country. It was often marked by Brazilian frustration and uncertainty regarding U.S. willingness to provide economic and military assistance, let alone military backing in an international confrontation. From 1914 to World War II Brazil repeatedly doubted the U.S. commitment to assist it in case of an attack. On the eve of both wars, Brazil was frustrated by the slow and tentative U.S. efforts to provide it military and economic aid as well as the deployment of U.S. forces. It was a lopsided approximation. Brazil was more committed to a formal alliance and close cooperation than the United States at any one point.[213]

BRAZILIAN MILITARY POWER AS *QUANTITÉ NÉGLIGEABLE*

The Paraguayan war had revealed serious defects in Brazil's military organization. Victory came at a terrible cost. Military leaders recognized the defects and their costs. A year after the war was concluded, Marshall Viscount de Pelotas reminded his colleagues that the human and material costs Brazil suffered could have been minimized if the country had a prepared standing army based on obligatory military service. War Minister João Junqueira added that the "Paraguayan War revealed just how limited and imperfect" the army was.[214] The Brazilian military after the Paraguayan war entered a period of decline and internal disarray. The country's ability to free ride on U.S. and Chilean power, as well as Argentina's westward preoccupation, hid its military weakness.

The Paraguayan war is generally cited by Brazilian military historians as the point at which the Brazilian military acquired a sense of corporate

---

[211] See, for example, diplomatic exchanges between the state department and the U.S. Embassy in Rio de Janeiro during March–December 1924 in, *Foreign Relations of the United States* (FRUS), vol. 1, 1924.

[212] Quote cited in Joseph Smith, "American Diplomacy and the Naval Mission to Brazil, 1917–1930," *Inter-American Economic Affairs* 35, no. 1 (Summer 1981): 73–91, 86.

[213] Smith makes this argument in *Unequal Giants*.

[214] Ministério de Guerra, *Memorial*, 1871, 6 and annex, 47.

identity.[215] The war had raised expectations among the officer class, who expected that the monarchy's neglect of the armed forces would end in view of their sacrifice.[216] The war brought neither prestige nor greater expenditures; only neglect and civilian hostility. (Most Brazilian military historians agree that the emperor distrusted the military and opposed a large, modern permanent army that could possibly block royal pretensions or, more likely, upset the delicate federalist balance between the central government and the semi-independent, powerful states.)[217] In the first decades after the Paraguayan war, military reforms as well as the military's political role became key issues of public debate. The issues involved in the so-called *questão militar* (military question) that emerged in the mid-1880s were part organizational and part political.[218] With regard to modernization, not much changed after the 1889 military coup d'etat overthrowing the monarchy.

Between 1870 and 1906 the army stagnated. The navy did not fare any better, save for the 1904/1906 modernization. The army's deficiencies did not go unnoticed inside and outside Brazil. Brazil's military weakness became a constant theme in military thinking during the Old Republic.[219] The war ministry's annual reports of this period contained frank and critical assessments of the state of the military. The first major internal review of the state of the military came right after the Paraguayan war. The reviews, contained in the *Relatório* of 1870 and 1871, were prepared under the direction of the then acting war minister, the Viscount Rio Branco, father of the future foreign minister by the same name. As part of the 1871 review of the military's performance in the Paraguayan war, Viscount Rio Branco distributed a survey to field commanders soliciting their comments regarding the organizational, doctrinal, and technological deficiencies of the army as well as recommendations on changes that should be adopted. The common conclusion among the field commanders was that reforms were needed in every area of the army, from arms to regulations. In his final report, the elder Rio Branco focused on modernizing the army's armaments in light of the lessons of the Franco–Prussian war. He recommended the adoption of breech-loading Krupp cannons.[220] Commander Gastão de Orleans concurred, noting that the German cannons "have in their favor the sanction of splendid

[215] See, Magalhães, *Evolução militar do Brasil*; Coelho, *Em busca de indentidade*. On intellectual developments within the army, see McCann, "The Formative Period."

[216] Coelho, *Em busca de identidade*, 46.

[217] Magalhães, *Evolução militar do Brasil*. See also essays in Keith and Hayes, eds., *Perspectives on Armed Forces in Brazil*.

[218] See Coelho, *Em busca de identidade*; Hayes, *The Armed Nation*, chaps. 2 and 3; Hahner, *Civilian-Military Relations*.

[219] Frank McCann, "The Brazilian General Staff and Brazil's Military Situation, 1900–1945," *Journal of Inter-American Studies and World Affairs* 25, no. 3 (August 1983): 299–324.

[220] Ministério de Guerra, *Relatório do Ministério de Guerra*, 1870, 11.

experience," in reference to the Franco–Prussian war.[221] Notwithstanding these recommendations, nothing was done. Over the next three decades the military languished.

Deterioration set in everywhere, from basic equipment and supplies, to administrative structure, to officer formation. Corrupt practices persisted. Officer recruitment and advancement were based on particularist criteria such as family connections and political appointments. The great majority of the corps lacked not just technical training but also general secondary and baccalaureate education.[222] The army lacked even basic training and campaign manuals. Training and conscription were nonexistent; both officers and ranks were poorly and irregularly paid.[223] Not only did the army lack basic equipment (uniforms, footwear, housing), but it was greatly undermanned. Desertion was rampant. The ranks continued to be filled by slaves, illiterates, and petty criminals. The national guard, which was essentially controlled by the states and which acted as an instrument of patronage and means for the well-to-do classes nominally to fulfill military service, had more privileged access to resources.[224]

Despite the introduction of important reforms during 1906–14 and during the war in Europe, Brazil's military system remained poorly organized and ill equipped. Raw figures on army size, number of warships, and the like, do not tell the whole story of Brazil's military inferiority, because the quality of armaments and personnel are not so easily summed up. A British diplomat reported to the foreign office in 1913 that "there has been little improvement in the condition of the army during the past year." He added, in an even more disparaging tone, that "I do not suppose for a moment that the Brazilian army, undisciplined, undrilled, of degenerate black blood, officered by commanders as conceited as they are ignorant, would have a ghost of a chance against any ordinary fighting force." This assessment echoed those made by Brazilian officers. He concluded that "I do not, for instance, believe that [it] could hold [its] own even against the 7,000 military police of São Paulo, who have been carefully drilled and exercised by a French commission during the last seven or eight years."[225] The 1912 Contestado rebellion by barefoot illiterate peasants and their messianic leaders pushed the army to a breaking point for four long years. An editorial in *A Defeza Nacional* was severe in its criticism of the army's organization and performance,

[221] Ministério de Guerra, *Relatório, 1871*, annex, 33.
[222] For a superb study on the formation of the Brazilian officer corps, see Motta, *Formação*.
[223] Sena, "O desenvolvimento do Exército."
[224] On the national guard see Sodré, *Historia militar do Brasil*.
[225] Annual Report from British legation in Brazil to Foreign Office, 1913, *British Documents on Foreign Affairs: Reports and Papers From the Foreign Office Confidential Print*, pt. I, series D, *Latin America, 1845–1914*, vol. 9, *The Latin American Republics, 1910–1914*, ed. George Philip (Bethesda: University Publications of America, 1991): 121–22.

describing the federal forces as nothing more than "an organization of irregular troops."[226]

BRAZIL, ARGENTINE POWER, AND THE CHANGING BALANCE OF POWER, 1870–1914

Since colonial days, Luso Brazil's diplomatic and strategic position on the continent was an uneasy one. Historically, Spanish America viewed Brazil as expansionist; its population as land-grabbing and alien. Brazil's neighbors had good reasons to worry. Similar to early U.S. settlers in places like Texas, Brazilian settlers and entrepreneurs pushed inland into neighboring countries and undefined land where they established permanent settlements and trading posts. Distrust of Brazil was open and widespread. Anti-Brazilian sentiment was a favorite topic of Brazilian diplomats in their regular reports to the foreign ministry.[227] Border disputes with its Spanish-speaking neighbors were the primary source of diplomatic and security concerns during the 1870–1906 period. While the sources of its principal military threats were Argentina, pre-1883 Peru, and pre-1870 Paraguay, its relations with all neighboring countries were strained by border tensions. Brazilian diplomacy was adept at settling most of these disputes peacefully, largely through a combination of superficial compromise and bilateralism.[228] The strategy of preventing boundary disputes from becoming multilateral (since it would be outnumbered against a Spanish American coalition) remained an enduring aspect of Brazil's regional diplomacy.[229] This strategy of phony compromise and bilateralism, and the fact that Brazil came to have such a skilled and professional diplomatic corps that could capitalize on (and fuel) Spanish America disunity, allowed Brazil to expand without always relying on military force or triggering an encircling coalition.

Argentina was Brazil's single most important security threat since independence. Their relations were tense and militarized since independence. Brazil always regarded Argentina as its most likely opponent in an international war. Their rivalry was all-encompassing. Territorial disputes were

---

[226] *A Defeza Nacional* 4, no. 47 (10 August 1917): 357.

[227] See diplomatic cables in the foreign ministry historical archive, in *Correspondência*, in Arquivo Histórico do Itamaratí.

[228] This perspective comes through in the views of Brazil's famous foreign minister, Barão do Rio Branco, *Obras do Barão do Rio Branco*, vol. 1, *Questões de limites entre o Brasíl e a República Argentina* (Rio de Janeiro: Ministério de Relações Exteriores, 1948). See also Burns, *The Unwritten Alliance*.

[229] On Brazilian diplomatic history, see Delgado de Carvalho, *História diplomática do Brasíl* (São Paulo: Cia. Editôra Nacional, 1959); Hélio Vianna, *História diplomática do Brasíl* (São Paulo: Edições Melhoramentos, 1958); *História geral da civilização brasileira*, 10 vols., ed. Sérgio Buarque de Holanda (São Paulo: Difusão Européa de Livro, 1972); *Brazil: Empire and Republic, 1822–1930*, ed. Leslie Bethell (Cambridge: Cambridge University Press, 1989).

inseparable from their struggle for regional control. Their first war, the 1825 Cisplatine war, was for control of what eventually became Uruguay. Argentina and Brazil would subsequently spend the next two centuries vying for dominance in the La Plata Basin, jockeying for control over the buffer states of Uruguay and Paraguay. Armed clashes were frequent during the years of the Argentine dictator Juan Manuel de Rosas. Brazil frequently intervened militarily and politically in Argentina's interprovincial strife and civil wars, and in the early 1850s joined rebel provinces and foreign (mainly European) powers in an armed intervention to overthrow the Argentine dictator. As late as 1874, Brazilian warships bombarded Argentine towns. Argentine rebels often used Brazil as a base of operations and refuge. Their territorial disputes dated back to the 1700s, and turned for the worse by the early 1890s. A border dispute over control of the Misiones (or Palmas) territory brought them close to war. Argentina claimed possession of most of the present-day Brazilian states of Paraná and Santa Catarina.

"If any South American republic seeks supremacy or hegemony," the foreign ministry reported pointedly in 1895, "it is a noble motivation for us to invigorate our efforts for the purpose of finding effective and permanent means to block it."[230] Undoubtedly, the foreign ministry was making reference to Argentina, at a time when both were ensnared in a worsening dispute over Misiones. It was only with the onset of Argentina's massive military buildup, however, that the fear of an Argentine attack became a permanent and constant feature in Brazilian thinking. The period stretching from 1904 to World War II was marked by continual worries on the part of Brazilian leaders of an imminent Argentine assault.[231] It was in its southern states (Rio Grande do Sul, Mato Grosso, Santa Catarina, and Paraná) bordering Argentina where Brazil deployed the bulk of its forces up into the Second World War. As the chief of the general staff put it in 1934, Argentina was "the principal adversary."[232] This element in Brazil's strategic thinking remained fixed up to the 1970s.[233] The critical phase of Brazilian modernization, 1906–18, coincided with near-war crises, arms racing, and invasion fears in Brazil. The risk of war was so great by 1908 that the United States warned Argentina that it would send a naval squadron to the region to prevent a clash.

Brazil's military weakness was exposed as Argentina embarked on its modernization. Brazil's military attention had always been turned southwest toward Argentina.[234] As in the case of Chile, Argentina was a negligible

---

[230] Ministério de Relações Exteriores, *Relatório, 1895*, 4.
[231] On this point see the superbly researched studies of McCann, "The Brazilian General Staff."
[232] Quote cited in McCann, "The Brazilian General Staff," 308.
[233] McCann, "The Brazilian General Staff," makes a similar point.
[234] On Brazilian–Argentine relations, see Estanislao S. Zeballos, *Diplomacia desarmada* (Buenos Aires: Editorial Universitaria de Buenos Aires, 1974); Stanley E. Hilton, "The Argentine Factor in Twentieth Century Brazilian Foreign Policy Strategy," *Political Science*

threat as long as it remained a collection of warring provinces. The combination of national unification and military modernization turned it into a serious and immediate threat. Relations soured by the mid-1890s, but Argentina had to contend with Chile in any confrontation with Brazil. The next decade would witness a rapid and extensive growth in Argentine military power. It was no coincidence that the first sustained effort by Brazil to reverse decades of military decline would occur during the definitive phase of Argentina's own modernization. Nor was it happenstance that the first decade of the new century would mark a period of escalating arms race between the two countries. Argentina had been building a huge and well-armed army and a blue water navy, primarily in preparation for war with Chile. That power now threatened Brazil. The security dilemma was inescapable. Argentina had amassed this power with a view toward sustaining multitheater combat operations against both archrivals. The Brazilians knew it. "What is Argentina's motive to take advantage of the hard experience of [Germany] to arm itself," asked an *A Defeza Nacional* editor in 1915, "in a way so that it can wage war on two fronts, against Brazil in the East and against Chile in the West."[235] The spiral of insecurity deteriorated uncontrollably. Relations reached near-war conditions for most of the first decade of the twentieth century. Argentina openly opposed Brazil's acquisition of the disputed Acre territory on the border with Bolivia in 1904. Relations reached the nadir in 1907–08, and both states locked themselves in an intense and expensive naval arms race that also brought financially strapped Chile into the spiral.[236] In 1907 Rio Branco cabled to Joaquim Nabuco, the ambassador to the United States, that war with Argentina was imminent.[237]

Thus Brazil's security situation worsened quickly in the first decade of the new century. The big change was the rise of Argentine offensive capabilities on land and on the high seas. Argentina's military modernization program gave it the capacity to project power on two fronts. Brazilian diplomatic and military correspondence during the decade is marked by a growing sense of alarm and despair at their lack of military preparedness. Brazil closely monitored Argentina's military buildup and preparedness. A widely read and extensive study on the Argentine military was prepared in 1901–02 by an influential general staff officer, Major Armando Duval. By 1909 Brazil had assigned another influential and highly skilled general staff officer, Augusto Tasso Fragoso, as military attaché in Buenos Aires. Fragoso, a vocal and

Quarterly 100, no. 1 (Spring 1985): 27–52; Seward W. Livermore, "Battleship Diplomacy in South America, 1905–1925," *The Journal of Modern History* 16, no. 1 (March 1944): 31–48.

[235] Maciel da Costa, "Asegurar a Paz," *A Defeza Nacional* 3, no. 25 (January 1915): 7.

[236] On the naval arms race, see Livermore, "Battleship Diplomacy"; Robert L. Scheina, *Latin America: A Naval History, 1810–1987* (Annapolis: Naval Institute Press, 1987).

[237] Quoted in Burns, *The Unwritten Alliance*, 185.

respected reformer, was perhaps Brazil's leading expert on foreign military systems.[238] During his stay in Buenos Aires he compiled several studies on the progress of Argentina's military modernization and sent warnings of Brazil's own growing inferiority.[239]

By the First World War Argentina had amassed an impressive offensive military force. Brazilian leaders became alarmed at Argentina's extensive rail network, much of which concentrated in the Buenos Aires province and along the border with Brazil.[240] According to one Brazilian observer, Argentina had some 34,000 kilometers of track in 1914, more than double the 14,000 kilometers it had in 1897.[241] By 1914 Argentina ranked in the top ten in the world in total rail mileage. Though much of this rail network was created as an economic infrastructure, it had dual-use, military potential. This rail network allowed Argentina to mobilize and concentrate its forces rapidly and decisively. One Brazilian officer observed in 1910 that "There is in South America no other army which can mobilize as rapidly and completely as that of Argentina."[242] Another army officer noted, with some alarm, in 1917 that "Argentina established a rail system that allows it to realize in any of its three frontiers a rapid mobilization or concentration of all its forces. No other state in South America is better equipped in this area," estimated to be around 35,000 kilometers of track.[243]

Argentina's growing military strength was in sharp contrast to the disrepair and internal chaos of the Brazilian armed forces. Brazil's leading statesman, the Baron Rio Branco, told an audience at the military club in 1903 that "after twenty years of neglect, it is necessary that we seriously undertake to reorganize [our] national defense, following in the example of certain neighboring countries, who in short time have managed to equip themselves with elements of defense and attack much more superior to ours."[244] The 1906 annual report of the war ministry began by stating that the country's frontiers "are in precarious conditions of defense."[245] Comparing Brazil's situation in view of developments in Argentina, Rio Branco described Brazil in 1906 as in a "state of military weakness."[246] He warned in 1909 that war does

---

[238] On Fragoso, see Araripe, *Tasso Fragoso*. See also McCann, "The Brazilian General Staff."

[239] McCann, "The Brazilian General Staff."

[240] See, for example, an article by a general staff officer in *Boletim Mensual do Estado Maior do Exército* 1, no. 2 (May 1911).

[241] Sargento Albuquerque, *Em caminho da guerra: a cilada argentina contra o Brasíl* (Rio de Janeiro: Editores S.A. Monitor Mercantíl, 1917): 117. Given Albuquerque's jingoistic and alarmist attitude, his figures may be open to question.

[242] Quoted in Araripe, *Tasso Fragoso*, 459.

[243] Alburquerque, *Em caminho da guerra*, 117, 118.

[244] Barão do Rio Branco, *Obras do Barão*, vol. I, xviii.

[245] Ministério de Guerra, *Relatório*, 1906, 8.

[246] Barão do Rio Branco, *Obras do Barão*, vol. 1, 104.

not depend on the wishes of one country alone but also on the intentions and ambitions of neighbors; Brazil could not continue to lack basic "elements of national defense" and leave itself vulnerable in the face of Argentina's military buildup and modernization.

General staff officer and military attaché to Argentina, Tasso Fragoso, authored a 1910 study on the military balance between the two countries and concluded that Brazil stood in a position of "absolute military inferiority," given the disorganization of its army, the lack of obligatory service and reserve system, and incapacity to mobilize and concentrate forces effectively.[247] By 1910 the reports dispatched from Buenos Aires by Brazilian attachés were pronouncing Brazil's "absolute military inferiority." Fragoso warned that Argentina could assemble a first line force of 50,000 troops on the border within thirty days, before Brazil could even mobilize and deploy a token defense force.[248] In his 1911 general staff study on the "Present State of the Army," 1st Lieutenant Mário Clementino described the state of military affairs as the "disorganization of the army," and warned against the "precarious state to which our military organization has reached."[249] He argued that Brazil's main strategic problem and military threat was Argentina, from which Brazil can derive lessons about strategy, regional military organization, and the rail network that converges on Brazil's southern frontier. Between 1910 and World War I, the topic of rail transport was prominent in military debates. The war ministry's 1912 report focused heavily on the need to build a national rail network to meet military objectives.

The World at War and Fears of Invasion

Brazil responded to the Argentine threat with a combination of internal and external balancing measures. Abandoned by Chile, it quickly turned to the United States. In 1904 it put in motion a sizable naval buildup, followed by an armaments acquisition program. The reforms of the Young Turks made some dent in reversing military disorganization. The new round of naval acquisitions begun in 1907 helped close the imbalance with its powerful neighbor. Notwithstanding these efforts, the reality between 1914 and the 1930s is that Brazil continued to find itself in a position of military inferiority relative to its principal rival.

As war approached in Europe and relations deteriorated with Argentina, Brazilian concern with Argentine power grew desperate as did its assessment of its own military capabilities. Fear of the gap in capabilities intensified. The general staff's *Boletim Mensual do Estado Maior do Exército*, the main

---

[247] McCann, "The Brazilian General Staff," 304.
[248] Ibid.
[249] Ministério de Guerra, Estado Maior General do Exército, *Boletim Mensual do Estado Maior General do Exército* 1, no. 2 (May 1911): 84.

vehicle through which intelligence gathering and net assessments of foreign military systems were carried out, estimated that Argentina was capable of mobilizing a standing wartime force of 250,000 on the eve of the war in Europe.[250] An earlier study in the *Boletim* estimated that already in 1902 Argentina had over 700,000 males with some level of military training among the first line army, the national guard, and its territorial guard.[251] Brazil in 1914 was simply incapable of defending itself. Not much seemed to have changed by war's end according to the war minister's assessment in 1919 that Brazil was completely defenseless. Commenting on Brazil's army, a British diplomat noted in 1913 that "as a fighting force against a really disciplined army, it may be looked upon as a *quantité négligeable*," adding that "neither the army nor the navy is of any military value."[252]

Despite the strides made during the 1906–18 reform phase, Brazil continued to find itself in a position of military inferiority as war erupted in Europe in 1914. Many reform measures were never implemented or only partially implemented. Brazil's military unpreparedness was further revealed after it declared war on Germany in October 1917 – after much prodding and reassurance from the United States – and attempted to mobilize a token naval force to participate in the war effort. Brazil's still small, aging navy was not able to conduct even minor operations.[253] United States naval personnel found Brazilian vessels in disrepair and their crews untrained. Its two main battleships were in such questionable seaworthy conditions that they barely made it to New York for general repairs in early 1918.[254] Both British and U.S. military and diplomatic observers had the same dismal assessment of Brazil's military preparedness and potential. One U.S. diplomat commented in 1916 that the Brazilian army was in serious need of instruction and was inferior to that of its neighbors.[255] The long-serving United States ambassador Edwin Morgan cabled Secretary of State Robert Lansing in November 1917 that "[i]n esprit, technical knowledge and general efficiency [the Brazilian army] is inferior to similar organizations in Argentina and Chile and would be at a disadvantage in a trial of strength."[256]

[250] Ministério de Guerra, Estado Maior General do Exército, *Boletim Mensal do Estado Maior General do Exército* 5, no. 3 (March 1913).

[251] Lieutenant Gensérico de Vasconcellos, "Notas sobre a organização militar da República Argentina," *Boletim Mensal do Estado Maior do Exército* 1, no. 3 (June 1911): 146.

[252] Annual Report from the British legation in Brazil to foreign office, 1913, cited in Philip, ed., *British Documents on Foreign Affairs, The Latin American Republics, 1910–1914*, 121–22, 151.

[253] On this point, see Healy, "Admiral William B. Caperton"; Smith, *Unequal Giants*, chap. 3; Albuquerque, *Em caminho da guerra*.

[254] Healy, "Admiral William B. Caperton," 316.

[255] Quoted in Smith, *Unequal Giants*, 107.

[256] Quoted in Smith, "American Diplomacy," 76.

The war in Europe, together with Argentine military might, suddenly magnified threats to the country's safety. The threats were an interplay of old and new, external and internal. As war broke out in Europe, Brazil was gripped by fear of external invasion from Germany, hitherto its main supplier of armaments.[257] Germany's practice of unrestricted submarine warfare had a devastating impact on Brazilian shipping. The sinking of Brazilian shipping, along with pressures from the United States, eventually forced Brazil to break relations and declare war on Germany and the Central Powers in October 1917.

Fear of attack was magnified by the power of its ancient rival to the south, an unambiguously pro–Axis Argentina. As discussed above, Argentine military power loomed large, as did its expenditures. Argentine military spending nearly doubled between 1916 and 1922.[258] The size of the first line forces increased significantly, with a 40 percent annual increase in the number of conscripts incorporated.[259] Its armaments buildup was even more impressive, ballooning from 353,000 pesos in 1925 to nearly 28 million pesos in 1930.[260] In sharp contrast, Brazil's states bordering Argentina were both poorly defended and lacked essential infrastructure, such as rail networks for mobilization and concentration of forces. As late as 1907, the war ministry was complaining about the "military problem of our states of Mato Grosso and Rio Grande do Sul," urging that "we prepare those two southern-most states of the Republic with the necessary elements for their complete defense."[261]

Brazil's southern states, bordering its principal military threat, were home to a large German émigré population. For Brazil, it was a nightmare scenario: an Argentine–German invasion combined with a secessionist rebellion of its southern provinces. Making matters worse, the same southern states near the Argentine border were in open rebellion, the Contestado, sweeping across Santa Catarina and Paraná during 1912–16. That is, Brazilian leaders feared not only an assault across the Paraná River, but a combined Argentine blitzkrieg into the southern states coordinated with a "fifth column" rebellion in the provinces. Brazil had always been concerned with the vulnerability of its southern states bordering Argentina. States like Rio Grande do Sul, moreover, were traditionally hotbeds of rebellion and flammable jealousies in the fragile coalition politics of the Old Republic. Concerns over the south

---

[257] The war experience stimulated Brazil to pursue the goal of absolute independence in the area of military resources. Brazilian military chiefs recommended that Brazil pursue a strategy of military self-sufficiency by establishing a military industry. On this point, see Ministério de Guerra, *Relatório, 1918*, 36.

[258] Robert Potash, *The Army and Politics in Argentina, 1928–1945: Yrigoyen to Peron*, vol. 1 (Stanford: Stanford University Press, 1969): 7.

[259] Potash, *The Army and Politics*, 6.

[260] Ibid.

[261] Ministério de Guerra, *Relatório, 1907*, 10.

were aggravated by its uncertainty over the loyalty of these provinces, home to a substantial but poorly assimilated German émigré population. The reaction of Brazilian leaders never reached the extreme of their counterparts in the United States in the case of its Japanese citizens. During the war, Brazilian leaders raised concerns about Argentine (and German) espionage and subversive activities in the southern provinces – which became a real problem during the Second World War.[262] To be sure, realist theory does not expect a state's security concerns to be directed inward. It was Argentine power, however, that compelled Brazilian leaders to factor into their calculations its unassimilated immigrant population of unknown loyalty. The real fear was external invasion by Argentina and Germany, and the chance that they would play on the native loyalties of the immigrant population – in a region undergoing a rebel movement.

Relations between Brazil and Argentina during the interwar period continued to be marked by the same rivalry and distrust of the pre-1914 era. There were brief lulls and superficial détente, such as the short-lived ABC treaty. For Brazilian civil and military leaders, there was only one purpose for Argentina's growing military power – war with Brazil. "Let us have no illusions about Argentina's plans," warned the Brazilian legation in Buenos Aires.[263] As relations grew tense in the latter part of the 1920s as a result of renewed arms racing, Brazil's embassy in Chile warned in late 1927 that Argentina would attack Brazil within five years.[264] The problem for Brazil was the same as Chile's: neither could hope to keep up with Argentine military potential.

Brazil's relative military weakness was unchanged at the start of the 1920s despite some shallow reforms during the war. One U.S. diplomat cabled Washington in the early 1920s that Brazil was "clearly inferior" in comparison to its main neighbors.[265] General Maurice Gamelin, head of the French military mission, had no illusions about the uphill battle facing him in reorganizing the Brazilian military, given its "flagrant inferiority."[266] Argentina outclassed Brazil in every category of military capabilities, as Brazilian officer and former attaché in Buenos Aires, Major Armando Duval stated in his influential study on Argentine military capabilities.[267]

Brazil's military inferiority worsened in the 1920s and into the 1930s, as Argentina launched several spurts of arms buildup, troop expansion, and

---

[262] Stanley E. Hilton, *Hitler's Secret War in South America, 1939–1945* (Baton Rouge: Louisiana State University Press, 1981).

[263] Hilton, "Brazil and the Post-Versailles World," 350.

[264] Ibid.

[265] Quoted in Smith, *Unequal Giants*, 140.

[266] Quoted in Hilton, "Brazil and the Post-Versailles World," 347.

[267] Major Armando Duval, *Argentina, potência militar*, 2 vols. (Rio de Janeiro: Imprensa Nacional, 1922). Duval's study became a standard text for general staff courses in the military academies during the 1920s.

other improvements.[268] The general staff estimated that Argentina had an army of ten combat-ready active and reserve divisions in 1922, while Brazil had only two active and one reserve. Argentina's efficient military organization allowed it to mobilize a force of 380,000 men, and deploy them on Brazil's borders within a few weeks before Brazil could patch together a force of 136,000. Argentina, moreover, outdistanced Brazil in number and quality of artillery. Despite its naval modernization during 1904–10, the Brazilian navy totaled 65,000 tons, but most of the warships were aged. Argentina's navy, in contrast, totaled an estimated 114,000 tons.[269] Predictably, Brazil's 1924 naval modernization provoked Argentina to launch an even larger naval expansion in 1926.

Notwithstanding the heroic efforts of the French mission, the general staff issued a report in 1927 making dire assessments of Brazil's position. The report noted that "the military advances realized in recent years by the Argentine Republic oblige the general staff to call respectfully the attention of the government to the precarious situation in which our national defense finds itself."[270] Brazilian concerns during 1932–35 rose sharply as a result of Argentina's open meddling and material support to Paraguay during the full-fledged Chaco war between Bolivia and Paraguay. Brazilian leaders feared that the war, the second largest war on the continent after the war with Paraguay and costing an estimated 130,000 battle related deaths, would spill over into Brazil and drag in superior Argentina.[271]

Brazil's emulation during 1906–30 provides ample empirical support for the theory of emulation's predictions about the timing, pace, and scope of military emulation. More so than in Chile and Argentina, however, the process of modernizing the armed forces suffered as a result of the country's internal turmoil. The terrible instability the military and the country experienced between 1922 and 1934 meant that most of the reforms and work of the French were not realized until after 1934. The Brazilian military from the 1922 *tenentes* revolt to 1934 was an institution simultaneously renovating and disintegrating. The military was in a state of permanent rebellion.[272] The decade-long violent implosion of the Old Republic, and the fratricide within the army in the wake of the *tenentes* revolt, obviously throttled the modernization program. Last, Brazil's other misfortune was to lack an Emil Körner or Pablo Riccheri, larger-than-life individuals who singlehandedly guided the emulation process.

---

[268] On Brazil's military situation in the interwar years, see Stanley E. Hilton, *Brazil and the Great Powers, 1930–1939: The Politics of Trade Rivalry* (Austin: University of Texas Press, 1975).

[269] On the 1922 general staff report, see Hilton, "Brazil and the Post-Versailles World."

[270] Quote cited in McCann, "The Brazilian General Staff," 307.

[271] Hilton, *Brazil and the Great Powers*, 12.

[272] Motta, *Formação*, 282.

It was not until World War II that Brazil finally closed the gap in military capabilities. As in 1917, it joined the United States in declaring war against Germany. The country became host to U.S. military installations, and its expeditionary force fought alongside U.S. troops on the Italian front. Its forces turned to U.S. armaments and equipment. The war thus became another historical marker in the Brazilian military's emulation of foreign models. The United States had been serving as a model for its navy since the early twenties. Heavy U.S. organizational and doctrinal influence on its army since the war would become a point of political and scholarly controversy. The military's overthrow of civilian rule in 1964 was interpreted by many as a product of the Cold War–inspired training its officers received at places like the School of the Americas and incestuous relationship that existed between the two officer corps. Such controversies aside, the Brazilian military was once again accompanying global transformations in military technology and organization.

7

Conclusion

Military emulation is an enduring phenomenon in the international system. Its causes are to be found, not in the character and internal conditions of states or in their shared cultural norms, but in the nature of the international system they occupy. This study developed a neorealist theory of emulation to explain crossnational emulation and its variance. The essence of this work has involved uncovering and developing a hidden and neglected dimension of neorealism. The work builds on the foundations laid by Waltz. It corrects many of the flaws in Waltzian neorealism while remaining faithful to its structural logic and economy of explanation.

The theory directs our attention to how adverse shifts in the state's external security prompt it to undertake large-scale internal balancing efforts such as military emulation. The study shows that military emulation is a form of balancing behavior, specifically internal balancing. It is thus a product of the security competition inherent to anarchic systems. Unlike explanations that focus on unique attributes of individual states or global cultural norms, the neorealist theory of emulation offers a clean, testable, and economical account of why a variety of states emulate the same military system. Equally as important, and unlike social theory accounts, the theory explains the variance in their emulation process – its timing, pace, and scale. Whether states emulate, whom they emulate, when, how much, and how often are dictated by their external security environment – not historical peculiarities, domestic concerns, ideological whims, or cultural predilections. The theory predicts that states will emulate only the military systems that have been tested and proven successful in war. This is an important corrective to Waltzian neorealism. This study shows that states emulate prevailing international best practices, rather than the practices of their adversaries or the most powerful, as Waltz suggests. In addition, it explains why states emulate particular models, and why even states of great power and innovativeness will also emulate.

This study makes a number of important contributions to international relation theory, and the main debates in the field today. First, its primary contribution is to construct a neorealist theory of crossnational emulation. The work strengthens neorealism by developing a neglected but vital area of the theory, and by bringing greater determinacy to its explanatory framework on balancing behavior. Second, the study shows that neorealism can address a much wider set of dependent variables. Not only does it provide a powerful and economical account for crossnational convergence, but the theory of emulation offers a fruitful avenue through which neorealism can address one of its main units of analysis – the state. The study shows why and how the theory's core predictions about state behavior – balancing and emulation – generate dual effects on the organization and development of the state. Third, the study contributes to the central debate today in IR between neorealism, on one hand, and theories that give causal primacy to cultural and social forces in international politics. Social theory has developed elaborate accounts of crossnational emulation and convergence, even in military-security matters, while neorealism has been silent. Debate has thus far been one-sided. Our collective knowledge progresses when both sides in the debate have meaningful, coherent, and testable claims and accounts. Fourth, the study widens the empirical base, or stock, of IR theory today by offering dense and original historical cases. Fifth, the historical story of large-scale military emulation is itself interesting and of theoretical relevance, especially with regard to questions about military organizational behavior, the spread of European military organization and technology, and the behavior of secondary states.

A SUMMARY OF THE FINDINGS

While this study extracted the wider theoretical and historical implications of crossnational emulation in the course of the narrative, its primary objective was to develop a neorealist theory of emulation. Its goal was to develop a theory of emulation that can provide a more coherent and powerful explanation for the four main facets of emulation: why states emulate; whom they emulate; when, how extensively and quickly they do so. In other words, this theory goes beyond merely telling us why states emulate. It provides a discriminating account of variance in emulation across countries and in their individual emulation efforts. The study tested the validity of the theory's predictions by applying it to three historical cases of large-scale military emulation: late-nineteenth-century Argentina, Chile, and Brazil.

The historical cases studied here, based exclusively on archival evidence, confirm the theory of emulation. The three main cases of large-scale military emulation from turn-of-the-century South America fall closely within the predictions of the theory. The theory performs without much effort in explaining why we see military emulation taking place in the region at this time; why it displays a cascading or sequential pattern across the three states; why they imitate the German and later French systems; and why they do so to varying degrees. Any theory that emphasizes the role of external threats and security-driven behavior would easily capture the behavior of the big South American powers, enmeshed in interlocking rivalry since their independence. Military emulation, as predicted in Chapter 1, will tend to display both a clustering pattern and a knock-on effect among contending states.

Military emulation was a recurring practice in South America since the wars of independence. The difference in the last decades of the century was the scale and reach of emulation. Chile's innovation move – to adopt in full Germany's mass army and outfit it with the most advanced weapons of the day – had a domino effect on the rest of the region. Not only did it trigger an immediate arms race among the three major powers of the region, it spurred Argentina to upgrade its military power. Argentina's large-scale emulation, in turn, prompted its other historic rival, Brazil, to do the same. Chile's decision in 1885 to modernize its military power was prompted by an array of national security challenges. Geographic exposure and encirclement by historic enemies already made the country perennially insecure and attentive to the quality of its arms. Even while the Pacific war (1879–83) was still under way, Chilean leaders recognized the need for a fundamental retooling of the nation's military power. The army and navy were performing poorly. More significantly, as victory and territorial expansion came within grasp, the wartime meddling of the United States, other great powers, and archrival Argentina made it plainly visible that an anti-Chilean coalition was emerging to roll back its gains. Victory and conquest were thus double-edged swords. The postwar decades brought with them a stretch of near-war crises (with the United States and Argentina), territorial disputes, diplomatic ostracism, and escalating arms racing. Not surprisingly, the pace and scale of Chile's military emulation was equally intense.

As the theory predicted, all three countries emulated the German army between 1870 and 1914 as they modernized their armies (and emulated the British Royal Navy). Victorious military systems generate the greatest emulation appeal, since they set the standards of competitive effectiveness. From the time of its defeat of France in the Franco–Prussian War to its own submission in World War I, the German system attracted the most widespread emulation in the system. All three South American powers emulated the German army, though Brazil's was both limited and brief. Brazil turned to the French in 1918.

The theory of emulation tells us the emulation appeal of any one system will wax and wane with its fortune in wars. Brazil is the clearest empirical example of switching midstream, but all the cases switched models. Prior to 1870, the three regional powers emulated the French army. Chile, whose attachment to the German system came to be seen as bordering on religious cultism, had actually hired a French training mission in the late 1850s. Brazil moved sluggishly to modernize its forces, and began emulating the German system during 1906–14. As predicted, it switched (or returned) to the French system in 1918, after using the German model as the basis of its modernization program during 1906–14. That emulators switch – when prompted by major threats – confirms the point that states put a premium on proven effectiveness.

As the theory predicted, and consistent with insights from balance-of-threat and offense-defense theories, there was variance in timing, pace, and scale of emulation across the three countries. Indeed, given the interlocking rivalries of the South American system, it is no surprise emulation processes in the region were characterized by a wavelike, domino pattern. The three big powers did not experience the same threat at the same time, but different threat sources at different times. Even more crucial, each major distinctive phase in their emulation process corresponded to new adverse changes in external security conditions. By the 1880s the three powers were locked in a tripolar power balancing system. As Schweller nicely shows, tripolar systems are naturally unstable.[1] Slight changes in power differentials, let alone qualitative jumps in capabilities such as Chile's innovation move in 1885, trigger an immediate chain reaction.[2] As I show in this study, the timing, pace, and scale of military emulation (and all forms of internal balancing) will be affected by the availability of external balancing options. Some like Brazil had viable, if ultimately temporary, external alliance options that dampened the severity of gathering threat, in this case the rise of Argentine power. Argentina, though sandwiched by its two historical enemies, was able to derive respite from the United States–led anti-Chilean coalition despite the rapid rise of Chilean military power. By the early 1890s, it could no longer put off the required military retooling to meet the Chilean challenge.

The theory accounts for the overall pattern of variance in emulation, including its distinctive phases. Variance in the timing, pace, and scale emulation in all three cases fell within reasonable ranges. Indeed, that it does, despite all the wider social and political ramifications and domestic reasons arrayed against such a large-scale undertaking, is testament to the primacy of structural forces. The theory of emulation cannot and does not pretend to tell us every detail of the emulation process of individual states. From the standpoint of the theory, what is far more significant is that the study's findings fall within expected ranges, in accord with its expectations in cases

---

[1] Randall Schweller, *Deadly Imbalances: Tripolarity and Hitler's Strategy of World Conquest* (New York: Columbia University Press, 1998).

[2] On the interplay between power differentials and polarity, see Dale C. Copeland, *The Origins of Major War* (Ithaca: Cornell University Press, 2000).

where structural theory should perform less well. South American leaders had numerous reasons not to undertake large-scale emulation. Organizational change of any kind is difficult, let alone major reconfiguration of the state's central edifice. The distributional effects were significant, especially in terms of political power inside the military, inside the state apparatus, and between state and society. The political risks alone were sufficient to sway leaders to opt for a politically more congenial solution to the country's military problems.

Nonetheless, the theory of emulation cannot tell us, for it cannot predict with pinpoint precision, the exact timing of emulation nor how promptly states will respond. No theory can. The theory does not deny that domestic factors play a role in driving the residual or unexplained variance in military emulation. Given the nature and ramifications of large-scale emulation, it is unreasonable to expect that the process will be unaffected by domestic-level factors. These unit-level factors, as the study shows, do not overwhelm structural imperatives. Yet the process of emulating was difficult, contentious, and disruptive. Indeed, in the case of Brazil, the process was tortuous – though very little of its difficulties had to do with military emulation and reform per se. The most common manifestation of domestic factors was to affect the timing, pace, and scale of military emulation. Military organizational and domestic political factors were the most salient among unit-level factors. Naturally, political opposition inside and outside the military was the most common factor. Military modernization involed the redistribution of power. It should be recalled that military modernization in all three countries entailed a parallel legislative process, with all the political battles, inefficiencies, and distortions that attend such matters.

The weight of internal factors was particularly salient in the case of Brazil, which was attempting to remake its military system at a time when both the country and military were becoming unglued. Reinventing an entire military establishment, or any bureaucratized institution for that matter, is never easy anywhere. Reformers everywhere faced the dilemma of how to reform – how to get rid of the old and introduce the new – without triggering fratricide or worsening military ineffectiveness. More problematic for reformers in Chile, Argentina, and Brazil was how to remake their country's military power by importing alien practices. Large-scale military emulation has enormous distributional consequences inside and outside the military – leaving winners and losers in its wake. Its ramifications for political power, inside and outside the military, are great. Indeed, what is surprising is that modernization in South America did not directly result in internecine bloodshed and political disorder. Reformers everywhere were forced to scale back the original project. In South America, much opposition naturally stemmed from those who stood to lose the most from modernization – from provincial governors to old guard officers.

STATE-MAKING MILITARY EMULATION

The process of large-scale military emulation implicates a number of other, more complex issues and subject matter, none of which can be meaningfully treated in the present work. Involved are a number of broader historical and theoretical implications. Large-scale emulation entailed changes far beyond military organization. Yet, though beyond the purview of this study, some of these wider implications cannot escape notice.

First, one of the more interesting aspects of the historical process in all three cases is that these countries were very much aware of the potential pitfalls and wider ramifications of large-scale emulation. It is interesting to note that leaders in South America were cognizant of emulation's state-making impact and, in some cases, deliberately promoted it. Some, like Brazil's Young Turks, deliberately sought to use military emulation as an instrument of nation building. South American leaders may have been unduly optimistic about their ability to manage and control these ramifications and spinoff effects. They equated military modernization with positive aspects of nation building, itself viewed as a foundational piece of national power. Of the three major powers, the Brazilians were more explicit and enthused by the state-making and nation-building results, as they saw them, which would come from military modernization. Brazil's Young Turks believed that adopting the modern mass army would spur economic and social development, improve the country's human capital, release the total energies of its people, engender patriotism, integrate the nation, and prompt the building of its infrastructure. All these benefits, in turn, would boost national power and enhance the country's capacity to defend itself in a hostile world. The Young Turks may have been too cerebral, overly ambitious, and wildly optimistic, compared to their fellow reformers in Argentina, Chile, and the United States. That they had their own theory of state making, which viewed military modernization as its principal driver, is both interesting and instructive for theory.

Second, large-scale military emulation in late-nineteenth-century South America, as a historical process, did produce state-building effects. A far more focused and ambitious study is required to assess the nation-building and state-making impact of large-scale military emulation in South America. State making in Latin America remains an understudied subject matter. As Centeno observed, that state making in the region may have taken different paths is itself theoretically interesting and fruitful for our understanding of the full range of state making.[3] Moreover, Latin American states may have bypassed many other organizational effects of war making by their reliance on easy taxation of primary products exports rather than more demanding forms of extraction.

[3] Miguel Angel Centeno, *Blood and Debt: War and the Nation-State in Latin America* (University Park: Pennsylvania State Press, 2002).

Nevertheless, large-scale military emulation resulted in the elimination of the old military and its replacement by a modern, powerful, professional, and much larger apparatus of state power. The ancillary parts and arrangements in the state apparatus altered accordingly. During this period, large-scale military modernization in South America was accompanied by an equally impressive process of social and economic modernization, especially in Chile and Argentina. Some of this modernization predated military emulation and as unrelated to it. These countries were flush with cash. From the last quarter of the nineteenth century to World War I witnessed a tremendous expansion in world (European) demand for raw materials and primary products, which the economies supplied.

Theoretically, we expect the type, extent, and depth of state-making effects to correspond with the scale and longevity of the military modernization process. In general, the theory predicts that the primary locus of state-making effects is the fiscal-coercive-administrative organs and functions of state. We expect the effects to be quantitative and qualitative, human as well as organizational, fiscal as well as managerial. Military modernization in South America was both extensive, especially in Chile and Argentina, as it was enduring, spanning several decades.

The most direct impact was in military organization and the ancillary organs and functions of the state pertaining to its coercive capacity. The military's size grew. So did its resources and its elaboration within the machinery of state. Growth in size necessitated new and expanded methods of internal control, management, and accountancy. Universal conscription, and all other demands arising from building and maintaining a mass army, forced states to expand their reach, to build infrastructure, and even to establish universal primary education. The greater fiscal (extractive), administrative, and logistical requirements of military modernization everywhere necessitated modernization and elaboration in other parts of the state and economy. The greater extractive capacity necessary to launch and sustain military modernization, aside from the diversion and reallocation of resources, was a straightforward outcome.

Consequently, the size and reach of the central state grew. War and war preparation have always triggered organizational rationalization and expansion, even among constitutional democracies, which are presumably inoculated against centralization and expansion of state power. The mustering and husbanding of national military power pushed the South American states to become involved in a broad range of societal and economic areas hitherto neglected or nonexistent. Long before the Great Depression, the unquestioned laissez-faire ideology of the past loosened its grip on these South American governments. For the first time they began to adopt an activist role in the economy and society. They began to see the state as an agent of national development. For instance, large-scale military modernization was accompanied by a wide range of infrastructural development, especially in terms of rail, roads, and ports. Prior to this period, the rail system was typical of postcolonial primary exporting countries. The greater mobilizational and defense demands of military modernization spurred the development of a national rail network. Ports and coastal fortifications were improved or expanded. Telegraph networks appeared. In Brazil and Argentina a national armaments industry was one of the more salient spinoffs of the process. Brazil's success today as a major arms producer and exporter dates to this formative period. Far more difficult to calculate and trace were the developmental and multiplied effects of improved human capital.

The creation of the mass army altered the traditional relationship between the military and society in terms of service, but the nature and impact of military service itself changed. The relationship between state and society, between people and nation, changed. More people were serving under arms and getting military training. What they experienced radically changed during the time they served. It was not simply a matter of more people receiving better training. By integrating primary education, health and physical training into mass conscription, the military, literally, became a school of the nation. It was the first systematic project in Latin America to build human capital. A number of Latin American governments began to make mass primary education their business. Additionally, we can expect that mass conscription might leave cognitive, emotional, or other ideational residue on those who serve. There is some debate on this question in the wider literature.[4] South American military leaders were explicit about these kinds of nation-building outcomes they wanted to pursue through the vehicle of obligatory mass conscription. Reformers in Brazil, for example, saw it not only as a way to mobilize the productive energies of the people but as the only mechanism to integrate Brazilian society. Their larger agenda was the manufacturing of nationalism and patriotism. There was nothing unusual in such efforts. The use of mass conscription served a dual purposes. Leaders everywhere believed secular nationalism and patriotism enhanced the state's military power. But giving the masses guns and training in how to use them worried kings, dictators, and democrats alike, a problem only solved by using mass conscription to generate loyalty to the state.

Politically, all this meant a far more powerful central government and an altered domestic balance of political power. Since it is Latin America, we must ask about the political impact on the military itself. The political ramifications of military modernization – and professionalization in Huntingtonian terms – are inescapable, even if their precise nature and direction are ambiguous or impossible to measure. Huntington notwithstanding, there has never been a politically sterile military anywhere. But this is not the same as saying emulation led to militarism, whereby the military came to have excessive

---

4 Ronald Krebs, "A School for the Nation? How Military Service Does Not Build Nations, and How it Might," *International Security* (Spring 2004): 85–124.

influence over the society and politics. We need not accept the thesis that military emulation in South America gave rise to the "new professionalism," whereby, contra Huntington's thesis, the Latin militaries suddenly became politicized and developed a corporate identity as the only institution capable of leading the nation.[5] Long before and long after military emulation, the Latin militaries were involved in politics, including political rule. Modernization, or professionalization, did not appear to make a difference either in the nature or timing of military interventions. It is impossible to generalize in a region as large and varied, with an equally varied history of civil-military relations. Nevertheless, it is noticeable that by the 1920s we see a good deal more restiveness and upheavals on the part of the military in the three cases studied here. Military modernization shifted the political balance of power inside the military, inside the state apparatus, and between state and society. The precise ways in which this shift played out politically remains to be studied, but the trend everywhere in the region by the 1930s was toward greater central power and concentration in the executive.

Other Findings and Implications of Large-Scale Military Emulation

An aspect of crossnational emulation that has theoretical bearing was, upon closer inspection of the historical record, the extent to which states studied and evaluated the military systems and innovations of each other. For realism this is not surprising, for it is premised on the assumption that states pay close attention to their relative power. But what does this mean in practice? Emulation shows that states are continually monitoring, searching, evaluating, and observing their own experience and strategic environment as well as the experience of others. Episodes of military emulation are literally characterized by direct study and learning on the part of emulators – either through close study and evaluation of the prospective foreign model or under the tutelage of foreign military advisers.

No suggestion is made here that the theory of emulation, or more broadly neorealism, can or should incorporate unit-level variables and so-called process variables such as learning. It does mean that these structural forces materialize or translate into concrete choices, carriers, and strategies. There is a much bigger, and more problematic, theoretical issue involved here – namely, the connection between external imperatives and the domestic decision-making process. Neorealism is widely criticized for not accounting for how decisions are made or how leaders think and choose.[6] It does not and need

[5] Frederick M. Nunn, *Yesterday's Soldiers: European Military Professionalism in South America, 1890–1940* (Lincoln: University of Nebraska Press, 1983).

[6] Aaron L. Friedberg, *The Weary Titan: Britain and the Experience of Relative Decline* (Princeton: Princeton University Press, 1988).

not. Structural theories, by their very design, cannot. Neorealism does posit close correspondence between external imperatives and the logic of decision making. The findings support the presumption that the logic of decision making corresponds with exigencies of external competition. The decisions to emulate, the reasons given, the criteria leaders used to choose specific models to emulate, the timing of the decisions, all support the rather simple, if hidden, presumption in neorealism that the domestic decision logic will generally correspond with structural logic of security competition.

Military emulation suggests that the organization and technology of violence in the international system tend to follow similar transformations and trajectory. The large-scale military emulation in turn-of-the-century South America marked the founding of the modern militaries in these countries. The founding pillars of the modern professional armies were put in place. The heavy imprint of foreign military influence in the region has given rise to a good deal of debate in the literature of Latin American studies as to the organizational and political consequences. Whatever may be the hypothesized political fallout of military emulation, the theory and historical process themselves point to much broader questions about the development and change of military organizations over time. That is, crossnational emulation suggests that the military organizations of countries – or at least clusters of competing states – tend to follow similar and simultaneous transformations. In other words, notions about a national military, about an organization that is sui generis, are at best, conditional claims.

Military emulation, in addition, suggests that military organizations undergo deep change or innovation. The theory cannot settle the debate over the rate or ease of change in military organizations. That any kind of change takes place at all, let alone organizational remaking on the basis of foreign practice, is telling. Few other organs of state are as closed, secretive, and wary of outsiders than the military. Militaries are spurred to change by external competitive pressures, by developments in rival organizations that enhance their relative size and effectiveness.[7] That states would remake part or all of their military establishment on the basis of foreign arrangements suggests they attach greater value to their ability to compete externally than to the sanctity or purity of their national institutions and mythology. In addition, the theory posits that military change on the scale studied here, like change in the wider state apparatus, are marked by a punctuated equilibrium. It is broken, uneven, episodic, rather than slowly accreting over time. Military organizations, like states as a whole, develop through an evolutionary, albeit punctuated, patchwork and through cycles of innovation and emulation. As the examples from South America illustrate, military organizational change is marked by periodicity. Major change such as that experienced in South

---

[7] Kimberly Marten Zisk, *Engaging the Enemy: Organization Theory and Soviet Military Innovation, 1955–1991* (Princeton: Princeton University Press, 1993), makes a similar argument.

America occurs in phases, in bursts sparked by strategic junctures in the state's external security. The next major period of transformation for most of the regional militaries, for example, began during World War II when the United States locked in the region under its sphere of influence.

A NEOREALIST THEORY OF THE STATE?

What does the theory of emulation tell us about the state's development? As noted earlier, crossnational emulation provides an important avenue for studying the state's historical development. However, it must be stressed at the outset that the conceptual and methodological impediments to developing a neorealist theory of the state are many. Moreover, we must caution against drawing extended conclusions from such indirect, limited evidence. Few other subject matters have received as much scholarly attention and generated as much debate as definitions and conceptions of the state.[8] There are different kinds of theories of the state, and each addresses different questions.[9] The neorealist theory of the state need not make overly ambitious claims, but should limit its explanatory purview to those aspects of state formation and organizational development that it is best equipped to address directly – macrohistorical changes in the state's central organizational structures. I do not pretend to offer a theory of the state, nor do I introduce new facts or new concepts. Rather, I tie together widely rehearsed ideas, unearth and extend insights in neorealist theory in new ways to address one of the theory's main units of analysis. A brief excursus on such a large subject matter necessarily involves simplifications, abstractions, and generalizations.

Developing the neorealist theory of emulation is an important first step for building a neorealist theory of the state. Key insights are present in Waltz's original formulation. The first is neorealism's organizational conception of the state. The second is the theory's emphasis on the dual organizational effects of competition in anarchic realms. Nonetheless, the impediments are many. Not the least being the lacunae in the theory's treatment of the state, and the second tier of structure as a whole. Neorealism's neglect of the state

---

[8] The literature on the state is as vast as it is Eurocentric. Among the works referenced in this study include: Michael Mann, *States, War, and Capitalism: Studies in Political Sociology* (Oxford: Basil Blackwell, 1988); Charles Tilly, *Coercion, Capital, and European States, A.D. 900–1990* (Cambridge: Basil Blackwell, 1990); Theda Skocpol, *States and Social Revolutions: A Comparative Analysis of France, Russia, and China* (Cambridge: Cambridge University Press, 1979); F. H. Hinsley, *Sovereignty* (Cambridge: Cambridge University Press, 1986); Martin Van Creveld, *The Rise and Decline of the State* (Cambridge: Cambridge University Press, 1999); *Bringing the State Back In*, ed. Peter Evans, Dietrich Rueschemeyer, and Theda Skocpol (Cambridge: Cambridge University Press, 1985); *The State and American Foreign Economic Policy*, ed. G. John Ikenberry, David A. Lake, and Michael Mastanduno (Ithaca: Cornell University Press, 1988); Fred Halliday, *Rethinking International Relations* (Vancouver: University of British Columbia Press, 1994).

[9] Michael Mastanduno, David A. Lake, and G. John Ikenberry, "Toward a Realist Theory of State Action," *International Studies Quarterly* 33, no. 4 (December 1989): 457–74.

has been widely and correctly criticized. Waltz famously denies that a theory of the state is needed or even desirable. His position on the theory of the state is actually quite simple to explain: consistent with his microeconomics analogy, he conflates a theory of the state with a unit-level, inside-out explanation of world politics. He resists the idea of a neorealist theory of the state because he associates it with a reductionist theory of foreign policy.[10] His notion of a theory of the state is an inside-out theory of foreign policy, where the state (its internal conditions) is an independent variable, as opposed to one where the state and its internal conditions are dependent variables. This position conflates levels of analysis and units of analysis. As a result, the state and the second tier of structure are conceptually undeveloped, and the "unit level" becomes a dumping ground for all he deems reductionist, inconsequential, or outside the purview of the theory. A neorealist theory of the state is possible, albeit partial, and is consistent with neorealism's third-image logic, because the state and its organizational makeup are dependent variables.

Rudiments of a neorealist theory of the state may be gleaned from the theory of emulation, but a more serious treatment will require reversing neorealism's underdevelopment of the state and the second tier of structure. Nowhere is there a concise definition of the state, making neorealism even more vulnerable to criticisms of treating the state as a black box. At best, the state and second tier of structure are subjects of limited and rudimentary conceptual treatment, both receiving a mere four pages in *Theory of International Politics*. The problem for a potential neorealist theory of the state is the lack of any theorizing on the causal interplay of the three tiers of structure. Ruggie was first to point out that the three tiers of structure are arranged according to causal depths, with ordering principle as the first and deepest causal tier.[11]

The significance of *Theory of International Politics*, and Waltz's real accomplishment, is developing a truly structural theory. He conceives the international system as consisting of a three-tier structure, on the one hand, and interacting units (states) on the other. In Waltz's three-part definition of system structure, the first tier is the ordering principle – anarchy – according to which the state-units are arranged. The first tier is the deepest causal tier and the least mutable. The second tier of structure – functional similarity – is the organizational nature of the primary units or actors in the system, the states. The second tier is conceptually the least developed and most controversial. In sweeping statements, Waltz claims that states are "like units," in

[10] Waltz, *Theory of International Politics* (Reading, MA: Addison-Wesley, 1979); 71–72, 89, 93, 121.

[11] John Gerard Ruggie, "Continuity and Transformation in the World Polity: Toward a Neorealist Synthesis," *Neorealism and Its Critics*; Keohane, ed., (New York: Columbia University Press, 1986): 131–57. See also Barry Buzan, Charles Jones, and Richard Little, *The Logic of Anarchy: Neorealism to Structural Realism* (New York: Columbia University Press, 1993).

that, as sovereign entities, they all duplicate the same functions. The third tier – the distribution of capabilities – distinguishes state-units according to their most relevant and weighty attribute pertaining to their placement in the system. In Waltz's formulation, the third and most superficial tier emerges as the only tier of structure that undergoes change.

Waltz famously noted that the second tier of structure "drops out." Since states are functionally alike, the second tier of structure is not needed in defining structure nor in constructing a theory of international politics.[12] By implication, the internal conditions of states are either unimportant to such a theory or outside its explanatory purview. Waltz prematurely closes off the second tier to theorizing. In fairness, he closes off the second tier as a locus of causation of international political outcomes as well as definitional components of structure. The second tier drops out in the theory as a source of independent variables; the move is premature only in that it unnecessarily removes it as a potential locus of dependent variable. The theory of emulation shows that neorealism can speak to the state's historical development.

The state is conceptually undeveloped in neorealism, but Waltz lays important groundwork. A closer reading reveals a number of ideas, some rudimentary, upon which a more coherent organizational conception of the state can be constructed. First, consistent with the wider realist tradition, Waltz embraces the fundamental idea that the state is an organizational solution to the insecurity of international life. Implicit in this conception is the notion that this organizational form has differentiated internal structures and hierarchy. Waltz views the state as having differentiated governing structures and hierarchic political ordering.[13] It is difficult to imagine that someone who wrote *Foreign Policy and Democratic Politics* would treat the state as a proverbial "black box."[14]

Second, one of Waltz's biggest accomplishments is to treat states as states. He conceives states as comprising a much wider category of territorialized forms of political organization than just the typical Westphalian modern state. The theoretical progress he makes is to develop a structural theory of behavioral and organizational effects applicable to any realm characterized by anarchic ordering principles – be they premodern states, tribes, city-states, leagues, empires, firms, ethnic groups in collapsed states, or street gangs.[15] The concept of state in neorealism is a generic one, encompassing the great variety in forms and internal composition. Their functional similarity and behavioral regularity unite them in common across historical time. In other words, Waltz's restrictive definition of structure's second tier contains useful

---

[12] Waltz, *Theory of International Politics*, 93.
[13] Waltz, *Theory of International Politics*, 80.
[14] Kenneth N. Waltz, *Foreign Policy and Democratic Politics: The American and British Experience* (Boston: Little, Brown, 1967).
[15] Waltz, *Theory of International Politics*, 67.

insights and conceptual building blocks. Treating the second tier in terms of like units allows us to trace their organizational changes over time.

Last, neorealism makes four simplifying assumptions about the nature, goals, and role of the state in world politics: that it is rational, unitary, and the main actor in world politics; that its overriding goal is security; that its logic of action is self-help. These are as familiar as they are contested. One of the three core neorealist assumptions is that states are the primary actors in the system and can be treated as reasonably rational and unitary. While the logic of anarchy applies to a variety of settings and organized collectives, neorealism presumes an international system populated by hierarchically organized states.

Thucydides, Hobbes, and Machiavelli laid the conceptual foundations for a potential neorealist theory of the state. The neorealist theory of the state begins with familiar realist verities: the centrality of war and competition, and the importance of the external anarchic realm in the life and death of states. The theory of emulation suggests that a partial neorealist theory of the state is possible – one that can illuminate the ways in which the anarchy of the external realm shapes the articulation of hierarchy in the domestic realm. The pillar assumptions and claims of structural realism – the primacy of anarchy in the external realm, balancing, the centrality of organized violence, and emulation – constitute a built-in second-image reversed thesis. These basic insights realism shares with the so-called war-centric accounts in historical sociology and the German historical school. The theory of emulation builds on and extends these long-standing verities. By highlighting the role of crossnational emulation, the theory of emulation extracts the full implications of internal balancing.

The theory of emulation, I have argued, suggests that neorealism is not just a theory of state behavior but, more broadly, a theory of organizational effects in anarchic systems. Competitive realms spur states continually to attend to how well they are internally organized and equipped. In so doing, states deliberately imitate each other's best practices, thus pushing their organizational and technological transformations toward a common trajectory. The theory of military emulation traces the development of the state's central edifice, the fiscal-coercive-administrative backbone of its relative competitive effectiveness. The theory argues that the organization of violence is defining not just for relations among states but also for the state's own organizational development. It may be an exaggeration to depict the state as nothing more than a machine organized for war. The Mongol ideal of the army-state has been few and far between – at least by way of replicas. Not all of state making can be reduced to the recommendation of the U.S. Council of National Defense in 1918 to organize "the Nation as a machine for making war."[16] Yet

---

[16] U.S. Council of National Defense, *Second Annual Report* (Washington, DC: Government Printing Office, 30 June 1918): 6.

war and war preparation – defined as a continuing activity – are major driving forces in overall organization and historical development. Tilly's tense, moreover, is misleading, for the theory of emulation tells us that the state is always in the making. State making is not a single-shot episode, a point made clear by Tilly. Since emulation (and deep internal balancing in general) is a response to threats, the pattern of organizational development is likely to be discontinuous, irregular, jagged, and uneven across states at any one point in time. Anarchy's dual organizational effects, in other words, come in spurts. The state's organizational development is punctuated by periods of lull and periods of intense activity, by stasis and renovation.

"CHANGE" IN THE INTERNATIONAL SYSTEM

In what ways do neorealism's expectations about the twin organizational effects of anarchic competition speak to the issue of "change" in the international system? As noted in Chapter 1, neorealism is famously presumed to be incapable of explaining change of any kind. A serious response to this charge must necessarily begin with definitional matters, for the debate about change is hampered by imprecision as to what change might mean and of what observables it is constituted. What is the nature of change that critics believe neorealism is incapable of explaining? At which tier of structure? How might change in one tier, or other aspect of the system, be caused by another, and what might be the effect of the change on another tier? I argue that neorealism is a theory about certain types of change in the international system. Sterling-Folker has proposed that neorealism contains under one theoretical narrative both change and stasis, history and structure.[17] The theory of emulation helps to account for an important category of change.

Waltz readily announces that neorealism cannot explain change, only continuity.[18] Such statements are not helpful, but his original formulation contained powerful insights and useful classifications. Change in the system may take any number of forms and quality, from garden variety changes to more complex change, a point Waltz recognizes.[19] I suspect that critics have in mind one particular form of change – structural, or epochal, transformation. As the initial exchange between Waltz and Ruggie revealed, social theorists in particular insist on anarchy-transcending change.[20] To simplify our discussion, we can delimit three levels of change, corresponding to each tier of structure: change in ordering principle, functional similarity of units, and distribution of capabilities. Upon closer inspection, Waltz does not deny

---

[17] Jennifer Sterling-Folker, "Realism and the Constructivist Challenge: Rejecting, Reconstructing, or Rereading," *International Studies Review* 4, no. 1 (Spring 2002): 73–97.
[18] Waltz, *Theory of International Politics*, 69.
[19] Waltz, *Theory of International Politics*, 70.
[20] Ruggie, "Continuity and Transformation."

the possibility, prevalence, or even significance of changes at all three levels. Indeed, he sees change possible at all three levels, or tiers, of structure, but changes in each tier differ according to their structural significance and their probability.[21]

The distinction Waltz makes is useful. For neorealism, there are two kinds of changes that take place in the international system: epochal change or changes of system and within-system changes. Change of system constitutes an epochal transformation of the first tier's ordering principle, from anarchy to hierarchy, or some other form.[22] More than once he refers to this as "systems change," a somewhat awkward term to denote a change of structure's ordering principle. Such a change alters the logic of behavior and outcomes in the system; that is, the behavioral regularity of anarchic realms is replaced. States would no longer stand in relation of coordination to one another, but in relation of command. Such a change alters the functional arrangement of the state-units, going from self-help to a division of labor. For Waltz and nearly all realists, change of system is possible but highly improbable. For Waltz it is possible only through one avenue or source – deep and irreversible transformations in structure's third tier. In such a circumstance, difficult as it may be to imagine, revolutionary technologies may allow one state to amass enough capabilities to impose universal hegemony, turning the system into an hierarchic order. Though it cannot be ruled out, such change is improbable because of the operation of the balance of power. Moreover, for Waltz as for all realists, such a transformation is the product of raw material power, not social construction or ideational forces.

Changes within systems comprise everything else, presumably all changes in the second and third tiers. Here neorealists need to do more and better work, for it is fertile ground to extend the theory. The most weighty, albeit infrequent, within-system change are shifts in polarity, such as change from multipolar to bipolar structures. Waltz refers to this kind of change, alternatively, as "structural change" and "systems change," a rather confusing language. Third-tier changes occupy nearly all of Waltz's explanatory attention. Waltz's careless language is the source of confusion, despite his insight. Likewise, his discussion at times is marked by ambiguity. For example, he observes that "international structures vary only through a change of organizing principle or, failing that, through variations in the capabilities of units."[23] (In other words, structural change may alternatively denote polarity shifts or ordering principle alteration.)

Changes in the second and third tiers of structure do not constitute epochal change, however significant some of them may be. They are not

[21] Waltz, *Theory of International Politics*, 100.
[22] Daniel Deudney, "Dividing Realism: Structural Realism versus Security Materialism on Nuclear Security and Proliferation," *Security Studies* 1 (1993): 7–37.
[23] Waltz, *Theory of International Politics*, 93, 161.

anarchy-transcending, even though they may be the source of epochal change (the hierarchy example above). The first tier is durable and unchanging, and generates the same behavioral and functional imperatives regardless of the nature and magnitude of changes in the lower tiers. As Waltz says, states change endlessly in size, shape, and internal conditions; their numbers expand and contract as they rise and fall, emerge and die. None of these changes, however significant they are in their own right, constitute epochal change, for they are unable to escape the functional and behavioral uniformity imposed on them by the anarchy of their external realm. This matter was the crux of the Waltz–Ruggie debate, subsequently picked up by Kratochwill, Fisher, Hall, Cronin, and others. This study is located at the nexus between the first and second tiers, and explains how the former induces organizational and technological transformations in the latter.

Waltz's treatment can be misleading. As he noted in his exchanges with Ruggie and others, the second tier is a potential source of anarchy-transcending change. Waltz limits the second tier of structure to functional similarity, however. Thus change in the second tier necessarily becomes epochal, anarchy transcending.[24] Functional similarity is a structural variable, an attribute of the system, and not a unit-level attribute. In other words, the first and second tiers are bound together; one implies the other. Anarchic realms necessarily and automatically produce functionally similar units. Put differently, anarchic realms, by definition, are realms in which the constituent parts are functionally similar; functional differentiation, or a division of labor, is possible only under hierarchy. As long as the system is anarchic, states will be functionally similar, and vice versa. This leaves only the third tier as a source of within-system change. Yet, as the theory of emulation proves, significant change is possible at the second tier. States undergo substantial changes in how they are organized and equipped, but do not cease to be self-help units grappling with the pressures of competition under anarchy. How then can we treat, classify, and locate the many changes the system's units, states, undergo over time?

The question is: What is the significance of changes in the internal conditions and organizational attributes of states? Without delving into this debate, the neorealist answer is simple: these changes, important as they might be, do not constitute epochal change.[25] The states of medieval Europe behaved no differently, and were functionally no different, from those of the ancient Mayan state system, or the city states of ancient Greece, the imperial systems of classical India and China, the city-state system of Mesopotamia, or the modern state system today. Issues relating to overlapping authority, poorly defined territorial space, or conflicting claims to sovereignty reflected,

---

[24] Waltz, *Theory of International Politics*, 93, 110.

[25] On this point, see Markus Fischer, "Feudal Europe, 800–1300: Communal Discourse and Conflictual Practices," *International Organization* 46, no. 2 (Spring 1992): 427–66.

as they do today and have always, differences in capabilities. Waltz recognizes that changes continually take place among the state-units of the system. States change widely in form, purpose, and internal conditions, but these constitute changes within system rather than epochal transformations. Much of this change is captured by the theory of emulation and the neorealist theory of the state. The theory of emulation tells us that states have always, and will into the future, undergo continual transformations in how they are internally organized and equipped, and that these transformations will follow similar trajectories.

THE WORK AHEAD

This work constructed a neorealist theory of emulation. It refined and amended aspects of neorealist theory to explain the main aspects of cross-national military emulation. It did so while preserving neorealism's elegance and economy, and remaining faithful to its materialist structural logic. Work remains to be done to sharpen the neorealist theory of emulation.

The most immediate challenge for both the theory of emulation and the neorealist theory of the state is to continue the work of minimizing indeterminacy in predictions and explanation. In general, neorealists must continue working to sharpen neorealism's conceptual toolbox, and operationalize key concepts, such as threat. The principal challenge, however, is how to do so while avoiding twin dangers: undermining the theory's parsimony and violating its structural logic by introducing reductionism. There are three subject areas, or questions, that the theory of emulation must address next. They are outcomes that it cannot capture as presently constituted, or that occur outside the conditions laid out by the theory. The first involves reducing the indeterminacy over which balancing strategies states are more likely to choose and under which conditions. Related to this, theoretical work is required to bring more precision to the relationship between emulation and innovation strategies. The second, directly relevant to emulation, is the question of effectiveness, or success, of military emulation.[26] Why is military emulation successful in some countries and not in others? From the standpoint of policy makers, especially in innovator states, it is useful to know how quickly and effectively their innovations spread, that is, how rapidly the advantages of innovation dissipate. Third, are there anomalies, and what is their theoretical implication? A related, perhaps more interesting, question is why do some states rise to the occasion and respond to external pressures with renewed vigor and retooling, while others collapse? China during this period is frequently cited in the literature as an example of states that failed to balance, or to do so vigorously. Mid- to late-nineteenth-century Mexico

---

[26] Jeffrey Taliaferro and a number of other classical realists are working in this area.

might be an example of both. The theory does not presume that states will rise to the challenge, for it rests on the claim that structure selects through rewards and punishment. As Feaver points out, theoretical work is needed on neorealism's concept of structural selection. After all, international competition can and often does lead to implosion. We have a good understanding of the process when states respond and thrive. But we need a better understanding of cases when the outcome is collapse. Waltz's structure punishes, but neorealists have not operationalized the proposition in order to determine the various gradations of punishments states suffer as well as why some states are punished, others rewarded.

The last two areas pose a more serious theoretical challenge, and suggest an opening for the role of unit-level factors. The theory of emulation provides an elegant framework to understand the pressures states face to reorganize and retool, and it explicates the expected range of responses, but it cannot tells us with certainty whether states will respond effectively. It cannot because, ultimately, a number of intervening variables stand in the way. The work many realists today, working in the classical tradition, have taken up is to specify the interaction between systemic and domestic factors in shaping behavior and choices.[27] To the extent that some realist scholars want to preserve neorealism intact, the challenge is to do so in a way that minimizes the indeterminacy of the theory but remains consistent to its structural logic and economy.[28] The bigger, more complex theoretical question involved here is how to connect structural forces to the decisions and actions of states. Friedberg cautions that there are strong empirical and theoretical grounds to reject theories that move directly from structure to behavior without incorporating or giving weight to how national-level factors affect how structural forces and incentives are filtered and translated into behavior.[29]

What about the future? What are the implications for processes of military emulation in the future? As long as the system remains anarchic, states will emulate the best practices of one another. What changes is the nature of the best practices and the spin-off effects that come from their emulation. Military technology has changed, and continues to change at an accelerated rate, especially in the direction of true dual use and miniaturization. The age of information warfare means that the lines of distinction between civilian and military technology are nearly obliterated. These are technologies that are at the core of modern economic production. One implication here is that the future of weapons proliferation will be much more difficult from the standpoint of nonproliferation regimes.

---

[27] Jeffrey Taliaferro, "Neoclassical Realism and Military Emulation: The Case of Meiji Japan and late Qing China," unpublished manuscript.

[28] Mastanduno, Lake, and Ikenberry, "Toward a Realist Theory of State Action."

[29] Friedberg, *The Weary Titan*, 7.

Another implication is that, as the nature of warfare changes more and more to information warfare and capital-intensive technologies, military emulation in the future may be more confined to the emulation of technologies rather than the kind of large-scale military emulation of the past that covered all areas of the military system. On the other hand, these technological changes may also induce deep organizational restructuring. The rate of military emulation in the future may also be much more rapid. The miniaturization and capital-intensive quality of military technology (or all dual-use technologies) will mean cheaper import and start-up costs for would-be emulators, though perhaps far more difficulty in managing and sustaining such expensive and complex systems. What is clear is that military emulation will continue to characterize the behavior of states in the system. States in anarchy will continue to turn to military emulation as the surest and most direct strategy to enhance their security.

Index